Trial of
Simon, Lord Lovat
of the '45.

EDITED BY

David N. Mackay

Writer, Glasgow

REPRINT 1995
GAUNT, INC.

GAUNT, INC.

International Standard Book Number: 1-56169-120-8

Library cf Congress Catalog Number: 95-80133

NOTICE

Printed and bound in the United States of America.

The paper used in this publication meets the requirements of the American National Standard for Permanence of Paper for Printed Library Materials Z39.48-1984.

Reprint 1995
GAUNT, INC.
Gaunt Building
3011 Gulf Drive
Holmes Beach, Florida 34217-2199
U.S.A.

Notable English Trials

Simon, Lord Lovat
of the '45

Lord Lovat in old age.

(After Hogarth's Portrait.)

Trial of

Simon, Lord Lovat

of the '45

EDITED BY

David N. Mackay

Writer, Glasgow

EDINBURGH AND GLASGOW

WILLIAM HODGE & COMPANY

PRINTED BY
WILLIAM HODGE AND COMPANY
GLASGOW AND EDINBURGH
1911

TO THE RIGHT HONOURABLE

DONALD JAMES, LORD REAY

K.T., G.C.S.I., G.C.I.E., LL.D.(EDIN.), D.LITT.(HON. OXON.)

CHIEF OF THE CLAN MACKAY

THIS VOLUME IS

RESPECTFULLY DEDICATED

BY

THE EDITOR.

EDITOR'S NOTE.

The publishers' decision to include this volume in their list of Notable English Trials has called forth criticism from some of the Editor's Scottish friends. It is surely an overstrained patriotism which grudges England the record of a criminal trial. It is admitted that the impeached peer, the evidence which overwhelmed him, and the Rising in which he was involved, were all unassailably Scottish; but the trial took place in Westminster Hall, and the procedure adopted was purely English in origin. The Lord Chancellor presided, the Managers who conducted the prosecution were led by the English law officers of the Crown (one of whom happened to be a Scotsman). The prisoner was impeached by the Commons and tried by the Lords—a method of judging which has no historic parallel in Scotland, as Lords and Commons in Scotland before the Union were members of one House.

It has not been considered desirable to prefix an elaborated record of Lord Lovat's life. The Editor has endeavoured to give a condensed account of the doings of the accused peer, long enough to give a fair estimate of his strangely assorted characteristics, but short enough to leave the reader with the desire to peruse the full biographies by Dr. Hill Burton and Mr. W. C. Mackenzie. A short account of the wider literature of the subject is given in an Appendix.

D. N. M.

Glasgow, *September*, 1911.

CONTENTS.

CONTENTS.

APPENDICES.

LIST OF ILLUSTRATIONS.

LORD LOVAT.

INTRODUCTION.

LORD LOVAT'S condemnation to death for treason marked the close of an epoch in Scottish history, the end of the clan period in the Highlands. When a hundred and seventeen peers answered, with weary monotony, "Guilty, upon my honour," the public career of the last Scottish clan dictator came to an end. Thenceforward the name of "chief" was to be a thing of polite conceit, except when the bearer had other claims to respect. Till then clan feeling had been a matter of vital importance, now it was to become one of the sentiments. Ordered government had prevailed over MacShimi. The era of the humdrum had arrived.

Simon, Lord Lovat, had taken the fancy of the populace in London in 1747. For fifty years he had been a kind of political abstraction, a man whose name was better known than his character, and one whose visits to the metropolis had been, except during a few years of favour, like those of the fox to the farmyard—brave enough, but secret, wary, and ominously circumspect. Now this hazy being had been visualised. The great chief of the Frasers was in the Tower. Soon certain well-known and very ordinary peers were going to try this human portent. The people had a suspicion that a death sentence would follow. They began to inquire about Simon, and printing presses began to reproduce facts, fictions, and songs about the great man in the Tower. Lovat had been a man of portentous effrontery, and many persons, in various social ranks, could tell tales of his subtle doings. He was in durance for no mere personal wrongdoing. The charge against him was attempted subversion of the existing regal order. Political sympathy and hatred were in the balances the people used in weighing up his qualities. They knew that he would be executed in public if convicted, and that orgies of public passion would celebrate that day.

The people were interested in Lord Lovat's strange personality. His historical setting was to them either a matter of the commonest knowledge or of indifference. Neither attitude mattered; he had personal characteristics enough. Here was a man who had been sentenced to death decades ago, but had lived to be the recipient of a King's favour, had served and betrayed the two Royal houses of Britain at different times, if not at the same time, held bantering conversations with Madame de Maintenon, had been a priced fugitive on West Highland hills, and had held his own in intrigue with rulers, priests, and legates.

The year of Simon Fraser's birth is unknown. The places of his birth and his burial have been the subject of controversy, though it seems probable that he was born in Urray, Ross-shire, and it is now certain that he was buried in the Tower of London. Mystery was to him as a cloak to a traveller. To get beneath the cloak and find the traveller, to fathom the mystery and make the acquaintance of Lord Lovat, is the task that now confronts us.

Whatever may have been the actual year of his birth, he was born in stirring times. The period covered by the years between his mother's marriage and death (1665-1679) was full of great events. The best evidence seems to point to 1676 as his probable natal year. The boy was not a likely lord or chief when he learned the elements of the various languages necessary for the equipment of a Highland gentleman. He was a first cousin, once removed, of the then Lord Lovat, and he had an elder brother. His father, Thomas Fraser of Beaufort, was the fourth son of Hugh, the ninth Lord Lovat. While still a youth—and we may be sure that he was a picturesque youth—Simon was sent to college at Aberdeen. Whatever may have been the social exploits of his college days, he certainly acquired a good knowledge of Latin, for, through all the changing fortunes of his manhood, he was always able to quote aptly from the classics.

The year 1685 was an important one for Simon. His cousin Hugh, the eleventh Lord Lovat, then married Lady Amelia Murray, a daughter of the Marquis of Atholl. This year was a black one for the Protestants (among whom was Simon). King Charles II., when on his deathbed, avowed himself a Roman Catholic, and when James II. came to the throne he also showed strong Roman Catholic sympathies. In 1689 the fiery cross was out in Scotland, and on 20th November

Lord Lovat's Youth.

Simon drew a step nearer the peerage when his elder brother Alexander died from a wound received at Killiecrankie.[1] That Simon already held political views is indicated by his own statement that he was thrice cast into prison for "exertions in the Royal cause before he was sixteen." He also states that he served under General Buchan, but such early soldiering did not make the lad a fire-eater. He soon found the pen a mightier weapon than the claymore. He was ever a restless being, unfitted, both by disposition and circumstances, for maintaining during any great length of time a uniform motion in a politically straight line. So we find his college career, which lasted four years, abruptly coming to an end. He forsook his studies and again donned a uniform, that of the regiment raised by Atholl's son, Lord John Murray,[2] for the service of William and Mary. At first Simon had refused the commission. He had even prevented his cousin Hugh, Lord Lovat, from raising "so much as three men" for Murray; but on an uncertain date (probably about 1694, two years after Glencoe) he took the oath of service. He explains his conduct in this matter by stating that Lord John Murray, through Glengarry and Lord Lovat, induced him to join, and said that "it was impossible to render more important service to King James" than by taking a command in this regiment. Simon professes to have received from Lord John himself the assurance that the regiment was really meant for the service of the exiled King. After Queen Mary's death, which occurred on 28th December, 1694, we find her sworn defender from the hills writing thus—"I doubt not you will be in mourning for Queen Mary, but I am resolved to buy none till K. W. dies, which perhaps may serve for the next summer suit."

His autobiography (the "Memoirs," published in 1797[3]) gives an account of a romantic but fruitless plot in 1696 to obtain possession of Edinburgh Castle in name of King James, and of a ruse by which Lord John Murray persuaded Simon to visit

---

1 It will be remembered that in modern times various claimants of the Lovat estates have alleged that Alexander did not die as above stated, but fled to Wales, having stabbed a piper. Mr. William Burns deals with these claims, with apparent effectiveness, in his privately circulated Life of Lord Lovat. The Kirkhill parish register records Alexander's death on the date above mentioned, and the House of Lords has held the entry to be authentic.

2 See Biographical Notes, p. 301.

3 See Appendix No. IV., p. 308.

London and kneel to King William. Whatever may have been the fact, we find the life of arms being replaced by that of intrigue. Simon told Lord John (now created Earl of Tullibardine) to give his regiment to his footman, and began to ingratiate himself further with his cousin, Lord Lovat. His real aptitude, that of scheming, was beginning to assert itself. Lord Lovat is said to have been induced in March, 1696, to leave his estates to Simon's father, Thomas Fraser of Beaufort, and his issue, if he himself should leave no issue. A bond for 50,000 merks Scots was executed at the same time by the baron in Simon's favour "for love and affection." Neither of these provisions, however, proved in any way effective, and the documents were even said to have been forged by Simon. The friendliness between Lord Lovat and the Beauforts meant trouble with the Atholl family, who saw Lady Lovat's position being jeopardised, and the situation became acute. Tullibardine had Simon court-martialed for high treason either in connection with the plot to take Edinburgh Castle or because of some injudicious political letters which Simon had written. The accused officer was undoubtedly guilty of the crime of treason, but fortune favoured the bold, as she so often does, and Simon was acquitted. The lad was already learning how to play with fire.

Hugh, eleventh Lord Lovat, died on 4th September, 1696, leaving four daughters, but no son. There was a doubt, though ill-defined, whether the barony of Lovat was "a male fief"—one in which only the male line would succeed. Tullibardine, not unnaturally, denied that it was a male fief, and the question, as such questions will, drifted into the law Courts. To Simon it seemed to be a situation calling for strategy. He had acquired some confidence in his own manœuvring abilities. Like most men of his general type, he was quite willing to use women as pawns in the game, the objective here being no less than the full possession of the Lovat estates. Clearly the simplest way was to marry the child heiress, Miss Amelia Fraser, who was the late baron's eldest daughter. She must have been very young, because her father was born in 1666. She seems to have been born in 1686. Such a marriage would ultimately dispose of the question about the fief, bring him the estates, and very possibly the title also. Simon was always able to ingratiate himself with ladies, and ere long Miss

Amelia promised to elope with him. She did elope towards him, but, before the couple met, the intermediary, one Fraser of Tenecheil, thought better of it (probably he knew Simon), and returned the child to her mother. No reference to this escapade is made in the "Memoirs."

Amelia deserves our pity. Her heart was not to have the freedom of its kind. A certain Robert Fraser (who afterwards died, if Simon speaks truly, "under the visible judgment of God") conceived the idea of having her married to the son of Lord Saltoun, and got some Frasers to sign a letter to that peer making this antenuptial suggestion. Saltoun was himself a Fraser, with estates in Aberdeenshire, and to him the plan was big with possibilities. Seigneury in Inverness-shire, would be a good complement to sway in Aberdeenshire, so Saltoun set out for the Lovat country, accompanied by one of Lord Atholl's sons, Lord Mungo Murray. Amelia is again entitled to our sympathy. At the suggestion of scheming outsiders, a man was to bring his son to marry her; but the deliverer appeared, and in the person of her former wooer —Simon himself. It was no piece of knight errantry, for Simon, as we shall see, had a small supply of sentiment. His interference was selfish, but it was timely and effective.

After a meeting with some of the younger Fraser men, Simon took active steps towards his own objective, though also, by a happy chance, for the good of Amelia. Saltoun was taken prisoner at Bunchrew, 3 miles from Inverness, on or about 6th October, 1697, and borne to the Tower of Fanellan. In imitation of an ancient ruse, Simon erected a gallows in full view of the prisoner's window. It was meant for Saltoun's eyes rather than for his neck, but he was told to prepare for death. The grim joke was well stage-managed. Saltoun was induced by fear to sign a promise to give up Amelia and to abstain from scheming to get the lands. In his "Memoirs" (which contain some very excellent fiction) Simon alleges that he was the means of saving Saltoun's life from the fury of the clansmen. He makes no mention of his gallows. Clearly there had been no homicidal intent in the breast of any one; they only meant to frighten the Aberdeenshire gentleman, and they succeeded.

In all this, however, Simon did not attain his real object. He merely prevented Saltoun and Robert Fraser (not yet "visibly" rewarded for his plot) from securing a dominating position. A forward movement must now be made. His method of doing so was characteristic enough. He changed his whole tactics and married the dowager, Amelia's mother, or, to be brutally accurate, he went through two alleged marriage ceremonies, in which the dowager was an unwilling participant. His motive in "marrying" the dowager instead of laying more persistent siege to the heart of her daughter is not ascertainable. There is no suggestion of genuine affection for the former lady, and she could hardly have brought him into position for claiming the title or the lands, while the latter might conceivably have done so. Yet the fact remains that Simon chose the widow.

Various accounts of the nuptials have been given. They were stated by a contemporary to amount to "a most barbarous rapt." A writer in Somers' Tracts calls them "an ordinary cruel rape." Major Fraser's manuscript says, "The lady not yielding willingly, there was some harsh measures taken, a parson sent for, and the bagpipe blown up." Was it—to put the question bluntly—a wedding or a crime? I am inclined to think it was not a wedding, but, in spite of the bagpipe, I would not class it as a rape. Afterwards both Simon and the dowager at one time admitted the marriage and at other times denied it. A letter by Thomas Fraser of Beaufort to the Duke of Argyll says, "We have gained a considerable advantage by my eldest son being married to the dowager of Lovat."[1] On 23rd November, 1697, Simon wrote to the laird of Culloden, "I am very hopful in my dear wife's constancy if they do not put her to death."[2] On the other hand, Simon completely ignored the dowager when he wished to form another alliance.

The "marriage" with Amelia's mother had one important result. It focussed the hatred of the Athdolls, who now began active hostilities. On 26th October, 1697, he writes of "my implacable enemies." On 18th November of the same year Letters of Intercommuning were issued against him and his father. In those days Highlanders deferred to the Government only when they pleased. The earlier kings had never been able to dictate to the folk of the northern counties how they should mend their manners. The memory of the last clan fight—Mulroy, in 1688, when "MacDonald took the

[1] Carstares Papers, p. 434.
[2] Culloden Papers, p. 24.

brae on them"—was still in its first freshness. The territorial influence of the clan leaders was a far more potent force than any Royal warrant. A Fraser always considered himself first as a Fraser, and then as a Scotsman. The common people north of the Grampians had little idea of the great political movements of their day. They could be swayed, deceived, or goaded into war by any alleged insult to their immediate community. The larger issues were unrealised. Few could read or write, which mattered little, for there was little to read and no occasion to write. The keen religious antipathies of later days were then practically unknown. Neither Protestant nor Romanist had any idea of inward religion. They looked upon trade and commerce with contempt. When the southern counties burned with indignation against the commercial oppressions of the English, the Highlanders were concerned with their own tribal jealousies alone. Had the Lovat dowager been a Sassenach, her relatives had been as powerless as a Glasgow bailie's warrant would have been in Inverness-shire; but the dowager's Atholl folk were Highlanders, and Simon could not as yet exercise any real authority over his clansmen. He fled, and his name was added to the long list of well-known Scotsmen on whose heads a price has been put.[1] On 18th February following, a military expedition, with a Colonel Dalzell in command, was sent to hunt him down, but the colonel never had any real chance of out-manœuvring Simon. Only a very hostile Gael would have assisted a southern soldier against a Highland lad of his position and pretensions.

To this period belongs Simon's story of his alleged triumph over the official searchers at Altnigoir ("Memoirs," pp. 90-95). He would have us believe that this was an important military engagement which ended in complete victory for him, the enemy having to sue for mercy, which, he says, he granted after having inflicted on them the Roman humiliation of "passing under the yoke." He states that he made the soldiers swear "that they renounced their claims in Jesus Christ and their hopes of heaven, and devoted themselves to the devil and all the torments of hell, if they ever returned into the territories of Lord Lovat or occasioned him, directly or indirectly, the smallest mischief." It is not unfair to

1 Finlay MacLean's book of the stories of his father, "the Inverness Centenarian," states that Simon lurked for fourteen days among the rocks behind Clachnabarry (p. 57).

suggest that this piece of virile composition was the imaginative work of Simon when writing the "Memoirs" rather than an effort of a military leader under arms.

In spite of this so-called victory, Simon fled to Dunvegan, in Skye, where he had kinsfolk of his mother's family, the Macleods of Macleod. The power of the State did not succeed in arresting him, and in June, 1698, he was tried in absence for high treason, "by raising unlawful associations and continuing in arms when charged by a herald to surrender." The Court solemnly and ineffectually sentenced him to death.[1] Hugo Arnott tells us that this was the only case in Scotland since the Revolution in which a man was condemned in absence.

It is even possible that Simon never heard that the arm of the law had been outstretched at all. His flight can be explained by his fear of consequences other than mere judicial complication. The indictment was served under an Act of James VI., which made it permissible to serve summonses "against Islandmen, Highlandmen, and Borderers" by formal proceedings at the mercat cross of the head burghs of the next shires in the Lowlands. The Government was careful of the skins of its messengers-at-arms. Such means as these were necessary to disguise its impotence beyond the hills. It was easy to speak of "the wicked thieves and limmers of the clans" (Act of 1594, cap. 231); to govern them was quite another undertaking.

The doings of the Justiciary Court were more irksome than dangerous to Simon. He evaded capture for about two years, and then took steps to procure a pardon. Archibald, first Duke of Argyll,[2] writes to Forbes of Culloden on 5th September, 1700, "I have made it my chief concern to obtain Beaufort's (now I think I may say Lord Lovatt's) pardon, and the other gentlemen concerned with him in the convocation and seizing of prisoners . . . which I have at last obtained." The Highland outlaw was summoned to the Royal presence, apparently in 1700, to receive his pardon. He found the King at Loo, in Belgium, and received a document embodying the Royal clemency in respect of the charge of treason, but not absolving him from prosecution for rape. While on the Continent he visited the exiled

---

1 See State Trials, vol. xviii., p. 823.

2 See Biographical Notes, p. 300.

Jacobite Court at St. Germains, which proceeding, though clearly discourteous to the monarch whose grace he had just enjoyed, was not an act of treason. Had Simon been an Englishman, it would have been a crime to visit the Pretender; but the succession to the Scottish throne was still a matter of election, as it had been at King William's accession, so Simon was then (like every Scotsman till 1707) quite within his rights in visiting St. Germains.

He soon returned to the Highlands, and we may be sure that he did so with some ostentation. His star was temporarily in the ascendant, and Simon was never troubled by excessive modesty. His purse was nearly empty, but this was the plight of most Highlanders of that time. The years between 1696 and 1703 were the "seven lean years" of modern Scotland, when "the living wearied of the burying of the dead." Yet Simon was able in 1702 to raise some resources, mainly by granting bonds to the Fraser leaders, so cunningly framed that they could only be enforced if the creditor continued faithful to Simon's interests—an excellent way of securing a following.

Meanwhile, what of his domestic affairs? It is improbable that he ever met the Dowager Lady Lovat after 1700, though she lived till 1743. He was still only a claimant to the Lovat estates, though his father had died in Skye in May, 1699.[1] Yet he had led armed clansmen of his name. In his personality were concentrated brighter clan prospects than existed elsewhere, but he had not yet succeeded in becoming the unquestioned chief. He must have been a great hero among the younger Frasers, but that was not enough. The dowager and the Atholl family were ever in his way. Major Fraser tells us that, when Lord James Murray met his sister after the alleged wedding, he "took up his foot and gave her along the belly," asking if she owned herself married to such a villain. I think it is probable that the dowager had entertained a certain regard for Simon, but her family's hatred of him seems to have infected her after the separation.

---

1 A "pyramid," erected by Simon to his father's memory, formerly stood in the Parish Church in Durinish, Skye. It contained an inscription in characteristically Simonic language. Dr. Johnson and Boswell saw it in 1773, and the doctor described the inscription as "poor stuff, such as Lord Lovat's butler might have written." The monument fell to pieces, and was removed into the grounds of Dunvegan Castle. It has been re-erected by Macleod of Macleod.

The Fraser-Atholl spite continued keen, and the climax came in 1702, when Amelia, the Lovat heiress, wedded, with the consent of the Atholls, Alexander Mackenzie, son of Lord Prestonhall (a Court of Session judge, and brother of the Earl of Cromartie). The bridegroom took the name of Fraser with a view to conciliating Amelia's clan, and adopted the designation "of Fraserdale," by which he is known in history. Here was a great strengthening of the anti-Simon party. Steps were taken to attempt Simon's permanent discrediting. The old charge of rape was revived, and as he did not appear to thole his assize, he was denounced on 16th March as an outlaw, and "intercommuned" at the Inverness Cross. It was officially declared that he had forfeited any rights he had to the Lovat estates. Letters of fire and sword went out against him. Such was Scottish justice two centuries ago. In such facts are rooted the arguments, still advanced by Mr. William Burns and others, in mitigation of the verdict of posterity upon Simon's complex life. One cannot deny their plausibility. He certainly had a far sounder right to Fraser leadership than any man who opposed him. The Atholls were justly disliked for their landgrabbing and domineering propensities. His crime against the dowager, if it was a crime, was as well known at the time of his political pardon as it was in 1702, but the need of alleging it, for oblique purposes, had not arisen. Such treatment creates dourness even in less ambitious men than Simon.

He was deserted by his friends: even Argyll, the hereditary enemy of the Atholls, did not espouse the cause of his former *protégé*, and Simon did not fail to reproach him for his faithlessness or to become more determined in consequence. If the leading Highlanders had been neutral towards his pretensions he might have done without the smile of the official party, but he could not stand against both. It became desirable that he should shake the dust of Britain from his feet, and what was more natural than that he should proceed to the Stuart Court in France, where he might assist in brewing trouble for his present oppressors? He tells us in the "Memoirs" that he met the leading Jacobites before he left, and received their authority to represent them at St. Germains.

A Scot Abroad.

It was certainly a fit occasion for the presence of a capable Scottish Jacobite at the Court across the water. King William, who never really won the affection of the Scottish people, had died. The immediate future might bring many changes in its train. So, when Simon reached France by way of Holland, in September, 1702 (leaving his patrimonial claims in the keeping of his brother John, a very good custodian), he was welcomed. He soon had a meeting with the Queen. James had been dead for nearly a year.[1] James Francis Edward Stuart, afterwards known as "the Old Pretender," was then a child. His mother, Queen Mary of Modena, was head of the exiled Court.

In several respects Simon's arrival was opportune. England and France had been at war since May, and in October, 1702, the French and Spanish fleets were defeated at Vigo. An outlawed Scot could count on sympathy in France, and, with a little effrontery, he might secure patronage. Simon was received by Louis XIV. himself, and though that honour could not be truly styled "unexampled" (as Simon has it), the event was significant. St. Germains, however, was no abode of political peace and domestic goodwill, its whole atmosphere being charged by intrigues. Lord Middleton[2] and the Duke of Perth[3] were the leading courtiers, and were bitter rivals. Simon had to take sides, and, choosing the duke, he incurred the bitter hatred of Middleton, who was making a bid for Mary's favour, as Lovat himself did before long, by professing very devout Catholicism. Even for a man "naturally plain and sincere in his manners" (for so Simon describes himself in his "Memoirs"), the position was uneasy, but in his opening experiences he was fortunate. He was accepted as a man of influence. He tells us that at this time he got from the King of France a commission as brigadier-general. In 1703, when Jacobite prospects were excellent on account of the fiscal disputes between England and Scotland and the consequences of the

---

1 Major Fraser, in the Manuscript, says Simon was well received by King James II. (vol. i. p. 135). This is clearly wrong. King James died in 1701. Lord Lovat, in the "Memoirs," says he arrived in Paris in September, 1702 (p. 120).

2 See Biographical Notes, p. 305.

3 See Biographical Notes, p. 306.

Darien scheme's failure, he was sent back to his own country to feel its political pulse. If proof of his ability as a courtier were needed by the modern reader, this appointment supplies it. Though an outlaw, a mere claimant to Scottish territorial powers, this young man, in one year at St. Germains, had advanced thus far. The feeling between England and Scotland had become so bitter that the Scottish Parliament had rightly passed the Act of Security, providing that no English sovereign should rule in Scotland unless the northern wrongs were righted. Naturally the Royal assent was refused, but the passing of the Act showed how keenly the pride of Scotland had been touched. The chances of the Stuarts were brighter than at any time since the Revolution.

The Jacobites over the water were not without wisdom. They did not accept the envoy's estimate of his own nature as ingenuous and simple, so John Murray (not the Broughton fox, who was to follow his track so keenly at its end, but a brother of Murray of Abercairney) was sent to watch his movements.

One can guess what were the thoughts of Simon as he crossed the Channel. Here he was, the hunted outlaw of the previous year, playing for higher stakes than ever. He might soon be able to shape the destinies of Scotland, to win the Lovat lands, and to pay off old scores with Atholl. If he brooded over the devious courses of his personal enemies he must be forgiven, for Amelia's husband, and still more her crafty father-in-law, had resorted to methods that were low indeed. Knowing that the founts of Scottish Justice were poisoned, Lord Prestonhall, regardless of his honour and anxious to get a good infeftment in the Fraser lands, had himself purchased a debt incurred by a former Lord Lovat in 1669. An old form of legal diligence known as an "appraising" had been executed by the former creditor. Prestonhall, being now in right of it, had an opportunity that must have delighted his pettifogging mind. There was always a strong chance that Simon might return to found on the plea that the Lovat succession was "a male fief," and to serve himself the nearest heir male. This would have been awkward for the old judge and his daughter-in-law, but the "appraising" brought a splendid possibility. Prestonhall, knowing that Simon would not dare to appear as a litigant in any Scottish Court, raised before his own judicial brethren a ponderous action of reduction, improbation, and declarator, based on the appraising; and on 2nd December, 1702, he was found to be in right of the Lovat estates. He then executed a new entail of the lands, settling them on the issue of his son's marriage with Amelia. It was a pretty piece of trickery for a Senator of the College of Justice. More scrupulous men than Simon would be forgiven for vowing vengeance. The game was like to be keenly played. Prestonhall and Simon were well matched for such a contest, but the latter had to bide his time, for bearding a judge was too big an undertaking for an outlaw. During this excursion he must devote himself to politics alone, hoping by political scheming to reach a position whence he would enfilade that of the Mackenzies.

His journey north was adventurous, in the natural order of things. At Northallerton he encountered a suspicious justice of the peace. The outlawry could not be ignored, and a zealous magistrate was not a welcome visitor, but Simon was equal to the emergency. He plied his inquisitor with wine, an excellent sedative for such persons. The wheels of the law were thus put safely out of gear. In Durham and the north of England he interviewed the leading Roman Catholics, but found them far from "soople." Next we find him at Drummond Castle, dealing with a genuine meeting of Highland chiefs. Lochiel and other considerable folk were present, and kept council for three days. Simon says they decided to send him back to France to get a promise of military "succours," and that "in an evil hour" he consented, "in spite of the tears of the gentlemen of his clan, who, in despair, tore their hair when they saw him ready to abandon them a second time." The actual fruits of the Highland visit were unsubstantial. Simon returned south and interviewed Queensberry, who then held the post of Commissioner in Scotland, an office resembling the modern Lord Lieutenancy in Ireland. Simon says he went to amuse Queensberry and throw him on a wrong scent. The Commissioner, like his caller, had no reason to love either Atholl or Hamilton, so Simon gave him what purported to be reliable information that these nobles were traitors to the House of Hanover. In order to implicate Atholl, the Lord John Murray of former days, he affixed the address, "L—— M——Y," to an unaddressed packet handed him by Mary of Modena for conveyance to Scotland. He then informed Queensberry that he was under orders to deliver this packet to Atholl. The bogus address was accepted as corroborating the story, for Atholl, when in France, had been known as "Lord Murray." Simon says that Queensberry was delighted, and offered his visitor an amnesty, payment of his debts, a pension, and the command of a regiment if he would only become a Hanoverian. He tells us that he refused these numerous benefits for the present, saying he must first revisit the exiled King, and then he might return and submit to Queen Anne. On this footing he received a passport for France. Queensberry, on the other hand, states that Simon offered his services as a spy, and, as such, received the passport. One is inclined to give the preference to Queensberry's story. In any case, Simon had become a very efficient plotter, though he was not equal to the notorious Robert Fergusson, whom he met in London at this time. Fergusson, being a follower of Atholl, found Simon apparently very anxious to be reconciled to that nobleman, but Fergusson was no ordinary schemer. He saw through Simon's bold plan to ruin Atholl by securing his confidences. He warned Atholl, who, in turn, passed a hint to the Jacobite Court in France. A political adventurer in those days had need of keen wits.

Simon, who now decided to return immediately to the Continent, had succeeded in causing a good deal of commotion in the world, but he had overshot his mark. Even his St. Germains reputation was based more on cleverness than on trustworthiness, and the tide had turned against him. Sir John MacLean, a Jacobite from St. Germains (whom Lovat calls his "cousin-german," "Memoirs," p. 120), had just been arrested, and had laid bare the Jacobite plans. On 16th November, 1703, Lovat set out for France by way of the Low Countries, where, for the first time, he saw a great war in progress. Marlborough (in some respects as great a turncoat as Simon himself) was making Holland secure against attack, and preparing the way for continuing his great campaign.

Lovat seems (though with little reason) to have been confident at this time of a great personal success. He wrote to a clansman on 17th December, 1703, from Rotterdam—"Let no man's saying discourage you, for if we live both a year, you will, by God's help, see me the greatest Lord Lovat that ever was. I am so already out of my country, and I hope to be so in my country very shortly."[1] He also sent a manifesto to

1 Scottish Conspiracy Papers, pp. 33, 34.

the "Gentlemen of Clan Fraser," some phrases of which are very significant—"If you should not hear from me till I see you, let this letter be a faithful advertisement to you that I never resolve to quit my birthright and preserving of you while I live; and let it be a convincing exhortation to you to be united as one man to keep the possessions of your fathers, and resolve to dye bravely together, rather than survive your honour and the Mackenzies domineering over you, and transplanting you, which none of you is so ignorant but must see is their design and endeavour. But they never will do it while I live, and I hope to turn the chase on some of them before it be long."[1] Unfortunately for Simon, this letter and manifesto were captured, and never reached the Frasers, except, perhaps, in the official publication issued by the House of Lords in March, 1704.

Simon, with his brother John, passed through Holland in disguise and reached Paris in safety. An account of the visit to Britain was laid before Queen Mary, but it was soon clear that misfortune was in store for Simon. Murray's report was unfavourable, and received credit. Simon could no longer boast of his Continental importance. Still, he had great faith in his ability to deal with awkward situations by the use of his pen. He was ever a memorialist, and at this period his memorials were numerous. Yet they only sent him deeper into the political quagmire, for his correspondents were sometimes as unscrupulous as himself.

On 16th January, 1704, Lord Middleton had written to one of King Louis' Ministers, the Marquis de Torcy, making charges against Simon, and suggesting that he be arrested "without noise." On 3rd April the Duke of Berwick wrote to Queen Mary of Modena asking for his arrest. Murray's attitude at this time was afterwards dubbed by Lovat that of a "traitor," and "the creature of Lord Middleton." The situation prompted Simon to an impetuous act, which he must soon have regretted bitterly. He wrote to Queen Mary stating that he would never draw his sword while she ruled. Even Simon's recent adoption of the Roman Catholic faith did not save him from the consequence of this letter. The Queen was irritated, and asked the French King (whose coin sustained her Court) to

[1] See Mackenzie's "History of the Frasers," p. 283, and Mr. Burns' book, p. 54.

confine her overbold correspondent. The request was not granted immediately, but on 31st May Simon reached Bourges practically a prisoner, although he received a pension of a hundred crowns per month. Thence he was removed to Angoulême, where he remained for three years.

The political situation at this time was electric. The Scottish Parliament—by no means an easily suppressed force—was in a state of very proper indignation against England on account of commercial oppression. A formal proclamation had been issued in James' name claiming the thrones of Scotland and England. So keen was the tension that on 5th February, 1705, the English Parliament showed its foresight by providing for the military defence of the country in the event of troubles spreading from the north. The political flashpoint was nearly reached. War between the two countries became exceedingly probable, and though this crisis was met by saner methods, England had many other troubles. Political dispeace was omnipresent. Mr. Lecky states his opinion that had the Queen died at this juncture, the Pretender would have been called to the throne as her successor. It was seen that definite steps for a real Union of the two nations, politically and commercially, must be taken. The Commissioners for Union began their sittings on 16th April, 1706, and on 23rd July the Articles of Union were finally drafted. The movement for Union was very unpopular in Scotland. Towards the end of the year Queensberry's carriage was stoned in the Scottish capital, and the Jacobite Duke of Hamilton was publicly applauded by both Jacobites and Presbyterians.[1] The Union, consummated in 1707, was far from being an immediate success.

The prisoner at Angoulême, hearing of these events, must have chafed in his confinement. He had sought French favour by giving a fête in celebration of the birth of a daughter to the Dauphin. He "ordered a hogshead of wine to be brought out to the open street, and called on the townsmen to drink out with their caps and hats to the health of the cheild then born; and when he found that this had not fuddled them, he caused bring out two hogsheads more, and caused beat both the ends out of them, and made them all sprall on the streets drunk; which was caused be put immediately in the news."[2]

[1] Mr. Andrew Lang has given particulars of a strange alliance at this time between Jacobites and Cameronians.

[2] Major Fraser's MS. i. 150.

This display of loyalty had at least a partial effect, for Simon received a grant of five hundred livres and permission to choose his place of confinement. He chose Saumur, which had been till recently a Protestant stronghold. He went there towards the end of 1707.

In another respect good fortune came to Simon. Prestonhall had still further besmirched his own escutcheon by granting, in February, 1706, as a complement to a new deed of entail of the Lovat estates, a further legal document allowing the use by his son Fraserdale of the name Mackenzie, in place of Fraser. This naturally gave great offence to the Fraser clan, as such an act would do even in this twentieth century. There was a great French nobleman, the Marquis de Frezelière, who in a sense was a member of Clan Fraser,[1] and his favour naturally went out to his Highland cousin in France.

In 1708 there happened that strangely mismanaged Scottish invasion by James. Frezelière asked the Pretender's advisers to put Simon upon the staff, but, in spite of the Angoulême festivities, the reply came that if Simon had not been already a prisoner, Louis would have been asked to make him one. Doubtless they rued the decision before long. Simon's brains and energy would have been very valuable in an expedition where these assets were conspicuously absent. Frobin's fleet, with James and 4000 French troops aboard, was only successful in anchoring off Crail, in Fifeshire. The appearance of Admiral George Byng[2] sent the fleet again to sea, and with the loss of one ship it returned ignominiously to France.

The good graces of Frezelière were still with Simon, and he tells us[3] that in 1708 he planned an escape, intending to return to Britain and throw himself at the feet of Marlborough and Argyll,[4] but that he gave up the idea when he learned that, if successful, he would bring Frezelière into trouble. In 1709 he got another lesson in caution. He befriended an officer called Hamilton, who had killed his man in a duel. Believing that he could trust this object of his pity, Simon gave Hamilton the task of handing

1 The Lovat Frasers were descended from a Norman stock, and related to the house of Frezelière, in France.

2 Afterwards Viscount Torrington, and father of the unfortunate Admiral John Byng.

3 "Memoirs," p. 354.

4 John, second duke. See Biographical Notes, p. 300.

letters to some English and Scottish noblemen, including one to Lord Leven. The messenger was unfaithful, and the letters found their way back to St. Germains, where they were retained against an opportunity of using them to checkmate their writer. That they were so used is clear. Some authorities say they were produced in 1711, but Simon's own assertion that they did not emerge till 1714 is probably correct. At any rate, Simon was left in peace till the latter year, while English and Scottish politicians still quarrelled about the affairs of the two nations.

In 1714 happier days dawned for Simon. Fraserdale had exhausted the patience of the Fraser clan by his attempts to make them Mackenzie dependents. When Simon's brother John returned from the Continent the usurper had tried to capture him dead or alive. The irritation of the leading tacksmen became acute, and they began to long for the return of Simon. They knew that disaffection to the Government simmered merrily throughout the land, that a proposal to repeal the Union had only been defeated in the House of Lords in 1712 by a majority of three, that lords of Session, advocates, and lawyers in Edinburgh were ready for a change of ruler, that the Pretender's birthday had been celebrated in that city by bonfires and fireworks, that, in spite of the peace following the Utrecht treaty, the reigning dynasty would not rule for a week if a suitable Protestant Stuart could be found to replace the Queen. So they deputed one of their number, James Fraser[1] of Castle Ladar or Leathers (who in 1715 was to acquire the rank of major) to cross the narrow seas in quest of Simon.

Here we make the acquaintance of the major, whose crisp phrases (from his "Manuscript") have already been quoted. His is one of the quaintest figures in Scottish annals. One seldom finds a minor character in history in possession of a recorded personality. Usually he is little more than a name. The major, thanks to his partial autobiography, is a man whom we can know. Bombastic, chivalrous, vain, we find him self-revealed as clansman, traveller, courtier, soldier, publican, and farmer. In each capacity he is interesting to a wonderful degree. One is frequently tempted, when recording the deeds of Simon, to exchange the story of his treacheries

[1] See Biographical Notes, p. 302.

Major James Fraser, of Castleleathers.

(From a Portrait painted in 1723.)

for the quainter narrative of Castleleathers' exploits; but the major must be treated here only as Simon's associate, and the reader is advised to make his better acquaintance by direct perusal of the "Manuscript."[1]

Suffice it to say that, "upon the first day of May (1714) be four of the clock of the morning, the major" (he always writes in the third person) "took journey from his dwelling-house with his habersack, and left his wife and children spralling on the ground in tears, and proceeded on his journey till he came to Newcastle; from that went down to Shiels, and took occasion of a collier's vessel going for London." Soon he was on board a French ship bound for "Callies." "The major, not having tyme to bring in any provisions aboard, only a little bread and cheese, thought of no drink; the winds being contrary, was very sore put to it by the rascals. The major, not having their language, was like to fall foul of them, and, in end, their cruelty came to such a height that they would not give him drink, the bread and cheese drying him up, he was necessitate to draw his sword and was resolved to kill the three (being no more aboard) and to run the vessel to land, which, when they saw that he turned so desperate, gave him some small beer. But he was thereafter necessitate to watch for three nighs (nights) for fear they had attempted to kill him. But when they came in sight of Callies, the rascalls demanded his freight. He then stood to his guard, and resolved he would give them none untill they would land him, that he might have justice of them for using him so ill as not to give him drink and a bed to lay in, which was their paction at Gravesend." When he got ashore he visited a magistrate, and it is gratifying to learn that "the skiper was found guilty of oppression and fined in a gallon of wine, and not a farthing to be paid for his passage; which made us all very hearty."

In the beginning of July, after the adventures which were bound to happen to a traveller of his temperament, the major met his chief at Saumur, finding him "very low in his person." The message of the Fraser leaders was duly conveyed, but Simon replied that he could not leave France without the Pretender's permission. Discussion of the situation occupied several days, and then Simon fell a-writing. Always a great

1 Published by David Douglas, Edinurgh, in two volumes. Edited by Lieut.-Colonel Fergusson, 1889. See Appendix No. IV., p. 310 *inf.*, for notes as to this book.

penman, he produced on this occasion no less than eighteen letters, including "a whole sheet of paper, written back and fore, to the Pretender." Having got an introduction from Simon to an "Irish Cordileer," who might act as interpreter, the major set forth to move high personages in his chief's favour.

He first waited upon the Duke of Perth, who received him graciously and introduced him to his lady, but the Duke then showed him Simon's unlucky letter to Lord Leven—one of those that went astray through Captain Hamilton's treachery—yet so well did the major succeed that the duke said, "there was nothing like a tryall of the Queen's clemency," and sent him on his way. Like a dutiful clansman, the envoy pressed on to "Shallio" (Chaillot), and was soon before Royalty. "The major, never having the honour before to be so near a Queen, stood upon his good behaviour." Her Majesty, "be way of Jesuite," sent him on a fool's errand, pretending to wish him success in his mission. She sent him to find the Pretender where she knew no Pretender was, "which she might have spared if she had not been a real Jesuite, and, according to her belief, yet in purgatory till she make atonement to the poor major for the sweat he lost."

As a matter of fact, Queen Mary had just heard of the death of Queen Anne, and had sent a message to James summoning him to her side. The major was not to be outwitted. Perseverance won the day. He soon had an interview with James at Luneville. Castleleathers was becoming acclimatised to the Court atmosphere, and, when reference was again made to Simon's letter to Lord Leven, he mildly suggested that it was a forgery, probably perpetrated by one of the Atholls!

James had sized up Lovat, and roundly abused him to his clansman's face. The major pointed out how Simon's return would thirl the clan to the Jacobite cause. James indicated that the Frasers might be made useful without Simon; but the major said he could not betray his trust to his friends, who would never draw a sword for James or any of his house if they did not get back their chief. The Pretender then gave the major four medals, and said that he expected to see him die a colonel in his service, but ordered him to leave France without re-visiting his chief. The major's diplomatic progress was not at fault. Before he left he procured the recall of this command.

He further advanced in knowledge of courtly ways by meeting the Duke of Lorraine, who thought he could make sport of the rough Highlander. Lorraine soon found out his error. Physical prowess supplied any remaining want of social veneer in the major's composition. By taking part in a hunt, outstripping the hounds themselves and killing the hare with his riding whip, he showed such sporting mettle that the duke presented him with an excellent horse. As he was then forty-four years of age, the major's feat was a notable one, and he deserved the useful gift.

When two such spirits as these Frasers foregather, as they did again at Saumur, important developments might be confidently foretold. They absented themselves from Saumur for seven weeks and visited the south-west of France, an expedition that was probably meant to test the possibility of more definite action. After a brief reappearance at Saumur to take leave of the priests and to assure them, untruthfully, that Simon had permission to return to Britain, the adventurers "took the road," leaving a hint that inquisitive people should be told that Simon had gone to visit the Governor of Rouen.

The major exchanged shots with two highwaymen before that city was reached, but this was a mere incident in the travels of two such braves. They went next to Dieppe, but, finding no means of crossing the sea, they tried Boulogne, whence they sailed to England in an open vessel. An altercation took place about the major's demand for the transportation of his Lorraine horse, and the chief's yielding to his clansman must have increased the danger of the passage. A few years later the ungrateful Simon would have left both major and horse on a foreign shore had the opportunity recurred.

At this stage Simon entered on another period in his history. He soon became a servant of his former enemies, the Hanoverians, and the enemy of his former friends, the Jacobites. Here is one of the puzzles in his life. What is one to make of this rapid change of front? I regard his career as a kind of "beat to windward," to use a nautical metaphor. Like a sailing ship heading up channel against the wind, he was now on the port tack and now on the starboard. He pointed at one time almost directly opposite to his former course, but he was getting to windward all the time. It was not the compass bearing of the moment that really concerned him, but the ultimate point of arrival, which in his case was the undisputed possession of the Lovat estates. Many years afterwards he wrote to a friend as to the recovery of the lands, saying "that I did in such a venturous or rather desperate manner that none of my enemies or even friends and relations thought that ever I would be able to accomplish my design, but that I must die in the attempting of it."[1] Thus it was that Simon "went about" during his Channel passage.

He reached London, and, as soon as an opportunity occurred, set about preparing a petition for the remission of the sentences pronounced against him.[2]

It was obviously desirable that the petition should seem to be backed by some kind of public desire for clemency to the outlaw. The major was despatched to Scotland on 11th December, 1714, to have this document signed by the Jacobites as if it were meant for the king-over-the-water and by the Whigs as if for King George. Naturally, Fraserdale scented trouble, and, through the Justice-Clerk and Montrose, who was the Secretary for Scotland, frustrated Simon's plan. The Culloden Papers show that before the end of 1714 Fraserdale applied for an extract of the old sentence against his rival.

In this same month the sentenced man wrote to the Earl of Sutherland asking his help, being "fully resolved to expose his life for the Royal Family of Hanover." This, indeed, he did in the immediate future.

In February of the fateful year of 1715 the major returned to Simon in London with the petition, signed, he tells us, by "all the leading men of the five countys." He says that he and Simon were "forced then to make many a moonlight flitting from one part of London to another"; but they continued to remain in that city till the month of June, in spite

---

1 Letter to Lord Advocate Craigie, written on 3rd December, 1743. Major Fraser's MS. ii., Appendix, p. 196.

2 In the "Culloden Papers," p. 336, a petition is reprinted, with a list of its signatories, which was believed by the Editor of these papers to be the petition above referred to. Some of its words speak of special services rendered "by the influence he had over a numerous clan," "when the greatest dangers did seem to surround us." I am of opinion that this clearly relates to Simon's attitude during Mar's rising, and that, accordingly, this petition cannot be the one above mentioned.

of efforts by the Atholl faction to harry their lodgings on the 11th of that month, when they were living in Soho Square. Simon was busy with his pen. The major tells us that on 30th April Simon wrote to the Earl of Sutherland "a very creeping letter." He was an adept at such compositions.

When the petition was presented to the King on 24th July, that monarch very astutely placed it in his pocket and gave no opinion. His Majesty had many matters well fitted to weigh upon his mind. News of an intended Jacobite invasion had come from France nine days previously. Several of the dismissed Ministers were being impeached. Naturally the King was cautious. It may be noted that this incident of 24th July is the last recorded in Simon's "Memoirs."

Within a few days two men left London independently and with equal secrecy. One was the disappointed and revenge-obsessed Earl of Mar, and the other was Simon, who bore a pass from Lord Townshend. On 17th August Mar passed the Tay, with forty horsemen. Nine days later the Jacobite leaders met at Braemar, and the rising of the '15 was definitely begun, though the war standard did not wave till 6th September. Fraserdale was now a Jacobite. To pardon Lovat would have been simple, but the King was afraid of the Atholl family.

Simon's doings during September are unrecorded, but it is clear that he reached Dumfries early in October by way of Newcastle, accompanied by the faithful major. His long Continental absence saved him from ready recognition by ordinary wayfarers, but at Dumfries he met a member of the Atholl house, who promptly informed a magistrate. A guard was placed over his lodgings till the Marquis of Annandale's wishes could be known. The marquis, after interviewing the major, was prepared to trust Simon, and reprimanded the magistrate. Simon's next known halt was at Lanark, where he received very different treatment. He and five of his party were made honorary burgesses on 15th October.[1] Argyll, in

[1] The Burgh Council seem to have been lavish in their grant of the dignity of honorary burgess. On this occasion the recipients were—"Ane noble lord, Simon, Lord Lovatt; Mr. James Frazer, his brother german of Colshill; Mr. John Frazer, Esquire; Daniell Frazer, servitor to ye Lord Lovatt; Alexr. Frazer, also servitor to ye said lord; Hugh Frazer of Lillshoum; John Campbell, son of Capt. John Campbell of Wallwood; Cornet William Campbell, Jr., Wallwood; Dr. John Stevenstoun in Air; John Carnachan, servitor to Capt. John Campbell of Wallwood; David Ross, servitor to Capt. John Campbell of Wallwood; William Lauder, Quarter Master in Lord Portmore's Regiment of Dragoons."

command of the King's forces, was now at Stirling, and thither Simon hastened. A mutually satisfactory interview took place, and he then went to Edinburgh, where a temporary reverse of fortune awaited him. He was arrested by order of the Justice-Clerk, but quick wits and an elastic conscience prevailed. He assured his captor that he was a "Captain Brown." The Provost knew it was false, but he was a Campbell, and loyal to his chief, Argyll. He arranged Simon's release, and procured him a passage for the north. Sailing from Leith, with his brother, the major, John Forbes of Culloden[1] (brother of the future President), and about a dozen other passengers, he had a romantic though uncomfortable voyage. If we may believe the major's narrative, the skipper (a Portsoy man, and probably a Roman Catholic) wished to allow a Jacobite search party to come alongside as they sailed along the coast of Fife. "The major immediately presented a gun to his breast, and desired him to higher all sails. . . . Lord Lovat and Culloden, hearing a noise, put out their heads and asked what the matter was; the major commanded them to keep their room, he knowing by that time that they were sea-sick. The boat being in rear of them, they let fly three or four shots more, they having plenty of ammunition. In a short time the ship outrun the boat—and so they were quit of her."[2]

Next day they reached Fraserburgh, near the Saltoun country (very excellent sailing), and "the wind turned a pick-teeth, so that they were forced to drop anker before that town. Then a counsell was held by my Lord Lovat and Culloden what method to take. My Lord Lovat would rather go to sea than land at the man's door, for whose father he had erected a gallews. Culloden answered that he believed he would not hang him; and for his share he was so seasick that he would rather fight his way and dye at land than keep the sea any longer. Whereupon the cock-boat was put out, and as many as it could carry went ashore, namely, my Lord Lovat, his brother, Culloden, and the major."

They visited an inn for refreshments, and there a pretty affair began to develop. Lord Saltoun, the man whom Simon most wished to avoid, came to the door inquiring who the

---

1 See Biographical Notes, p. 302.
2 MS. ii., p. 50.

strangers were, as he was in the neighbourhood with a Jacobite force on the look-out for Royalists. The major was sent to deal with Saltoun. He assumed the rôle of drover, probably because some of his late fellow-voyagers were drovers from the county of Sutherland returning from the south. His party, he said, were Mackenzies, Mackays, and Sutherlands returning from the southern markets. A little whisky was found useful in keeping awkward subjects out of the discussion, and soon Saltoun not only accepted the drovers at their face value (though it is certainly not clear why he should have looked with favour on Mackays and Sutherlands, who were nearly all Hanoverians), but supplied them with horses for their journey. It was a smart piece of trickery, which Simon should have remembered for the major's benefit in after days.

The rest of the journey was safely accomplished, though the major had to make some further use of his talent as a romancer. They reached the house of Hugh Rose of Kilravock, who was "mighty fond to see them." Simon remained there, as the night was stormy, "he being always tender of his carcass," in the major's opinion.

These were great days for Simon. After years of intrigue, he was about to grasp the prize. The "beat to windward" seemed well-nigh completed. The long-looked-for anchorage seemed close at hand. Fraserdale had joined the Jacobite army with some of the Frasers, but three hundred had declined to join their would-be chief, and were now in Stratherrick awaiting developments. It was important that they should come to heel at once, so the major went post-haste to meet them and bring them to Culloden House. He found them determined to know exactly how Simon stood with regard to the ruling party in the State. For a man who had successfully tackled Lorraine and Saltoun, the management of a few hundred of his own clansmen was mere recreation. Let me take his own words—"The querrie then to the major was, on what terms had my Lord Lovat come home. 'Gentlemen, you are all my friends and relations,' said the major, 'and I am bound to tell you truth.' Which be the by, he did not, but dissembled with them all. For had he told them that my Lord Lovat had not got his pardon, but had run off from England, as he did from France, not one man of them would have joined. So that the major told that my Lord Lovat had remission of all former crimes.

And that he had his promise of his estate upon proper behaviour, if Fraserdale had gone to the rebellion; and moreover the major told them that he got £500 to bear his charges; whereupon quart-stoups of whiskie went round to the King's health who had given their chief his peace."[1]

In a short time the major and his men were at Culloden House, where a council of war was held. Simon was now an example of loyal energy, resolved "to do some signal action for the Government, or die on the spot." He sent a prompt message of recall to those of his clan whom Fraserdale had enlisted for Mar, and three hundred men were thus lost to the Jacobites two days before Sheriffmuir.

He turned his attention to Sir John Mackenzie of Coul, who held Inverness Castle for the Pretender. The movement required some assurance, for a MacDonald army, under Keppoch, was hurrying to Inverness. Had this force co-operated with the garrison Simon would have had a difficult task, but he stood so firmly that the MacDonalds turned their attention to plundering the Grants' country, and left the garrison to take care of themselves. This was done so feebly that on Saturday, 12th November, the day before Sheriffmuir, Simon was in full possession of the Highland capital and its dominating castle. The Grants, eight hundred strong, had threatened the town from the south, and Culloden's men were on the east, so the taking of Inverness was not a bloody affair, or an epoch-making event in military history. Still less was it as Simon declared in a letter to Ilay,[2] "the greatest piece of service that was done in this country to any King." But it was a useful feat, and it entitled its doer to gratitude, though not to laurels. The modern reader will agree that Simon's subsequent appointment to command the Government troops at Elgin was an adequate recognition of the performance.

The Earl of Sutherland, with his own clan and the Mackays, reached Inverness soon after its capitulation, and the prospering Hanoverian chiefs learned of Sheriffmuir. Like their enemies, they regarded that fight as a victory. The news that "we ran and they ran" took long to percolate the Highland counties.

---

1 Major's MS. ii., 67/8.

2 Archibald, Earl of Ilay, afterwards third Duke of Argyll. See Biographical Notes, p. 300. This letter is printed in Hill Burton's Life of Lord Lovat, pp. 115 and 201.

The Rising of 1715.

But little military duty remained to Simon and the major (who, as already stated, attained his military rank during this campaign). Simon prepared to prevent Seaforth from causing further trouble, and when he and his men came home from Sheriffmuir Simon offered to fight them. Terms, however, were arranged, and no blood was shed. He also "reduced the Duke of Gordon," but that was no difficult undertaking as matters stood.

Thus began and ended the military services rendered by Simon to his former enemies, and of which he afterwards tried to make so much when his life hung upon the record of his actions. It must be remembered, however, that Mar's estimate of Simon's services was candid enough. He wrote—"Lovat is the life and soul of the (Hanoverian) party here. The whole country and his name dote on him, and the Frasers have left us since his appearing in the country."

Simon had no part in suppressing the futile attempt to renew the rising, after the Pretender's arrival in Scotland with six followers at the end of 1715 or beginning of 1716. Auchterarder, Crieff, Muthil, and other places were burned by the insurgents, but the attempt was inefficiently organised, and the Pretender fled on 3rd February to France. Even the just indignation caused in Scotland by the action of the Government in taking the Scottish prisoners to Carlisle for trial, did not fan into flame the dying embers of Jacobitism.

With the Fraser leader the personal element was, as usual, supreme. He tried to strengthen his position by making, on 10th January, 1716, a bond of friendship—that old-world bargain—with William, Lord Strathnaver. On 5th March he wrote to Duncan Forbes of Culloden—"For its most certain, I keep'd ye Macleods at home, which was considerable service to ye Government. . . . If you suffer Glengarry,[1] Frazerdale or ye Chisholm[2] be pardon'd, I will never carry a musquet any more under your command though I should be oblig'd to go to Affrick."[3]

Five days later his pardon was signed. Hill Burton has described it as "an astounding and horrible enumeration of all the crimes and abominations to which the human animal is

---

1 See Biographical Notes, p. 305.
2 See Biographical Notes, p. 301.
3 Culloden Papers, p. 101.

liable," but this statement is too strong. On 23rd June of the same year Simon was accorded the honour of a Royal audience. He was now busy trying to get a grant of the life-rent escheat[1] of Fraserdale's goods. At this time he did not press his claim to being the only rightful Fraser chief. He found it easier to begin by claiming the income of the lands forfeited by Fraserdale's rebellion. It was another aspect of the beat to windward. On the day of his visit to the King he wrote to Duncan Forbes—"I want but a gift of ye escheat to make me easy." On 28th June he wrote to him stating that the King had given him a grant of the escheat, and, uniting the practical side of life with the emotional, he foreshadows a matrimonial alliance with a sister of the Laird of Grant. On 23rd August the Royal warrant was executed putting him in possession of the liferent use of all goods formerly possessed by the hated Fraserdale, "for the many brave and loyal services done and performed to his Maty, by Simon, Lord Lovat, particularly for the zeal and activity he showed in suppressing the late unnatural rebellion."[2] He had thus been formally recognised as Lord Lovat, and though the possession of the income was not very stable, it represented a great advance on any former position he had occupied.

Fraserdale showed a great amount of cunning and persistence, almost equal to that of his opponent. On 28th January, 1717, we find Lovat imploring Duncan Forbes for legal assistance. "I beg you may give me some prospect," he wrote, "of not being again forc'd to leave ye kingdom or to fight against ye King's forces. The one or ye other must be, if I do not find any legal pretence of possessing the estate but by this gift, which I now reckon as nothing."[3] Six months later, on 20th June, the liferent was confirmed to Lovat by the House of Commons, but it was no more than a liferent. "Lovat's gift run the gantlet this day in the House of Commons,"

---

1 Liferent escheat is the forfeiture to a superior or to the Crown of a vassal's rents while he remains an outlaw. Liferent escheat follows upon sentence of outlawry, if not recalled within a year. The fee, or real ownership, of the lands remains with the outlawed vassal unless expressly taken away. He may therefore dispose of the fee by will, or otherwise, provided he does not thereby prejudice the rights of the party entitled to the liferent escheat. See MacRae, 1839; MacL. and R. 645.

2 Culloden Papers, p. 339.

3 Culloden Papers, p. 70.

writes John Forbes of Culloden to his brother Duncan, "by reason of a resuming clause in favour of Fraserdale's lady, presented by Lord James Murray and strongly supported by Cockburn, Halden, and the squad: who in the debat, which lasted two hours, were pleased to belch out many scurrilous reflections against Lovat; but all to no purpose, for the gift subsists as it did, in a great measure owing to Mr. Walpole."[1]

Almost exactly coincident with Lovat's entry upon recognised territorial power was his marriage with Margaret, fourth daughter of Ludovick Grant of Grant. The beginning of 1717 saw the couple duly wedded, and the union lasted till 1729. It seems to have been the most successful of Lovat's matrimonial experiences. When a man writes to the relations of a deceased wife roundly abusing her successor, one may presume that the former union was at least peaceful. The Laird of Grant was Lovat's chief correspondent when a later marriage proved painful, so we may believe that Margaret Grant had some virtues in her husband's eyes.

It is unnecessary, in describing the life of this great political schemer, to deal in detail with his many private quarrels and litigations. He went to law with the major respecting that worthy's claim for boarding John Fraser of Lovat during an illness that terminated fatally in April, 1716; with the creditors of Fraserdale, who vindicated their right to share in the escheat to the amount of their debts; with the factor appointed to secure the Dowager Lady Lovat's interests;[2] and with Fraserdale's chamberlain about the family plate. Very probably Lovat enjoyed these lawsuits, for some people have an unnatural zest for litigation. He had, in 1721, the further experience of having objection taken to his proxy for the election of Scottish representative peers. Murray of Broughton, in his "Memorials," says Lovat was so hated in Edinburgh that his men had to carry arms in that city.

During the picturesque years that saw the birth of Prince Charles Edward Stuart, the making of General Wade's roads in the Highlands, Voltaire's visit to England, the Shawfield riots in Glasgow, the death of George I., and other important events, Lovat was mainly "up north" performing his duties as Sheriff of Inverness, to which he had been appointed, drilling

---

1 Culloden Papers, p. 72.

2 This gentleman's granaries were, not surprisingly, burnt down by unidentified persons in December, 1719.

his company of men-at-arms, looking after the estates, and quarrelling bitterly with Fraser of Phopachy and his old benefactor, Major Fraser. General Wade, in his report of 10th December, 1724, said Lord Lovat then had eight hundred men able to bear arms. For nine years after his return to Royal favour he had retained his half-pay and a pension of £400, which he says he owed to the personal friendship of King George I. (see letter to Lord Ilay of 27th May, 1737, Hill Burton, pp. 204-5). In his speech after the verdict of the peers he said he had had a pension of £300 which had never been withdrawn.

He seems to have been a good landlord. Dr. Charles Fraser Mackintosh[1] reproduces a lease granted by Lovat in 1732 with a provision about inbringing barren ground. He says, "Simon, Lord Lovat, must be included in the category of improvers of land a century before it became common" (to improve it). The major, in an affidavit, sworn after Lovat's death, tells us that his chief went freely about the countryside conversing with all and sundry. It is also on record that he always kept a supply of farthings for gifts to beggars, and in those days that humble coin was not despised. On 3rd July, 1730, the peerage litigation had been decided by the Court of Session in his favour.[2]

He seems to have maintained his political equilibrium unshaken for nearly two decades. One need not accept the statement made at the treason trial by Chevis of Muirtown that Lovat was privy to the farcical Jacobite invasion of 1719. Chevis's statements were not in themselves entitled to much respect, were unconfirmed at the trial, and it must be remembered that even Lovat's accusers at this trial alleged in their Articles of

1 Antiquarian Notes, 1st Series, p. 2.

2 The case involved an interesting point. The Lovat title had not been created by any known patent, but had come down from immemorial days. Till 1696 the direct male line had never failed. Simon argued that all such baronies descended in the male line only, as they must be presumed to have been granted for services in council and in battle, which could only be rendered by men. Fraserdale contended that, in the absence of a definite restriction to heirs male, it must be held to descend to "heirs whomsoever." Simon's contention prevailed. Readers who find Boswell's "Life of Johnson" more entertaining than Bell's "Principles of the Law of Scotland" will find in the former work an interesting discussion of the relative merits of a fief to "heirs male" and one to "heirs whomsoever." Lord Auchinleck and his son differed as to an intended entail, and Dr. Johnson gave his views.

Impeachment no fall from political grace earlier than 1743. It is true that the Attorney-General and other speakers alleged complicity in the rising of 1719, although no such crime was in the charge. According to modern practice, the Attorney-General should have been severely censured for introducing such an accusation, since no notice of it had been given to the accused, and he had been granted no opportunity of preparing rebutting evidence.

Lovat became a widower in 1729, and, after an unsuccessful attempt to win the hand of a daughter of Lord President Dalrymple, he married Primrose Campbell of Mamore.[1] The wedding took place in 1733. A worse-assorted couple has seldom existed. One cannot at this date find evidence from the wife's point of view. That of the husband is made only too plain by his published letters[2]—" Lady Lovat, whose head was never right, turned completely wrong since I saw you. Her behaviour looked rather like a mad woman, full of folly and malice, than like a woman of common sense and religion." " I knew her hellish temper." " Poor Lord Lovat has for his wife a mixture of a devil and a daw." He makes various charges against her—fitness for Bedlam, an intrigue with a minister, turning her room into an apothecary's shop, and in September, 1739, he " blesses God " that he is now very near being "separated from that incarnate devil," his wife. In May, 1740, they finally separated. The reader will doubtless rejoice that he is not compelled to give a verdict as to the cause of the unhappiness, but it must be remembered that Simon was strongly disposed to quarrelling.[3] When one finds him referring to the poor old major in terms of the vilest abuse, one is inclined to sympathise with the unlucky Primrose Campbell.

As examples alike of Lovat's pungency in description and his forgetfulness of old promises, the following characterisations of Major Fraser may be culled from the letters:—" A wild,

1 Margaret Grant, Lady Lovat, had four children—Simon, the Master of Lovat (see Biographical Notes); Alexander (1729-1762), called by his father " the Brigadier "; Janet, who married Cluny MacPherson, of the '45; and Sybilla, who died, unmarried, in 1755. By Primrose Campbell there was only one child, Archibald Campbell Fraser, who succeeded his elder brother as head of the clan.

2 See letters printed in " The Chiefs of Grant."

3 Finlay MacLean's book of the recollections of " the Inverness Centenarian " records that Lovat was dealt with publicly for misconduct and placed on " the cutty stool " in church, and that in consequence he forsook the church of Kiltarlity for that of Kilmorack (p. 66).

unnatural, and ungrateful wretch;" "That known notorious liar and monster of ingratitude, Major Cracks;" "A known liar, romancer, knight of the post, and a double spy whom no man in this country regards more than they would do a madman that runs up and down the fields;" "I will make a faithful memoir of the history of that ruffian since I knew him." Those phrases are directed against a man whose conduct was clean, and whose career was honourable. They are therefore significant as signs of their writer's capacity for rounding upon his friends. His treatment of Castleleathers was even more remarkable as a display of unjustified aversion, almost amounting to mania.

High court was held at Castle Dounie, the family stronghold, then standing on a site near which is the present Beaufort Castle. One of the guests has given a graphic account of a dinner in the castle hall, where the chief was surrounded by his retainers in the ancient mode. Each received liquor appropriate to his social standing, and Lovat is said to have shown great tact in preventing the lesser clansman from feeling slighted by the gradation of his tipple. In one direction Lovat was nearly always lavish—in his use of terms implying intimacy. "Dear cousin," and similar phrases, were constantly on his lips. It must have been a pleasant period of his life, contrasting strongly with the restless years that preceded and followed it.[1]

Here the student of Lord Lovat's life finds the state of matters suddenly becoming complex. Practically every former course taken by "the old fox" (as Highlanders called him) is easily explained. He had thought, when he took it, that therein lay the quickest road to the chiefship and the lands. Yet now when these were in his grip, when further worldly advancement must have seemed the certain reward of political consistency, we find him risking the very prizes he had so laboriously gained. Whatever may have been his secret attitude during the previous twenty years, in 1739 he took sides with the Jacobites. An "association" was formed by him, with Lord John Drummond, Lord Traquair, Lochiel, and others, for furthering the regal claims of the Stuarts. These secret communings must have been known to the Government, for in the

[1] See Donald Macleod's Narrative, pp. 47/48, and Fraser Mackintosh's Antiquarian Notes, 2nd Series, p. 7.

same year Lovat was deprived of the command of his company of soldiers, a loss which he deemed a most bitter insult, and which must have undermined his local prestige. Previously he had written to Lord Ilay—" I always loved Sir Robert Walpole more than all the Ministers I ever knew in England." That opinion was now reversed. He complains of being turned out of the King's forces " in a manner not known in any army." He never forgot the incident. To the end he referred to it as justifying all his subsequent conduct. During 1740 he visited Argyll and Ilay, and assured them of his continued loyalty to King George, but about the same time the King over the water issued a patent creating him Duke of Fraser, Marquis of Beaufort, and Earl of Stratherrick. The double deal had begun. In January of the following year he wrote to a confidential friend—" You see me embark'd over head and ears with the noble party of the patriots."[1]

What was Lovat's motive here? I believe he experienced an outbreak of that inherent Jacobitism which had already caused his early imprisonments, his troubles with Tullibardine in Edinburgh Castle, the subsequent court-martial, and which though dormant at times, was never extinct. During the years of his outward loyalty, the irritation at his French confinement had not died away, and, what was more important, his enemy Fraserdale had become a Jacobite, and so opened a way for Lovat's material advancement. Lovat's Jacobitism was like the sectarian spirit of Highlanders in later days, a survival from the historic past, a sentiment subject to strong outbursts, an attachment not necessarily in relation to the other ruling conventions of its possessor, but never permanently forsworn. Lovat was like the man who agreed that honesty was the best policy, but declined to be bigoted in his opinion. He was ready to make exceptions.

He had become involved in local politics some years previously, and found in them a new field for tactical operations. Many of the prominent Highland magnates were engaged in moulding public opinion, or, more accurately, in vitiating its expression, by creating "barons." Pieces of land were trans-

1 See Mr. Mackenzie's Life and Times of Simon, Lord Lovat, p. 313, and New Spalding Club Historical Papers relating to the Jacobite period, vol. ii., pp. 10/27.

ferred to the names of trusted inferiors, who would vote as they were bid when the Parliamentary elections recurred. The records of the Court of Session contain much buried information which may yet be used to show in what strange burrows Scottish democracy took root. It was natural that Lovat should also engage in the sporting employment of voter making.[1] He declared, "I'll make twenty new barons . . . for I am resolved to keep a sort of ballance in ye shire, as my ancestors have done." The inevitable result followed. Lovat was at best a suspect. The Government, aided, we may presume, by carefully circulated Atholl and Mackenzie rumours—began to denude him of the honours it had formerly bestowed. He became more and more involved in Jacobitism. Few men, in the circumstances, would have maintained any show of loyalty, but Lovat was a prince among deceivers of historic importance. As his Jacobite operations became more pronounced he drew nearer in professed friendship to Duncan Forbes of Culloden, who had been Lord President since 1737, and was the best friend the House of Hanover ever had in the north.

On 23rd December, 1743, James appointed Lovat his lord lieutenant "of the country north of the Spey." Soon afterwards we find him dining with Lord President Forbes.

Prince Charles Edward reached Eriskay, near Barra, on 23rd July, 1745, and set foot on the mainland two days later. On 3rd August Lovat wrote to Lord Advocate Craigie expressing his eagerness to serve the King and the Government; but before many days had passed he informed Lochiel that, if the Macphersons rose, he would bring out the Frasers to help them. The spinning of his tangled web went merrily on. A letter to the Lord Advocate, dated 23rd August, contains a complaint that his clan had been so neglected that he had not "twelve stand of arms in the country." On the 27th he wrote to Forbes about "Lochiel, who, contrary to his promise to me, engages in this mad enterprise. . . . I have always been a declared enemy against this mad project."[2] How deceitful were his expressions is shown by the letter to Lochiel of September, 1745, saying, "I fear you have been overrash in

---

1 Culloden Papers, p. 131.
2 Culloden Papers, p. 214.

going ere affairs were ripe. I'll aid all I can, but my prayers are all I can give at present."[1]

The Lord President was acting the part of a true friend at this time, for surely there is no more worthy service than trying to dissuade a headstrong man from a ruinous course. He wrote frequently to Lovat, and saw him as frequently as possible, but the self-confident chief took his own course still, and Forbes had to test him more definitely. He offered to Lovat's second son a commission in the regular Army. Lovat declined it, though in subtle words meant to veil his meaning. The contrast in those men—the two most able Highlanders of their day—is very vivid. Forbes was a good man in the fullest sense of that phrase. No matter what ill-fortune had overtaken the cause of King George, Forbes would have remained true to it. He was not concerned with results, but with principles as he understood them. With Lovat it was a case (subject, of course, to his general bias towards the Stuarts) of forecasting the political future, and acting accordingly.

On 23rd September, 1745, two days after Prestonpans, he says, "I truly believe P.C. master of all Scotland." So 700 men were drilled at Castle Dounie. On 7th October he writes to the President asking that they may go on "communicating to one another what news we hear and inquiring for one another's health."[2] That was Lovat's attitude epitomised. He asked for news and pleasantry. The people might do the fighting. He would wait to have his principles decided for him by the success of either party. He would see what side was likely to win, and then pretend that all the while he had been its friend.

On 10th October Lord Loudoun landed at Cromarty, and took up the supreme command of King George's forces in the north. This nearer approach of armed authority made it necessary for Lovat to temporise still further. Many years before he had advised a correspondent to write "in fair generals." He now wrote (doubtless in "fair generals") asking Forbes for his advice, and on 16th October he wrote to Cluny Macpherson[3] (who was his son-in-law) of "my extra-

1 Anderson's Family of Fraser, p. 150.
2 Culloden Papers, p. 227.
3 See Biographical Notes, p. 305.

ordinary zeal in this affair." Prestonpans had given a fillip to his zeal, though he still continued to mystify the President by requests for advice. Early in November, in a letter bursting with flattery, he announced to the Lord President his intention "to list 200 of my men that stay's at home, and put pretty gentlemen at their head, that they may watch and guard the country from all robbers and thieves and loose men that come from the Highland army; and to seize them and to send them to Inverness."[1]

There is little room for wonder that the authorities did not know whether to treat this arch-schemer as a rebel or a loyalist. Men were drilling on his green, but only he knew why, and the law's arm was restrained till he should be forced to declare his choice. Even the fact that his son, the Master of Lovat, and a number of Frasers were off to join Tearlach Og was not conclusive, for their chief grimly declared, "I would be very glad that the fifth man of them were hanged."

His position lacked dignity, and, in the light of history, it lacks even decency. Mr. Facing-both-ways may rouse interest, but never admiration. Down south they were making history. Every man who followed the rash Prince had at least the grace of courage. Though he may have been a dupe, he was a soldier, earning the meed of admiration due to those who put their fate in a balance. Lovat (too old for carrying arms) was at home playing with written words, regardless of his clansmen's lives. One wonders what he said when he got the Lord President's letter of 11th November, intimating that Lord Loudoun had promised not to molest him except on getting express orders to do so. Lord Loudoun wrote on the same day, concluding, "Your lordship will by this time see that I am willing to show all the lenity that is consistent with the service of my King and country." Lord Lovat was beginning to learn that even the great chief of Clan Fraser was a possible subject of discipline. The national pressure from beyond the Grampians was about to display its power. Lord Lovat's sense of the Hanoverian momentum is shown in several "very creeping letters," as the major would have said. That of 23rd November recounts all the previous services rendered to the reigning house. The writer, who so persistently accused other men of double dealing, was ever wont to quote these

[1] Culloden Papers, p. 240.

good deeds of 1715 as proving the utter impossibility of bad ones ever after. His other theme, constantly reiterated, was the injustice done him by the very suggestion of Jacobite complicity or blame for the departure of the Master to join Prince Charles.

On 26th November he sent to Loudoun the following homily:—"According to your lordship's way of reasoning, any particular clan or country may be convict of rebellion and exposed to the dismall consequences of it, if any number of rascalls, less or more, that live among them shall be so audacious to attempt that crime, let the rest be ever so quiet and peacable, and according to that doctrine one universall attainder may be direct in the present unhappy conjuncture agt. all Scotland. God forbid, my lord, that any man in power, and much less the Earl of Loudoun, should reason or act upon such principles, and especially when the Lord Lovat and his country are to be made the first instance in Scotland of such proceedings. . . . I shall rest satisfied that neither I nor they shall meet with any distress from your lordship for the misconduct of some rascalls that live in this country. As to my unhappy son, I wish from my heart that my paternall advices or authority could influence his conduct."[1] The reader will find it interesting to compare this epistle with Lovat's letter to the Prince, written in the course of that very month of November, 1745.[2] As for the "unhappy son," we know that just before he left Castle Dounie he "damned the white cockade" in his father's presence.

One cannot have any sympathy for the crafty old man in respect of his arrest by Loudoun on 10th or 11th December. He had great political influence in the north. Probably none of the contemporary chiefs had greater influence. He was related by blood or marriage ties to some of the most powerful clan leaders. The Government could not afford to allow him to plot without restraint, so he was taken to Inverness in a carriage and imprisoned in a private house. The wonderful patience of the Government had given out. Lovat promised to deliver up some arms, but failed to do so. Accordingly, on 19th December sentries were placed at his door. He was visited by Lord Loudoun himself, and was threatened with

1 The Transactions of the Gaelic Society of Inverness, xiv., p. 13, &c., contain this interesting correspondence with Lord Loudoun.

2 See p. 212.

removal to the Castle prison, but the wily old brain was still alert—too alert, indeed, for his captors. He escaped before the end of December by a back passage, which was unwatched, probably because the authorities thought him too ill to make the attempt. The old man's hiding-place, whether in town or country, remained unknown for some time, though it was believed he had perforce to be carried off on men's shoulders. The correspondence with his son still continued, and Lovat received a filial warning against "losing on both sides." He had been called upon by Lochiel to appear openly with the Jacobites, and the Prince himself had joined in that request. The President and Loudoun had showed that they were no longer gullible, so Lovat took a side at last. There was no more letter writing, so far as we know, and many of his further doings are in consequence unrecorded. He seems to have lived mainly, if not solely, in wild Stratherrick, within a day's march of Inverness.

Three months of military effectiveness were still left to the Jacobite army. After the victory at Prestonpans they had returned to Edinburgh and spent golden days in trivial display. They had marched into England, where every day brought bitter disappointments, and where the Prince suffered hourly from that worst of insults—public indifference. They had made their masterly retreat from Derby into Scotland. Met and followed from the English Midlands by three well-equipped armies, this scratch body of mountain soldiers, with no effective horsemen, had made good its return to Scotland not only without serious loss but even with some minor successes. They were re-entering their native land, a formidable though a retreating force, about the date of Lovat's escape to the mountains, and when 4000 men gathered at Perth under Lord Strathallan, they had some cause for renewed anticipation of ultimate success. The Master and the Frasers were with the Prince at Falkirk on 17th January, and on 10th February in Badenoch. Lovat must have been in communication with them. Had he been younger he would certainly have drawn the sword, after the crowning insult of arrest. He was never a coward, but he was too old for military service. He must have got news of the two Jacobite armies, one coming by Speyside and the other, led by Lord George Murray, moving north by the east coast towards Aberdeen; and of Cumberland following Lord George, and, wisely enough, remaining at Aberdeen until the spring should make his Highland operations easier. He knew, no doubt, that the Prince's men were much more active, compelling Loudoun and the Lord President to retreat before them—the former to Dornoch and the latter to Skye. Very probably the old chief had a small corps of swift-footed young clansmen who kept him in touch with the doings of those stirring days. They may have brought news of Cumberland's march from Aberdeen, and we may imagine the old man's anxiety if he heard of the intended raid on Nairn, followed next day by the tense excitement of Culloden's fatal hours.

On that evening (16th April, 1746) the Prince arrived at Lovat's lonely residence at Gortuleg, in Stratherrick, a fugitive, the victim of the defeat, and, what was worse, its cause. Had he left the campaign to be conducted by that brilliant soldier, Lord George Murray, the cruel butchery of Culloden would have been avoided; but he had displaced his only tactician, preferring the counsel of smooth-speaking incapables. Prince Charles was a broken man, not because he had lacked the essentials of success, but because he had failed to use them. The night march to Nairn had resulted in mere weariness; the field of battle had been ill chosen; no use had been made of the proximity of mountain moorlands (so useful for a possible retreat, during which the Highlanders could have laughed at south country soldiers); the men had been put starving into the battle line; the action had been begun before hundreds of approaching allies had arrived.

It was Lovat's first meeting with Prince Charles. A short conversation in French followed an equally French embrace. Lovat apologised for his absence from the fighting force, but assured the Prince that he had done his best for him. The Prince drank three glasses of wine, and soon the flight had to be resumed, the Prince going towards Invergarry, which was reached next morning. No record of Lovat's immediate doings has been preserved, but he must have left Gortuleg without delay. He was too important a Jacobite to be able to rest long in the very line of the Prince's headlong course. We next hear of him at Loch Muilzie, in Glenstrathfarrar, where he was carried by his clansmen, being unable to walk.

Robert Fraser, the second witness at the subsequent trial, says his chief had a meeting with Murray of Broughton and other Jacobite leaders, ten days after Culloden. This statement seems to be inaccurate, for Murray says he did not see

Lord Lovat for "some weeks" after the final battle. Lord Lovat found a temporary resting-place in Glen Mely (now known as Glen Mallie), a valley watered by one of the streams that run into Loch Arkaig. About the beginning of May (if Robert Fraser is not again inaccurate) he went further into "the Rough Bounds," and took up his abode in one of the islands in Loch Morar, a fresh water loch, separated from the sea by a narrow neck of land. If tradition speaks truly (and I have the story of men whose great-grandfathers took part in the doings now narrated), the Fraser band, numbering about twenty men, commandeered all the boats on the loch side and rowed them to their island for greater safety. Lord Lovat had now, though weak and ill, to be content with a cave as a temporary home.

During the second week of May several conferences took place at Mortleg, otherwise known as Muirlaggan, on the shores of Loch Arkaig. The paths of Lochiel, Glenbucket, Roy Stuart, Murray, and Barrisdale converged at this lonely spot. These men, some of whom had taken part in the ceremonials at Holyrood and the romantic march into England, and all of whom had lately commanded hundreds of warriors, were now hunted outlaws, meeting by stealth to concert measures of safety. Lovat was carried to the meeting place, but in spite of his obvious bodily infirmities his words were received with respect.[1] It was proposed that 3000 men be raised, and Glen Many (or Glen Mely, according to Murray) was selected as the rendezvous for ten days later. Lovat's optimism seemed to be unquenched by his many troubles, and he said he believed they would soon have 8000 or 10,000 men under arms.

It is said that he had a definite scheme of operations, and he afterwards stated that, had his plans been adopted, the Jacobites could have treated His Majesty's troops with derision. Certainly if a good leader, with tact enough to command the Highlanders without arousing intertribal jealousy, had appeared after Culloden, the Hanoverian gibbets would have been robbed of some of their eighty victims; but there was no one able and willing to fuse the beaten and jealous clans into an army effective in retreat. Only a few hundred men were at the

---

[1] Murray says Lovat here used "the privileged custom which he had assumed to himself for so many years of being the oracle of the country" ("Memorials," p. 274).

rendezvous when the time of meeting came, and the 300 Frasers, who were expected, were among the absentees. Had a few companies of dauntless men gone forth, regardless of personal safety, they might have lured the duke's regulars deep among the hills, and ultimately, by Boer-like determination, have compelled a grant of honourable terms for themselves and of pardon for those who were no longer under arms. Now there was only one course open—continued flight.

The search for Jacobites continued. The old man returned to his island, after spending a period at a house belonging to Lochiel on the south slope of Glen Dessary, at the west end of Loch Arkaig.

There may have been a scheme for escape to France. A body of over a score of men could not expect to remain long in one hiding-place, even on the island, for the men of the King's ships were searching from the neighbouring seaboard. As the old plotter spent those summer days in his lonely retreat, many schemes must have occurred to his still fertile imagination, but Fate—which he had often outgeneraled—intervened to frustrate all his plans. Towards the end of May or beginning of June the searchers came, led by a naval captain. Possibly their suspicions had been aroused by the absence of boats on Loch Morar-side. One was procured from the seashore, hauled overland, and launched in the fresh water. Lovat and his men, now accompanied by Bishop Hugh MacDonald, made a hasty retreat to the opposite shore, on the Arisaig side. There seems to have been some firing, but Lord Lovat is said to have ordered his men to desist, and to have taken shelter in a dense birch wood near Ceann-Camuis-Ruaidh. The searchers were baffled, and the fugitives enjoyed some days' respite.[1] Near Meoble, on the southern shore of Loch Morar, Lord Lovat was seized by illness, and all chance of continued flight immediately vanished. He was captured on 7th June (the day the Prince reached Island Ouia) by a Captain Millar, at a spot near Meoble, either when hiding in a hollow tree, or, according to another tradition, when resting after sending to the searchers a message of surrender. Had he been young he could have escaped with ease. It was a tragedy of old age. Advancing years had made his movements slow,

1 An account of these events is given in Father Charles MacDonald's most interesting book on "Moidart, or Among the Clanranalds" (Oban: Duncan Cameron, 1889).

and corpulence had rendered him conspicuous. He was still his pursuers' equal in cunning, but he was now in a land which he described as "a desert," and an escape would only have been rendered possible by superior physique.

He surrendered his sword, a weapon carried as a sign of rank, and with no lethal possibilities in such hands as his. He was taken on board the sloop "Furnace." Unluckily, his "box," with its incriminating contents, was found and conveyed aboard. His luck had deserted him as ruthlessly as he himself had deserted his old friend the major. He was taken in a litter to Fort-William, and there, as usual, he resolved to do some writing. He thought Cumberland might prove as lenient as Loudoun. On 12th June he wrote to "the Butcher" these pitiful words, "I can do more service to the King and Government than the destroying a hundred such like old and very infirm men like me, past seventy, without the use of my hands, legs, and knees, can be advantage in any shape to the Government."[1] Cumberland was not the man to be moved by such a plaint, and the prisoner was removed to Fort-Augustus, and afterwards to London (by way of Stirling, Edinburgh, Berwick, Newcastle (where he was hissed by the crowd), Leicester, and Barnet), to stand trial for high treason. Months of seclusion in the Tower of London, and the concentration of a great public interest in his character and past deeds, were the next events in his strangely varied life.

"Death doth discover virtue," said Francis Bacon. His coming doom brought out the best in Lovat's character. In the Tower he played a man's part. If there is virtue in a light heart, it is surely thrice admirable in an old man spending in a prison the last days of his earthly course. Lovat showed "uncommon gaiety and jocoseness." He made merry with his visitors, joked with his jailers, and never shivered at his impending fate. If he had been asked to sum the total of his days, he would doubtless have said, "It was a keen life, but it was worth having. I have lost the prize, but I have enjoyed the game, and I am ready for my fate." He must have had one bitter annoyance, however, for his old friend and enemy, the major, was now Crown factor on the forfeited Lovat lands!

---

[1] Hill Burton, p. 249.

The Impeachment.

The peers were convened on 9th March, 1747, to try him on an impeachment by the Commons.[1] Lords Kilmarnock, Balmerino, and Cromartie had been tried by their peers, but not on impeachment by the Commons. It has been suggested that the more cumbrous procedure was adopted in Lovat's case because there was some doubt if he were really a peer, and thus entitled to be tried by the lords alone. This suggestion seems ill-founded, for Lord Lovat's right to the peerage was recognised in the articles of indictment themselves. The great gravity of his offences, and his superior influence in Scotland, seem to have caused the Commons to adopt the process of impeachment.

Like all human judges, the lords were concerned with facts and crimes, and not with the larger problem of assaying a human soul. Here was a traitor, who had written lying words and helped the enemies of his King. Here was black treason, proved beyond all chance of cavilling. They knew the penalty and they passed their sentence, in all its strange union of quaintness and cruelty. No one can say that they did wrong. Lord Lovat had come within the law, and no consideration for his grey hairs or his past good service, no admiration for his coolness in face of death, could relieve the blackness of his treachery. He had gambled for power with his country's fate as a mere counter on the gaming table. They could have pitied an honest fanatic obsessed by exaggerated notions of real or imaginary wrong, but here was a man who had been a Jacobite with reservations, a friend without constancy, a citizen with a price. It was right that men such as he should be shown that they "had a lith in their neck."

---

1 See Appendix No. III., p. 307, as to Procedure in Impeachments.

Gorthlick House (formerly known as Gortuleg House), the meeting-place of Prince Charlie and Lord Lovat on the evening of Culloden.

IMPEACHMENT.

PRELIMINARY PROCEEDINGS.

I.—In the House of Commons.

On 11th December, 1746, the Chancellor of the Exchequer, by the King's command, communicated to the House of Commons a letter signed "Lovat" relating to the Pretender and to the late rebellion. The letter was read, witnesses were examined to prove the handwriting, and the House immediately resolved to impeach Simon, Lord Lovat, of high treason. It was announced that Lord Lovat was already in custody in the Tower of London.[1]

II.—In the House of Lords.

Die Jovis, 11° Decembris, 1746.

A message was brought from the House of Commons by Sir William Yonge and others to acquaint this House that they, having matters to communicate to their lordships of great importance to the King and Kingdom, do desire that their lordships will continue sitting for some time.

To which the House agreed.

And the messengers were called in again, and acquainted by the Lord Chancellor that the Lords will continue sitting for some time, as desired.

The House was adjourned during pleasure.

The House was resumed.

A message was brought from the House of Commons by Sir William Yonge and others as follows:—

"My Lords,

"The Commons of Great Britain in Parliament assembled, having received information of divers treasons committed by a Peer of this realm, Simon, Lord Lovat, have commanded me to impeach the said Simon, Lord Lovat, of high treason, and I do here in their names and in the names of all the Commons

[1] See "Parliamentary History." vol. 13. p. 1436.

of Great Britain impeach the said Simon, Lord Lovat, of high treason, and I am further commanded to acquaint your lordships that they will, with all convenient speed, exhibit Articles to make good the charge against him."

Die Mercurii, 17° Decembris, 1746.

A message was brought from the House of Commons by Sir William Yonge and others, who said he was commanded by the House of Commons to deliver to this House Articles of Impeachment of high treason against Simon, Lord Lovat. He said he was also commanded by the Commons to acquaint their lordships that they were ready to maintain their charge; and he delivered in the said Articles, which Articles being read, the Duke of Newcastle acquainted the House that the said Lord Lovat was already under commitment for high treason in His Majesty's Tower of London.

Then the following order was made:—

> Whereas the Commons, assembled in Parliament, have this day exhibited to this House Articles of Impeachment of high treason against Simon, Lord Lovat, it is ordered by the Lords spiritual and temporal, in Parliament assembled, that the said Lord Lovat be brought to the bar of this House to-morrow at two of the clock in the afternoon to hear the said Articles read, and to abide such further order as this House shall think fit to move concerning him.
>
> To Charles, Lord Cornwallis, Constable of His Majesty's Tower of London, and in his absence to the Lieutenant of the said Tower, or his Deputy.

Die Jovis, 18° Decembris, 1746.

The order being read for bringing Simon, Lord Lovat, to the bar of this House to hear the Articles of Impeachment of high treason exhibited against him yesterday by the House of Commons, the said Lord Lovat was accordingly brought to the bar by the Deputy Gentleman Usher of the Black Rod, where he kneeled until the Lord Chancellor directed him to rise, then the said Articles of Impeachment were read unto him; which done, the Lord Chancellor asked him what he had to say thereunto, and informed him that if he had anything to request of the House this was his proper time. Whereupon he acquainted the House with his infirmities occasioned by old age, and particularly alleged his deafness, that he could not hear what the contents of the said Articles were. Wherefore, having a Petition prepared to make known to the House his requests, he desired the same to be read, which, being delivered in, was read by the Clerk, and is as follows:—

"To the Right Honourable the Lords spiritual and temporal, in Parliament assembled.

"The humble Petition of Simon, Lord Fraser of Lovat.[1]

"Sheweth,

"That your petitioner, by reason of his great age, labours under many infirmities and weakness, and, being entirely ignorant of the forms of law and method of proceedings in this august Court, is unable to make any defence, or give in a proper Answer to the Articles of Impeachment exhibited against him, without the assistance of able counsel and solicitors.

"That your petitioner, during his close confinement in the Tower of London for now near five months, has not been able to obtain one shilling either out of his estate or otherwise, which has been occasioned, as your petitioner has been informed, by some grants of a very extraordinary nature, and which your petitioner hopes shall never again in this island be drawn into precedent, authorising and empowering other persons, strangers to your petitioner, to take possession of his estate, and to levy the rents thereof, whilst such as had in their hands any money or effects of your petitioner's were prohibited and restrained from paying any part thereof to your petitioner or his order.

"That your petitioner applied several times to one of His Majesty's principal Secretaries of State, complaining of the hardships your petitioner suffered by means of such proceedings; and your petitioner is informed that two several orders were made thereupon, in order to remove the said prohibitions and restraints, and to recall the said powers so granted as above; but, notwithstanding thereof, your petitioner is still in the same deplorable circumstances, without any money even to procure him the common necessaries of life, and is wholly indebted to General Williamson for his support.

"That your petitioner, when he was apprehended by a party of His Majesty's troops in Scotland, had, in his strong-box,

---

1 From the time of the first recorded use of the Scottish title (early in the fifteenth century) until it was forfeited in 1747, the holders used on formal occasions the title, first of "Lord Fraser of the Lovat," and afterwards of "Lord Fraser of Lovat." In 1837 the title was restored to Thomas Alexander Fraser, tenth of Strichen, in the form of a peerage of the United Kingdom, in the style of "Baron Lovat of Lovat." In 1857 the Scottish peerage was regranted to the same chief.

money and jewels to the amount of seven hundred pounds and upwards, which they seized, and retain, insisting the same is lawful prize.

"Your petitioner therefore humbly prays that your lordships, moved by your innate goodness, may be pleased to assign your petitioner such and so many counsel and solicitors as your lordships shall think proper, that your petitioner may have a copy of the Articles of Impeachment, and may not be ordered by your lordships to begin and enter upon his defence while he remains stripped and deprived of all the necessary means which the law allows him for his defence and support, but that such a reasonable time may be allowed your petitioner to prepare and put in his Answer that he may be enabled to receive money sufficient to retain and fee his counsel and solicitors, without which your petitioner affrends he cannot have their assistance and advice, and that, for that purpose, the money and jewels contained in the strong-box, and unjustly taken as above, may be immediately restored to your petitioner by your lordships' order.

"And your petitioner shall ever pray, &c.

"The counsel that Lord Lovat desires may be assigned are Mr. Starkie, Mr. Forrester, Mr. Ford, and Mr. Wilmott, and the solicitors are Mr. George Ross, Mr. Hugh Fraser, and Mr. Godfrey."

The Petition being read, the said Lord Lovat was asked by the Lord Chancellor if he had anything further to offer, to which he, answering in the negative, was directed to withdraw, and the House, taking the requests of the said Petition into consideration, *ordered* that the said Lord Lovat may have a copy of the said Articles of Impeachment exhibited against him, and that he do put in his Answers thereto in writing on or before Tuesday, the 13th day of January next, and that Mr. Starkie, Mr. Forrester, Mr. Ford, and Mr. Wilmott, the counsel mentioned in the said Petition, be assigned to assist him in preparing his Answers, and likewise in his defence, in matters of law; and that Mr. George Ross, Mr. Hugh Fraser, and Mr. Godfrey be also assigned solicitors for him, and that such counsel and solicitors may have access to him at all seasonable times, and that the said Lord Lovat have liberty to cause search to be made and copies of records and journals to be taken out in order to his defence, and that he shall have summonses issued for such witnesses as he shall send in the names of, to be by him made use of at his trial, which witnesses shall have the protection of this House for their safe coming and going during the time of the said trial.

Preliminary Proceedings.

Ordered that the Lord Chancellor do acquaint the Lord Lovat that it is expected by their lordships that he would send in the names of such witnesses as he shall desire to be summoned as soon as conveniently he can, and that, in case he do not, he must not expect to be indulged with any further delay on that account. *Ordered* likewise that the said Lord Lovat be permitted to receive the rents and profits of his estate by his factors or agents in like manner as if he was not under accusation for high treason, and that His Majesty's Advocate for Scotland do take the proper methods to carry this order into execution.

Then the Lord Lovat was called in again, and the Lord Chancellor acquainted him with what the House had ordered, and then he was a second time directed to withdraw.

Ordered that Lord Lovat do stand committed to His Majesty's Tower of London, to be there safely kept in order to his trial, till he shall be thence delivered by due course of law, and that no person shall have access to him without the special leave of the House.

Ordered that the Lord Chancellor do write letters to all the lords who have not been present in the House either this day or yesterday in the usual manner, requiring their attendance on the service of this House, all excuses set apart, on Wednesday, the 21st day of January next, on occasion of the proceedings now depending in the House against Simon, Lord Lovat, who stands impeached by the House of Commons of high treason.

Die Martis, 23° Decembris, 1746.

A Petition of Simon, Lord Fraser of Lovat, was presented and read, praying that he may be allowed to the 1st day of February for answering the Articles of Impeachment exhibited by the House of Commons against him, within which time he hopes that the care and diligence of his agents in Scotland will, notwithstanding the season of the year, furnish him with the papers and materials necessary for that end, and thereupon Mr. George Ross, one of the petitioner's solicitors, being called in and heard at the bar touching the contents of the said Petition, he was directed to withdraw. *Ordered* that the said Petition be rejected.

Ordered that the Lieutenant of the Tower of London, or his deputy, do bring the said Lord Lovat to the bar of this House on Tuesday, the 13th day of January next, at two of the clock in the afternoon, in order to the putting in his Answer to the Articles of Impeachment of high treason exhibited against him by the House of Commons.

Trial of Lord Lovat.

Die Martis, 13° Januarii, [1747].[1]

The order of the day being read for bringing Simon, Lord Lovat, to the bar of the House, in order to the putting in his Answer to the Articles of Impeachment of high treason exhibited against him by the House of Commons, he was brought to the bar accordingly, where he kneeled till the Lord Chancellor acquainted him he might rise. He then delivered in his Answer to the said Articles, and the same was read. Then Lord Lovat was asked by the Lord Chancellor if he had anything further to offer, whereupon he acquainted the House he had caused to be prepared two Petitions to their lordships, which he conceived did concern the justice as well as the honour of the House; and his lordship, delivering in the said Petitions, the same were severally read—the first complaining that the order of this House of the 18th of December last relating to the factory or receivership of the petitioner's rents had not been obeyed so as to be effectual to him, nor had the contents of the strong-box taken from him and now in Captain Ferguson's possession been delivered to his agent, as had been promised him, and praying that obedience to the said order might be compelled, and an immediate restitution of the money taken out of the said box, or that such order might be made concerning this matter as to the House should seem meet, the other Petition setting forth that Mr. William Fraser, Writer to the Signet, who for many years had acted as his chief agent, and had the management of his estate in Scotland, was by his direction come to town, but could not have access to him without the permission of this House, and praying that the said Fraser might have liberty to come to the petitioner at all seasonable times.

Then the Lord Lovat was directed to be taken from the bar; which done, the first Petition was again read, and, after debate and reading the said order relating to the receipt of the rents and profits of the said Lord Lovat's estate, *ordered* that the said Petition be rejected. Then the other Petition being likewise read, *ordered* that the said William Fraser be permitted to have access to the petitioner at all seasonable times between the hours of ten of the clock in the forenoon and

---

[1] In the House of Lords' records the date here given is 1746, the reason being that 1st January was not adopted as the commencement of the new year in England till 1752. Prior to that date the new year in England began on 25th March The change had been made in Scotland in 1600. Prior to the change such confusion was caused that it was common to give both years thus: "1746/7," the last figure indicating the year according to the present reckoning. The year figures here enclosed in brackets have been altered to conform with the modern usage.

two of the clock in the afternoon, in the presence of such officer belonging to the Tower of London as the Constable thereof shall appoint.

Ordered that a copy of the Answer of the said Lord Lovat to the Articles of Impeachment of high treason exhibited against him by the House of Commons be prepared, and that, when the same has been carefully examined by the Clerk, it be sent by a message to the House of Commons and left with that House.

Ordered that the said Lord Lovat be conveyed back to the Tower of London[1] by the Lieutenant of the same or his deputy, to be there kept in safe custody until he shall be thence delivered by due course of law.

Die Veneris, 16° Januarii [1747].

A message was brought from the House of Commons by Sir William Yonge and others to acquaint this House that they have considered the Answer of Simon, Lord Lovat, to the Articles of Impeachment exhibited against him by the Knights, Citizens, and Burgesses assembled in Parliament, and do aver their charge against the said Simon, Lord Lovat, for high treason to be true, and that the said Simon, Lord Lovat, is guilty in such manner as he stands impeached, and that the Commons will be ready to prove their charge against him at such convenient time as shall be appointed for that purpose.

Die Jovis, 22° Januarii, [1747].

A Petition of Simon, Lord Lovat, stiling himself Simon, Lord Fraser of Lovat, was presented and read, praying that Mr. William Fraser may be appointed one of his solicitors in room of Mr. Hugh Fraser, he being necessarily required to go into the country. *Ordered* that the said Mr. William Fraser be assigned the petitioner's solicitor in room of Mr. Hugh Fraser as desired, and that the said Mr. William Fraser may have access to the petitioner at all seasonable times. *Ordered* that Monday, the 23rd day of February next, be, and is hereby appointed for the trial of Simon, Lord Lovat, in Westminster Hall, upon the Articles of Impeachment exhibited against him

1 The *Scots Magazine* of January, 1747, records that Lord Lovat was abused by the mob both when going from the Tower to the House of Lords and when returning therefrom.

by the House of Commons for high treason, and a message was sent to the House of Commons by Mr. Spicer and Mr. Edwards to acquaint them therewith. Then the House appointed a committee to inspect the journals of this House, and to consider the proper methods of proceeding on the Impeachment against Simon, Lord Lovat, and to report to the House what they shall think proper thereupon.

Die Lunae, 2° Februarii, [1747].

The Earl of Warwick reported from the Lords' committee appointed to inspect the journals of this House relating to former cases of impeachment and to consider the proper methods of proceeding on the Impeachment of Simon, Lord Lovat, and to report to the House what they shall think proper thereupon, that the committee had met and inspected the journals of this House in former cases of impeachments, and considered the matters to them referred, and had come to several resolutions, which his lordship reported. And thereupon several orders were made touching the course of proceeding to and at the ensuing trial, and for preserving the peace, and amongst them as follows, viz.:—

Ordered that an humble address be presented to His Majesty to acquaint His Majesty that this House hath appointed the trial of Simon, Lord Lovat, upon the Articles of Impeachment of high treason exhibited against him by the House of Commons to begin in Westminster Hall on Monday the 23rd day of this instant February, and humbly desire that His Majesty will be pleased to appoint a Lord High Steward to continue during the said trial.

Ordered that the said address be presented to His Majesty by the Lords with white staves.

Ordered that the counsel assigned the said Lord Lovat may be present when he is at the bar in order to be heard touching any point or matter of law, if any such shall arise, during the said trial.

Ordered that the witnesses which shall be produced by the Lord Lovat to be examined in his defence shall be examined upon oath, which oath shall be administered in the like form as an oath was directed by this House to be administered to any witness who should be produced by the Earl of Winton [1] at his trial.

[1] George Seton, fifth Earl of Winton, who was taken prisoner at Preston, and impeached in March, 1716, for high treason in respect of his conduct during the Rising of 1715. He was sentenced to death, but escaped to France, and died at Rome in 1749.

Preliminary Proceedings.

Ordered that the Lord Great Chamberlain be desired to take care and give order that accommodation be made in the scaffold already erected in Westminster Hall for the Commons, as hath been used in trials in Westminster Hall upon impeachments.

Die Mercurii, 4° Februarii, [1747].

The Lord Steward reported that the Lords with white staves had, according to order, presented to His Majesty the address of this House on Monday last for the appointment of a Lord High Steward to continue during the trial of Simon, Lord Lovat, and that His Majesty had been pleased to give orders accordingly. *Ordered* that the said commission for appointing a Lord High Steward shall be in the like form as that for the trial of the Lord Viscount Stafford as entered in the journal of this House the 30th of November, 1680, except that the same be in the English language.

Die Mercurii, 18° Februarii, [1747].

A Petition of Simon, Lord Fraser of Lovat, was presented and read, setting forth that upon the appointment of his trial he immediately despatched one of his solicitors to summon the petitioner's material witnesses, who are at great distances from each other, inhabiting the counties of Inverness and Ross, but by reason of the inclemency of the weather, the badness of the roads, and other unavoidable accidents, none of them as yet arrived nor can possibly be got to London by the time of trial, and praying that this House will appoint some more distant time for that purpose.

And thereupon William Fraser and William Godfrey, two of the petitioner's solicitors, were called in and heard at the bar, to verify the truth of the allegations of the said petition; and being withdrawn, *ordered* that the time appointed for the petitioner's trial be, and is hereby, enlarged till to-morrow fortnight, the 5th day of March next.

Ordered that a message be sent to the House of Commons to acquaint them that, upon the humble Petition of Simon, Lord Lovat, for putting off his trial to a further day, for the reasons therein alleged, the lords have enlarged the time appointed for the trial of the said Lord Lovat till Thursday, the 5th day of March next: and a message was accordingly sent to the House of Commons by Mr. Holford and Mr. Bennet to acquaint them therewith.

Trial of Lord Lovat.

Die Lunae, 2° Martii, [1747].

A Petition of Simon, Lord Fraser of Lovat, with an affidavit of Hugh Fraser thereto annexed, was presented to the House and read, as follows:—

"To the Right Honourable the Lords spiritual and temporal, in Parliament assembled.

"The humble Petition of Simon, Lord Fraser of Lovat.

"Sheweth,

"That your lordships having appointed your petitioner's trial for the 23rd of February, your petitioner did lately take the liberty humbly to represent the impossibility he was under to prepare so soon for trial, in respect his witnesses, from the badness of the road, were not then arrived, and your lordships were pleased to indulge your petitioner with a delay till Thursday next.

"That Hugh Fraser, whom your petitioner had directed to serve your lordships' summons upon your petitioner's witnesses, arrived in town with sundry of them late on Friday night, having duly served your lordships' said order upon several other persons who were all material witnesses for your petitioner.

"That Thomas Fraser of Struy, and Donald Fraser, *alias* Down, two of the witnesses served as aforesaid, were prevented by sickness from setting out as early as some of the rest, but had declared to the said Hugh Fraser their willingness to obey your lordships' summons as soon as they were able to travel, which your petitioner hopes will soon be the case.

"That William Fraser of Belloan, Alexander Fraser of Belnain, Thomas Fraser of Garthmore, Alexander Fraser of Beleloyne, and the Reverend Mr. Donald Fraser, minister of Killearnan, who are all material witnesses for your petitioner, and without whose testimony your petitioner cannot safely proceed to trial, have absolutely refused to attend, though regularly served with your lordships' summons, as by affidavit annexed appears, and that the persons named as aforesaid are material and necessary witnesses your petitioner is ready to make affidavit of; but being strictly confined in the Tower, and no person having access to him without your lordships' order, he has no opportunity so to do.

"That under these circumstances, and that your petitioner, without your lordships' interposition, cannot compel the said persons to attend his trial, he is under a necessity to apply to your lordships for relief, without which he must, as to the charge in some of the aforesaid Articles, remain defenceless should your lordships in the interim proceed to trial.

"Your petitioner therefore humbly prays your lordships would be pleased to appoint a more distant day for the trial, and that your lordships would be pleased to compel the said William, Alexander, Thomas, Donald, and Alexander Fraser to attend your petitioner's trial at such time as your lordships shall think fit, or to grant him such other relief as to your lordships in your great wisdom shall seem meet.

"And your petitioner shall ever pray.

"LOVAT."

"In the House of Lords upon the Impeachment for high treason against Simon, Lord Lovat.

"Hugh Fraser, of Gray's Inn, in the county of Middlesex, gentleman, maketh oath—That he, this deponent, did on the 10th day of February last personally serve Thomas Fraser of Struy, and on the 10th day of the said month of February, did also personally serve William Fraser of Belloan, Alexander Fraser in Belnain, Thomas Fraser of Gathmore, Alexander Fraser of Beleloyne, and David Down, *alias* Fraser, with an order of this honourable House, bearing date the 16th of January last past, whereby it was ordered that the said several persons and others named in such order should attend this House as witnesses for the said Simon, Lord Lovat, who stands impeached of high treason by the House of Commons, by delivering to each of them a true copy of the said order, and at the same time showing to them the said original order. And this deponent further saith that the said William Fraser of Belloan, Alexander Fraser of Belnain, Thomas Fraser of Garthmore, and Alexander Fraser of Beleloyne, though served with the said order as aforesaid, absolutely refused to obey the said order, and this deponent verily believes will not attend the said trial. And the Thomas Fraser of Struy and Donald Down, *alias* Fraser, were both at the time of such service sick and unable to travel, and declared themselves incapable of complying with the said order. "HUGH FRASER."

Sworn the 2nd day of March, [1747], before me, at the Court of Requests. M. THURSTON.

Afterwards the said Hugh Fraser and Mr. Godfrey, one of the prisoner's solicitors, were called in and examined at the bar, and being withdrawn, *ordered* that the said petition be rejected, *ordered* that the Lieutenant of the Tower of London, or his deputy, do bring to the bar of this House, in Westminster Hall, on Thursday next at ten of the clock in the forenoon, Simon, Lord Lovat, in order to his trial upon the Impeachment of high treason exhibited by the House of Commons against him. Then a message was sent to the House of Commons by the former messenger to acquaint them that the lords will be ready to go down into Westminster Hall at the time above-mentioned, in order to the trial of the said Lord Lovat.

Die Martis, 3° Martii, [1747].

A Petition of Simon, Lord Fraser of Lovat, with affidavits of Mr. George Ross and Mr. William Fraser thereto annexed, were presented and read as follows:—

"To the Right Hon. the Lords spiritual and temporal, in Parliament assembled.

"The humble Petition of Simon, Lord Fraser of Lovat.

"Sheweth,

"That nothing but the utter impossibility the petitioner and his agents are under of preparing his defence against Thursday, the fifth of the instant March, could have induced him to trouble your lordships with this second application for some days further time. But none of your petitioner's witnesses coming to town till late on Friday night last, and one of your petitioner's agents having received an account by last night's post, that two other persons, who were summoned as witnesses for your petitioner, set out from Edinburgh on the 24th and 25th of last month, and are not yet arrived in London, but expected here by the end of this week, your petitioner cannot possibly be prepared to take his trial before Monday next.

"The petitioner begs leave, further, to represent to your lordships that in the present unhappy situation of his affairs he has no means of furnishing himself with money either for applying to counsel, bearing the charges of his witnesses, or other necessary expense, but from the supply afforded him by his agents, who have already advanced him considerable sums for the above purposes which are already expended, that the solemnity and unavoidable length of the proceedings, making further sums of money still necessary, the petitioner is afraid that his defence may suffer on that account unless your lordships are pleased in compassion to his present difficulty to give some kind of encouragement to his agents to hope they shall be repaid what they already have, or may hereafter disburse on the petitioner's account, it being by the loss of the petitioner's moveables, out of his own powers, to give them any kind of indemnification.

"The petitioner also prays your lordships to assign Mr. Charles Hamilton Gordon to be one of his counsel in place of Mr. Starkey, who, on account of the bad state of his health, has declined giving the petitioner his assistance.

"May it therefore please your lordships in consideration of the premises to put off the petitioner's trial until the next Monday, and to make such other order upon this application as to your lordships shall seem meet.

"And your petitioner shall ever pray, &c.

"LOVAT."

In the Impeachment of the Commons of Great Britain against Simon, Lord Fraser of Lovat, George Ross, one of the solicitors, assigned by the Right Honourable the House of Lords to the said Simon, Lord Fraser of Lovat, maketh oath—That since his appointment he has at different times laid out and expended upwards of six hundred pounds out of his own pocket in feeing of his lordship's counsel, bringing up his witnesses, and other charges attending the several steps already taken towards preparing for the said lord's defence, without receiving any money or security whatsoever for his indemnification.

"GEORGE ROSS."

Sworn at the Public Office, 2nd March, [1747], before
"W. KINASTON."

In the Impeachment of the Commons of Great Britain against Simon, Lord Lovat, in the House of Lords, William Fraser, Writer to His Majesty's Signet, maketh oath—That last night he received advice from Edinburgh that Thomas Fraser of Struy and Mr. Donald Fraser, two of the witnesses summoned on behalf of Lord Lovat, are now upon the road, and will be here by Saturday or Sunday first, which information this deponent believes to be true. "WILL FRASER."

Sworn at the Public Office, 3rd March, [1747], before
"THO. BENNET."

Trial of Lord Lovat.

Ordered that the trial of the Petition be put off to Monday next, as desired. A message was sent to the Commons by Mr. Burroughs and Mr. Allen to acquaint them that this House, upon the Petition of the said Lord Lovat for the reasons therein contained, hath enlarged the time of his trial upon the Impeachment of high treason exhibited against him by the House of Commons to Monday next at eleven of the clock in the forenoon, and that their lordships will be ready to go down into Westminster Hall at the time above-mentioned in order to his trial.

Ordered that the Governor of the Tower of London, or his deputy, do bring the said Lord Lovat to the bar of this House in Westminster Hall at ten of the clock in the forenoon on Monday next in order to his trial upon the said Impeachment.

THE TRIAL.

Managers for the House of Commons.

Sir Dudley Ryder, Attorney-General.
The Hon. William Murray, Solicitor-General.
Lord Coke.
Sir William Yonge.
Sir John Strange.
Sir Richard Lloyd.
Mr. William Noel.
Mr. Lyttleton.
Mr. Yorke.
Mr. Grenville.
Mr. Legge, and others.

Counsel for the Accused.

Mr. Forrester.
Mr. Ford.
Mr. Wilmott.
Mr. Charles Hamilton Gordon.

Solicitors for the Accused.

Mr. Wm. Fraser, W.S.
Mr. George Ross.
Mr. Hugh Fraser.
Mr. Wm. Godfrey.

First Day—Monday, 9th March [1747].

The lords met in the House of Lords in their robes, and, after prayers, adjourned into Westminster Hall.

Trial of Lord Lovat.

About eleven of the clock the lords came from their own House into the Court created in Westminster Hall in the manner following:—

The Lord High Steward's Gentlemen Attendants, two and two.
The Clerks Assistant to the House of Lords and the Clerk of the Parliament, with the Clerk of the Crown in the Court of Chancery bearing the King's Commission to the Lord High Steward.
The Masters in Chancery, two and two.
The Judges, two and two.
The Peers' eldest sons, two and two.
Peers' minors, two and two.
York and Windsor Heralds.
Four Sergeants-at-Arms, with their maces, two and two.
The Yeoman Usher of the House.
Then the Peers, two and two, beginning with the youngest Baron.
Then four Sergeants-at-Arms, with their maces, two and two.
The Sergeant-at-Arms attending the Great Seal, and Purse-bearer.
Then Garter King-at-Arms and the Gentleman Usher of the Black Rod carrying the white staff before the Lord High Steward.
Philip, Lord Hardwicke,[1] Lord High Chancellor of Great Britain, Lord High Steward, alone, his train borne.

The lords having taken their places in the Court according to their degrees, the Lord High Steward being upon the uppermost Woolsack, and the Commons and their Managers being also in the seats respectively prepared for them;

The Clerk of the Crown in Chancery having His Majesty's Commission to the Lord High Steward in his hand, standing before the Clerk's table, with his face towards the State, made three reverences, the first at the table, the second in the midway, and the third near the Woolpack; then kneeled down, and, on his knee, presented the Commission to the Lord High Steward, who delivered the same back to him, who, rising, made three reverences, and returned with it to the table, and then proclamation was made for silence in this manner.

SERGEANT-AT-ARMS—Oyes![2] Oyes! Oyes! Our Sovereign Lord the King strictly charges and commands all manner of persons to keep silence upon pain of imprisonment.

Then the Lord High Steward stood up and spoke to the Peers:

LORD HIGH STEWARD—His Majesty's Commission is about to

---

[1] See Biographical Notes, p. 303.
[2] Originally "Oyez!" but corrupted to the form above given.

Philip, 1st Lord Hardwicke.

(Lord High Steward at the Trial of Lord Lovat.)

be read. Your lordships are desired to attend to it in the usual manner, and all others are likewise to stand up uncovered while the Commission is reading.

All the Peers uncovered themselves, and they and all others stood up uncovered while the Commission was read, which is as follows:—

GEORGE R.

George the Second, by the grace of God, of Great Britain, France, and Ireland, King, Defender of the Faith, and so forth, to our right trusty and well-beloved counsellor, Philip, Lord Hardwicke, Baron of Hardwicke in our county of Gloucester, our Chancellor of Great Britain—greeting. *Whereas* Simon, Lord Lovat, before us in Parliament by the Knights, Citizens, and Burgesses in our Parliament assembled with many of the said knights, citizens, and burgesses, and in the name of all the Commons of our Kingdom of Great Britain, is and stands impeached and accused of high treason by him, the said Simon, Lord Lovat, committed and perpetrated; we, considering that justice is an excellent virtue and pleasing to the Most High, and being willing that the said Simon, Lord Lovat, should, before us in our present Parliament, according to the law and custom of this our Kingdom of Great Britain, and according to the custom of Parliament, be heard, sentenced, and adjudged touching and concerning the said high treason whereof he stands impeached and accused as aforesaid, and that all other things which are necessary in this behalf should be in due manner done and executed; and forasmuch as the Lords, spiritual and temporal, in our present Parliament assembled, have most humbly besought us that we would vouchsafe to appoint a Steward of Great Britain for the time. We, very much confiding in your fidelity, prudence, provident circumspection, and industry, have for the cause ordained and constituted you Steward of Great Britain, to hear, execute, and exercise for this time the said office, with all things to the same office in this behalf due and belonging; and therefore we command you that you diligently set about the premises, and for the time do exercise and execute with effect all those things which belong to the office of Steward of Great Britain, and which are required in this behalf. In witness whereof we have caused these letters to be made patent. Witness ourself at Westminster the ninth day of March, in the twentieth year of our reign.

By the King himself signed with his own hand,

YORKE AND YORKE.

SERGEANT-AT-ARMS—God save the King!

Trial of Lord Lovat.

Then Garter and the Gentlemen Usher of the Black Rod, after three reverences, kneeling, jointly presented the white staff to His Grace the Lord High Steward, and then His Grace, attended by Garter, Black Rod, and the Purse-bearer (making the proper reverences towards the Throne) removed from the Woolpack to an armed chair, which was placed on the uppermost step but one of the Throne, as it was prepared for that purpose, and then seated himself in the chair, and delivered the staff to the Gentleman Usher of the Black Rod on his right hand, the Purse-bearer holding the purse on the left.

Clerk of the Crown—Sergeant-at-Arms, make proclamation.

Sergeant-at-Arms—Oyes! Oyes! Oyes! Our Sovereign Lord the King strictly charges and commands all manner of persons to keep silence upon pain of imprisonment.

Lord High Steward—Is it your lordships' pleasure that the judges have leave to be covered?

Lords—Ay.

Then another proclamation was made.

Sergeant-at-Arms—Oyes! Oyes! Oyes! Lieutenant of the Tower of London, bring forth your prisoner to the bar, according to the order of the House of Lords to you directed.

Then Simon, Lord Lovat, was brought to the bar by the Deputy-Governor of the Tower, having the axe carried before him by the Gentleman Gaoler, who stood with it on the left hand of the prisoner with the edge turned from him. The prisoner, when he approached the bar, made three reverences, and then fell upon his knees at the bar.

Lord High Steward—Your lordship may rise.

Then the prisoner rose up and bowed to His Grace the Lord High Steward and to the House of Peers, which compliment was returned him by His Grace and the lords, and, proclamation being again made for keeping silence, the Lord High Steward spoke to the prisoner as follows:—

Lord High Steward—Simon, Lord Lovat, you stand impeached of high treason by the Knights, Citizens, and Burgesses in Parliament assembled, in the names of themselves and of all the Commons of Great Britain, and your lordship is now brought to the bar of this House to receive your trial upon that impeachment. The weight of this accusation, the solemn manner of exhibiting and prosecuting it, and the awfulness of this supreme Judicature, the most illustrious in the world, are circumstances that may naturally strike your mind with anxious and alarming apprehensions. Reasonable and well founded must those apprehensions be, if they proceed from that greatest of all terrors—a consciousness of guilt. But if your lordship is innocent, if you have really preserved yourself untainted furth the heinous crimes laid to your charge, as you have averred by your Answer, these very awful circumstances, when duly considered, ought to have a contrary effect, and to afford you support and consolation.

Your lordship can never doubt the greatest fairness and candour in the management of a prosecution carried on by the House of Commons, instructed and highly concerned to preserve the rights and liberties of their fellow-subjects. Neither can you entertain the least doubt of a just and impartial trial where the law of the land and the custom and usage of Parliament (an essential part of that law) constitute the rule of proceeding, and the decision and judgment rest in the breasts of those noble lords, your peers, who are to try you upon that honour which is inseparable from them, and to judge you by that law, which is the great security of themselves and their posterity.

It is my duty to put your lordship in mind of some things which may be of use to you in the conduct of your defence, but in this I shall be the shorter since at your own request counsel have been already assigned you, with whom you must be presumed to have advised.

Your lordship must give due and patient attention to the reading of the Articles of Impeachment, and what shall be said by the Managers for the House of Commons, or offered in evidence against you, without giving any interruption, but when the Managers shall have finished the examination on their part of any witness produced by them, you will have liberty to cross-examine that witness.

When the managers for the Commons shall have gone through their evidence and closed what they shall think fit to offer by way of charge, then will be your lordship's time to make your defence. In doing this you and your witnesses will be heard with the greatest attention and equity.

But your lordship must take notice that your counsel are not to examine or cross-examine any witness nor to give you any assistance, while matter of fact only is in question; but if any point or matter of law shall arise during this proceeding they will, according to the known rules in such cases, be heard to it on your behalf, and for that purpose are permitted to be present whilst your lordship is at the bar.[1]

The witnesses produced in your defence must be examined upon oath, pursuant to a very just and wise provision made by Act of Parliament in the first year of the late Queen Anne,

---

1 Immediately after this trial the rule was altered. In 1747 Sir Wm. Yonge (one of the managers in the case) moved in the House of Commons that impeached men be allowed the full use of their counsel as in ordinary Courts. Horace Walpole's comment was "Thank God! we are a better-natured age than that of William III., and have relinquished a savage privilege with a good grace."

and according to the form established by their lordships in former cases of impeachment.

By command of their lordships, I am further to acquaint you and all other persons who shall have occasion to speak to this Court, that they are to address themselves to the lords in general, and not to any lord in particular. Before I conclude I must beg the indulgence of the House to add one thing more. If your lordship shall desire to have the use of pen, ink, and paper to make notes in order to your defence, I presume it will be permitted, and if in the course of your trial you should happen to omit any advantage which in law and justice ought to be allowed to you for your defence, such is the candour of my lords, your judges, that I trust I shall meet with their approbation in giving you notice of it.

The Articles of Impeachment and Lord Lovat's Answer thereto, as also the Replication of the Commons to the said Answer, were, by command of the Lord High Steward, read, and the same are as follows:—

Articles of Impeachment for High Treason against Simon, Lord Lovat.

WHEREAS the Imperial Crown and Government of these kingdoms have been long duly and happily established in the Royal Family of His present Most Sacred Majesty, upon principles equally conducive to the honour and safety of the Crown and to the protection and liberty of the subject, whereby settled laws are made the common measure of justice to both, and a prerogative wisely calculated to promote the greater good of the people and answer the exigencies of government, has been ascertained and secured:

And WHEREAS the reign of His present Majesty and his Royal Father have given the strongest and most illustrious proofs of the happy effect of those principles in the exercise of their legal, mild, and equal administration under which every subject, from the highest to the lowest, has had his religion, his person, and his property fully protected by the most inviolable observance of the laws, which have had their free course without the least interruption on the part of His Majesty or of his Royal Father:

NOTWITHSTANDING which, there have been found many wicked and ungrateful persons, who have themselves enjoyed all these blessings in common with the rest of their fellow-subjects, and yet have been weak and desperate enough, from time to time, to contrive the subversion of this happy establishment, in order to introduce popish bigotry and superstition, instead of the Protestant religion, and an arbitrary, tyrannical power, instead of a free government; and as the only means of establishing and perpetuating these great evils, to place the Pretender to His Majesty's Crown upon the throne of this kingdom; and the more easily to obtain these ends, have from time to time taken advantage of the distresses which in the course of human affairs have happened to their native country to set on foot and prosecute their traitorous designs.

And WHEREAS divers of the said traitors to His Majesty have laid hold of the opportunity arising from the just and unavoidable, but difficult and expensive, wars in which this nation has been for some time engaged, to renew their treasonable conspiracies for the bringing their wicked purposes to effect by the assistance of troops and money from His Majesty's enemies abroad and by raising a rebellion at home:

And WHEREAS by the instigation of, and in concert with, the said traitors, a great number of French troops, accompanied by the eldest son of the said Pretender, were ready, and had in part embarked and actually set sail, to invade this kingdom in the year 1743, but were then prevented from accomplishing their design by the wise prevautions of His Majesty and the good providence of Almighty God:

And WHEREAS the same traitors, restless and indefatigable in the prosecution of their wicked and traitorous purposes, hoping that the French, by great superiority of their numbers in Flanders, might be able to invade this kingdom, and at the same time to prevent the return of His Majesty's troops from abroad for the defence of the nation, did, in the year 1745, encourage the said eldest son of the Pretender to His Majesty's Crown, to land, at that critical juncture, in this kingdom, who in pursuance of such encouragement did actually land in Scotland and put himself at the head of a large body of armed traitors, and commence and carry on for a considerable time a cruel, unnatural, and bloody war against His Majesty within this realm, which has at last been happily suppressed.

Article I.

Simon, Lord Lovat, being a subject of His said Majesty, one of the said traitors and rebels, and conspiring and joining with them in their said traitorous designs, and having withdrawn that due obedience, fidelity, and allegiance which, as a loyal subject, he owed, and of right ought to bear to His said present Most Sacred Majesty, the only true, lawful, and undoubted Sovereign of this kingdom, his true and natural Lord, did, upon the 31st day of December, in the year of our Lord, 1743, in the shire of Inverness, and on the 28th day of October, in the year 1745, in the same shire, and at divers other days, times, and places, wickedly, maliciously, falsely, and traitorously compass and imagine the death of His said Majesty.

ARTICLE II.

And for accomplishing his said wicked and traitorous purpose he, the said Simon, Lord Lovat, upon the said 31st day of December, in the said year 1743, in the shire of Inverness aforesaid, did traitorously correspond with the said Pretender, obtain and accept a commission from the said Pretender to be a Lieutenant-General of his forces, and another commission from the said Pretender to be General of the Highlanders, and did also accept from the said Pretender a patent or grant importing to create him, the said Simon, Lord Lovat, Duke of Fraser; and then and there did traitorously conspire and enter into an association with many other traitors, in order to raise a war and rebellion against His Majesty within this realm, and to obtain troops, money, and succours from France for that purpose.

ARTICLE III.

And the said Simon, Lord Lovat, did further, falsely, and traitorously, at the times and places before particularly mentioned and at divers other times and places, assemble himself, with divers other false traitors and rebels, against our said Sovereign Lord the King, being armed and arrayed in a warlike manner, and did raise, and cause to be raised and assembled, great numbers of armed men, His Majesty's subjects, for the service of the said Pretender and his said son; and arrayed and caused them to be arrayed in a warlike manner against His Majesty, and did traitorously levy, and cause to be levied, cruel and unnatural war against His Majesty within this realm at the times and places aforesaid, in favour of the said Pretender.

ARTICLE IV.

And for the more effectual bringing his said treasons and traitorous designs to effect, he, the said Simon, Lord Lovat, did, in the month of November in the said year 1745, traitorously compose, write, and send, and caused to be composed, written, and sent, a treasonable letter to the said eldest son of the said Pretender, then in arms within this kingdom, and joined by, and at the head of great numbers of His Majesty's subjects, false traitors and rebels against His Majesty, then also in arms and rebellion against His Majesty within this kingdom; in which letter he, the said Simon, Lord Lovat, among other things, expressed the great pleasure it would give him to end his days in the service of the said Pretender's said son, that he was resolved to send to him his, the said Lord Lovat's, eldest son to venture his life in his service, and deliver up his clan to him, and further expressed and represented his own great zeal and attachment to the said Pretender and his said son, and their cause and interest, and the service he had done, was doing, and intended to do for the said Pretender and his said son, with intent and in order to confirm, animate, and encourage him, the said Pretender, his said son, his adherents, and all the said traitors in the prosecution of their said treasons and traitorous designs.

Article V.

And the said Simon, Lord Lovat, in further pursuance of his said treasons, did, at the times and place before-mentioned, and at divers other times and places, after the said war and rebellion began, and while the same was carrying on, traitorously compose, write, and send, and cause to be composed, written, and sent, divers other treasonable letters and papers to divers false traitors then openly in arms in this kingdom against His said Majesty, and to divers others of His Majesty's subjects and other persons to assure them of his own zeal and firm attachment to the cause and interests of the said Pretender and his said son, and to confirm, solicit, excite, and persuade them to engage in, continue, and prosecute the said war and rebellion, and to promise and assure them of his assistance therein.

Article VI.

And the more effectually to attain the end of the said treasons and treasonable designs the said Simon, Lord Lovat, did at the said times and place and at divers other times and places, traitorously aid and assist the said Pretender's son and the said other false traitors and rebels in the carrying on the said treasons, war and rebellion, and furnish and provide them with great quantities of arms, ammunition, implements of war, clothes and other things useful and necessary for that purpose, and also sent his eldest son and many of his name, family, and dependants to the assistance of the said Pretender's eldest son and the said other rebels, and also gave them advice, directions, and instructions in the prosecution of the said rebellion.

Trial of Lord Lovat.

ARTICLE VII.

And the said Simon, Lord Lovat, further, at the times and place aforesaid and at divers other times and places, did unlawfully and traitorously hold, entertain, and keep intelligence and correspondence, both in person and by letters and otherwise, with the said eldest son of the said Pretender, well knowing him to be so, and also with divers other persons who were employed by the said Pretender's said son, and particularly with John Murray of Broughton, Esq.; Donald Cameron, the elder, of Lochiel; Donald Cameron, the younger, of Lochiel; Alexander Macleod, advocate, of Edinburgh; John Roy Stewart, Dr. Archibald Cameron, and divers others, all which persons were employed by the said eldest son of the Pretender in this kingdom in the said rebellion, the said Simon, Lord Lovat, well knowing that they were severally employed.

ALL WHICH SAID TREASONS AND CRIMES abovementioned were contrived, committed, perpetrated, acted, and done by the said Simon, Lord Lovat, against our said present Sovereign Lord the King, his peace, crown, and dignity, contrary to the duty of his allegiance and against the laws and statutes of this kingdom.

OF ALL WHICH SAID TREASONS AND CRIMES the Knights, Citizens, and Burgesses in Parliament assembled do, in the name of themselves and all the Commons of Great Britain, IMPEACH the said Simon, Lord Lovat.

And the said Commons, by protestations, saving to themselves the liberty of exhibiting at any time hereafter any other accusation of impeachment against the said Simon, Lord Lovat, and also of replying to the Answer which he shall make to the premises, or any of them, or to any impeachment or accusation that shall be by them exhibited according to the course and proceedings of Parliament, do pray that the said Simon, Lord Lovat, be put to answer all and every the premises, and that such proceedings, examinations, trial, and judgment thereupon may be had and used as shall be agreeable to law and justice.

THE ANSWER OF SIMON, LORD FRASER OF LOVAT, TO THE ARTICLES OF IMPEACHMENT OF HIGH TREASON EXHIBITED AGAINST HIM BY THE NAME OF SIMON, LORD LOVAT, BY THE KNIGHTS, CITIZENS, AND BURGESSES IN PARLIAMENT ASSEMBLED IN THE NAME OF THEMSELVES AND ALL THE COMMONS OF GREAT BRITAIN.

The said lord, saving and reserving to himself all benefit and advantage of exception to the uncertainties and insufficiencies in the said Articles contained, and also to all advantages and privileges belonging to him as a Peer of this realm, in answer to the aforementioned article, says, that being as fully sensible as any British subject of the many blessings these kingdoms have enjoyed under His present and late Majesty's mild and equal administration, and having, in the Rebellion of 1715, given the strongest proofs of his zeal for, and attachment to His late Majesty, and the succession of the Crown in his illustrious family, and against such as had undertaken the destruction of both, he cannot but lament his misfortune to have his fidelity questioned at the end of his days, and himself, when near worn out with age and infirmities, charged with intending the subversion of a Government he had in the strength and vigour of his age exerted his utmost power and address to support. Under this heavy pressure, attended with many other calamities and misfortunes, particularly his own inability to manage his defence, his only resource is in your lordships' justice, who will, he is well assured, regard only plain facts, not as aggravated by skill and oratory, but as clearly and manifestly proved by the testimony of credible and unexceptionable witnesses.

Under this firm persuasion, therefore, the said lord, in answer to the first and second Articles, denies that he did wickedly, maliciously, falsely, and traitorously compass or imagine the death of His said present Majesty or correspond with the Pretender, obtain or accept any commission or commissions, grant, or letters patent from the said Pretender, or traitorously conspire or enter into any association whatsoever for raising a war or rebellion against His said Majesty within this realm, or for obtaining troops, money, or succours from France for that purpose in manner and form as by the said Articles is alleged.

To the third Article the said lord denies that he did assemble himself with any traitors or rebels, or raise or cause to be raised or assembled any armed men for the service of the said Pretender or his eldest son, or array or cause to be arrayed any person or persons whatsoever against His said Majesty, or levy or cause to be levied any war against His said Majesty in this realm in manner and form as in this Article is charged.

To the fourth Article the said lord denies that he did compose, write, or send, or cause to be composed, written, or sent, any letter, paper, or writing whatsoever to the said Pretender's eldest son to any such purport or effect as by the said Article is supposed, or to any other purport or effect whatsoever.

To the fifth Article, he denies that he did compose, write, or send, or cause to be composed, written, or sent, any letter or letters, paper or papers, to any person or persons to such purport or effect as by the said Article is alleged.

To the sixth Article he denies that he ever did furnish or provide the said Pretender's elder son or any traitors or rebels, with any arms, ammunition, implements of war, or other things useful or necessary for the purpose in the said Article mentioned, nor did he send his eldest son, or any of his name, family, or dependants, to the assistance of the said Pretender's eldest son, or any rebels whatsoever, nor encourage, advise, direct, or instruct any of them in the prosecution of the said rebellion.

To the seventh Article, the said lord denies that he ever did hold, entertain, or keep any intelligence or correspondence with the said Pretender's eldest son, either in person or otherwise, nor did he entertain or keep any correspondence with any other of the persons mentioned in the said Article, or with any person employed by the said eldest son of the Pretender in the said rebellion, knowing any of them to be so employed.

And as to all other matters and things in the said Articles contained, and which is not herein particularly answered (if any such there be) the said lord avers that he is not guilty of them or any of them in manner and form as laid in the said Articles, or in any other manner or form whatsoever; and humbly submits himself to your lordships' judgment.

The following Extract from the House of Lords records was then read:—

Die Veneris, 16° Januarii, [1747].

A message was brought from the House of Commons by Sir William Yonge and others to acquaint this House that they have considered the answer of Simon, Lord Lovat, to the Articles of Impeachment exhibited against him by the Knights, Citizens, and Burgesses assembled in Parliament, and do aver their charge against the said Simon, Lord Lovat, for high treason, to be true, and that the said Simon, Lord Lovat, is guilty in such manner as he stands impeached, and that the Commons will be ready to prove their charge against him at such convenient time as shall be appointed for that purpose.

Lord High Steward—The distance of this place from the bar is so great that I am obliged to ask your lordships' leave to come down to the table for the convenience of hearing.

Lords—Ay, ay.

Which was done accordingly.

Lord High Steward—Gentlemen of the House of Commons, you will be pleased now to proceed.

First Day.

SIR WILLIAM YONGE[1]—My lords, as I was commanded by the House of Commons to lay before your lordships the Articles of Impeachment of high treason against the noble lord at the bar, which have been just read, so it becomes my duty to open the general charge to your lordships, together with some of the inducements which prevailed with the Commons to think this accusation necessary. Sir William Yonge

In the first place, my lords, I cannot omit observing that as every Impeachment is said to be in the name of all the Commons of the land, so this may most emphatically be declared to be so, as I am confident there is not a single subject of the United Kingdom of Great Britain who has not demanded justice against this notorious offender, excepting a few miscreants who may still be intestine enemies to His Sacred Majesty on the throne, His Royal Family, and, by necessary consequence, to the religion and liberties of their native country. The crime of high treason has at all times been considered in the most civilised and in the most free countries as an offence of the blackest dye, and as such the severest punishments have been inflicted on such offenders, and this, my lords, with the greatest reason and justice. Government was instituted for the happiness and security of mankind, to rescue them from the rapine and disorder, the murders and distractions which must be the consequences of anarchy and confusion.

Treason tends to destroy all Governments, whether monarchical or that of a commonwealth of any denomination, to introduce confusion and bloodshed, and if he that murders one man is by the laws of God and man to be punished with death how much more every rebel, every fomentor and abettor of rebellion, who is a murderer of thousands? By our law, he that but imagines the death of the King (in whose person all the bonds of society are united) and discovers his wicked imagination by any overt act, is a traitor. If this be proved against the prisoner (as I doubt not it will be to your lordships' full satisfaction), the noble lord at the bar is then a traitor.

Raising rebellion and levying war is another species of treason, by our law, or rather the plainest and most notorious overt act of imagining the death of the King, and we doubt not to prove the noble lord at the bar to be a rebel. It is high treason by statute to correspond with the Pretender to His Majesty's Crown, or with the sons of the Pretender, or those employed by them. But we shall amply prove it to your lordships that the noble lord at the bar has boasted that he received a patent as Duke from the Pretender, an authority

---

[1] See Biographical Notes, p. 307.

Sir William Yonge

as Commander-in-chief of the Highlands, is a general officer in the Pretender's service, and that he has openly corresponded with the son of the Pretender and his followers, then in open war against His Majesty within this realm, and given them harbour, encouragement, and assistance.

Your lordships have, I am persuaded, given due attention to the preamble as well as to the Articles that have been read. The Commons have there asserted that, most unfortunately for this nation, we have amongst us an obstinate, bigoted, restless faction, who are not, and will not be, contented with the enjoyments of liberty, peace, and prosperity, but who are perpetually watching for every favourable opportunity to overturn our Constitution and the present happy establishment. This is not only the principal, but has been their constant endeavour at different times from the late glorious Revolution to the present hour, by plots and conspiracies, by fomenting frequent rebellions, by inviting our enemies to invade us, and by that detestable crime of assassination. These facts require no proof. Our annals will afford and your lordships' memories will furnish numerous instances of some or other of these attempts. But, my lords, we shall, in the course of our proceedings, make it appear that the noble lord at the bar, so long as seven or eight years ago, joined in an association with other traitors, under their hands and seals, for dethroning His present Majesty and placing the Pretender in his stead. Not contented with this, the association so signed and sealed was transmitted by a faithful hand to the Cardinal then Prime Minister of France, in order to excite those, our natural enemies, to give their assistance and to invade this country with a foreign force, even at a time when we were in actual peace with that kingdom. His lordship and the other conspirators, justly imagining that this might be a favourable conjuncture, a war with Spain at that time being commenced, wisely concluded that when we were engaged with one branch of the house of Bourbon, the other would not long be neuter.

So early was his lordship in fomenting a rebellion at home and inviting an invasion from abroad! Nor was he only active in promoting and active in supporting, but zealous in endeavouring to prevent the extinction of the late rebellion, for when the rebels were broken, and their chiefs fugitive from the victory at Culloden, his lordship found means to be present at a sort of council of war held by those chiefs, where he earnestly encouraged them to reassemble the remains of their scattered troops and to revive the war, which was resolved on, and might have happened, had not the vigilance of His Royal Highness the Duke prevented its taking effect, thereby showing his own superior abilities in using, as eminently as his courage and conduct in obtaining, victory.

Sir William Yonge

The noble lord at the bar was at the time of this victory within 14 miles of Inverness. What would have been the conduct of any loyal subject on this occasion? Would he not have hastened thither to congratulate His Royal Highness on the success of that glorious day? What was the conduct of the prisoner at the bar? He received the young Pretender, flying from his defeat, embraced him with open arms, assisted him in his flight, and the next news we hear of his lordship is that he fled from justice himself, and appeared at the meeting of the rebel chiefs I have just now mentioned. This is the substance of our charge; and when I have said this much your lordships will not be at a loss for the strongest inducements to the Commons to impeach. But, my lords, there are other inducements. The Commons look upon it not only as their duty, but as a duty of the greatest importance to this nation, to take this opportunity to let the world know by the unanimous voice of the representatives of all the Commons of Great Britain their sincere and hearty abhorrence of every attempt to disturb His Majesty's auspicious Government, either from abroad or at home; to convince all the world that we are determined to be a free people under our own King; that we are determined to continue a Protestant nation; and that we never will suffer an arbitrary Government or popish superstition to be imposed on us by any power whatsoever; that we will give convincing proof to all Europe that we are not that dissatisfied, disaffected, turbulent people they have been vainly made to believe, by having adopted as truths all the seditious, discontented, and traitorous libels which have at different times and on various occasions been industriously scattered through the nation, and that our enemies did foolishly and ignorantly imagine these libels and calumnies to be the general sense of the people.

Permit me, my lords, to put you in mind that that scandalous declaration of the young Pretender published at Edinburgh, which your lordships, with the hearty concurrence of the Commons, ordered to be burnt by the common hangman, was but a short abstract of those very libels. This belief of our enemies was their folly. The relying on it has proved, thanks be to God, their destruction. Had they not been thus infatuated, would such a nation as France have attempted or thought it possible to overrun, much more to conquer, a brave and warlike people with a handful of men so poorly provided at first, and throughout so weakly supported? To convince mankind of these false and vain imaginations was one of the inducements which prevailed with the Commons to vindicate the people they represent from these vile aspersions in the most solemn manner in presence of your lordships and this great assembly. But, my lords, the body of the people themselves,

Sir William Yonge

from the highest to the lowest, have vindicated their own loyalty and honour.

After a small body of the regular troops had received a check, when it was apprehended the rebels would venture to march southward, what a noble spirit immediately arose throughout the nation! Not an artificial false clamour for liberty, but the old British spirit of liberty, the true Revolution spirit that asserted and signalised itself out of hatred to popery and arbitrary power. And, thanks be to God, it still remains in its full vigour amongst us. It cries aloud in our streets for justice against those that would have made them slaves and papists. It cries aloud for justice against the prisoner at the bar.

Calumnies of the like nature preceded the great Rebellion in the year 1715, and most justly may our present gracious King now say, in the words of his Royal Father of glorious memory, to both Houses of Parliament—"My greatest comfort is that I cannot reproach myself with having given the least provocation to that spirit of discontent and calumny that has been let loose against me or the least pretence for kindling the flame of this rebellion. Let those whose fatal counsels laid the foundation of all those mischiefs, and those whose private discontents and disappointments, disguised under false pretences, have betrayed great numbers of deluded people into their own destruction, answer for the miseries in which they have involved their fellow-subjects."

I have chosen to make this quotation because it will appear to your lordships that the noble lord at the bar, since his being taken, has frequently declared that one of the causes of his late behaviour was revenge to the Ministry for having taken from him the command of an independent company which he enjoyed. Now, my lords, if there is such a principle, that men must be paid for being loyal and hired to live free and happy, whom no sense of religion or love of their country can engage, whom no ties of conscience, oaths, or abjurations can bind, if there *is* such a principle, it is the lowest, the basest, and the meanest, as well as the most mischievous and wicked, that can enter into the heart of man!

My lords, the Commons have still further inducements for impeaching this particular criminal. Your lordships have already done national justice on some of the principal traitors who appeared in open arms against His Majesty by the ordinary course of law. But this noble lord, who in the whole course of his life has boasted of his superior cunning in wickedness and his ability to commit frequent treasons with impunity, vainly imagined that he might possibly be a traitor in private and a rebel only in his heart by sending his son and his followers to join the Pretender and remaining at home himself to endeavour to deceive His Majesty's subjects, hoping he might be rewarded for his son's services, if successful, or his son alone be the sufferer for his offences if the undertaking failed. Diabolical cunning! Monstrous impiety! Sir William Yonge

My lords, secret criminals of this sort, and of all others, it is the peculiar business of the Commons to explore and to bring to justice. This is the first and great offender, but should hereafter other concealed criminals appear who encouraged and supported the late rebellion, but who, either through cowardice of their hearts or fondness for their estates and riches, durst not join the rebels, I make no doubt but the zeal and loyalty of the Commons will prompt them with equal ardour to bring them to condign punishment.

Having thus opened to your lordships the nature of the crime of which the noble lord at the bar is accused, and several inducements the Commons had for this accusation, it is needless for me to awaken your lordships' attention by enumerating the miseries which the late rebellion occasioned, or the utter ruin which might have attended its success. It is too fresh in your lordships' memories to need any aggravation, and I pray to God that your lordships, this great assembly, and the whole nation may for ever remember it. It has too often been the misfortune of this country to be involved in civil wars, a calamity of all others the most to be dreaded. In ancient times these unhappy divisions have arisen from contests between princes and great men without the least view to the liberties or the benefit of the people. Let who would be victors, they were sure to be slaves, and only fought for different masters. The powers and imperiousness of Rome they were sure to submit to, while each contender exerted his influence there for the confirmation of his title. Henry VII. united the two branches of the contending families. During his reign and those that followed, the Commons began to grow rich, and consequently powerful; they became jealous of their liberties and of their property. When they had something of their own to lose they were too wise to risk their fortunes or their lives in vain for quarrels of the powerful and great. They shook off the yoke of Rome. Laws were enacted to limit the power of the Crown, and the days of freedom began to dawn.

Still, there was another struggle when the Crown began to encroach upon those laws and exert despotic power. These struggles, virtuous at first, soon degenerated into faction. Civil war and anarchy ensued, and ended (as it always will) in the most absolute tyranny. The Restoration established the power of our Government, and new privileges were gained for the people. But in the next reign the impatient lust of power and the abject bigotry of the Prince produced the happy Revolution. The glorious Prince of Orange came to our

Sir William Yonge

rescue. The people received him with open arms, and then, and not till then, was established our present free Constitution.

Pardon, my lords, this short deduction, and be pleased to reflect how odious and detestable the late unprovoked rebellion must appear—a rebellion calculated to overturn this Constitution, so hardly acquired, and so carefully preserved, by all the succeeding princes to this present hour—a rebellion against our present indulgent Sovereign, whose study has been the happiness of his people, under whom the boldest rebel cannot complain of the least violence and oppression. The laws of the land have had their full course, except where their rigour has been restrained by the Royal mercy. Under such a prince, and for the destruction of such a Constitution, has the noble lord at the bar conspired and rebelled!

Be pleased, then, to remember, the degradation, the bloodshed, that spoiled and stained those countries through which the rebels passed. Let us remember the distress of public credit, the stagnation of trade, the loss of our manufactures, the reasonable yet dangerous apprehensions which seized on the minds of all the loyal inhabitants of these great and opulent cities of London and Westminster. Let us remember the loss of lives, the blood and the limbs of gallant and brave officers and soldiers who conquered, for our sakes, in the famous battle of Culloden. They are, and will be, a perpetual memorial for whom, and by whom, they suffered.

Let us remember their calamities and endeavour, as it is our duty, to prevent the like evils for the future, by doing justice on criminals, by putting a stop to the growth of popery (that bloody religion), by preventing the education of our youth in those principles which the prisoner at the bar has instilled into his son, and by lessening the power in those hands which have ever been ready to disturb this Government. These and such other provisions as the wisdom of the Legislature shall suggest are necessary to prevent the future mischiefs which may arise from the frequent disturbance of the Government. While we are in this state it is vain for this country to hope to make the figure it ought to do, or retain her due dignity among the States of Europe, or to preserve the peace and hold the balance among foreign powers.

If, while her armies are employed abroad to humble the pride of an assuming nation, her fleets to protect our trade or to annoy our enemies; if, then, our troops are to be called home to preserve domestic peace and our fleets to prevent invasion by these patricides, what ally can depend on our assistance, or what pretence can we have to be umpires in the common cause of Europe? Britain, united within herself, may from her situation, her wealth, her naval power, and the bravery of her troops, justly claim that title, but

Sir William Yonge

divided, torn to pieces by civil discord, must fall under the ancient reproach of this country, and, while we are contending among ourselves, become an easy prey to our most inveterate enemies.

Let us now, my lords, turn our thoughts from these gloomy reflections which the time and circumstances of the late unhappy rebellion of necessity must furnish, and let us then call to mind with thankfulness the good providence of God which put an end to these calamities and a glorious period to our terrors. Let us acknowledge with duty and gratitude all His Majesty's labours for the safety and happiness of his people, and let us remember, with honour and praise, his Royal offspring, who, by his courage and conduct, has secured and established His Majesty's Throne, your lordships' honours, our liberties and privileges, and the Protestant religion. Thus ended this wicked and unnatural rebellion, of which the noble lord at the bar will appear to your lordships to be one of the first contrivers and promoters and a very considerable support.

All I have said, I know, will avail nothing with your lordships unless the evidence we shall bring against the noble lord at the bar be clear and full, as we doubt not it will appear to be. In cases where life is concerned it is painful to be a judge, it is uneasy to be the accusers, but there is a duty encumbent on both. I know, such is the generous compassion of your lordships' noble hearts, that you will acquit with pleasure but condemn with reluctance. And as I am persuaded, from the fulness of our proofs, the latter will be your lordships' judgment, give me leave to add a few words to lessen that concern which your lordships may feel as judges, and we as accusers.

When I look at his lordship at the bar I pity his age and infirmities, but, when I consider that, at his years, pride, vanity, avarice, or ambition are so rooted in his heart as to tempt him to risk his honour and estate, to sacrifice the religion and liberty of his country, to those mean passions, that pity is mixed with indignation. But when I reflect on his having been already pardoned for this very crime, that he has been amply rewarded by His Majesty's Royal father, and entrusted by His present Majesty in preserving the peace of those Highlands where he rebelled, I own I feel the strongest resentment of such heinous ingratitude.

The bringing his grey hairs with sorrow to the grave seems to be a distress to human nature, but when we consider how different the distress when that expression was first used, and that the prisoner at the bar is not brought into that wretched circumstance by the misfortune or loss of a darling child, but by sacrificing his eldest son to his own ambition, and by endeavouring to save his own worthless life by his son's destruction, it must almost harden the most tender breast.

Sir William Yonge

One word more and I have done. When your lordships look towards the bar you will please to reflect that had the design of the noble lord who stands there had its effect, it would probably have happened to many of your lordships' noble body, who should not have perished in the defence of your country, to have stood in that very place, while his lordship, with a number of mock peers, had sat in judgment on your lordships for the very crime for which he is now accused.

Thus far, my lords, I have gone in pursuance of the trust reposed in me by the Commons. I am now, my lords, for myself, humbly to implore your lordships' indulgence for any errors I may have been guilty of, either in matter or in words. If I have omitted anything material I am sure it will be supplied by the great abilities of those who are to follow me, and who will lay before your lordships the particular evidence to support our charge.

Lord Coke

Lord Coke—My lords, I am likewise commanded by the House of Commons to assist my honourable friend in maintaining the Articles of Impeachment against the noble lord at the bar, and, my lords, if I commit any errors in what I shall offer to your lordships I hope I shall meet with your lordships' indulgence. I in return promise you they shall not be wilful. It is a business, my lords, to which I am an entire stranger, nor should I have undertaken it in a case of so high importance if I did not think that my duty to my country, as well as my allegiance to His Majesty, to which I shall ever be faithful, equally called upon me to be instrumental, if I could, to find out concealed treasons and to bring the contrivers of them to justice, as to have ventured my person and fortune, if necessary, when the rebels were in the field. What I shall chiefly endeavour to prove to your lordships is that the last rebellion was not the effect of chance only, entered into by a few rash, inconsiderate men, without thought or previous design, but the result of long-considered and well-weighed consultation, and of schemes not so ill-concerted as to make their success either impossible or without some degree of probability in them; and, my lords, the reason why I choose to mention this general design to your lordships is that, though I am not very old, I have twice seen this country in very great danger from the disbelief of Jacobitism prevailing in it. In 1743 I with grief remember, when a message was sent from the King to a certain place in this kingdom, that an invasion was projected from France, what popular declamations were made to show that the scheme was impracticable, and that it ought to be looked upon only as a terror thrown out by the Ministry, because, as there was neither the colour nor appearance of truth in it, there could be no reality. And in the beginning of the last rebellion there was a disbelief prevailed even among those who ought to have been more certain of the truth. But that was not the case of the prisoner at your bar. He did believe it. He sent one of his chief agents into Lochaber to the young Pretender to go and receive his commands, and ordered him to express the greatest satisfaction at his being come over. He did not content himself with beginning the rebellion then, but in 1736 an association was sent by him to Rome, signed and sealed by many of the people of that country, to invite the Pretender then to come over, and that was afterwards carried to Paris and showed to the Cardinal, and, I believe, met with approbation at both these places. Lord Coke

My lords, I say nothing to aggravate the case of the prisoner at your bar. He is already oppressed with misfortunes enough, and it is not in my nature, I hope, to add to them. Nor should I, my lords, make the following observations did I not think myself obliged in justice to an unfortunate young man whom this noble lord has forced into the rebellion. He did write a letter that he was afraid the disobedient behaviour of his son would bring down his grey hairs with sorrow to the grave, and therefore it will not appear astonishing to you that when he had forgotten that tenderest tie of human nature, the love of a father to his child, so far as to desire to save the wretched remains of a life almost worn out, by the destruction of his own son, that he should forget his allegiance to the son of a King who saved his forfeit life, the remainder of which he has since employed in endeavouring to overturn and destroy his family and the Government established by him. I shall therefore conclude, with my honourable friend, in saying that we are ready to make good our charge against the prisoner at the bar.

The Attorney-General (Sir Dudley Ryder[1])—My lords, I have likewise the command of the House of Commons to assist in the prosecution of the noble lord at the bar. The charge has been fully stated and opened by the Managers who have spoken before me. The prisoner has denied every part of it, and thereby put the proof upon us, to be made out, not as he rightly says in his Answer to the Articles by facts aggravated by skill and oratory, but by credible and unexceptionable witnesses, in a plain and legal way, against which he will have the full benefit of any just defence he can state. I shall therefore avoid dwelling upon those many circumstances of aggravation either in respect to the rebellion in general or to the noble prisoner's own particular conduct in it, which will neces- Attorney-General

[1] See Biographical Notes, p. 306.

Attorney-General

sarily occur in the progress of the prosecution. The honourable Managers who have preceded me have very properly pointed them out to your lordships. They have had their effect already—all that effect which your lordships' wisdom and justice would suffer them to have, all that the Commons would wish them to have. They have awakened your lordships' attention, if that could possibly be wanting in the least degree on such an occasion. They have balanced that compassion which the age, appearance, and quality of the noble prisoner must materially raise in your lordships' humane breasts, that is, they have cleared the way for that justice which the nation calls for, and the Commons of Great Britain and the people whom they represent, on behalf of themselves, now demand at your lordships' bar.

All, therefore, that I shall offer to your lordships' consideration will be a plain narrative of facts, with the nature of the evidence to prove them, and some short observations to show the force of those facts to maintain the charge which the Commons of Great Britain have undertaken to make good. The facts will be very numerous, to be proved by a variety of witnesses and writings, and therefore must necessarily in the course of the evidence be intermixed. I shall therefore, in the opening, endeavour to disentangle them, and that your lordships' attention may be the more easily fixed, and the facts as they shall arise in the evidence be the more readily applied to the several parts of the charge, I shall divide them into three distinct periods of time—(1) those which happened precedent to the Pretender's son's landing; (2) what happened after that time, and before the battle of Culloden; and (3) what arose since that happy event; and within each of those periods your lordships will find many things which it will much concern the prisoner at the bar to give a satisfactory answer to.

The first will open to your lordships a wicked and traitorous scheme, begun and carried on for many years, for bringing over the Pretender by the assistance of a foreign force, in which his lordship will appear to have had a principal hand. The second will include the more immediate scene of action in the late wicked rebellion, and the particular parts which the prisoner took in it. The third will show him in the circumstance of a defeat; and the measures he then thought proper to take, and in every part of this whole scene he will appear plotting, associating, and supporting all the steps that were taken for subverting this happy establishment, dethroning His Majesty, and substituting a popish Pretender in his room.

To begin with, the first of these periods (and here I shall be under the necessity of going some years back in order to lay before your lordships a view of those traitorous schemes that have been set on foot, and prosecuted for some time past, in order to prepare the way for and bring on the late rebellion). As soon as the war with Spain was declared, the Pretender and his agents thought that a favourable opportunity offered to promote his interest, and a project was immediately set on foot by several of his friends in the northern parts of Scotland for bringing in the Pretender by the assistance of France, and seven of the chiefs of them entered into an association for that purpose. The prisoner at the bar set himself at the head of them, and himself, together with the Earl of Traquair, Sir James Campbell of Auchinbreck, Cameron of Lochiel the younger, John Stuart, brother to Lord Traquair; Lord Perth, and Lord John Drummond signed and sealed an association in writing, in which they engaged to venture their lives and fortunes to restore, as they called it, the Pretender, whom they styled their King, and his family. They agreed to send one Drummond, *alias* MacGregor, of Bochaldie, a relation and intimate friend of the prisoner's, to Rome, in order to have the scheme for bringing over the Pretender digested there, and from thence carried to Paris, for completing the execution of it. It was there to be delivered to Cardinal Fleury, then Prime Minister of France, with a memorial pressing in the strongest terms for her assistance.

Attorney-General

In order to engage the French Court he was to represent the great interest and strength of the conspirators in the Highlands, to assure the Cardinal that they could raise 20,000 Highlanders for the service, and wanted nothing but a few French troops and some money to secure the success. The conspirators, at the same time, sent over a list of many other heads of clans, who, they pretended, would join in the same design.

Drummond accordingly went over, and carried with him the association and list, and, after he had obtained the sanction of Rome and the Pretender, he came to Paris, where he was introduced to the Cardinal by one Semple, whom they called Lord Sempill,[1] an agent at that place for the Pretender. He delivered the association and list to the Cardinal, with an assurance that any of the seven who had signed the association would come over and confirm it in person whenever he desired it.

Any scheme to disturb the peace of this nation is but too acceptable to that Court at all times. The Cardinal received it with great attention and encouragement, and promised their assistance as soon as the conspirators could show a reasonable

[1] Lord (Robert) Sempill, who must not be confused with Lord Sempill, who succeeded to his title in 1716, and was a Hanoverian. Robert Sempill was created a peer of Scotland by the Pretender in 1723.

Attorney General

prospect of success. Drummond continued at Paris, and kept a constant correspondence with those who had joined in the association. Nothing, however, appears to have been finally resolved on till about the latter end of the year 1742, or the beginning of 1743, when the Court of France, finding how necessary it was to their views of oppressing Europe, to take off the weight of our assistance from our allies upon the Continent, thought it worth their while (though then at peace with us) to enter seriously into this design, and Drummond was about that time sent over hither by the Cardinal to assure the conspirators and the rest of the Pretender's friends in Scotland that if they could procure encouragement from England they might depend upon being assisted by France with an invasion the autumn following.

Drummond came accordingly over to Edinburgh, where he had a meeting with the Earl of Traquair, Lochiel the younger, and Cluny, and gave them an account of his negotiations, and particularly of his last message and promise from the Cardinal. Upon this it was agreed that the Earl of Traquair should go immediately to London and try what encouragement he could meet with there. The Earl went accordingly, and Drummond accompanied him. The Earl, after some time spent in England, returned to Edinburgh, and assured his friends there that the people here were well inclined to the Pretender, and would join in the design, provided they could depend upon assistance from France.

About the same time Drummond went over to Paris to satisfy the Cardinal of the success of his negotiation, and he gave him such satisfaction that a project for an invasion was soon after agreed on. The plan was that the French should send over 3000 men under the command of Earl Marischal,[1] who were to be joined with large bodies of Highlanders, which the conspirators had undertaken to raise. Fifteen hundred of the French were to go directly to Inverness, where the prisoner at the bar was to join them with his clan of Frasers; the remaining 1500 were to land in the west, near Sir James Campbell's, who was to go to the Isle of Mull and raise the clans there, who, all together, were to march and join the Frasers and the other body of French. At the same time, 12,000 French, under the command of Count Saxe, were to march to the coast of Flanders and France, and from thence embark and land in England within two or three days' march of London.

As soon as this scheme was agreed upon, Drummond, about the middle of the summer of 1743, wrote letters to the Earl of Traquair to inform him of the resolution that had been taken, to direct him to acquaint his friends of it, and to

[1] See Biographical Notes, p. 305.

assure them that it would very soon be put in execution. The Earl communicated this intelligence to John Murray of Broughton, Lochiel, and several others, who immediately sent the same Mr. Murray to France in order to settle matters beforehand for the execution of it. He went over accordingly, but the death of the Cardinal about that time suspended the prosecution of it for a little while. As soon as he arrived at Paris he was assured by Drummond of the Cardinal's good intentions and zeal for the Pretender's cause, and that nothing but his death could have prevented the immediate execution of it, and that the Cardinal's first design was that the army under the command of Maillebois should be employed in it, but that some persons about the King of France had prevailed upon him to order that army to march towards Hanover. Murray of Broughton was then introduced to Cardinal Tencin, and afterwards to M. Amelot, who assured him of the late Cardinal's sincerity in the proposed invasion, and that the French King had ordered him to acquaint the gentlemen who had entered into the association that he had the Pretender's interest very much at heart, and would certainly execute the scheme which had been settled as soon as his affairs would permit. M. Amelot, at the same time, entered into a discourse concerning the number of Highlanders that might be expected to join them. Attorney-General

With these assurances Murray returned to Edinburgh and made a report of his proceedings to the Earl of Traquair, Lord Perth, and others of the Pretender's friends. Drummond was sent at the same time with the like assurances to the Pretender at Rome in order to engage him to send the young Pretender to come and put himself at the head of the expedition. Drummond soon after came back to Paris, and from thence to London, in order to settle matters here for the intended invasion, and returned again to Paris, from whence he acquainted the Earl of Traquair by letter that the French Court had now settled everything for the invasion, that it would be executed immediately, and that the Pretender's son was come from Rome to accompany it.

This was in January, 1743, and in February following an invasion was attempted by a large embarkation from Dunkirk, where a great number of transports were got ready. Many of the troops actually embarked with a design to have come up the river Thames, and a fleet of men-of-war actually sailed from Brest to support the descent or to divert our fleet, while an army of 12,000 men might land without interruption. Nobody can have forgot how that expedition was happily disappointed by the good Providence of God and the vigilance of His Majesty, nor what terror it struck while it was depending, at a time that our own troops were necessarily engaged on the

Attorney-General

Continent, in the defence of our own and the liberties of Europe, and consequently when we had so few left to defend ourselves at home.

After this disappointment no letters appear to have come from France for a considerable time, which made the conspirators and their friends here very uneasy, and the Earl of Traquair engaged Murray to go again to Paris in order to know in what situation their affairs stood there, but before he was actually gone a letter came from Sempill to account for and excuse the miscarriage of the invasion, and desiring that fresh assurances might be sent from the Pretender's friends both in England and Scotland in order to engage the French Court in a new one.

This did not prevent Murray's intended journey, and in June, 1744, he went over to Paris, where he was introduced to the Pretender's eldest son at the house of one MacDonald, a banker, and had soon after a second meeting with him. The young Pretender then assured Murray that the French had been very serious in the invasion, which had been disappointed by nothing but wind and weather and other inevitable accidents, but, however, he had the strongest promises, both from the French King and the Ministry, that the scheme should be put in execution the then next summer, in the year 1745, and, as for himself, whether it was or not, he was determined to come over, if he brought but a single footman with him. And though Murray represented to him the rashness and danger of such an attempt, he was so fully satisfied of assistance from the Highlands whenever he appeared in person, that he would, in all events, come over at that time.

Murray returned to Scotland from Paris, and communicated what passed to the Earl of Traquair, Lochiel, Lord Perth, and others of the Pretender's friends, and at the same time brought along with him several letters from the Pretender's son, but with blank addresses, in order to be delivered to such as it should be thought proper, when Murray came over, and they were accordingly soon after delivered to such as, it was apprehended, would make the best use of them.

The time, however, running out, and no preparations yet appearing in France for an invasion, the Pretender's friends, who were acquainted with the design, began to fear the French would deceive them, and, in June, 1745, Murray received a letter from the Pretender's son, in which, without taking notice of any invasion from France, he informs Murray that he was determined himself to come to the northern part of Scotland immediately, and desired his friends might be informed of it, and be ready to join him with all the forces they could raise. He tells him that it would be the latter end of that same month, and appoints the place where he designed to land, together with the signals that were to be given and taken. Attorney-General

This letter was immediately communicated to the Pretender's friends in the north, and, amongst the rest, to the noble lord at the bar. So unexpected a resolution, without mentioning any assistance from France, much surprised them. They thought it, as was natural, rash, precipitate, and dangerous to come without force, and therefore determined, most of them, if they could not prevent his landing, to advise him to return and wait till he could be better prepared. About a fortnight after, the Pretender's son actually arrived, and landed in the north-west part of Scotland upon the 25th of July, 1745.

Your lordships will permit me now to make a little stand. I have stated these facts as a short view of the commencement and progress of several wicked and treasonable correspondences, plots, and schemes contrived and carried on from the year 1740 for bringing over the Pretender by the assistance of the power of France.

I have hitherto, my lords, but just named the noble prisoner at the bar in the account I have given of them, and I have avoided it on purpose that, when your lordships should have before your eyes, in one view, the general plan of that series of treasons which have been contriving, and in part executing, for so many years, I might the more easily point out to your lordships, as it were in a map, the particular precise parts which the noble lord acted in them, which is what I shall now apply myself to. And in order to do this the more clearly and agreeably to the evidence which will be produced, I shall be under the necessity of going back to some yet earlier parts of his life, and which, my lords, I should not do if your lordships would not necessarily, in the course of the evidence, see the prisoner himself taking pains to connect the early with the latter parts of his life in order to prove the uniformity and consistency of his conduct, all tending to and uniting in one great centre, the overturning of the Protestant succession, excluding or dethroning His Majesty and his Royal father, and setting up the Pretender to their throne in their room.

So long ago as the reign of Queen Anne, when the nation was involved in a war with France, and invasions from thence were continually set on foot, and it became material for the Pretender's service to arm his friends in the northern part of the island, the prisoner, who had been from his youth bred to war, accepted of a commission from the Pretender of a general officer. It must be owned that it does not appear that the prisoner made any particular use of it; and the first time any opportunity did offer, when the rebellion broke out on the death of Queen Anne, the noble lord at the bar did important services to His late Majesty. He himself will likewise admit that he was

Attorney-General

amply rewarded for them, but he seems very soon to have repented of those services, even while he was in the full possession of the reward of them.

In 1719, when a Spanish invasion was undertaken in favour of the Pretender and Spanish forces were actually landed in the north, the prisoner thought proper to engage in it, and, while the Earl of Seaforth was raising his men to assist in it, the prisoner himself wrote a letter to that Earl, with a promise to join him with his clan, but before he had actually done it that attempt was defeated. From that time till the year 1736 the Managers don't take upon themselves to state to your lordships anything concerning his conduct but that general account which your lordships will find him giving of himself in his own letters, that he had, ever since he had the use of his reason, been the most faithful and zealous subject to the person and interest of the Pretender. But in that year, when one Roy Stuart, who had escaped out of prison, to which he had been committed for high treason, and been afterwards harboured in the prisoner's house, then High Sheriff[1] of the county where he had been imprisoned, was going to the Pretender to Rome, the noble lord sent by him an assurance to the Pretender of his constant fidelity even to death, and desired a commission from him to be lieutenant-general of the Highlands and to have a patent of dukedom, which he had before solicited, expedited, and which he claimed as a matter of right for the services he had done that cause.

In the year 1740, when an invasion was projected, the noble lord was not only one of those that signed the association and corresponded with the persons that negotiated it beyond sea. but himself proposed it, and seems to have been the original projector.

In the year 1743, when the invasion was actually resolved, and a person of figure and interest was necessary to conduct it in the Highlands, the prisoner was pitched upon as the most proper for that purpose, and accepted two commissions from the Pretender at Rome in December, 1743, one to be lord lieutenant of all the counties north of Spey, and the other to make him a lieutenant-general. He likewise, about the same time, obtained the patent, which he had been long soliciting, for creating him Duke of Fraser. And, though the disappointment of that expedition prevented his immediate use of those powers, they did not lie idly by as a private ornament to his person and to gratify his vanity only. They were made use of by him to propagate the principles of treason and rebellion, to sow the seeds of disloyalty to His present Majesty and his

[1] The Attorney-General should have said "Sheriff." No office of High Sheriff existed in Scotland.

Government, to discipline his dependants in the service of the Pretender and make them ready whenever his master's projects were ripe for execution

Attorney-General

He was, as your lordships will see him expressing himself in his letters, always the most zealous and active partisan that the Pretender had in those parts.[1] He was, in his own words, the life and spirit of the Pretender's affairs in that country. He made it, as he says, his sole business to keep up the hearts of his King's friends, though it was both fatiguing, troublesome, and expensive, and appeals for the truth of it to the knowledge of all the gentlemen in the Pretender's interest in the north. He did, as he expresses himself in another letter, more service to the Pretender's cause than any one of his rank in Britain.[2] He constantly made it his business, as he says in another, to promote his master's interest and to engage faithful subjects to him. So that he had done, as he expresses in a still higher strain of language, more against this Government than would hang fifty lords and forfeit fifty estates.[3]

I have now pointed out to your lordships the particular share the noble lord will appear to have had in the steps towards the late rebellion, in which you must have observed him to be a most active friend to it. I shall now open to your lordships a state of the facts that affect the prisoner since the young Pretender's landing, which was, as I mentioned, upon the 25th of July, 1745.

Notice was immediately sent of it to the chiefs of the clans known to be in his interest, and the prisoner at the bar was one of the first to whom it was communicated. The conspirators, who expected an attempt at the head of a French army, were surprised at his coming in a single ship, without soldiers and without any material friends, or even many servants, accompanying him, and were at first shocked at the danger of a design so prematurely executed. However, some of the clans came in soon; and the prisoner at the bar seems to have early determined to have done so too, not, indeed, at first in person, which he excused from his age and supposed infirmities, but by sending his son at the head of his clan. For that purpose he directed the Master of Lovat, his son, who was then at, or but just come from, the University of St. Andrews, to get ready. He likewise directed the inferior heads of the clan of Frasers to send in lists of their numbers and names, with severe threats on such as neglected or gave him incorrect ones. He ordered the arms which he had in his house to be cleaned and mended, bell tents and camp colours to be made, and the arms of the Fraser's family to be painted on them.

---

1 See his letter to the Prince, p. 215 *inf.*
2 See letter to Lochiel, p. 216 *inf.*
3 See letter to the Master of Lovat, p. 220 *inf.*

Attorney-General

He appointed his son the colonel, and directed his tenants and dependants to follow him, exhorted them to be true to the Pretender's cause, and encouraged them with an assurance of success.

The men were brought together and twice rendezvoused. Officers were appointed, who were entertained in his house and at his table, where he used to call the Pretender's son by the name of "Royal Prince" and "Prince Regent," and drank to his success. He ordered the Pretender's declaration to be read, and, when the person whom he had commanded to do it declined it, he declared it was high treason to refuse it. He provided the men with arms, meal, provisions, and money, sent for ribbands to make white cockades for them, and had tailors and other workmen in his house to make them caps, bonnets, and brogues. He went still further, and, as some of his dependants were unwilling to engage, he ordered the fiery cross, as it is called, to be sent about his country to force them. This is the last and most extreme customary, though illegal and cruel, sort of process, if I may so call it, that the Highland chiefs use to compel their dependants to perform their arbitrary commands, and is a general public denunciation of plunder, fire, and sword on all that do not obey; and several were actually forced into the rebellion by taking away their plaids, beds, and cattle and turning their wives and children out of doors. While he was using threats to some, he tempted others by the promises of rewards to their wives, and commissions to themselves.

Soon after the last rendezvous of the men the Earl of Cromartie's clan marched near the prisoner's house in their way to the Pretender's son. The Earl, his son, and some of the officers called at the house, where they were entertained as friends, and the prisoner told the Earl that his clan should follow soon after, laying the blame, at the same time, upon his son, the Master of Lovat, that they were not yet ready.

The prisoner, however, did not think fit as yet, either by himself or his son, actually to join the Pretender. The rebels were now but beginning to march southward. The King's troops were endeavouring to intercept them, and, till they met, the event, he thought, might be doubtful. The rebels, however, escaped them, and upon the 17th of September got possession of the capital of that part of the United Kingdom, and in a few days afterwards the unfortunate battle of Prestonpans seemed, in the opinion of those deluded people, to turn the scale in their favour.

At that time one Hugh Fraser, who had about a year before been secretary to the prisoner, was at Edinburgh, where William Fraser, a relation of the noble prisoner's, happened then likewise to be. They had both heard of his design of sending the Master of Lovat into the rebellion, and both were desirous of preventing it, for which purpose William Fraser thought of an expedient for getting the Master of Lovat out of the way by sending him to Holland to complete his education, the expense of which he was willing to be at. With this message Hugh Fraser went to the prisoner, and made him the offer. My Lord Lovat at first seemed to yield to it, but at last told him he was too far engaged, and was resolved that the Master should go with his clan to the young Pretender. Attorney-General

The prisoner had early notice of the battle of Prestonpans, and Barrisdale, one of the heads of the rebellion, came to his house and told him he was going to raise more of the Highlanders for the service. This battle seems to have determined his resolution, and when Hugh Fraser was to return to Edinburgh he charged him with a verbal message to the Pretender's son to inform him that his age and infirmities would not permit him to travel, and therefore hoped he should be excused attending him in person, but that he would send his son at the head of his clan, which would be a much greater mark of his loyalty, and the message was delivered accordingly.

The rebels continued at Edinburgh till the 31st of October, when they were beginning their march towards England, but the prisoner's son not having yet joined them, it was thought necessary that John Murray of Broughton, the young Pretender's secretary, should write to the prisoner to hasten his men and meet them at Carlisle. The letter was written and sent, and soon after delivered by Hugh Fraser, who at the same time represented to him the bad condition of the rebel army, the state of His Majesty's forces, and the arrival of the Dutch troops, which he did, in order to prevent the prisoner's going on with his engagements. But the prisoner told him it was now too late to go back, and forbade him to mention anything to his son against it. He, besides, told him that he had put his name down as a captain-lieutenant in his son's company, and ever after called him by that title.

His dilatoriness, however, had made some of the Pretender's friends uneasy, and apprehensive that he was playing a double game, and as they thought it would be of great service to their cause if the noble prisoner would make a public avowal of his taking part with them, applied to him for that purpose, and told him that a great deal depended upon his throwing aside the mask, upon which he pulled off his hat and threw it on the ground, saying "There it is then!"

In the month of November he sent a letter to the Pretender's son to assure him of his fidelity, and about the same time two others to Lochiel and Murray, the secretary, both of them to the same effect. Though the two first of these letters appear by the dates to have been written in November, and the latter

Attorney-General

probably at the same time, yet, as the rebels were then going into England, they don't seem to have been sent till their return. The prisoner in the meantime went on with raising his men, till it was universally known in that country that the Master of Lovat was to go at the head of them and join the rebels.

My Lord Loudoun and the President of the Session were then at Inverness collecting a body of men to oppose them, and were then superior to the rebels in those parts. The prisoner well knew that the design of the Master of Lovat's joining the rebels could not be unknown to them, and that they must suspect at least that he himself was at the bottom of it. This made him afraid for his own person as soon as his son began to march. These apprehensions made him suspend the time of their march till he could be better informed of the measures the Lord Loudoun and the President would take in that event with respect to himself. And, therefore, after he had once ordered them to march, and those of his country of Eirth[1] had actually begun it, and proceeded as far as Strathannan in the way to Perth, which the rebels were then in possession of, his courage began to fail, and he sent orders for their return, which they immediately obeyed, excepting twenty, and he thought it more prudent, before they finally marched, to send Hugh Fraser to Inverness to sound the inclinations of Lord Loudoun and the President, and to represent to them that the intended march of his son was against his inclinations and contrary to his commands, that his son was obstinate and disobedient, and that it would be unjust that a father should suffer for an undutiful child.

The Lord Loudoun and President took it to be, as it really was, a pretence only, and the effect of that double part which the prisoner was acting till he thought it worth his while to throw off the mask in reality. They knew that a young man of nineteen years old, that had lived at the University and but just come home, could have no power over his father's tenants and dependants, but just so far as his father gave it him, and that the prisoner was himself the most absolute superior in all the Highlands. They therefore gave Hugh Fraser to understand there could be no safety for the father while the son was in open rebellion.

Hugh Fraser returned with this answer to the prisoner, and delivered at the same time a letter from the President to the same effect. About the same time news came that Lord John Drummond, with French troops, was landed, which seems to have determined the prisoner's resolution, and he told Hugh Fraser that the threats of the Lord President were but a bugbear, and immediately gave the Master of Lovat his final

1 "The Aird."

orders to march, which he instantly obeyed, and marched accordingly. And Lord Loudoun and the Lord President found means soon after to secure the prisoner's person, who was carried a prisoner to Inverness, from whence, however, he soon after made his escape. Attorney-General

The Master of Lovat was now got to Perth, at the head of the clan of Frasers, whither Hugh Fraser attended him as his captain-lieutenant, and, upon notice from the Pretender's son, who was then come as far as Glasgow in his return from England, was sent thither by the Master of Lovat for a supply of arms. Hugh Fraser, on his return from Glasgow, was charged by Murray, the Pretender's secretary, with a packet, in which were enclosed three letters—one from the Pretender's son to the prisoner, referring to a second enclosed from Murray, Lochiel, and Cluny, to him likewise, and a third to the Master of Lovat. There were also three commissions enclosed, two of which were dated at Rome, 23rd December, 1743, from the Pretender himself, one of which was to make the prisoner lord lieutenant of all the countries north of Spey, and the other to make him a lieutenant-general.

The rebels, as soon as they had collected all their parties together, marched towards Inverness. His Royal Highness the Duke of Cumberland followed them as fast as the season of the year and the nature of the country would permit, till he came up with them, and obtained that signal and complete victory at the battle of Culloden upon the 16th of April, 1746, when all the noble lord's schemes of grandeur and power and for a new Revolution were put an end to at once.

I am now come, my lords, to that last period of time—from the battle of Culloden. The prisoner was waiting not very far off the event of that important day. The night after the Pretender's son came to Gortuleg, where the prisoner then was, and had an interview with him. The noble lord did not even then disavow his cause, but received him as his prince, excused his not joining him in person, and, after the tenderest embraces, parted from him as a faithful subject to his royal master.

The prisoner, as well as those who had been in open arms, was now obliged to fly. He knew his guilt was the same, and therefore deserved the same treatment. The rebel army, and their chiefs who escaped from the battle, were now dispersed, but some correspondence among them was kept up, and upon the 15th of May a meeting was had at a place called Mortleg, where there were present the prisoner, Lochiel, his brother Dr. Cameron, Murray the secretary, and several others. The end of the meeting was to consider what was proper to be done for their common safety.

The noble prisoner met them himself, not as an innocent person, to advise them to lay down their arms, confess their

Attorney-General

guilt, and beg for mercy, not as a neutral person, if neutrality, in the cause of our King, religion, liberty, and this happy establishment can be attended with a less degree of guilt, but as one involved in the same common crime and calamity, as a chief whose age and experience entitled him to the lead, and he took it. He advised them to raise a sufficient number of men to defend themselves against the King's troops till they could make terms for themselves, and, after computing what each of those present was capable of procuring, he proposed the number of 3500, of which each was to raise a certain proportion, and he himself proposed that his son should raise 400, and desired Lochiel, as he himself had not been in arms, to answer for his son. Lochiel did so, and all the company agreed to the proposal, and, there having been then lately come from France 35,000 louis d'or, it was likewise agreed that each should have ten days' pay for their men out of it, which was immediately distributed, and the share of the Master of Lovat was paid to the prisoner's servant. In consequence of this about 400 men, in the whole, only were raised. But the rebels made no stand afterwards.

The Master of Lovat had afterwards a meeting with his father at Kilbogie, when the Master proposed to surrender to His Majesty, but the prisoner dissuaded him from it, and reflected upon his son as a person of mean spirit to think of so dishonourable an action, and determined to fly himself, but with a guard of about twenty soldiers, whom he took into pay for his defence. However, he was pursued and taken by a party sent by the duke, under the command of Captain Ferguson, who treated him with great humanity. During the time of his being in his custody they had frequent conversations together concerning the rebellion. He was asked by the captain how he could act as he had done after all the favours he had received from the Government. He answered, it was not against the King but the Ministry he had acted, that they had taken away his company, and when he was told it was a bad revenge to endanger his own life and fortune, his answer was, "Who could have thought but that they" (meaning the rebels) "would have carried all before them?" and that if the young Pretender would have taken his advice he might have laughed at the King's forces, and none but a mad fool would have fought that day; that they might have gone into the mountains, and lived on butter and cheese, and given the duke twelve months' work; besides, that they were in daily expectation of assistance and money from France.

The prisoner was afterwards brought before Sir Everard Falkener. He did not then think of denying his treason. On the contrary, he gave the same account of the motive to it which he had done to Captain Ferguson, but with this addition, that he resented the loss of his independent company so much that, if Kouli Khan[1] had come, he should have been for him. He talked much of the King's mercy, of the former services he had done to this Royal Family, and that he could still do greater than twenty such old heads as his were worth. However, he concluded with the following passage out of Virgil:—

Attorney-General

In utrumque paratus,
Seu versare dolos, seu certæ occumbere morti.

I have now, my lords, gone through those three periods of time which I proposed, in which your lordships have observed many things of great moment to the present cause. The Managers have with the greatest care endeavoured, amongst that great extent of evidence which has come to their knowledge, to discover the truth, and I have with the utmost fidelity stated to your lordships no fact but what I take to be so. I know, my lords, how unjust it would be to endeavour to mislead your lordships. I know how idle and fruitless it would be to attempt it.

I have likewise endeavoured to throw all the facts together in such an order that they may serve to give light to each other and ease your lordships in the attention you will give to the evidence that will prove them.

I shall now, therefore, endeavour to give your lordships a short view of that evidence. It will be of two sorts, parole and written evidence. The former will consist of a great number of witnesses concurring in the account of the secret preparations towards the rebellion, the steps taken in it, and many in charging the noble lord as the principal actor in both. What they say will be supported, confirmed, and illustrated by the written evidence.

As to the first sort, it will be tedious and unnecessary for me to give your lordships a detail of the names and characters of each witness or the particular facts they speak to. It will be sufficient to say in general that I don't know of one circumstance that I have opened which will not be fully proved by some or other of them, that some of the witnesses were principal actors in the steps leading to the rebellion, as well as in the prosecuting of it, that some have been long acquainted with the prisoner, seen his life and conversation, and had, from his own mouth, the truth of many of the facts that preceded their own time, and have attended his person, and been eye and ear-witnesses of many others, that others of the witnesses have heard and received his commands, felt the weight of his power, or been employed by him in divers of those acts of treason wherewith he is charged, that all have had full

1 A Persian conqueror who defeated the Great Mogul. His name was used several times in Lord Lovat's letters. In the "Memoirs" he says Argyll knew as much of Atholl's doings as "the Khan of Crim Tartary."

Attorney-General

opportunities of knowing the facts to which they will be called, and none have any imputation on their characters but that of having some of them been accomplices in the same treason.

The written evidence which the Managers have been able to collect and produce consists of letters from and to the noble lord. The former are of the handwriting of Robert Fraser, one of his secretaries, dictated and signed originally by himself, though the signatures of some appear now torn off.

They were all written during the rebellion, not at the beginning, when the prisoner, surprised by the sudden appearance of the son of him, whom he had formerly called his King, might be drawn into expressions of affection and zeal beyond his real meaning, but after the rebellion was grown to a great height, and the noble lord had full time to look about him, to foresee, weigh, and balance all consequences to his country, himself and his family, and upon the whole had deliberately chosen the side he took. Of this sort of letters there will be many produced to your lordships. One of them written and sent to the Pretender's son himself, dated November, 1745. The signature and some parts of the body of it are torn off, but that will be supplied by a copy under the same secretary's hand taken by his lordship's own order. Two others were written about the same time to Mr. Murray, the Pretender's secretary, and to Lochiel. Two of the rest were written to the prisoner's own son.

Your lordships will excuse my mentioning a few passages out of them as specimens of the whole. That to the Pretender's son, which is itself in the Articles made a distinct overt act of treason, is addressed to him by the title of "Most Royal Prince," and in the conclusion calls him "His Royal Highness." It mentions the prisoner's having been made a general offer by the Pretender himself above forty years before, excuses his incapacity of serving him in person by his age and infirmities, and his resolution to give him the next mark of his zeal by sending his eldest son, the bearer, to venture his life in his service, with a great number of gentlemen and heads of families of his clan, and 800 of his common people.

The letter to Murray is to engage him to become his son's patron at the young Pretender's Court. It boasts of the same merit in sending his son and clan, and sets out his own long services to the Pretender in the strongest light.

The letter to Lochiel complains greatly of the treachery, as he calls it, of an honourable person in engaging on His Majesty's side, and of the mischief his conduct had done to the cause, and magnifies his own clan and services to the Pretender.

His letters to his son open the secrets of his heart, acquaint him with the association he had formerly signed to venture his life and fortune to restore the Pretender, informs him of the promised assistance of France, the commission from the Pretender to make him general of the Highlands, the more favourite patent for a dukedom, and sets them all in a light that would render him, as he says, "a monster of ingratitude if he was not attached to the Pretender more than ever." Attorney-General

The rest of his letters are written in the same strain and founded upon the same principles of treason and rebellion. The letters written to the prisoner are one from the Pretender's son himself, referring to another written to him by Lochiel, Murray and Cluny, and one from the prisoner's own son. The two former were written by way of acknowledgment for his services and to engage him in an open personal appearance on that side as the best means to secure the success of their cause, and will show the Pretender's son's employment of those persons with whom the prisoner treasonably corresponded. The son's letter is part of a correspondence with the father upon the subject of the rebellion, and was the occasion of the letters before mentioned to have been written by him.

My lords, I have now done with that general view of the evidence which I proposed to give your lordships. I would not anticipate what the noble lord may say by way of defence, but as the evidence, on the part of the Commons, will necessarily mention one sort of defence, which the prisoner formerly made use of when he apprehended his person in immediate danger from the President and Lord Loudoun on account of the Frasers rising to join the Pretender, I can't help just taking notice of it here. His pretence to them was that his clan was raised by his son alone without his direction and against his command, and that the whole conduct of the clan of Fraser was an act of disobedience in his son to him, as well as of treason to His Majesty, and that it would be hard that a peaceable father should be answerable for the guilt of his son.

If this should be any part of the noble lord's present defence I shall obviate it only so far as to observe to your lordships that it is as false as it is unnatural, and will appear to be so, not only by the parole evidence we shall produce, but by every one almost of the prisoner's own letters, in which he takes to himself the whole merit of his son's services, and values himself to the young Pretender according to the strength and zeal of his clan.

What remains, my lords, is only to make a few observations tending to show how the facts and the evidence I have been stating will maintain the particular charges which the Commons have undertaken to make good, for which purpose it will be necessary very shortly to point out the precise nature of the charge itself.

It contains three species of treason—(1) Compassing the

Attorney-General

death of His Majesty; (2) levying war against him within the realm; and (3) corresponding with the Pretender's son and his agents.

As to the first of these, the wisdom of this Constitution, foreseeing that the general happiness must be most intimately connected with the safety of that Royal person, and providing against the remotest dangers to which it may be exposed, has made the very imagination of the heart, when directed to its destruction, an act of treason, but as the intent by itself alone can be known to none but the great Searcher of Hearts, it has, with equal prudence and justice, provided that this imagination must be discovered by some external act, which, in the ordinary language of the law, is called "an overt act."

The Commons have pursued in their impeachment the law in both respects. They have charged the prisoner with that traitorous imagination, and they have stated many facts that manifest it, such as by the established rules of law have in all times been held sufficient.

The overt acts particularly charged are—his entering into an association to raise a war and rebellion against His Majesty by the assistance of French troops; his corresponding with a Pretender to His Majesty's crown; his obtaining two commissions from the Pretender, one to be general of the Highlands, and the other a lieutenant-general of his forces; his sending a treasonable letter to the Pretender's son with expressions and assurances of that fidelity and loyalty to his father which was due to His Majesty alone; his sending many other treasonable letters to his fellow-subjects to engage and persuade them to join and continue in that rebellion, which was then begun and raged in the northern parts of this kingdom; his assisting the Pretender's son with arms and sending his own son with his clan into the service of the Pretender.

Your lordships will be beforehand with me in distributing the various matter I have before opened to these several heads. I would only observe that, besides the evidence arising from the witnesses who will appear in person at your lordships' bar, the prisoner's own letters are not only special overt acts of treason themselves, but will be the clearest proof of the most material of the others.

When the prisoner, in the fulness of his heart, opens himself to a son, whose parts and proficiency were his own pride, upon a subject the most of all interesting to both, to the future as well as present happiness of his family, its honours and estate, your lordships can have no possible doubt of the reality of that association, those honours, those trusts, and that attachment to the Pretender on which he builds and communicates the resolution he had then taken.

Attorney-General

When he writes to the Pretender's son himself, then in the capital of one part of the United Kingdom at the head of an army of rebels, acting the part of Royalty, and subduing His Majesty's faithful subjects, to boast of his former, and promising him future, loyalty, your lordships must see in the clearest manner what side he had chosen, and whose life and throne he was striking at.

As to the treason of levying war, the prisoner seems to have thought that nothing but an open personal appearance in arms would bring him within that sort of guilt, and, in fact, whether out of greater caution on that account, or from peculiar views of management with the Pretender, or more probably from both, he seems studiously to have avoided that particular precise mark of treason. But the law, which, in words, though not in punishment, distinguishes in some sorts of crimes between principals and accessories, makes no such distinction in this of the highest nature. They are both in treason equally criminal, and the various acts of encouragement, persuasion, and assistance given and done by him to those who were personally engaged, do, in the eye of the law, as indeed they do in reason, make their guilt his own.

The last species of treason charged is founded on the breach of the late Act made in the seventeenth year of His Majesty, on occasion of the invasion attempted from Dunkirk in that year in favour of the Pretender, and accompanied by his eldest son. This Act extends the treason made by the Act of the thirteenth of King William, of corresponding with the Pretender the father, and his agents, to a correspondence with his sons and their agents.

The proof of this treason will be manifest to your lordships both from the written and parole evidence. The same letters, which afford such conclusive proof of the other treasons, are direct and immediate proof of this; besides the personal interview between the prisoner and the Pretender's son, and the many more personal correspondences with the Pretender's servants and officers.

I have now, my lords, finished all that I proposed to lay before your lordships. The great variety of matter must be my excuse for the length of it. I am not under any apprehension that the evidence will be insufficient to convince your lordships of the justice of the prosecution. I am more afraid lest your lordships and the world should inquire, "Why all this load of evidence?" when one of those many facts fully established would be enough to convict the noble lord of this highest of crimes, and draw down upon him from your lordships that heaviest of sentences which is the consequence of it. If that question should be asked, the answer I would give to it should be shortly this. The Managers did not think

Attorney-General

it consistent with their duty to the Commons of Great Britain, whose commands they are to execute, that regard they owe to your lordships at whose bar they are to execute those commands, nor to the people of Great Britain whom the Commons represent, and who are greatly interested in the event of this impeachment, to suppress any part of that evidence, extensive as it is, which came to their knowledge material to the prisoner's cause. The Commons have thought this a matter worthy their own interposition, and therefore have taken it into their own hands not to deprive the noble lord of any legal defence. The candour of the Commons and your lordships' justice will secure him against any danger of that kind, not because they wanted that evidence, which would be sufficient in the ordinary Courts of justice (for far would it be from them to throw their weight into the scale of evidence), but because of the wide, extensive part the prisoner has had in this great scene of treason as its contriver, promoter, and finisher, so far as Providence suffered it to go.

As to your lordships, the Managers did not think it becoming them to prejudge your opinion or deprive your lordships of that full daylight in which the crimes of this lord appeared to them, and of that greatest of all satisfactions which every judge would wish to have in every cause, of being certainly right in the sentence he is to pronounce.

As to the people in general, it is of no small moment that they should be enabled to behold in one view the pernicious schemes that have for many years been concerting between Rome, France, and unnatural traitors at home that they might see a rebellion, which they have so lately and severely felt, traced, in some measure, to its source, and be fully convinced that, whilst they are themselves enjoying, at their ease, and too often asleep, their religion, their liberties, and their properties, under the protection of the best of princes and the influence of the wisest Constitution, they have enemies, both abroad and within their own native country, who are constantly awake for the subversion of them all, and learn this certain truth, which should be imprinted in everlasting characters on the mind of every Briton, that there is no effectual security against those determined and perpetual enemies, but in a vigilant and firm union of honest men, and be persuaded that every attempt to prevent, weaken, or dissolve such a union is little less than treason in its beginning, and if it takes effect must end in a real successful one, the worst that can happen to this land of liberty, the total destruction of this Royal Family, and of this happy establishment.

Sir John Strange—My lords, the Managers do not think it necessary to take up any more of your lordships' time by way of general opening of this case, but propose to go directly to their evidence, and the first witness we desire may be called is Robert Chevis, Esq., of Muirtoun, a near neighbour of the impeached lord, but one at a very great distance from his way of thinking or acting.

Lord Lovat—My lords, I have not had the use of my limbs these three years. I cannot see; I cannot hear; and I beg, if your lordships have a mind I should have any chance for my life, that you will allow either my counsel or solicitors to examine my witnesses and to cross-examine those produced on behalf of the Crown, and to take notes.

Lord High Steward—What your lordship says, if I understand you right, is that, by reason of your age and infirmities, you cannot examine the witnesses yourself, but pray that either your counsel or solicitors might have liberty to cross-examine the witnesses against you, and to examine your own witnesses. It is my duty to acquaint your lordship with what is the known and clear law in these cases, and I did acquaint your lordship with it in what I mentioned to you at first, that by the order of this House you had counsel and solicitors assigned you, who had liberty to assist you in all matters of law that might arise in the course of your trial, but that, by the known rules of law in proceedings of this kind, they have not liberty to assist you in matters of fact or in the examination of witnesses. As to taking notes, I have observed that one of your solicitors has, during the time that the Managers for the House of Commons have been speaking, taken notes, and that has been allowed.

Lord Lovat—My lords, it is impossible for me then to make any defence, by reason of my infirmities. I do not see; I do not hear; I came up to your lordships' bar at the hazard of my life. I fainted away several times, I got up so early. I was up by four o'clock this morning, and I am so weak that, if I am deprived of the assistance I ask for, your lordships may do as you please; and it is impossible for me to make any defence at all if you do not allow my counsel or solicitors to examine the witnesses. I will therefore submit myself to the lords.

Lord High Steward—Gentlemen of the House of Commons, you have heard what has been asked by my Lord Lovat, with his reasons for it. Have you anything to offer on that head?

Sir William Yonge—My lords, it has been determined by your lordships that the prisoner at the bar cannot in this case be allowed counsel to assist him, except in matters of law, and, as that is known to be part of the law of the land, whatever inclination the Managers may have to indulge the noble lord at the bar, it is not in our power to depart from the law of the land. We therefore hope your lordships will excuse us in not consenting to what is contrary to the law of the land. We cannot do anything of this kind without repairing to our own House.

Robert Chevis

The witness being produced,

LORD LOVAT—My lords, I object to this witness being examined, because he is a tenant of mine, and I am informed that my tenant cannot be evidence against me.

LORD HIGH STEWARD—My Lord Lovat, there is no rule of law for that in England.

LORD LOVAT—My lords, I am told that there is an Act of Parliament that no vassal, tacksman, or tenant shall be a witness against his lord.

LORD HIGH STEWARD—Your lordship will please to name that Act of Parliament.

LORD LOVAT—My lord, I am told it is in the first year of King George the First, cap. 19.

Then the Clerk, by direction of the Lord High Steward, read the title of the Act of Parliament passed in the first year of His late Majesty King George the First, entitled "An Act for encouraging all superiors, vassals, landlords, and tenants in Scotland, who do and shall continue in their duty and loyalty to His Majesty King George, and for discouraging all superiors, vassals, and landlords and tenants there, who have been, or shall be, guilty of rebellious practices against His said Majesty; and for making void all fraudulent entails, tailzies, and conveyances made there for barring or excluding the effects of forfeitures that may have been, or shall be, incurred there on any such account; as also for calling any suspected person or persons whose estates or principal residence are in Scotland to appear at Edinburgh, or, where it shall be judged expedient, to find bail for their good behaviour, and for the better disarming disaffected persons in Scotland." And also the first section, whereby it is enacted "That if any of His Majesty's subjects of Great Britain, having lands or tenements in Scotland in property or superiority, has been, or shall be, guilty of high treason, by holding, entertaining, or keeping any intelligence or correspondence in person, or by letters, messages, or otherwise, with the said Pretender, or with any person or persons employed by him, knowing such person to be so employed, or shall, by bill of exchange or otherwise, remit or pay any sum or sums of money for the use or service of the said Pretender, knowing such money to be for such use or service; and that whether the said facts or things be done within or without this realm, or has been, or shall be, adherent to the said Pretender in this realm, giving him aid or comfort in this realm, or elsewhere; every such offender who shall be thereof duly convicted and attainted shall be liable to the pains, penalties, and forfeitures for high treason. All and every vassal and vassals in Scotland who shall continue peaceable and in dutiful allegiance to His Majesty, his heirs and successors, holding lands or tenements immediately of the Crown, shall be vested and seized, and are hereby enacted and ordained to hold the said lands or tenements of His Majesty, his heirs and successors, in fee and heritage for ever, by such manner of holding as any such offender held such lands or tenements of the Crown at the time of the attainder of such offender; and where lands or tenements belonging to any such peaceable and dutiful subjects to His Majesty, his heirs and successors, lie within any regality or constabulary in Scotland, the same shall be, and they are hereby, dissolved from every such regality or constabulary for ever; and, in like manner, all and every tenant and tenants in Scotland who shall continue peaceable and in dutiful allegiance to His Majesty, his heirs and successors aforesaid, bruicking and occupying any lands, milns, mines, woods, fishings, or tenements, as tenant or tenants, tacksman or tacksmen, from and under any such offender, shall, and they are hereby ordained to, bruick and occupy all and every such lands, mines, milns, woods, fishings, and tenements for the space of two years or crops, to be accounted from and after such attainder, freely, without payment of any rent, duty, or service for the said two years or crops; and the Court of Exchequer in Scotland is hereby authorised and required, on production of any such attainder, to revise, compound, and pass signatures, and that without paying any composition, in favours of every such vassal or vassals, and his, her, or their heir or heirs of the said lands and tenements above-mentioned respectively to be holden of His Majesty, his heirs and successors, in fee and heritage for ever, and by such holdings as is above-mentioned, with clauses of *novodamus*, and (where such lands or tenements hold ward or few *cum maritagio*, or with clauses irritant) with change of holdings from waird to taxed-waird, according to the rules now observed in the Court of Exchequer in Scotland, dispensing with recognition and clauses irritant in favours of the Crown in time coming, in the most ample and best form, to the end that chartours and infeftments may be thereupon duly exped"; and also the ninth section, whereby it is "Provided always, and be it enacted, by the authority aforesaid, that no person or persons who may reap, or have any benefit or advantage by the attainder, conviction, or forfeiture of any person or persons, by virtue of this Act, shall be capable of being a witness or witnesses against any person or persons, by whose attainder, conviction, or forfeiture, any benefit shall or may accrue to such witness or witnesses."

Lord High Steward—My Lord Lovat, are those the clauses your lordship means, or will you have any other clause read?

Lord Lovat—My lord, that is what I mean.

Lord High Steward—What your lordship insists upon seems to me to be that, by this Act of Parliament, as you understand it, a person who is a tenant or tacksman to any lord, if his lord is convicted of rebellion, and such tenant remains peaceable, the tenant is discharged from two years' rent of the lands held by him, and by the ninth section, no person can be a witness who may reap or have any benefit by the attainder of the person he is to be a witness against. I am not now going to give any opinion upon that section, neither is it proper that I should, but it is necessary for me to inform your lordship that it is incumbent upon you to lay a foundation of fact to show that the person produced as a witness is a tenant or tacksman under your lordship within the description of this Act of Parliament, and your lordship may either prove this fact by calling witnesses of your own for that purpose, or by putting the question to the person now produced by the Managers. Has your lordship any witness to prove this fact, or will you examine the gentleman produced upon a *voire dire?*

Lord Lovat—I will ask it of this gentleman.

Lord High Steward—Gentlemen of the House of Commons, have you any objection to my Lord Lovat's asking the question of this witness?

Attorney-General—My lords, we have no objection to having that question asked of the witness.

Lord High Steward—As the question is to the competency of the witness, and he is to be examined touching that, he is not now to be sworn as a witness in chief, but the oath is to be administered upon a *voire dire.*

Then the witness was sworn by the following oath:—"You shall true answer make to all such questions as shall be demanded of you; and you shall speak the truth, the whole truth, and nothing but the truth. So help you God."

Lord High Steward—My lords, as my Lord Lovat's voice is low, whatever questions his lordship has to ask of this gentleman, your lordships, I presume, will (as you did upon a former occasion) let my Lord Lovat propose the question, and let the clerk repeat it to your lordships and to the witness. My Lord Lovat, you will now propose the question, and the clerk will repeat it to my lords and the witness.

Lords—Ay, ay.

Then one of the clerks was sworn to make true report of what should be said by the prisoner.

Lord Lovat—My lords, I beg this witness may be asked whether he holds any lands of me or within my regality, either by tack, lease, or otherwise.

Witness—I hold my lands of the Crown. I never had a tack of land of my Lord Lovat.

First Day.

Lord High Steward—Do you hold any lands, either by vassalage, lease, or tack, from my Lord Lovat?—I never had a tack of land from my Lord Lovat. Robert Chevis

You are to answer to the whole of the question, whether you hold any land, either by vassalage, lease, or tack, of my Lord Lovat. I never had a lease from my Lord Lovat. I was in possession of a farm of his there, which, by his own consent, was given to other people, but I never had a lease from him.

Did you hold that land of my Lord Lovat?—The farm belonged to my Lord Lovat.

How did you hold it of him—by tack, or lease, or how?—It was ceded to me by other people who were in possession before me.

Did you hold it by lease, or tack, or in what manner?—I never had any lease or tack from the lord.

Attorney-General—Do you now hold any lands from my Lord Lovat?—No, I hold none of him.

Have you held any lands of him since the beginning of the rebellion?—I have held none since the beginning of the rebellion, nor been in possession of a fur of land under him.

My lords, I should be glad to know of this witness whether he holds any lands within the regality of Lovat?—No, I hold no lands of my Lord Lovat there. I had that small farm I before mentioned.

Lord Cholmondeley—My lords, the question put to the witness at first was whether he held any lands of my Lord Lovat, either as vassal, tenant, or tacksman, according to the description mentioned in the Act of Parliament, and if he does, then he comes within the description there mentioned. He has told your lordships that he does not hold any lands by tack or lease from my Lord Lovat. My lords, I pray that the question may be now asked him whether he holds any lands of my Lord Lovat, either by vassalage, tack, or lease?

Lord High Steward—Sir, you hear the question proposed by the noble lord. Do you hold any lands under my Lord Lovat as vassal?—No.

Do you hold any lands under my Lord Lovat as tenant?—No.

Do you hold any lands under my Lord Lovat as tacksman?[1]—No.

Lord Talbot—My lords, I desire this witness may be asked whether he apprehends he can receive any benefit under this Act of Parliament by my Lord Lovat's being convicted of high treason.

Lord High Steward—Sir, you hear the question asked by the

1 A "tacksman" was a holder under a "tack" or lease of a large area of land, which he sub-let to the lesser clansmen, either on the "runrig" system or as sub-tenants in the modern way. See "Home Life of the Highlanders, 1400-1746," p. 34.

Robert Chevis noble lord?—I never heard the Act of Parliament mentioned till this day. I know of no benefit I am to receive under it.

Do you know of any benefit that you are to receive, or do you apprehend that you can receive any benefit, from the conviction of my Lord Lovat?—No.

Do you hold any lands at all within the regality of Lovat? —No.

Proclamation for silence.

LORD LOVAT—My lords, I beg this witness may be asked whether he owes me any money.

ATTORNEY-GENERAL—My lords, on behalf of the Commons we do object to that as an improper question, because I must submit it to your lordships that no question is proper to be asked but what tends to the discovery of something material to the point in controversy. Now, my lords, the question proposed to be asked, be it answered one way or the other, cannot tend to prove anything material to the present purpose.

Lord Lovat here interrupted.

LORD HIGH STEWARD—My Lord Lovat, you are not to interrupt the gentlemen of the House of Commons. You shall be fully heard in your turn.

ATTORNEY-GENERAL—My lords, I say your lordships will not permit a question to be asked which is totally immaterial to the present purpose, and I apprehend this question is totally immaterial, because the questions now to be put to the witness are only for the purpose of disqualifying him to be an evidence, which this question does not in the least relate to, and, be it answered the one way or the other, it cannot tend to disqualify the witness. Whether it be answered yea or no, it cannot tend to disqualify the witness.

LORD LOVAT—My lords, I beg that the witness may be asked whether he receives any rents or other profits from those lands lying within the regality of Lovat.

ATTORNEY-GENERAL—My lords, if this amounts to a question to bring the witness under the description of the Act of Parliament, it is a question that has been already put by your lordships and answered particularly and precisely. If the question tends to any other matter, I cannot conceive to what purpose it is to be asked. But, my lords, it is incumbent on the noble lord at your bar to mention what he intends to show by the question he asks.

LORD HIGH STEWARD—My Lord Lovat, the witness on this examination hath sworn that he holds no lands or tenements under your lordship, either as vassal, tenant, or tacksman, and your lordship would now have him asked whether he receives any rents or other profits from any lands lying within the regality of Lovat. As what the witness has already sworn does fully answer all the disqualifications mentioned in the Act of

Parliament which your lordship has quoted, what do you intend by the present question? Robert Chevis

No answer being made by the prisoner, Robert Chevis of Muirtoun was sworn in chief.

SIR JOHN STRANGE[1]—My lords, I desire this witness may inform your lordships how long he has been acquainted with the noble lord at the bar.

WITNESS—From about the year 1733.

Whether he has been acquainted with him ever since the year 1733?—Ever since.

Do you live near the noble lord at the bar?—I live within 2 miles of him.

Whether he has not been often in his company since the year 1733?—A great many times.

Whether he went to his house frequently?—Yes.

Whether he has had any conversation, and what conversation, with him in relation to public affairs?

LORD HIGH STEWARD (to the witness, perceiving him to have a paper in his hand)—What paper is that in your hand?—Notes of my own.

Are they of your own handwriting?—Yes.

To what purpose did you take them?—Only to refresh my memory.

Was that the only reason you took them for?—The only reason.

SIR JOHN STRANGE—My lords, I beg this witness may be asked what was the general turn of the conversation of the noble lord at the bar.—The general turn of his conversation was in favour of the Pretender and his family.

Whether the witness speaks of the conversation so far back as the year 1733?—Yes.

Whether the witness had ever any conversation with the noble lord at the bar in relation to the year 1719?—I had.

My lords, I beg he will give an account of what the noble lord at the bar has said to him in relation to what was going to be done in the year 1719.—My Lord Lovat told me of a letter he had written to the late Lord Seaforth, and that he had sent it by his own lieutenant to Lord Seaforth, to encourage and desire him to come down with his men, and that he, Lord Lovat, would join him with all his, in favour of the Pretender.

Notice being taken by some lords at the upper end of the Court that they could not well hear the witness, the Lord High Steward directed the Clerk to repeat the answers of the witness as he delivered them, which was done accordingly.

SIR JOHN STRANGE—Whether the noble lord at the bar acquainted him with his having sent such a letter?—He told me he had sent such a letter by his lieutenant.

---

[1] See Biographical Notes, p. 307.

Robert Chevis My lords, I beg he may be asked whether he ever knew from the noble lord at the bar that that letter was delivered or not?——Lord Lovat told me that the letter was delivered.

To whom did he say the letter was delivered?—He said the letter was first shown to Chisholm of Knockford, and after that it was delivered to my Lord Seaforth.

I shall be glad to know whether my Lord Lovat said anything to the witness in relation to any affidavit that had been made concerning that letter.

Lord High Steward—Gentlemen of the House of Commons, the transaction now inquired of happened in the reign of His late Majesty, and there is no charge in the Articles of Impeachment of any high treason committed against His late Majesty. You will, therefore, open to my lords how you would apply the evidence which you are now examining to.

Sir John Strange—My lords, your lordships will please to observe that, in the answer of the noble lord at the bar, he does particularly mention his great duty and affection for His late Majesty, and his behaviour from time to time in that respect, and we are now introducing this particular evidence in regard to that matter by first taking it up so long ago as the year 1719 to show what was then the disposition, behaviour, and conduct of the noble lord at the bar. My lords, we say that in the year 1719 there was that letter, written with a view to assist the Spanish invasion then intended, in favour of the Pretender, that that letter was sent, but before it was delivered to the person to whom it was addressed there was a communication of it, in the manner the witness hath mentioned, and that person gave proper notice and made affidavit of it, which was sent up to the Government, giving an account of it, and by the great dexterity of the prisoner at the bar he got the letter back again. My lords, the use we make of this is to show that this is no new matter arising from the present rebellion, but by deducing it from the year 1719 we shall make the noble lord's conduct to be one continued act of treason consistent with the Article of the charge.

Lord High Steward—Then I apprehend you apply this piece of evidence to encounter and contradict the allegation in my Lord Lovat's Answer, which you have mentioned.

Then the Lord High Steward repeated to the House that allegation out of the prisoner's Answer.

Sir John Strange—My lords, that is what we propose to show by this evidence. The witness has gone so far as to acquaint your lordships that that letter, before it was delivered to the person to whom it was addressed, was shown to one Chisholm of Knockford. My lords, I desire he may inform your lordships what the noble lord at the bar said was done in consequence of that communication.—Chisholm made affidavit of it, which was sent up to Court. **Robert Chevis**

Did Lord Lovat acquaint you whether he heard of such affidavit being transmitted?—He did.

Did he tell you what he did upon that occasion?—That he went immediately to Court and got himself introduced there; and Lady Seaforth being then in London, she applied to him to do something in favour of her son, which he then absolutely refused till her son should return him that letter, which being done, he showed it to a certain friend who read the letter, and who told him that there was enough to condemn thirty lords there, and threw it into the fire.

My lords, I desire he will give an account whether the noble lord at the bar said anything at that time whether he had signed and sealed the letter.—He said he had not signed it, and therefore they could not fix him with it.

I desire this witness may inform your lordships whether, when the noble lord at the bar told him that he had not signed it, he said anything further to him upon that occasion than that he had not signed it?—He said that he could not be fixed with it, and that that was the way he intended to get off, by its not being signed.

I desire you will please to inform their lordships whether you remember the time when Roy Stuart broke out of Inverness gaol.—Yes, it was in 1736.

Who was Sheriff at that time?—My Lord Lovat.

After Roy Stuart had escaped out of Inverness gaol where did he go to live? By whom was he entertained?—He came to my Lord Lovat's house, and was entertained there.

How long was he entertained there?—Much about six weeks, to the best of my remembrance.

Were you often at my Lord Lovat's during these six weeks? —Frequently.

Were you ever there when Lord Lovat and Roy Stuart were together?—Very often.

Do you remember whether Roy Stuart was going abroad about that time?—He was going abroad then, and the ship was prepared for him before he left Lord Lovat's house, and he went in my Lord Lovat's chaise or chariot.

I desire you will inform their lordships whether any message was sent from the noble lord at the bar by Roy Stuart, and to whom.—I heard the noble lord at the bar charge him with a message to the Pretender.

What do you mean by charging him with a message?—To assure the Pretender, whom he called his king, of his fidelity, and that he was determined to live and die in that cause.

I beg that he may inform your lordships whether there was anything said at that time in relation to any commission or patent.—He charged him to expedite his sending his commis-

Robert Chevis sion of lieutenant-general of the Highlands and his patent of a duke.

I beg he may inform your lordships whether at any other time or times he heard the noble lord at the bar say anything whether he had, or had not, succeeded in what he had sent for.—About 1742 he owned to me that he got his commission and patent to be a duke.

What commission did he tell you he had got?—A commission of lieutenant-general of the Highland clans.

From whom did he say he had received this commission and patent to be a duke?—From his lawful Sovereign King James the Eighth.

Pray recollect yourself. Did he make use of that expression which you have now repeated, that he had it from his lawful Sovereign King James the Eighth? Are you certain he did?—Yes.

Did he tell you anything what he would do now he was invested with that command and had got such a commission and patent?—He said that he was in a condition thereby to humble his neighbours.

Have you at any other time heard him speak of this patent or of this commission?—Several times.

Is it often that you have heard him?—Often. He has told me that he had a right to it by his services for that family, and that he had the like commission from the Pretender's father from St. Germains.

I desire the witness may inform your lordships whether, during the time that the noble lord at the bar and Roy Stuart were together, they diverted themselves with composing anything, and what.—They did, in composing burlesque verses that, when young Charles came over, there would be blood and blows.

You have not mentioned it in a poetical manner. Pray, can you recollect the lines?—

When young Charley does come o'er,
There will be blows and blood good store.

I beg that you will acquaint their lordships whether this verse that you mention is a translation, or whether this is the original language in which it was composed.—It was framed in Erse,[1] and this is the substance of one verse.

I beg this witness may inform your lordships whether he has at any time heard the prisoner say anything in relation to any association.—I have.

Please to tell the time you heard this discourse, and what the noble lord at the bar said.—It was between 1737 and 1740.

What did you hear the noble lord at the bar say then?—That there was an association of the Highland clans in favour

[1] Gaelic.

of the Pretender, whom he called his lawful Sovereign King James the Eighth, and that he had entered into that association, and would live and die in that cause. Robert Chevis

I beg he may be asked whether, at the time he is speaking of, one Drummond of Bochaldie was at Lord Lovat's house. —Drummond of Bochaldie was there much about this time, and used to drink "success to the association."

Do you remember Bochaldie's being at Castle Downie, and staying there any time?

LORD HIGH STEWARD—What place is Castle Downie?—It is Lord Lovat's place of residence.

SIR JOHN STRANGE—My lords, it is sometimes called Beaufort and sometimes Castle Downie. To whom does it belong?—To my Lord Lovat.

Do you know whether you heard my Lord Lovat say anything to Bochaldie at that time?—He mentioned an invasion of Britain in favour of the Pretender.

What year are you now speaking of?—The year 1739.

You say that Drummond was then at Lord Lovat's, stayed there a considerable time, and heard my Lord Lovat propose an invasion of Britain in favour of the Pretender?—I did.

Did you hear him propose it? And did you hear of anybody else he proposed it to?—I have heard the like was proposed to Cameron of Lochiel and others.

From whom have you heard it?—From my Lord Lovat himself.

Do you remember anything to have happened at Lord Lovat's about the time of Ostend's being taken by the French?—I was not there then, but he wrote a letter to me and told me that the whole coast of Flanders was now clear.

Did you hear my Lord Lovat say anything in relation to the coast of Flanders upon Ostend's being taken?—I have heard him say as much as he wrote in that letter.

What have you heard him say?—That the coast of Flanders was then cleared, and that the French would be over in one night's time and carry all before them.

I should be glad you would inform their lordships whether, at any time in the year 1745 Lord John Drummond was at Castle Downie or not.—To the best of my memory he was about that time at Castle Downie.

I should be glad you would inform their lordships about what time of the year this was, whether it was summer or winter.—I think it was summer, to the best of my memory, between summer and harvest.

I beg you will inform their lordships whether at any time, and in what month, in the year 1745, the Master of Lovat came to my lord's house, or whether you saw him at my lord's in 1745.—I saw him there several times in 1745.

Robert Chevis

Did you see him there when any paper or manifesto was produced?—I saw him there when the manifesto was produced.

At what time was this?—It was in September, 1745. The manifesto came in a packet enclosed to Lord Lovat.

What manifesto was it?—The Pretender's manifesto and Declaration, which he ordered the Master immediately to read.

Was it read accordingly by the Master of Lovat?—It was accordingly read.

What did Lord Lovat say when it was read, or before it was read?—I objected to the manifesto's being read, and Lord Lovat told me I talked treason.

Did he tell you what was his own disposition in regard to that manifesto after it had been read?—He told me after reading the manifesto that he was to join the Pretender's party in that cause, and that he would live and die in that cause.

I beg the witness may mention to your lordships whether the noble lord at the bar expressed his opinion in relation to the good or ill success of it.—He said he thought success was morally sure, as sure as light, as sure as God was in Heaven, the Pretender would prevail.

I beg you'll recollect, and give my lords the very words. Did he say the Pretender?—Not the Pretender; but his right master.

What was the expression he made use of?—As sure as the sun shined.

That who would prevail?—That his master (the Pretender) would prevail.

I beg you will inform their lordships whether anything was offered to you upon that occasion.—I was offered a captain's commission.

By whom?—By Lord Lovat, in that service.

In what service?—In the service of that person, whom he called his lawful prince.

My lords, I beg he may inform your lordships whether my Lord Lovat said anything in relation to the Pretender to recommend him to the witness at the time he says Lord Lovat offered him a commission.—I have often heard Lord Lovat say that whoever looked the Pretender, his lawful king, in the face, he would own he was his only rightful king, as he himself owned him to be.

I beg he may be asked whether he can recollect, during the time of the late rebellion, any number of Frasers being assembled.—I cannot say, for after the time of reading the manifesto I did not visit my Lord Lovat. I discontinued going to his house.

For your own sake, I desire to ask you, did you accept of the commission offered you by Lord Lovat or not?—I did not indeed. I refused it.

Robert Chevis

What healths have you heard the prisoner toast in your company?—" Confusion to the white horse and all the generation of them."

Are you certain you heard my Lord Lovat propose that health?—I have heard him propose it, and drink it.

What did you understand was the meaning of that expression, " confusion to the white horse "?—Confusion to the present Royal Family. It could mean nothing else. It was in allusion to the arms of the family.

I should be glad you would inform their lordships whether you know of any message sent by my Lord Lovat by Drummond of Bochaldie besides what he has mentioned, anything concerning the Reformation or Revolution.—He was to execute the message, and that with respect to his commission and patent.

With whom was he to execute that commission?—With the Pretender at Rome.

Did he at that time say anything more to him, and what was it?—He talked of the association and of the invasion.

Did my Lord Lovat say anything of religion at that time?—I heard him say frequently he believed there was no true religion in the world but one, which was the Church of Rome.

Was anything said of the Revolution?—He cursed the Reformation and the Revolution, too.

What did he curse the Reformation for?—Because he said it brought a false religion upon us, and the Revolution involved us in a load of debt.

Did he then propose any scheme to get rid of this grievance? —The scheme he proposed was by favouring the invasion and by taking part in it.

Did he say for what purpose that invasion was to be?—To restore the rightful king.

Did he name him?—To restore his lawful Sovereign King James the Eighth.

I beg you'll give their lordships an account whether you ever heard Lord Lovat say anything in relation to a marriage contracted for his daughter.—I heard Lord Lovat say that when his daughter was married to M'Pherson of Cluny he took it to be an accession of strength by the adding one Highland clan more to the number.

Please to inform their lordships whether, through the progress of the rebellion, you heard the Lord Lovat say anything as to what he would do with his tenants that would not join.—He said it was very easy for him to cut them off in a moment, as he was in such a capacity now.

What did he mean by that?—Any tenant that should oppose him or any of the clan or neighbours.

I beg you will inform their lordships what is the power and

Robert Chevis authority that Lord Lovat insists to have over his own clan, or whether they are under his power and command or not.—Lord Lovat certainly has the power of an absolute king over them.

Inform their lordships whether you apprehend the command of the clan is in my Lord Lovat, or his son the Master.—It is entirely in my lord's own hands.

Do you know what age my Lord Lovat's eldest son is?—Much about nineteen.

Was he at home at the beginning of the rebellion, or was he then at any other place, and where, for education?—He was at St. Andrews, the place of his education, and was called home about that time.

How long was that before Lord Lovat made his son read the manifesto which you have mentioned? How long was he at home before that?—Not very long before that.

You say the young gentleman was at St. Andrews, and was sent for home by his father, and that his father set him to read the manifesto. Pray how long had the young gentleman been at home before he was ordered to read the manifesto?—It might have been about two months, to the best of my memory.

Do you think it was so long?—I believe it might have been about two months.

When my Lord Lovat offered you a captain's commission did he acquaint you who was to be your colonel?—He did not acquaint me at that time who was to be my colonel, but he said he was in that service in that cause himself, and I understood that I was to serve under him.

My lords, as the witness has informed your lordships that he did not go to Lord Lovat's after he told him it was high treason to object to the reading of the Pretender's manifesto, I shall not examine him to anything subsequent, in point of time, to that, and therefore I shall not trouble your lordships with asking him any more questions.

Attorney-General—My lords, I beg this witness may inform your lordships whether he has heard anything of any threats made use of by the noble lord at the bar to his tenants or clan to come down upon them if they refused joining.—I saw a party of the MacDonalds in the country, and I think they came to the place where I lived. And I take the design of them to have been that they should be there to overawe the country.

Who commanded that party of the MacDonalds?—MacDonald of Barisdale.[1]

[1] See Biographical Notes, p. 303.

Simon Fraser, the Master of Lovat.

(From a Miniature.)

Did you hear anything said by my Lord Lovat to MacDonald concerning him or his clan?—He said, in general, that, upon being invested with this patent of duke, he would be able not only to humble and keep in awe his own clan but his neighbours. Robert Chevis

I beg he may inform your lordships whether he knows anything of Barisdale's going about to the clans to encourage them to join?—I saw him at Lord Lovat's house the day of the rendezvous.

What did he do there?—He spirited up the country people, and carried them along to the rendezvous.

Who was that?—MacDonald of Barisdale.

What do you know in relation to that rendezvous?—I saw the rendezvous at a distance, but I was not upon the spot.

Who was at the rendezvous?—Four, or five, or six hundred men.

Whose men were they?—The Frasers.

Under whose command were they?—I was told they were under the Master's command, but I was not personally present.

Lord High Steward—Gentlemen of the House of Commons, have you done with this witness?

Manager—My lord, we have done with him.

Lord High Steward—My Lord Lovat, the gentlemen of the House of Commons have gone through with their examination of Mr. Chevis. Has your lordship any questions to ask him?

Lord Lovat—My lords, he has said so many false and wicked things that I do not know what questions to ask him or where to begin.

Lord High Steward—Your lordship will be pleased to propose the questions, and then they will be asked of the witness.

The Clerk repeated the prisoner's questions to the witness.

Lord Lovat—My lords, I pray he may be asked whether or no since my arrival here, and being before the House of Lords, and that many witnesses had been summoned to give evidence against me, whether this witness did not go about to solicit witnesses against me, and whether he did not examine witnesses himself.—I refuse it.

Manager—You mean, you deny it?—I deny it.

Lord Lovat—My lords, I offer to prove it.

Lord High Steward—My Lord Lovat, your lordship must do that when you come to make your defence. Your lordship will then have an opportunity, by witnesses, to contradict or invalidate the testimony of this or any other witness produced against you.

Lord Lovat—I beg this witness may be asked whether he knows or ever heard that several people were threatened to be put in prison, and were put in prison, if they did not come up to be evidence against me.—I deny it.

Robert Chevis

I beg he may be asked whether he discovered to any person belonging to the Government the Declaration which he says he heard read at my house.—In September, 1745, I told it in common conversation, but I never went to any of the Government to inform them of it. The rebellion broke out then immediately.

LORD LOVAT—My lords, I beg this witness may be asked whether he ever said himself, or has heard others say, that the late plot by the Master of Lovat against me was to hang the old man and save himself.—I never heard of such a plot, but have often heard of a plot of my Lord Lovat's to try to hang his son, the Master of Lovat, and save himself.

A LORD—My lords, I do not doubt the witness designs to pay the money he owes to my Lord Lovat, but I pray he may be asked whether he expects to be forgiven that debt if my Lord Lovat is convicted.

LORD HIGH STEWARD—My lords, while this witness was examined upon a *voire dire* there was a question proposed by my Lord Lovat to be asked him, which was whether he owed my Lord Lovat any money. That question was objected to by the gentlemen of the House of Commons, as not tending to discover anything material to the point then in question; and what is now proposed by the noble lord to be asked of the witness is whether this gentleman owes my Lord Lovat any money, and if he does, whether he expects to be forgiven that debt in case my Lord Lovat should be convicted.—In regard of that debt it was condescended some years ago that my Lord Lovat should accept a gentleman who was my debtor for the payment of that money.

LORD HIGH STEWARD—Do you owe my Lord Lovat any money?—A mere trifle. This which he speaks of was to be compensed another way.

LORD HIGH STEWARD—Whether the debt be more or less, do you expect to save that debt, or to be favoured in the payment of it, if my Lord Lovat should be convicted?—Not at all. I deny it.

A LORD—How long have you been in town?—Since Tuesday last about noon.

A LORD—Whether have you lived at your own expense since that time, or who hath supported you?—I did design to have lived at my own expense, but I have been supported at the expense of the Government.

Then the witness withdrew.

SOLICITOR-GENERAL (the Hon. William Murray[1])—My lords, the next witness we beg leave to call is Robert Fraser, late secretary to my Lord Lovat.

1 See Biographical Notes, p. 306.

ROBERT FRASER was called in, and sworn in chief.

Proclamation was made for silence.

The prisoner rising up, the LORD HIGH STEWARD said—My Lord Lovat, do you object to this witness?

LORD LOVAT—Yes.

LORD HIGH STEWARD—What is your objection?

LORD LOVAT—He holds a tack of land of me.

LORD HIGH STEWARD—Is it true? Do you hold a tack of land of his lordship?

WITNESS—No; I do not hold any tack of land of my Lord Lovat.

LORD LOVAT—I am ready to prove it.

LORD HIGH STEWARD—Gentlemen of the House of Commons, my Lord Lovat may have liberty to examine a witness to prove that fact. It has been frequently done after a witness has been sworn in chief. My lords, at the common law where a witness is tendered by the plaintiff to be sworn the oath to give evidence in chief is administered to him unless the defendant makes an objection to his competency, and then he may be examined touching that objection upon a *voire dire*; but, after the witness has been sworn in chief if any objection is then made to him he may be asked the same question by virtue of his oath in chief as he might have been asked upon a *voire dire*. I have known it done both ways. But after the witness has been examined by the defendant to the fact of the objection and has denied it upon his oath it is not usual to give the defendant liberty to call a witness to prove it in order to repel him from being a witness unless the other side acquiesces in it.[1]

LORD LOVAT—I have sent for my witness.

The House having waited some time, my Lord High Steward asked the prisoner where his witness was, who said he was at the coffee-house, and a little time afterwards said—My lords, the witnesses are all gone about an hour ago, not expecting to be called.

LORD HIGH STEWARD—How came your witnesses to go away whilst your trial is going on?

LORD LOVAT—My lords, they did not know that they would be called to-day.

SOLICITOR-GENERAL—My lords, the objection made by the noble lord at the bar having been positively denied by the witness, and there being no evidence here to contradict him, we hope we may proceed to examine him.

ATTORNEY-GENERAL—My lords, we hope your lordships will not permit the prisoner at the bar to suspend your lordships'

1 The Editor of the "State Trials" here refers to Peake's Law of Evidence, chapter 3, sections 2, 3, and 6.

Robert Fraser proceedings whenever he pleases. And we hope the candour of the Managers, in not opposing his going into this objection after the witness has denied it upon his oath, shall not be extended to delay his examination under a pretence of this kind. The witness produced denying the objection upon his oath, and there being no evidence here to contradict it, we hope we shall be permitted to go on with the witness. My lords, the Managers were aware of this, nevertheless did not, at first, oppose any indulgence to the prisoner that might tend to justice. But as it is now known what point the witness is called to, though I do not suppose the witness capable of being influenced, yet if a bare allegation of this sort is sufficient to put off your lordships' proceedings, I must submit it to your lordships whether it will not give an opportunity of something to be done which ought not to be done.

Mr. Noel[1]—It is with great difficulty and disinclination that we can prevail upon ourselves to object to the utmost candour that can be shown to the noble lord at the bar. My lords, this is an occurrence which, in my little experience, I never knew to arise. My lords, I apprehend the way is, upon this occasion, to ask the questions of the witness upon a *voire dire.* The noble lord at the bar made the objection, and applied to the witness for an answer to that question, who has positively denied it. If, after that, the prisoner is to say, "I can falsify what the witness has now sworn; allow me time for it," and your lordships should indulge him with it in this manner, there is nobody but must be apprehensive of very dangerous consequences attending it, for any kind of evidence may, by that means, be prevented.

Lord High Steward—My lords, the gentlemen of the House of Commons may proceed in their examination of this witness, and my Lord Lovat will be at liberty to ask what questions he pleases in his cross-examination, and will likewise be at liberty to call witnesses to prove this particular fact in his defence in another shape, for he may prove this fact in order to impeach this witness's credit, and probably have as much effect of it as if it had been properly taken advantage of.

Solicitor-General—My lords, I beg this witness may be asked when he first came to live in Lord Lovat's family, and how long he lived with him.

Lord High Steward—Sir, you hear the question.

Witness—I entered into Lord Lovat's service in October, 1744.

Solicitor-General—How long did you continue with him?—I continued in his service till his lordship and I were taken prisoners, the 7th of June last.

I beg you may inform their lordships whether, in the month

[1] See Biographical Notes, p. 306.

Robert Fraser

of July, 1745, you knew of any information that was given to my Lord Lovat of an intention of an insurrection and invasion, and what intimation was given of it.—Some time after the 25th July, 1745, I heard a gentleman came to my Lord Lovat's house to tell him that the Pretender's son was landed somewhere about Lochaber. I heard my Lord Lovat say he did not land like a prince, that he had no army with him, and only a few servants.

What did my Lord Lovat say upon that occasion? Was his son at home?—He was at home, or was then sent for.

Do you know of any person that was sent by my Lord Lovat to see the Pretender at that time?—Not at that time; I cannot say that I knew of any.

Do you know of any endeavours that were then used to raise men upon my Lord Lovat's estate; and, if you do, please to mention the times?—I remember, some time after, he dictated a letter to me to be sent to two of the heads of the tribes of the Frasers.

Name them?—James Fraser of Foyers and John Fraser of Ferraline.

What was that letter for?—To get men ready to join the Master of Lovat.

Where were the men to go with him?—The letter does not particularise that.

Do you know of anybody that was sent to take lists of the men to be raised?—I took the lists of the names of the men. My Lord Lovat's chamberlain ordered me to make a list of the names of all the men capable of bearing arms north of Loch Ness.

For what purpose were those lists made?—To the best of my knowledge, to join the Master of Lovat with the Pretender.

Were such lists made out with my Lord Lovat's privity or by his direction?—I am sure he was acquainted with it.

How are you sure he was acquainted with it?—Because I went into the room and told him what I was doing, and that I was writing the list.

What did he say to you upon that occasion?—I cannot remember now.

Pray, did my Lord Lovat see the list after it was made out?—I can't tell. I returned it to John Fraser, my lord's factor.

Do you know of any message that was sent or passed between my Lord Lovat and Lord Loudoun and the Lord President?—Yes.

What was it about?—Several letters were sent by my Lord Loudoun and my Lord President to my Lord Lovat to dissuade him from entering into the rebellion.

What answer did my Lord Lovat make to these letters?—He said his son was so obstinate as to enter into the rebellion, but that he could not help it.

Robert Fraser

Was that fact true; was the son so obstinate?—No, I am sure it was not true.

Why are you sure it was not true?—Because, whilst I was preparing a letter to the Lord President, which my Lord Lovat dictated, wherein he acquainted them of his son's obstinacy in going into the rebellion (which letter my lord directed me not to let anybody see), his son, the Master, came in and asked me for the letter, and I refusing to give it him, the son took the letter out of my hand.

Who took it out of your hand?—The Master of Lovat took it out of my hand, and, after reading it, said, "Good God, how is this? Accuse me behind my back! To call me stiff-necked and disobedient! I will set the saddle upon the right horse."

Pray, repeat the answer you made last.—The Master of Lovat said, "If this letter goes, I will go and put the saddle upon the right horse, and will go and discover all to my Lord President."

What did he mean by putting the saddle upon the right horse?—That he would go and discover to my Lord President that his father, my Lord Lovat, had forced him to do what he had done.

Did the son say anything to my Lord Lovat upon that occasion?—Not that I know of. The words "stiff-necked and disobedient" were left out of the letter.

How came these words to be left out?—It was done by the Master of Lovat's order.

Did you hear anything that passed between Lord Lovat and his son about his backwardness in going into the rebellion?—I heard him blame the Master of Lovat for being dilatory.

Dilatory in what?—In raising men.

For what purpose?—To join the Pretender's son.

Do you know anything of Lord Lovat's sending for people, as painters, or of any sort, to prepare his tents?—Yes, I myself wrote a letter to his agent at Inverness, who was a painter.

By whose order did you write that letter?—By my Lord Lovat's order.

To what purpose was the letter written?—It was to order the agent, or the painter, to make some bell tents.

What did the painter do in consequence of that letter?—He made them.

Did my Lord Lovat know of it?—Yes.

How do you know he did?—Because I was with my Lord Lovat when the man was making them.

What are bell tents?—They are lodges to keep arms dry from the rain.

Did you know of any colours being made?—Yes; we had one pair of new ones made and another pair mended.

About what time was that, and what month?—About the month of September, I think.

Was it before the first rendezvous?—I think it was after the first rendezvous. Robert Fraser

Can you give an account of the men being rendezvoused, and whether it was done by my Lord Lovat's directions or under his authority?—They were rendezvoused.

Where were they rendezvoused?—Upon that part of Lord Lovat's estate near Castle Downie.

About what time was this—in what month?—In the month of August.

What was the particular purpose of their being reviewed then?—To see who was capable of bearing arms and who had any.

Were the officers appointed then?—No, I believe not.

How do you know that the prisoner was made privy to this rendezvous?—Because they came back to my lord's house afterwards.

Were they in officers' dress?—They had white cockades on.

How far was the place of rendezvous from Lord Lovat's house?—About a quarter of a mile.

Were the persons there tenants to my Lord Lovat?—They were his tenants.

What arms had they?—I can't say. I had my lord's liberty to go there and see them, but I did not stay there.

Do you know of any other rendezvous?—About a fortnight afterwards there was another rendezvous.

Do you know of any ammunition, muskets, or arms that were given to the men?—I don't know of any arms that were given them. There was a barrel of powder sent from Inverness.

By whose order was that done?—By my Lord Lovat's order. I wrote the letter.

What was done with that powder?—It was distributed among the men.

How do you know that it was done by my Lord Lovat's order?—Because the housekeeper being disgraced, I got the key of the place where it was, and saw the powder and bullets there.

Was the key delivered you for that use?—I told my lord of my having the key.

Do you know of any bonnets being provided?—There were bonnets provided for them.

By whose order?—By my Lord Lovat's.

For what purpose were they provided?—They were given to the men.

Do you know where the officers went after the last rendezvous?—The officers came back that night.

Where did they come to?—They came to my Lord Lovat's house.

Had they cockades?—They had white cockades in their bonnets.

Robert Fraser

Do you know for what sign or mark they wore white cockades?—It was a symptom of their being people to join the Pretender.

Do you know of anything that happened at my Lord Lovat's after the battle of Prestonpans?—Fraser of Dallcraig came to Castle Downie with an account of the battle of Prestonpans.

What did my Lord Lovat say to him upon that occasion?—He said that his men should be soon ready to go south.

For what purpose?—To join the rebels, I understood.

Do you know of any men passing by my Lord Lovat's house?—My Lord Cromartie's regiment passed by, and he and the MacDonalds, and several others were entertained there that night.

Did you hear anything that passed upon that occasion, anything that was said by my Lord Lovat upon it?—Yes, that it was owing to the Master of Lovat's disobedience that the Frasers were not ready as soon as any other.

Was there anything else that passed then or any particular healths drunk?—Yes, the health of the Pretender's son was drunk.

By what name?—By the name of Prince Charles.

Pray, at what time did the Master of Lovat go and join the rebels?—It was between the 10th and 20th of December that he went. My Lord Lovat was taken prisoner on the 10th or 11th of December, and escaped about the 19th or 20th, and at the same time the Master marched with the Frasers.

Was my Lord Lovat extremely displeased at his son's so marching, or did he disapprove of it?—No.

Did he send word for his son to come back again?—He did afterwards send for him back to raise more men.

Do you know of any person who was concerned in the rebellion that after the battle of Falkirk came to my Lord Lovat's house, and whether anything passed in company then, and what it was?—Yes, there was a French gentleman came that was said to be the French Ambassador.

Where did he come to?—To a place belonging to my Lord Lovat.

When was that?—It was after their retreat from Stirling.

Do you know who was there besides?—There were several others, particularly Lochiel, Keppoch, Cameron.

Do you know of my Lord Lovat's saying anything to them about his assisting them?—He told them he hoped they would excuse him on account of his age and infirmities.

Did he say anything to show his zeal for their success as he did not go himself?—Yes; he said, "I cannot go myself, but I will send my only son, the darling of my life."

Do you know of anything that passed between my Lord Lovat and his son after that?—Yes. The Master came to

Gortuleg, and my lord had lately received a letter from one Mr. Sheridan, who had some office under the Pretender's son, complaining of my lord's not getting his men ready. Robert Fraser

Do you know of anything that passed between them in relation to the men having leave to go home?—Yes, my lord was angry with the Master for giving them leave.

Pray, how long was this before the battle of Culloden?—This was in the month of February.

Do you know anything of the Pretender's son's coming to my lord's house[1] after the battle of Culloden?—Yes. The very night after the battle the Pretender's son came to my lord's.

Was my Lord Lovat there then?—Yes.

Do you know anything of what passed between them or what my Lord Lovat said to him?—He made some apology for not joining him in person.

Did he mention anything to show his zeal for him, though he did not join him in person?—He said he had sent his son to join him, whom he loved more than himself.

Did he mention his having sent any more?—Yes, he mentioned his having sent his clan.

Was the excuse accepted, or what did the Pretender's son say to him?—I cannot tell particularly. I do not understand French, and they spoke in French.

Did all the conversation which passed between them pass in French?—No, they spoke sometimes English and at other times they spoke French.

What language was that discourse spoken in which you have given an account of as to Lord Lovat's son and clan?—It was in English.

You have said you did not understand all their discourse. Pray, did you perceive any other demonstrations of friendship that passed between them?—Yes, they embraced one another.

Do you know of any consultation or meeting of the general officers of the rebel army which my Lord Lovat had at that time?—Yes.

Who were present?—There were several gentlemen present.

Name them.—There were Cameron of Lochiel, John Murray of Broughton, Barisdale, John Roy Stuart, Glenbucket, and others.[2]

How long was this after the battle of Culloden?—It was not very long.

How long was it?—A matter of ten or twelve days.

Was there anybody else there? Was the young Pretender there?—No, he was not.

Do you know anything of the conversation that passed

---

1 Gortuleg, in Stratherrick, now known as Gorthlick.

2 See Biographical Notes for information concerning these leaders.

Robert Fraser then or the result of the consultation?—No, I was turned out of the room. I did not hear.

Do you know of any money that was distributed? To whom was it distributed, by whom, and for what purpose?—I saw the Pretender's son's treasurer give money.

For what purpose was the money given?—To raise men.

Do you know what kind of money was so given?—It was French louis d'ors.[1]

Were you with the prisoner till the time he was taken? If you were, give an account of his retreat.—We stayed in an island for a month, and when we escaped we were obliged to take a boat to come down a loch.

What was the name of the island?—The island of Morar.

Had you been with Lord Lovat from the time of the battle of Culloden to that time?—We were in the island from the beginning of May till the 7th of June.

With what view did my Lord Lovat come there?—To screen him from the King's troops, which were then in pursuit of him, and several others of them.

Do you know of anything that passed between the Master of Lovat and him at that time?—I remember the Master proposed it to him to surrender himself to the duke, but my Lord Lovat advised him against it, and said he could not do it consistently with his honour, and he did not think he had been so mean spirited as to offer it.

Do you know anything of any advice that was given by my Lord Lovat about the raising of men?—Yes. My Lord Lovat was present at Morar, where they were speaking of the raising of men.

Had the prisoner any guard that attended him whilst he was in Morar?—Yes, he had a guard of twenty men to attend him.

Did they resist any of the King's forces that might oppose them?—Not that I know of.

By whom were they paid?—I paid them.

By whose directions did you pay them?—By my Lord Lovat's directions.

Did you apprehend that the Master of Lovat carried his men into the rebel army without his father's permission?—No; I am very sure he could not.

Why are you sure of it?—Because my Lord Lovat is a very strict man, and none of his children could have done it without his consent.

Had my Lord Lovat a power over them?—Yes, he had a very great power over them.

Pray, was the guard my Lord Lovat had armed?—Yes.

---

1 A louis d'or was a French coin worth about twenty shillings. It was first used by Louis XIII. in 1640.

You say there was no opposition given by them to any of the King's forces?—No; I think there were two or three of them fired, but my Lord Lovat sent me out to tell them not to fire. Robert Fraser

Do you know anything of my Lord Lovat's soliciting a commission from the Pretender to be lieutenant-general of the Highlands or a patent to be duke?—I remember, some time after I went into my Lord Lovat's service, which was the 18th of October, 1744, I saw in the desk a copy of an old patent which gave the title of duke to Lord Lovat only.

What other papers did you see there?—Some time after I saw a new patent, where the title was to descend to the heirs male of the family.

Did you hear from my Lord Lovat how he obtained the patent?—I have heard my Lord Lovat say that his patent lay in the hands of one Drummond in France.

Did he say what Drummond?—To the best of my knowledge, he said it was Drummond of Bochaldie.

Do you know anything of any other commission which my Lord Lovat had?—Yes; I saw a commission for his being lieutenant-general of the Highlands.

Where did you see that commission?—Lying upon a table in my lord's room. I read it, and made a copy of it by my lord's order.

Are you sure whether he himself ordered you to copy it?—I am sure he ordered me to make a copy of it.

Had you any other discourse with him about it? Did you hear with what view he had got it?—No, I had no other than what I have now informed you of.

Do you know of any complaint my Lord Lovat ever made about an independent company being taken from him?—I heard him complain that the Court did not use him civilly in taking away his company.

When did you hear him make that complaint?—Frequently in company in speaking upon the subject.

Pray, what did my Lord Lovat say upon that occasion?—I heard him say that it was entirely owing to General Wade, and that he did not blame the Government.

Did he draw any consequences from that?—I have heard him speak extraordinary well of his late master, King George.

What more did he say about this treatment?—He said that the Court used him so ill that he could not help doing what he was doing.

What was he then doing?—Raising men to join in the rebellion. He said he had no dislike to His present Majesty, but only to the persons who took away his commission.

Pray, what do you apprehend was the meaning of that expression of the Master of Lovat that he would go to the

Robert Fraser Lord President and discover all?—I understood that he meant that he would go and join His Majesty's forces.

My lords, we have done with the examination of this witness for the present. We shall have occasion by and by to call him to prove an exhibit or two.

Lord High Steward—My Lord Lovat, the gentlemen of the House of Commons have gone through their examination of this witness. Would your lordship ask him any questions?

Lord Lovat—I am not able to ask him any questions.

Then the witness, by order of the Lord High Steward, withdrew, and the Lord High Steward returning back to his chair, the House was moved to adjourn to the Chamber of Parliament.

Lord High Steward—Is it your lordships' pleasure to adjourn to the Chamber of Parliament?

Lords—Ay, ay.

The House was accordingly adjourned to the Chamber of Parliament, and the lords and others returned in the same order in which they came down, and the House being there resumed,

Ordered that this House will proceed further in the trial of Simon, Lord Lovat, in Westminster Hall, to-morrow at eleven of the clock in the forenoon. A message was sent to the House of Commons by Mr. Eld and Mr. Thurston to acquaint them therewith;[1]

Ordered that the Lieutenant of the Tower of London or his deputy do take back the said Lord Lovat, and bring him again to the bar of this House in Westminster Hall to-morrow at eleven of the clock in the forenoon.

---

[1] A book of Historical Papers published by the New Spalding Club in 1895 contains (vol. i., pp. 331, &c.) an "Account of the Trial of Lord Lovat, by One at the Trial." The anonymous writer says he was then a member of Parliament, and that his name was included in Lord Lovat's first list of witnesses. He tells us that he sat on two days hearing the trial, from between eleven and twelve till six o'clock, when the House rose, as there was no way of illuminating the hall.

Second Day—Tuesday, 10th March [1747].

The lords and others came from the Chamber of Parliament into Westminster Hall in the same order as on Monday, where the Commons and their Managers were in the seats prepared for them respectively as before. And the lords took their places in the Court, and the Lord High Steward in his chair.

Lord High Steward—The House is resumed. Is it your lordships' pleasure that the judges have leave to be covered?

Lords—Ay, ay.

Then the Sergeant-at-Arms made proclamation for silence, and afterwards the following proclamation:—Oyes! Oyes! Oyes! Lieutenant of the Tower of London, bring forth your prisoner, Simon, Lord Lovat, to the bar, pursuant to the order of the House of Lords to you directed.

The Deputy-Governor of the Tower brought the prisoner to the bar in the like manner as before. And then he kneeled down.

Lord High Steward—Your lordship may rise.

Then the Lord High Steward asked leave to go down to the table, which was granted.

Lord High Steward—Gentlemen of the House of Commons, you may proceed in your evidence.

Mr. Noel—My lords, the next witness we beg leave to call in support of the charge is John Murray of Broughton.[1]

John Murray of Broughton came into Court. **John Murray.**

Mr. Noel—My lords, we desire that he may be sworn.

Lord Lovat—My lords, I have objections against this witness, one or two I apprehend to be essential.

Lord High Steward—Make your objections.

Lord Lovat—As I cannot read myself, I desire your lordships will give leave to the Clerk to read them.[2]

Clerk reads—"My objection is that he is attainted by an Act of Parliament made in the last session, page 443, and that he did not surrender himself before the 12th of July last."

Attorney-General—My lords, I observe that the noble lord at the bar said that he had several objections to the examining this witness, and that one or two of them were essential, but the noble lord has not mentioned more than one. I presume, my lords, it would be proper that he should name all his

1 See Biographical Notes, p. 305. Murray was not called as a witness in the trials of the other Jacobites.

2 It is recorded that Lord Lovat was able to read by candle light in the Tower.

John Murray objections at once, that the Managers may have an opportunity of answering them all and receiving your lordships' judgment upon the whole; therefore if he has any other objections to offer it would be proper he should mention them now to your lordships.

Lord Lovat—My lords, I submit it to your lordships that that is a very odd proposition. I give your lordships an essential one now, and when that is answered I have another. I am not to be directed by those who are my persecutors.

Lord High Steward—My Lord Lovat, you are not to be directed by your accusers, but by the lords who are your judges, and the course of proceeding in this and all other Courts is that a person who objects to any witness should name all his objections at the same time, and it is the more material in this Court, as it tends to prevent the trouble of making several unnecessary adjournments.

Lord Lovat—My lords, as this objection is very essential, I pray that it may be answered before I make another.

Lord Talbot—My lords, if this is a material objection to the witness, then there will be no occasion for any other, but if it is an immaterial one, then your lordships may go into any other, but the way proposed by the Managers may be very detrimental to the unhappy person at the bar.

Lord High Steward—Your lordships hear what is proposed, and the question is whether the noble lord at the bar shall name all his objections now or take them one by one.

Sir William Yonge—My lords, I should hope that in any course of proceeding where objections of this kind are made they should be made all together, for if they are made separate we must consequently make distinct answers to them all, which may oblige your lordships to adjourn often to the Chamber of Parliament, which will create a great and unnecessary delay of time, and, my lords, there can be no objection to his naming the whole at once, since they will all be distinctly considered by your lordships, and undoubtedly receive distinct answers. I therefore humbly insist that he may be obliged to name all his objections at once.

Mr. Noel—My lords, what we are now upon is no point of law at all. It is simply whether the noble lord at the bar, as is usual, should not name all his objections at once. When he does name then, then to such as are clear points of law he must be heard by his counsel. But at present, my lords, we are upon a question concerning the course of proceeding, whether he shall name them all at once, that they may be taken into consideration at the same time. My lords, one thing struck me in a very extraordinary manner. It was said by the noble lord at the bar that he was not to be directed by his persecutors. My lords, we are no persecutors. We persecute no man. We are entrusted by the Commons, who carry on this prosecution against the noble lord at the bar for treason, and we prosecute for the preservation of the King's Government and the laws of the land. John Murray

LORD LOVAT—My lords, I said I was not to be directed by those who accused me. Your lordships cannot expect I can say what I have to offer in an eloquent manner. My lords, should the saving of a little time be a reason for taking away a person's life? I hope these will not act like the parricides who took off the head of both kingdoms in a day by their prosecution. I am a peer of this land, and I think no excuse of saving time should be allowed as a reason to destroy me.

LORD HIGH STEWARD—My Lord Lovat, the lords will use all the deliberation and give you all the time that is requisite for your defence, but I must beg your lordship will have so much consideration as to keep your temper and not suffer yourself to be hurried into passion, for that may greatly prejudice you in making your defence. Your lordship will find the advantage in your defence by keeping your temper.

LORD LOVAT—I give your lordship my humble thanks, and, since your lordships will not allow me counsel, I have spoken the little nonsense I had to say, but now your lordships shall hear me say nothing out of temper.

LORD HIGH STEWARD—My Lord Lovat, the question now is whether you shall name all your objections at once. I must acquaint your lordships that it is the rule in the Courts below, that if several objections are made to a witness they are all named at once, in order to prevent unnecessary delays.

LORD LOVAT—My lords, to show how much I desire to save time (though, according to the course of nature, my time can be but short) I am so far from desiring to give your lordships' trouble or to prolong time that I do insist upon this objection to the witness, and rely upon it as the only material objection.

Then the Lord High Steward directed the Act of the last session of Parliament for the attainder of several persons, and, amongst others, of John Murray of Broughton, to be read, and the same was read accordingly by the Clerk at the table.

LORD HIGH STEWARD—Gentlemen of the House of Commons, you hear the objection made by my Lord Lovat against this witness, which is that he stands attainted by the Act of Parliament just now read, and that he did not surrender himself before the 12th of July, the day prescribed by the Act. And this being a question of law, he desires to be heard by his counsel to it.

ATTORNEY-GENERAL—My lords, we have that which will appear to your lordships to be a plain and a clear answer to it. It appears that this is an Act of Parliament for attainting several

John Murray persons upon a certain condition, which is that if those persons do not, before the 12th of July, 1746, surrender themselves to one of His Majesty's justices of the peace, then every one so not surrendering himself shall be adjudged to be, and is thereby, attainted of high treason. And our answer to it is this, that the condition has been complied with by Mr. Murray. I shall readily own that, supposing the condition had not been complied with, according to law, in that case Mr. Murray being an attainted person, could not be a witness unless he had been pardoned. But our answer to that will be that he hath surrendered himself, and the surrender will appear upon record, and the manner of it is this—The last term Mr. Murray was brought by Habeas Corpus to the bar of the Court of King's Bench, and a transcript of the Act of Parliament being by *mittimus* and *certiorari* brought into that Court, and Mr. Murray brought up and personally appearing before the Justices of the Court of King's Bench, and being asked by them what he had to say why he should not suffer death according to law, upon a supposition that he was attainted upon that Act of Parliament, he pleaded in general that he was one of the persons named in the Act, and that long before the 12th of July, 1746, to wit, on the 28th of June then last, he did, at Edinburgh, in due manner, according to the meaning of the Act, render himself to Andrew Fletcher, Lord Justice-Clerk, and one of His Majesty's justices of the peace, and he says that the said Andrew Fletcher had then authority to admit him to make such surrender. He then states that on the said 28th of June, in consequence of this surrender, he was committed by the Lord Justice-Clerk to prison, according to the directions of the Act of Parliament, and that he had ever since that surrender remained in custody, and still continues in prison, and is ready to take his trial and submit himself to justice. My lords, he having pleaded this plea, the Attorney-General, by virtue of a warrant from His Majesty, confessed the plea to be true, upon which the Court of King's Bench made a record of it. He was remanded back to prison, and there remains to answer, according to law, when he shall be called to an account for this high treason. My lords, we have the record, and beg it may be read.

Lord Lovat—My lords, I object to the reading this record, because it is no evidence against me, and I beg my counsel may be heard to it. I am a stranger to the record, which is grounded only upon the confession of the Attorney-General, unsupported by any proof, and I desire my counsel may be now heard.

Attorney-General—My lords, as to the objection against reading this record, I apprehend there is no foundation for it. It is a record of the Court of King's Bench concerning the person to whom the noble lord at the bar has objected as being attainted, and, upon the face of the record, it will appear that he is not a person attainted. As to what the noble lord says, that he is no party to the record, it is true he is not, but it is a record notwithstanding. It is a record upon the point in question to show whether or no the person who is proposed as a witness is attainted, and there is no other way by which he can have an opportunity in a Court of justice to avoid that attainder but by being brought into that Court and asked what he has to say why execution should not be awarded against him upon the foundation of his being attainted by the Act. The law gives him a right to make his defence against that demand of execution. He has done it by averring a fact of a surrender pursuant to the Act, and the Attorney-General having confessed that fact, it appears that the witness is not attainted, and the whole is (as it ought to be) entered on record, which is the proper evidence of his not being attainted, and therefore must be proper to be read to your lordships to answer an objection founded on a supposition that he is, though the prisoner is not, nor could possibly be, a party to it. **John Murray**

LORD HIGH STEWARD—My Lord Lovat, you have heard what the Managers say. Do you now insist upon the objection to the reading of the record, or will you reserve your objection to the witness till after the record has been read?

LORD LOVAT—I desire that it should not be read.

LORD HIGH STEWARD—Do you desire that your counsel may be heard to that question as a point of law?

LORD LOVAT—Yes, I do.

ATTORNEY-GENERAL—To be sure, my lords, if it is anything, it is a point of law, but your lordships will judge whether it is a point of doubt, and therefore deserves to have counsel heard to it.

LORD HIGH STEWARD—If my Lord Lovat insists upon it his counsel must be heard to this point.

MR. FORRESTER—My lords, I am, by your lordships' order, assigned counsel to the noble lord the prisoner at the bar to advise and assist him in matters of law. The objection that the noble lord has made to the reading of this record is that it is grounded upon a plea of Mr. Murray, confessed by His Majesty's Attorney-General, to which the noble lord is no party, that nobody is bound by that confession but the Crown, and consequently that it cannot be read against the noble lord at the bar. And, my lords, I apprehend that a plea resting merely upon the confession of the King, and which, in fact, may or may not be true, ought not, in point of law or justice, to conclude any party but the Crown, in whom alone resided the power of confessing it. **Mr. Forrester**

Mr. Forrester My lords, I am ready to acknowledge that the law of England gives the greatest credit to proofs by matter of record, and that they are proofs of the highest nature, but, my lords, there is a great difference between records grounded upon the confession of the party and records upon verdicts.

The reason is that in records grounded upon confession the party may come in and suggest a thing that is true or false, and it would be extremely hard in regard to third persons who may be injured by it—I say it would be extremely injurious—if they had no method to be let in to falsify a plea thus confessed. But where a record is grounded upon a verdict and judgment given thereupon the case is very different, because there is always a full hearing before a Court of justice. The facts are proved by testimony of the witnesses, and the jury give their verdict upon such proofs, so that both the matters of fact and law, if any arise, being fully debated and determined, it is highly reasonable such proceedings should be conclusive upon the maxim, "*Expedit reipublicæ ut fit finis litium,*" since, if it was not, every fact might be called in question over and over again, and so Courts of justice would never come to an end of the business before them. My lords, the distinction that I make is not purely of my own imagination. Your lordships will find it in the best writers on the Crown law. My Lord Coke (in his Third Inst., fol. 231), and Lord Chief Justice Hale (in the first volume of his "History of the Pleas of the Crown," fol. 361) tell us that if a tenant in fee aliens his lands, and then is attainted of treason by verdict upon an indictment, supposing the offence committed before the alienation, the alienee cannot falsify the attainder upon a supposition that there was no treason committed before the alienation, but that, had the attainder been by confession, the alienee might falsify the attainder in the very point of the treason, there being nothing conclusive done by the alienor. This, my lords, I apprehend, is extremely strong to the present purpose. Your lordships will be pleased to observe how far it goes. It respects the Crown in point of interest, the lands actually forfeited to and vested in the Crown by the attainder, which yet being grounded only on the confession of the party cannot operate to injure a third person, but he may set it aside, and recover his lands again, notwithstanding the record by which it appears that the alienor committed treason, and sold the lands after the treason actually committed. My lords, I am aware of an objection that may be made. It will perhaps be said that it was in the power of the Crown to have fully established Mr. Murray's credit by taking another method, that of granting him a pardon, which would have removed all objections. My lords, I grant it would, and had it been done the noble lord at the bar nor his counsel would not have troubled your lordships with any objection. But, my lords, there is a very wide difference between the two methods. A pardon takes away, as Lord Hobart expresses it, both *pœnam* and *reatum*. It obliterates the crime as much as if there had been no crime at all, and when that has been once declared by the Crown it is conclusive to all people. A pardon removes all objections to the person and to his character, but the present case is extremely different, for the substance of Murray's plea, though confessed by the Attorney-General, still remains a matter of doubt and a matter of evidence. My lords, that Mr. Murray appeared in the Court of King's Bench, that he pleaded he was the person named in the Act, so far is true, and so far I allow. But, my lords, notwithstanding, he pleaded that he surrendered on the 28th June, and was then committed to prison, this may be false. Evidence might have been produced to the contrary, and upon that evidence it might have appeared that he did not surrender before the 12th of July. Mr. Forrester

My lords, should that happen to be the case, in what condition would a third person be? Was this proceeding to be conclusive against him? It is a maxim in law that *actis legis nemini facit injuriam*. The maxim holds equally strong as to the acts of the Crown, and, if our books are not so explicit on the latter as the former head, their silence proceeds from the great modesty of our laws, which, as they repose the highest trust in the honour and justice of the Crown, won't suppose its prerogative will ever be turned to the subject's detriment; and, indeed, right reason tells us that neither the acts of the Crown nor of any party whatsoever ought to affect a third person who was a stranger to them, and who has had no opportunity of controverting them.

My lords, I would trouble your lordships with a very short case to illustrate what I am contending for. A copyholder is attainted and flies, and the land escheats to the lord. Suppose that he is afterwards taken and brought up into the Court of King's Bench, and there pleads that he is not the man, and that plea is confessed by the Attorney-General, would this be evidence against the lord who had acquired a property in the land by escheat? Would he be concluded by that proceeding? Would the tenant, by saying "I have pleaded I am not the man, and the Attorney-General has confessed it," avail himself against the lord? My lords, here is to be an interest divested out of a person by a mere confession of the parties in a proceeding to which he is a stranger, and was never admitted to litigate. And as the lord by escheat would not be concluded in the case I just now put, I do not see any distinction can be made between that and the present.

The noble lord at the bar has a right to object to every

Mr. Forrester person attainted, and that right cannot be taken away by any proceeding between other persons to which he is no party.

My lords, the case is rather stronger here, because, by the same reason that Mr. Murray is enabled to be a witness, by having pleaded that he surrendered within the time limited by the Act, and that plea confessed by the Attorney-General, if a person actually attainted by verdict and judgment (which is the highest kind of attainder) should upon any occasion be brought up to the Court of King's Bench and asked why execution should not be awarded against him, that he should deny, as happened in Okey's case, his being the same person, and that denial be confessed by the Attorney-General, this man, whom the law disables by his attainder for an offence of the highest kind from giving testimony in any case, the Attorney-General would, by his bare confession, restore to credit and enable to give evidence in any case. This would be investing the Attorney-General with legislative power, and that, I believe, your lordships will scarcely think proper or reasonable.

Mr. Ford MR. FORD—My lords, I am likewise assigned of counsel for the noble lord at the bar, and the question before your lordships is whether the record now produced can be received in evidence to repel the objection that arises from the late Act of Parliament to Mr. Murray's evidence.

By that statute he is actually attainted unless he surrendered before the 12th of July, 1746, and, if attainted, it is admitted by the gentlemen of the House of Commons that he is incapable of being a witness.

My lords, the great consequence of questions of this nature is obvious to every one, the justice of all judicial determinations depending entirely on the veracity of witnesses who are to prove the facts upon which such determinations are to be founded. And there can scarcely arise a question relating to evidence of greater importance to any man than the present to the noble lord at the bar, whose estate, life, and honours depend on the evidence that may be received against him, and therefore your lordships will be particularly cautious that he shall not be affected by any but legal, unexceptionable witnesses.

As to the record now offered to be read, it consists only of a plea by Mr. Murray that he surrendered in due time, which Mr. Attorney-General has thought proper to confess. And it is argued that this plea and confession are proper evidence that such surrender was made, and the provision of the Act, so far as concerns Mr. Murray, absolutely defeated.

My lords, how far such a proceeding may bind the Crown is not material in the present question. But whether it shall conclude the noble prisoner, who is an absolute stranger to it, and who never had any opportunity of contesting the truth of the fact, is of the utmost importance. The Attorney-General, by his office, prosecutes and defends the causes of the Crown, and, as such, may make many admissions to bind the Crown. But it would be extremely inconvenient if such admissions should conclude anybody else. In some cases they are totally disregarded, and therefore, if things are confessed as errors in a record which appear not to be errors, the Court, where such record is depending, is bound to give judgment against such confession and according to law. **Mr. Ford**

So, if a matter of fact is offered to be admitted which the Court knows to be otherwise, it seems to be their duty to reject such admission; and therefore suppose, upon the statute of Edward VI., one outlawed for treason should be brought into the King's Bench in order to have execution awarded upon the outlawry, and should plead, what the Court knows to be false, that he surrendered himself within the year to the Chief Justice, according to that statute, and the Attorney-General should be disposed to confess it, ought not the Court to reject such an admission, or must they be concluded by what is well known to be untrue? Certainly the Court would not suffer such an attempt to prevail.

In the present case there is nothing offered to your lordships to prove Mr. Murray's surrender but the record of what passed between him and the Attorney-General in the King's Bench, and, if this record is permitted to be read, though the contents of it should be absolutely untrue, yet when once read it will be conclusive evidence of the fact it imports, and no proof can be admitted to contradict it, and if it is evidence to be received on this occasion, it must be evidence in all Courts and on all occasions where a question may arise about Mr. Murray's attainder.

My lords, Mr. Murray may have estates which, by the custom of the manors where they lie or by the grant of the Crown, may belong to the lords of those manors. If his surrender was not made in proper time, all such estates are forfeited to such lords, and yet, if this record is to be admitted, it will be evidence that cannot be contradicted by them, and must divest those rights and estates which by this attainder they were lawfully entitled to.

But the mischief of permitting such a record to be read will not stop here. For purchasers likewise must be concluded by it, and therefore, though lands may have been long since sold and enjoyed under a title arising from an attainder of the same nature with Mr. Murray's, yet, if this amicable proceeding between the Attorney-General and the party attainted is to prevail, no purchaser, even at any distance of time, can be secure.

Mr. Ford In this light the point seems of very extensive consequence, for it is to give the King's Attorney power to do more by the admission of a fact, which perhaps may not be true, than the King by a pardon can effect, for the King's pardon cannot restore lands forfeited to others, whereas, if the present attempt should succeed, the rights and titles of strangers may be destroyed, though never so justly founded.

My lords, whether Mr. Murray surrendered or not is a matter of fact capable of proof, is a fact of the utmost importance to the prisoner, and therefore, as the rule of law is general, that nothing done or transacted between two persons shall prejudice a third who does not concur in the act, nor has an opportunity of contradicting it, the present record, which, for anything apparent, may be an entire fiction, ought not to be received; and, my lords, supposing there was a possibility of proving this fact by matter of record, yet, by the constant rule of evidence, the record produced seems improper to be read, because it is not the best evidence the nature of the thing will admit of, and, for that reason, is not the proper record to prove the point in question.

That the judge or justice to whom Mr. Murray surrendered himself made a record of such surrender cannot be doubted. It was his duty so to do, and must be presumed to have been done, and therefore, if this fact is proper to be proved by any record, the original made by such magistrate who took the surrender ought to be produced.

My lords, it may be said this record in question imports an admission by the proper officer of the Crown of a fact which he must be supposed to have inquired into, and has therefore admitted, because he finds it to be true. My lords, this answer might have been given if Mr. Attorney had at this bar offered originally to confess the same thing, and suppose the record now attempted to be read had never existed, and, upon an objection to Mr. Murray's testimony, the Attorney-General had said, "Here I have the King's warrant to confess that he surrendered before the 12th of July," would your lordships have received such an admission? Would you conclude yourselves by the concession of a fact without knowing whether it was so or not? Would the Court have suffered the force of an Act of Parliament to have been defeated by such an acknowledgment? Or would not clear and positive proof have been required of an actual surrender?

My lords, if it could, upon what reason can such a confession in the King's Bench, in an inferior Court, in the absence of the prisoner, who may be prejudiced by it, be received in evidence against him? If it is true that Mr. Murray surrendered in proper time, it may be easily proved. If it is not, the present method by which it is attempted to be proved is a certain one to draw the Court into an error about it. Your lordships must perceive the danger of allowing such a proceeding, how mischievous it may be to the prisoner, to lords of manors, to purchasers, to all strangers, who never can have an opportunity of disputing the truth of it, and therefore, whatever effect it may have between the Crown and Mr. Murray, it is humbly submitted that it ought not to be read against the lord at the bar. **Mr. Ford**

MR. HAMILTON GORDON—My lords, I have likewise the honour to attend your lordships as one of the counsel for the noble lord at the bar, whose province it is to lay before your lordships and enforce with all humble submission what may occur to them in his favour in point of law. But the two learned gentlemen who have gone before me have spoken so fully and discharged their duty so well that I should trespass upon your lordships' time, and also do them injustice, if I consumed much of it. Besides, my lords, I am too diffident of my own abilities to speak long upon a question which is involved in the particular laws of this country; and therefore I shall, with your lordships' indulgence, confine my endeavours to serve my client by a few general observations which, I humbly think, must naturally occur to every man upon that point which the noble lord at the bar has taken the liberty to propose to your lordships by way of objection. **Mr. Gordon**

The noble prisoner at the bar has objected that Mr. Murray is not a competent witness against him, or, in other words, that, according to the rules of law, his evidence ought not to be received, and, to maintain that position, he has laid down another, namely, that the record of the Court of King's Bench, which proceeds singly upon the bare admission of His Majesty's Attorney-General, unsupported by any proof, ought not to be read as evidence of Mr. Murray's surrender so as to qualify him to give evidence upon this trial.

As to the first, I humbly apprehend it to be wholly unnecessary to use any arguments to prove that, if those proceedings in the King's Bench did not stand in the way of the noble lord at the bar, Mr. Murray must, of course, have been rejected as an incompetent witness.

It remains, therefore, only to be considered whether such proceedings, transacted only between the Crown and Mr. Murray, can affect the interest of a third person.

My lords, the consequences of this question are of the greatest importance to the subjects in general, and, although the noble lord is more immediately concerned in it, yet if it should be determined that this is proper evidence to affect him, the like evidence must be received against every other subject of Great Britain, for the law cannot distinguish between him and others.

Mr. Gordon And I beg leave, my lords, to say that it appears from the authorities which have been cited by the other gentlemen, and which have always been considered as of the greatest weight in this country, that the admission of the Attorney-General or any other cannot affect a third person, and I take it, my lords, to be a general established rule that the interest of one cannot be affected by the admission of another. My lords, I apprehend that my Lord Coke's sense of this matter is so extremely clear and obvious that it requires no explanation, and so is the opinion of another great lawyer, my Lord Chief Justice Hale.

My lords, the law gives an opportunity to falsify the verdict of twelve men where a third party, from the want of it, may be injured only in a pecuniary matter. How much more reasonable is it, therefore, that this kind of agreement should be set aside and held of no consequence in a case where the life, fortune, and honour of a noble lord are concerned?

My lords, I would humbly ask, what kind of acquittal was this? Not an acquittal by verdict, the legal acquittal in this kingdom, but by a bare consent, a consent that surely has not force enough to repeal an Act of Parliament.

My lords, the only way the Act of Parliament left for Mr. Murray to avoid the consequences of an attainder was the performance of a condition, that is, surrendering himself within a time limited. Now, I would suppose that this Act had been a deed granting an estate on a certain condition, must not that condition have been performed truly and effectually? Certainly it must by the rule laid down by Lord Coke. Shall not Acts of Parliament therefore be as strictly complied with as common deeds and conveyances? Surely the gentlemen of the House of Commons will hardly deny it. Consequently the Attorney-General could not by any consent of his make this record in the King's Bench tantamount to an actual surrender.

Suppose, my lords, the Act had attainted Mr. Murray of felony instead of treason, could this admission of Mr. Attorney-General have deprived the lord of the lands which would have escheated to him? No, my lords, it could not, if any regard is to be paid to the rule laid down in 5 Coke 96, that the estates of third persons shall not be divested by colourable or covinous payments, but by such as are true and effectual. And what are payments but performances of conditions? And the same law that guides one will the other.

The fact is not as the record states it, and the Attorney-General's consent, which is the fiat for this record, was a consent after the impeachment of the noble lord. I wish it rather had preceded it.

My lords, if Mr. Murray had held by copyhold from the noble lord at the bar, and had been attainted, the noble lord would have been entitled to the escheat or forfeiture of those lands, and no admission of the Attorney-General's could defeat him of it, any more than it could in the case of a forfeiture of lands in a county palatine, where the grantee of the Crown became entitled to the benefit of it. Shall, therefore, my lords, such admission be permitted to affect the life, honours, and fortune of the noble lord at the bar, or, indeed, of any other in his unhappy situation? No, surely, for it is against the common known principles of law, and of reason too, that a man shall be attainted as to some circumstances and free from attainder as to others, that he shall be incapable to hold his lands or chattels and yet be restored in credit so as to affect the life of an innocent man, for such, till conviction, every one is by law presumed to be. I say, my lords, this is a construction so unprecedented and new that we hope it will never receive the sanction of your lordships. **Mr. Gordon**

My lords, I hope your lordships will never countenance the admission of such an evidence, an evidence who is so strongly agitated by the hope of pardon and fear of punishment that to procure the one and avoid the other he may give up all sense of honour, humanity, and justice.

My lords, as the learned gentlemen who spoke before me on the same side have made it unnecessary for me to add anything more, I shall not give your lordships any further trouble at present, and I beg your lordships' pardon for that which I have already given you. But if any reply should be necessary to what shall be offered by the gentlemen of the House of Commons, I hope we shall have your lordships' indulgence.

Lord High Steward—Gentlemen of the House of Commons, you may proceed.

Attorney-General—My lords, the Managers do not dispute the prisoner's right to any good objection against the competency of the witness, or insist that it is not equally proper before your lordships on this impeachment as it would be on a trial in the ordinary Courts of justice, but they dispute the validity of the objection upon its own proper legal foundation. **Attorney-General**

As the objection is to the reading this record, the mere stating of the question will be an answer to it, and obviate or refute every argument used in support of it.

The original objection was against Mr. Murray's being examined as a witness upon the supposition of his standing attainted of high treason by the late Act in not surrendering within the time prescribed. The Managers allowed the consequence, if the allegation of his attainder were true, as that would render him infamous, not as it would prove him guilty of

Attorney-General

treason, for the guilt alone without the attainder would not render him incompetent, it being a clear established point that even a *particeps criminis* may be a witness to prove the guilt of those who joined with him in the same crime, and your lordships in the late trial of the Lord Balmerino admitted that sort of evidence, but the Managers answered the objection by denying the attainder, and produced this record to show the surrender pursuant to the Act, which attaints him only on condition of his not surrendering within the time limited. This record is of a proceeding commenced on the part of the Crown, on the footing of this very Act, in the proper Court of justice, against the witness, and defended, on the part of the witness, by this surrender, and that defence and surrender confessed by the Attorney-General by warrant from the Crown, and this allowed by the Court, who, instead of awarding execution against him, remanded him to prison, where he now remains, forthcoming to justice, according to the Act.

Now, to say that such a record relating to the precise point in question cannot be read to disprove the supposed attainder and support the competency of the witness, would be to deny one of the first principles of evidence, and therefore the counsel, aware of the absurdity, have not ventured in terms to assert a proposition so contrary to the known law of the land, as that such a record is not proper to be read, but seem rather, in the way of argument, to deny the consequence of it when read, and have insisted on reasons that tend to show that it is not conclusive evidence, and therefore that the fact of the surrender may be still controverted by evidence on the side of the prisoner rather than that it is no evidence at all.

Though this is more properly a subsequent question, and a very different one in its nature, yet, in the present case, it is really and in effect the same, and the necessary consequence of the other. For to insist that this record is not conclusive proof of Mr. Murray's not being attainted by that Act must proceed on this supposition that he may still be held attainted under the Act, notwithstanding this record. But, I presume, your lordships will upon no terms be induced to admit of that suggestion when it is considered that the certain effect of it must be that he may be called up again for execution, and put a second time on the defence of his life against the same charge.

But to consider the grounds on which the objection has been attempted to be supported, there are two general reasons insisted on—one that the surrender insisted on in behalf of the witness, when he was brought before the Court of King's Bench, was neither proved to the Court nor found by a jury, but only confessed by the Attorney-General; the other that the noble lord was himself no party to the record, and therefore not to be affected by it.

As to the first, in order to support that reason, a distinction is attempted to be set up between the case of a fact on which a judgment is grounded appearing by a verdict or evidence, and where it appears only by the confession of the party, and it is said that in the former case it may, but in the latter cannot, be conclusive to any other persons but those who were parties. And for this purpose the authorities of my Lord Chief Justice Coke and Lord Hale and others are cited to show the difference in point of consequence to third persons between an attainder by verdict or by confession, that in the one case the crime may be disputed by a purchaser under the attainted person, but in the other it cannot, though the time of the commission of it may. **Attorney-General**

It will be unnecessary for me to enter minutely into the nice disquisition how far and for what purposes the crime appearing on an attainder may be controverted by strangers whose interest is affected by it, because I am satisfied your lordships will see that the distinctions on that head are totally foreign to the present question, and one single observation would be sufficient to make that manifest—that is, that none of the cases cited or that can be cited prove that any stranger can controvert the attainder itself, whether founded on a verdict or confession or by default, and it is the attainder, and not the crime, that is the only material thing on the present objection.

All that will be necessary, therefore, upon this point will be to show that the confession in this case binds the Crown, and that if it does there is no attainder. The inference will then follow, of course, that the record may be read to prove Murray not attainted as the precise point to be proved in answer to the objection to his competency.

The authority of the Attorney-General to confess the truth of the plea of surrender has not been directly denied by the counsel, but as they have seemingly in consequence done it, and the clear establishment of that right in this case will, by certain inference, establish the right to read this record, I shall state a little to your lordships how that authority stands upon the nature and reason of the thing and the known constant practice.

The law and Constitution has entrusted the Crown, as the executive power, with the prosecution of crimes, and though oftentimes such prosecutions are carried on by private persons, even those are, for the most part, in the name of the Crown. But those, as well as civil suits, may be commenced sometimes without a just foundation, and the party sued may have a just defence to the one as well as the other. Where that appears it is equally just in both cases to put a stop to them, and as a subject plaintiff may confess the defendant's plea,

Attorney-General

so may the Crown, by the Attorney-General, its proper officer, confess the prisoner's defence, and such confession in both cases is and ought to be, both in law and natural justice, a security against any future action or prosecution for the same cause. Nor is there any reason that can be given for the power in the case of a subject but what will hold equally strong, and stronger, in the case of the Crown, as there could not be a greater grievance to the subjects in general than to have it established as a rule that when once a criminal prosecution is commenced, the defendant, how innocent soever or how willing soever to make satisfaction, must be put to the vexation of a trial or the charge of a pardon, which might in many cases be his ruin. And how strange would it appear to say that the King might not do the same justice to innocence that every honest man would do, or that he might not, for such wise and gracious reasons as would induce him to grant a pardon after sentence, stop the proceedings in the ordinary course of law before they come to sentence!

To avoid these absurdities the law entrusts the proper officer, the Attorney-General, with the power of confessing a defendant's plea where it appears to be true in charges of a lesser nature, and in the higher by the immediate warrant of the Crown, and such confession has the effect it ought to have of an absolute discharge, and I should imagine nobody who thinks of it for a moment would, for the sake of the subject, wish it otherwise.

And, my lords, this has been the constant practice not only in criminal prosecutions properly so called, but in all Crown causes even for civil rights; and whoever has had the honour of serving the Crown in the office of Attorney-General must have eased the subject on that head, when, on applications by the parties sued and attendances by the officers of that branch of the revenue which is in question, the plea has appeared to be a just one, and both the Crown and the subject find their account in this method of proceeding in the expense and delay that are saved by it; and such confession, being recorded, has to all intents the same effect as if, on issue joined, a jury had found the fact to be what the Attorney-General confessed.

The practice is the same in criminal cases where the Attorney-General confesses the plea, whether it be to the merits of the charge or only in order to let the defendant into an opportunity of trying those merits.

There is one sort of case frequently happens very parallel to the present, where a person is outlawed for treason or felony, which amounts in law to an attainder for the crime and equally affects the party both as to his life and estate as on a verdict. The party having no way of coming at the trial but by revers-

Attorney-General

ing the outlawry by writ of error, which cannot be allowed without His Majesty's consent, it is a frequent practice to apply for that indulgence, and it is very easily granted, provided there has been no great delay. If the party assigns an error in fact, as he may, the Attorney-General confesses it, if true, and the outlawry is reversed and the attainder avoided by it. And no one ever doubted but the record of that reversal is conclusive proof of his not being attainted.

Nay, the Crown has sometimes directed the Attorney-General to confess errors in fact, as the party's being beyond sea at the time of the outlawry, which have not been true, only that he may have an opportunity of taking his trial and not suffer for a default in not appearing only. And no lawyer ever said that such a confession was not as effectual to avoid the outlawry as the verdict of a jury impanelled to try it. And if in the present case the truth was that Mr. Murray did not actually surrender, but was apprehended before the day, and that should be thought in strictness not a compliance with the Act, and the Attorney-General was now prosecuting for the Crown only, I believe he would be under no difficulty of owning the truth or apprehensive that your lordships would say that the confession was either illegal or inequitable, or that when the end of the Act was answered by Mr. Murray's being ready to take his trial, it was not agreeable to His Majesty's royal justice and clemency to remove the only impediment to his having it. Nor can the exercise of this power be objected to from any reasons but what would equally affect the exercise of that great and excellent prerogative of pardoning.

What I have now said will fully show that the cases cited are not applicable to the present. They are the cases of innocent purchasers, whose estates were to be lost by the subsequent attainder and supposed guilt of the vendors.

It would be unjust in itself not to give them an opportunity of defending their property by controverting the fact on which it depended. The law, in conformity to natural justice, gives them in some cases liberty of disputing the crime itself where the conviction is by confession, and the time of the commission where it is by verdict. But in those cases the question was a matter of property between the Crown and an innocent subject, and depended on the crime's being committed before or after the purchase and not merely on the attainder, which would stand good, let that question be determined either way; but in the present case the question is on the incompetency of a witness, which depends solely on his attainder and not on the reality or time of his crime. Therefore, to make a parallel case it must be said that if the Attorney-General had confessed a plea of "Not guilty" to an indictment of treason,

Attorney-General

and the prisoner being thereupon acquitted should be brought as a witness either in a criminal or civil suit, his competency might be objected to and the objection supported by proof of his actual guilt. But this cannot be pretended. The contrary is so clear that if he had never been indicted or acquitted the clearest proof of his crime could not be admitted for this purpose, and no evidence can in any case establish such an objection but a record of an attainder.

The only colour of distinction between the case put and the present is that the attainder here appears *prima facie*, and must be avoided by a surrender to be proved. This is true, and therefore puts the proof on us to remove the objection, and it is for that reason this record is offered as the proper proof. And, as in the case where the proof lies on the side of the objection, the record of the attainder is the proper evidence, so in this, where it lies on the side of the witness, the record of his surrender is the direct proof that he is not attainted.

My lords, I come now to the second reason given for the objection, that the prisoner is no party to this record, and I shall have occasion to say very little upon this, because it is in effect answered by the first reason insisted on by the counsel themselves, which supposes, if the surrender had been found by verdict, the record would be proper evidence, and yet the prisoner would then have been equally no party. This, therefore, destroys the rule and supposition on which this reason is founded, which is that no record can be read against a man to which he was no party, and, indeed, there is not, nor can be, any such rule. It is most notoriously otherwise in the very instance in question, of the incompetency of a witness, on account of his attainder, which never can be proved by anything but the record, and yet the party to be prejudiced by it neither is, nor can be, a party to it.

The noble lord is controverting no property on the foundation of Mr. Murray's supposed attainder. He neither claims nor defends any right that is demanded on the foundation of his discharge. The record has no more relation to him than to all the world, and if the witness is disabled as to him, he is so with respect to all mankind, and in all causes, civil or criminal, and must be put on the trial of his surrender as often as he shall be called upon during his life to give his testimony in any Court and in any suit. What absurdities this would be attended with I need not mention. Your lordships will be beforehand with me in suggesting them to your own thoughts.

Sir J. Strange

Sir John Strange—My lords, the question arising upon the objection made by the noble lord at the bar is not what the

Sir J. Strange

consequence of this record will be when it is read, but singly, whether we shall be now admitted to read it or no? My lords, the objection made by the noble lord at the bar against this witness was founded upon this record. My lords, it was called for and read, which was the Act of Parliament made in the last sessions for the attainder of several persons, and, my lords, upon that sort of attainder no writ of error could lie, and therefore, my lords, there was no other way to take off the force of that attainder that was warrantable than the method taken in the present case. And, my lords, I must submit it to your lordships whether we are not entitled to read what we now call for, not as a distinct record, but as part of the whole record relating to the person now at your lordships' bar, for the record must come before your lordships in all its parts. Nobody can call for a particular part of a record to be read, but the whole must be laid before your lordships, and therefore, my lords, I beg leave to contend that this is part of the record of the proceedings against the person whom we now call upon as a witness, which the noble lord at the bar himself called for. My lords, what the consequence of it will be afterwards is a question of another nature, but I must submit it to your lordships that as part of the record of the proceedings against Mr. Murray we are certainly entitled to have it read.

My lords, one objection taken by the gentlemen on the other side is that it is not the record of the proper jurisdiction, but that it ought to be a record made by the person to whom Mr. Murray surrendered himself. But, my lords, I must beg leave to submit it to your lordships by way of answer that it is the record of a proper jurisdiction in a case of this nature. My lords, the Court of King's Bench as a Court of criminal jurisdiction, may have offenders of all sorts brought before them. My lords, in the present case a *certiorari* issues out of Chancery, and by *mittimus* the record is removed into the King's Bench. And I will call upon the counsel for the impeached lord if they will venture to say that a *certiorari* will not lie for that purpose. My lords, if it will lie, it must be for some end or purpose that a *certiorari* was brought and the record transmitted thither. That was the proper jurisdiction, and that Court then had a right to call upon the party brought up before them by *habeas corpus* to know what he had to say why execution should not be awarded upon the footing of the attainder by this Act of Parliament. My lords, the question was put by that Court to the person who was then a prisoner before them. He pleaded a surrender within the time, and insisted that there he was amenable to justice. He alleges that as a proper answer to that Court upon the question asked him, and whether it was or was not a proper answer, depended upon the fact. The

Sir J. Strange Court could have no doubt if the party surrendered himself in time and was amenable to justice, but that was an answer to their demanding to know of him why execution should not be awarded against him. And, my lords, if that fact had not been verified in a legal way, there must have been execution awarded, but if legal satisfaction was given by the then prisoner, it was the duty of that Court to record that as a matter of fact which was properly verified before them. And, my lords, there are two ways of verifying matters of fact. One is by the actual proof of the fact (if the other party denies it), or by confession. And if the party knows that he cannot in conscience deny it, then he ought to confess it, and not put the other to the expense and trouble of proving that which he knows to be true. If you know that to be fact that the party surrendered himself to justice and was forthcoming, will anybody say that it is not right and just to admit that fact as alleged? Therefore, my lords, the question of fact in this case has been properly determined by that Court, the consequence of which is that that Court ought to make a record of it, and that is to be considered, not as a distinct separate record of itself, but as the proceeding upon this record of this Act of Parliament which had thus been removed there by *certiorari*, and it is, to all intents and purposes of law, to be considered as a record of the proceedings, and they are to be considered as having the former proceedings before them upon the same record, and all Courts are bound to admit that record, which was thus made in a Court of legal proceeding. And therefore, my lords, if that Court was the proper jurisdiction, can anybody say that the record of what was there transacted is not as proper evidence as what the noble lord at the bar has called for, and which has been read to your lordships, which is the Act of Attainder of the last sessions of Parliament? My lords, the gentlemen on the other side say that this is an erroneous method. Say they, you have not gone to the proper person. Here is a particular jurisdiction to record a surrender, and you should have gone to the justice of the peace to whom the surrender was made. My lords, I have looked upon the Act of Parliament to see what the Legislature had thought proper to prescribe as the duty of the justice of the peace to whom the surrender is directed to be made.

My lords, all that is required of him by this Act of Parliament is—he is, upon the surrender, to commit the person so surrendering to prison for the high treason, there to remain till he is discharged by due course of law, and he is immediately to give notice of it to the Secretary of State. Your lordships will then be pleased to consider what it is that the gentlemen insist upon. My lords, will anybody say that what is mentioned in this Act of Parliament in regard to the justice of the peace will take away the jurisdiction from a supreme Court of original jurisdiction in cases of that kind, and that without a word being mentioned in the Act concerning it? Sir J. Strange

My lords, they say that the jurisdiction of recording the surrender is given to the Justice of the Peace, though the Act of Parliament does not say a word of his doing anything of this nature. And, my lords, if the Act of Parliament had made him the proper person whose duty it was to record the surrender, to what purpose is he to send an account of it to the Secretary of State? Was he to make up the record? No, all the Justice of the Peace was to do was to give notice of the transaction before him to those persons who are appointed to do what shall be done upon such a surrender. My lords, there is something that was said by the counsel for the noble lord at the bar which I will only just take notice of. They were pleased to put this case. Say they, suppose this record is now to stand, it is a matter transacted to which the noble lord at the bar is no party, and consequently ought not to be read against him. My lords, I will venture to say there is no such general rule. Nobody will contend (because there are numberless instances of it) that records are not constantly permitted to be read as evidence against persons who are no parties to them. My lords, suppose a man is charged with having harboured a person attainted of treason or felony, and, when he comes to be tried, say they, "Gentlemen, you shall not read the record of that person's attainder, because the man now charged is no party to it. Do not charge me with receiving or harbouring a man attainted by that record, for, though the record may be read as against him, yet it cannot be read against the person charged, who was no party to it." My lords, would any Court of justice make the least difficulty in admitting such a record to be read? My lords, the reason of the thing itself speaks it, for till the record is read it does not appear there is any person attainted, and consequently no charge against the prisoner. And, my lords, to make it a civil case, suppose a lord of a manor claims by escheat the estate of a person attainted, and another lord claims the same estate, cannot the record of the person's attainder be read as evidence in that case, though neither of them is party to it? My lords, there can be no doubt but it may, and therefore, my lords, that objection has no force upon the present question. My lords, the objection now made is to the reading of a record, or part of a record, which the noble lord at the bar himself called for, and I must submit it to your lordships that we are entitled to have it now read. What the consequence of reading of it will be is not now to be considered, for we argue singly upon the question whether it shall be now read or no.

Solicitor-General

SOLICITOR-GENERAL—My lords, whether the record which has been opened may be read at all, and what shall be the effect of it after it is read—I mean whether it may be falsified—are two separate and distinct considerations. Your lordships were pleased to ask the noble lord at the bar and his counsel whether they would rest their objection to the reading of it, or suffer it to be read and then object to the consequence of it. They chose to object to the reading, and the counsel were allowed to speak to that point only. And yet there is not an authority they have quoted which does not prove that, at least, it must be read.

The competency of all evidence in a great measure depends upon the nature of the question to which it is applied, for that is evidence in one case and to one purpose, which is not so in another kind of case or to another sort of purpose. The merits of this objection therefore will depend upon thoroughly understanding the purpose for which this record is produced.

The incapacity of a person attainted to give testimony does not arise from his life being thereby in the power of the King, or any presumption that, through the fear of death, he may be induced to exceed the bounds of truth, but it is one of those many incapacities which are the consequences of his attainder, He is cut off from the community. His blood is corrupted. He loses his credit, and therefore can be a witness in no case, neither for nor against a prosecution, nor in any civil suit between subject and subject.

All proceedings upon which a man can be attainted at the common law are between the King and the party only. But such proceedings are evidence, and the only evidence, to prove the attainder between all persons and upon all occasions, which shows the mistake the gentlemen proceed upon when they object that my Lord Lovat was no party to this record, and therefore it shall not be read against him.

The party who objects to a witness because he is attainted, undertakes to show that, according to the course of the public law and justice of the nation, he is so, and therefore may read any proceedings in the course of that public law to prove it. So likewise, in answer to the objection, and to show the person not attainted, any of the like proceedings may be read. If a conviction and judgment is read, it may be answered by reading the reversal of that judgment upon a writ of error, and yet the King must be the only party to both these proceedings.

The likest case to the present at common law is that of an outlawry. If an outlawry is produced to prove a man attainted the reversal of that outlawry may be given in evidence, as a full answer to that proof, and yet most of those reversals in high treason are grounded upon the Attorney-General's confessing an error in fact by the King's command, and this generally is a merciful confession, contrary to the truth of the case. Several noble families now enjoy their honours and their estates by virtue of such reversals. I will not mention instances, as your lordships have the assistance of the judges. I am persuaded they will inform your lordships that there are many. Would an objection be endured to the reading such a reversal? Solicitor-General

The present case is that of a Parliamentary outlawry, if I may so call it. Persons fled from justice are attainted in a more expeditious and summary way than could be done by the course of the common law, unless they come in and take their trials within a limited time.

The only Court in this part of the kingdom which can award execution against a person as attainted within this Act is the Court of King's Bench. There can be no party to such proceedings but the King, who is entrusted with the whole execution of the public law of the nation. A proceeding therefore in that Court which shows a man never to have been attainted within the Act is evidence to answer an objection which says he is. It proves conclusively that, in the eye and consideration of the public law, he is not an attainted man. He may inherit, he may purchase, he can't be put to death. By this proceeding the King is bound for ever. All magistrates are bound. No judicature can now consider the witness in any other light than he ought to be considered in, if the Act had never been made. Is it possible, then, to doubt whether (in answer to an objection that by the law of the land this witness is now looked upon as an attainted man) a record should be read which proves that by the law of the land he is not looked upon as an attainted man? He is either a person liable to all the consequences of an attainder or none.

Mr. Noel—My lords, I shall be very short in offering my sentiments to your lordships upon the present question, because three learned and able gentlemen have already spoken very fully to it. Mr. Noel

My lords, the question arises upon an objection taken by the noble lord at the bar against the competency of Mr. Murray's testimony, as he stands attainted by the Act of the last sessions of Parliament, which has been read to your lordships. But after that another objection arose in consequence of what we, on the part of the prosecution, offered, which was a record we proposed to be read, to the reading of which the noble lord objected, and has relied upon that objection that it cannot be read at all.

My lords, I was surprised at that objection, and the counsel for the noble lord have been so sensible that there was no great weight in it that they have prematurely, in the course

Mr. Noel of their arguments, run into a debate concerning the force and effect of it when read, and not to the actual reading of it, and, my lords, it was a very strange proposition to be insisted on before your lordships, that, in a question relating to Mr. Murray, and him alone, when an objection is made to his testimony, that he stands attainted by an Act of Parliament, that your lordships should shut your eyes and not receive evidence of the proceedings of a Court having proper jurisdiction to determine any question which might arise upon that Act of Parliament. I say, my lords, that would be a most extraordinary thing indeed, when the objection relates to Mr. Murray upon the attainder by Act of Parliament, and yet, they say, your lordships shall not see the record of the proceedings of a Court of justice founded upon that Act of Parliament. But, my lords, as the gentlemen have, under a notion of considering this objection, in some degree considered the force of the record itself if it had been read, though they have done it improperly, yet I doubt it will be expected that we should take notice of the foundation of that argument.

The question therefore seems to be whether Mr. Murray is to be considered under the Act, and the proceedings in the Court of King's Bench upon it, as an attainted person or not.

My lords, the Act of Parliament does not finally conclude any person. It names several persons whom the Act declares shall be attainted by the force of that law unless they comply with the terms expressed in it, and the proper Court of law must judge when the person comes before them whether he was a person within the meaning of the Act of Parliament or not. Therefore, my lords, when he was before a Court who had proper jurisdiction upon that question, whether he was an attainted person or not, and they have determined that question that he was not, then there is an end of that question. But it has been said that this may affect, in consequence, the property of a third person, and that the noble lord at the bar ought not to be affected by the proceedings in the King's Bench. But, I apprehend, this question relates personally to Mr. Murray, and to no other. It is merely a question as to his capacity or incapacity, that is, whether he be attainted or no, and therefore, my lords, that distinguishes this case from the cases of private property alluded to by the counsel for the noble lord in the course of their argument.

My lords, I beg leave to state this matter in a stronger light. If your lordships shall say that Mr. Murray is an attainted person, you must likewise say that he is liable to have execution awarded against him upon this Act, for when that is the question it must be considered entire with all its consequences.

My lords, if no execution can be awarded against him, your

lordships cannot say that he is an attainted person. Therefore your lordships see what difficulties will ensue if you should determine that he stands attainted with respect to the noble lord at the bar, but not to the consequences that the law draws from his being an attainted person. My lords, it would be the strangest case in the world if that should be your lordships' sentiments that he is not attainted in one respect, and yet that he is attainted in another respect. Mr. Noel

My lords, the counsel for the noble lord object that the proceeding which has been had has been by the confession of the Attorney-General, though they admit it was in the power of the Crown to make such confession. I must submit it to your lordships that, though it is by the confession of the Attorney-General, as it is by proper authority, and in a legal Court having proper jurisdiction, that it is as effectual and binding upon the Crown as any act they can possibly do. And can your lordships say that Mr. Murray shall not have the benefit of a legal proceeding of a Court of justice having complete and lawful jurisdiction, and who have determined the case?

My lords, it is said that there is some difference where it is upon the confession of the Attorney-General and where it is founded upon a verdict. My lords, your lordships will consider what are the circumstances of the case in regard to that matter. A gentleman is brought before a Court of justice to answer why execution should not be awarded against him upon a supposed attainder. He pleads a fact that is sufficient, if true, to exempt him from that attainder. Can the gentleman say that he must not avail himself of it, because the Attorney-General will not put him to the expense to prove it? My lords, it is said that if he had denied the plea the consequence to Mr. Murray must have been that he would not have appeared to have been a person exempted from the Act. No, but, say they, because the Attorney-General and the Crown are satisfied of the truth of the plea, and will not put him upon proving it, therefore he is not to have the benefit of the judgment of the Court upon that question. I must submit it to your lordships, that every man under those circumstances would be in a most fatal situation, and that it would be attended with very bad consequences. A man is asked what he has to say why execution should not be awarded against him, and pleads a fact that actually will clear him from the attainder. The Attorney-General confesses the plea, does not join issue, and will not give him an opportunity of proving it, and my lords, what is to be the consequence? Why, according to this doctrine, he must inevitably be condemned as a person attainted, whereas, if he had been put to the proof of it, it might have been determined that he was not attainted. I

Mr. Noel

apprehend your lordships will not suffer them to draw that inference, that because the Attorney-General has not put him to the proof of his plea he is to be considered as a person attainted, contrary to the judgment of the Court.

Sir R. Lloyd

SIR RICHARD LLOYD—My lords, the question has been so fully spoken to already that I shall not have occasion to take up much of your lordships' time. But I cannot forbear expressing my surprise at the objection now made, viz., that this record cannot be read against the noble lord at the bar, the reason given for which is that he is no party to it. Many answers have been given, and I will not repeat them, but shall offer a consideration or two to your lordships in order to show that the force and effect of Mr. Murray's attainder has been by this transaction on record totally taken off.

My lords, the whole argument on the prisoner's side is in this compass, they say that Mr. Murray (the person produced by us as a witness) is still attainted, and therefore, by the rules of law, cannot be a witness. And 'tis certainly true that if he stands now attainted he cannot by our law be admitted to give testimony. Let us come then to that question—Does he or does he not at this hour stand attainted by virtue of the late statute?

It cannot be doubted but that a Parliamentary attainder of this sort may be dissolved by some method or other, and the very statute directs one way, by surrender before a particular day, and the only way to ascertain that fact is a judgment on record that he did surrender.

I would ask the counsel for the noble prisoner whether Mr. Murray can by law be called to judgment for that high treason for which he was by the late Act attainted. They must own that this record of surrender would be an absolute defence on such an occasion; nay, it would be an absolute bar to such a demand of judgment. If this defence would not be his security, the consequence is that there would be no method at all of getting rid of such an attainder.

It has been objected that though this may be a good discharge betwixt the Crown and Mr. Murray, yet it ought not to affect others who are not parties to that proceeding. My lords, 'tis true others may be affected by Mr. Murray's being restored to his credit, but that is no objection, for though, by virtue of this record, he is so restored, yet that is only a consequence which necessarily follows from the facts ascertained by that record. The proceeding on the record was a legal transaction between the Crown and Mr. Murray, and no other person whatsoever had a right to be a party to it. The King at the time of Mr. Murray's pleading on the record was the only person to call him to account for his guilt. The only controversy at that time was betwixt the Crown and the party called down to judgment. The matter therefore being a legal transaction, a law controversy betwixt the only proper parties, its necessary consequences must follow, let who may be affected. Sir R. Lloyd

But 'tis said that if it had been found by verdict that Mr. Murray had surrendered in due time, then the record might have been read in evidence against all persons, but that, as 'tis founded on Mr. Attorney-General's confession of the surrender, it ought not. This is a strange distinction. I would ask the gentlemen who make it whether this record by confession is not a full and complete record. Has not His Majesty's Attorney a right to confess it? No lawyer will say that he has not such a right by the laws of our land.

My lords, let me argue this matter, not on the principles of law only, but on those of reason, abstracted from the law, and thence see whether Mr. Murray is not as much discharged from his attainder or his attainder as much avoided by this confession of the King by his Attorney as he would be by verdict. Is the King the only person in the kingdom who shall be compelled to say a thing is not true which he knows to be true? Or is His Majesty the only person who shall be hindered from owning that to be true upon record which he and all the world knows is true?

'Tis a point of legal controversy betwixt the Crown and one of his subjects, and supposing it to have been a fact notorious that Mr. Murray (the defendant in that controversy) had come in and surrendered in due time, according to the late Act, would it not be absurd to say that the Crown's Attorney should be bound by law to say that he did not surrender, that is, shall be bound to deny and put to trial a fact which he knows is indisputably true and needs no trial? Yet this, my lords, must be the doctrine to be maintained by the counsel for the noble prisoner, or else they must agree that this record of the fact of surrender by confession of the Attorney-General is of equal weight with any other record whatsoever.

My lords, His Majesty has a right to the life of every person attainted, and would it not be a cruel law that should prevent him from admitting any facts to be true, which such person insists on for the saving of his life, when the same, within his own knowledge, strictly are so?

There is no doubt but that a transaction of this kind betwixt subject and subject is good, where each party to a controversy (plaintiffs and defendants) admit such facts on the record which they know the certainty of, and never, unless out of a spirit of perverseness, put them in issue. Where is the difference, since the Crown and Mr. Murray are as to that matter then in controversy the only persons who could be

Sir R. Lloyd parties? The capacity to be a witness is only a consequence naturally flowing from the avoidance of the attainder. Mr. Murray is not restored to his credit by act of favour, but a necessary consequence of law, and such as the Crown could not prevent, for as the attainder was the only cause of his loss of capacity to be a witness, when the force of that is taken off, that capacity is, of course, restored, not out of favour, but of strict right and by necessary consequence.

My lords, I would ask one question, namely, whether the counsel for the noble lord at the bar will say that Mr. Murray has this present day any attainder against him, or whether he can ever be called again to answer on the foot of that Parliamentary attainder, in which he was included?

If he cannot, as most certainly he cannot, then there is nothing now existing which takes away his testimony, and, as the present record is of a controversy betwixt the only proper parties to it, and is produced only to manifest a fact then depending, and then by the rules of law ascertained, it ought to be read.

Lord High Steward—Gentlemen of the House of Commons, I suppose you have no objection to the counsels replying?

Sir John Strange—No, my lords, provided we have the last word, which is our right.

Mr. Forrester Mr. Forrester—My lords, I shall take up the less of your lordships' time at present, because I admit most of the propositions laid down by the learned Managers, though, I conceive, that none of them have answered the objection we made to the reading of this record, which was the possibility of damage that might ensue to the noble lord at the bar. My lords, the reason is plain why we object to it, because the credit of the fact depending merely upon the confession of the Attorney-General, if it be received in the present case, it must be so in every other, whether the questions relate to property or any other matter, and if it be conclusive to the noble lord at the bar, it is equally so to every man in this land. My lords, I admit every case put by the learned Manager who spoke first as relative to criminal proceedings, but what we insist upon is, that this confession of the Attorney-General does only bind the Crown and the parties to it, but binds no other person. And, my lords, they have cited no authority to your lordships to prove it binding upon anybody else. My lords, it was said by the learned Manager that if Mr. Murray was brought a second time into any Court of justice he would have the whole benefit of this record, and thereby, my lords, prove himself not attainted by this Act of Parliament. And there is no doubt of it, because the confession is the Act of the Crown, who is bound by it.

They likewise say that any person claiming under Mr.

Murray might entitle himself under this record. My lords, I admit that also, because such person would have the same right as Mr. Murray himself; but, my lords, that does not prove that it can affect any other person. Mr. Forrester

My lords, it is admitted that a pardon would have taken off all objection, but I humbly insist that by this method the gentleman still continues liable to be considered as an attainted person in another part of the kingdom—I mean in Scotland—where this record would be no evidence, for should he escape from his present confinement to Scotland, and be brought into the Court of Justiciary to show cause why execution should not be awarded against him, as attainted by this Act of Parliament, his plea in the King's Bench, confessed by the Attorney-General, would be of no avail to him. He must make out the fact insisted on by other proof, which, being matter of evidence, might as well come out one way as the other, that he did not, as that he did, surrender before the 12th of July last, that he was taken by the King's forces as that he did surrender himself as the Act requires. Thus your lordships see in how high a degree the question affects the noble lord at the bar, and your lordships will be very tender how this gentleman's testimony is admitted in a case of this nature until both his competency and credit be established by better authority than the bare confession of the Attorney-General.

My lords, I mentioned several instances where a record of this kind would not be evidence against a third person. But, say the gentlemen, that is not the case here, because my Lord Lovat is not affected by Murray's attainder. The King, who had the sole right of prosecuting, and had an interest in the attainder, has declared him not to come within the Act of Parliament. But I must submit to your lordships that my Lord Lovat is affected by and concerned in the consequence of the attainder. He has a right to set aside the testimony of Mr. Murray if attainted, and that right of setting aside his testimony is equally strong as a right to an estate, or any other right given by law, and the same methods must be used to deprive him of the one as the other. My lords, it is said that this method of confession is the proper course, that it is daily made use of, and that the Attorney-General, upon a writ of error brought and errors assigned in fact or in law, may admit them to be so. But, my lords, in none of the cases quoted by the gentlemen is there any wherein the Attorney-General has by his confession made that error, which is not so. And although the party should assign errors and the Attorney-General admit them, yet would not that bind the Court to pronounce them to be errors if they appear otherwise. My lords, as so much time has been taken up already I will not repeat any of the former arguments, but shall con-

Mr. Forrester clude with an observation delivered down to us by one of the greatest and most upright judges that ever sat in this hall. I mean my Lord Chief Justice Vaughan, who tells us that the artificial reasoning of law ought never to take place against the principles of natural justice and equity. And, my lords, it is a principle of natural justice that a third person should not be prejudiced by the acts of others. The same learned judge concludes his paragraph by adding that in cases which depend upon fundamental principles from whence plain and natural conclusions may be drawn, millions of precedents are to no purpose. But, my lords, there has not been one single precedent laid before your lordships where the right of a third person may be affected in the manner now contended for, and as nothing of that kind has been attempted I beg leave to insist that the right of the noble lord at the bar to set aside this witness is as much a right as that he has to any part of his own estate, and submit therefore to your lordships whether they ought not to substantiate this testimony by some better proof than so weak a thing as a record founded only on the suggestion of the party confessed by the Attorney-General.

Lord High Steward—Gentlemen of the House of Commons, the counsel for my Lord Lovat have done with what they had to offer by way of reply. Would you say anything to it?

Attorney-General

Attorney-General—My lords, it is said by the counsel for the noble lord at the bar that they do not deny any proposition laid down by us, but that they deny the consequence of those propositions. My lords, a denial of the premises would be a denial of the consequences, but an admission of the premises here is an admission of the consequences. They now say all they desire to contend for is that the confession in this case does not bind a third person, and that they shall not by that lose their right to this objection. My lords, what is that objection founded upon? It is founded upon this supposition, that the witness called is an attainted person. If he is not attainted their objection fails, for they cannot say that he is an improper person to produce as a witness upon any other ground. If the record therefore destroys the pretence of an attainder, it proves his competency. Now, the counsel for the prisoner have not been able to point out or suggest any one instance or respect in which he can be said to be, or affected as, an attainted person unless for the present single purpose. And it would be very extraordinary to say that a person who can lose neither his life nor estate nor the purity of his blood as a person attainted of treason should be deemed attainted for no other purpose but to render him infamous. My lords, what is the offence by this Act? It is not high treason. The offence is in not submitting to justice, and the record shows that he did submit himself to justice. This is stronger as to that point than a pardon, because it avoids the original guilt. The gentlemen say that this record cannot be made use of in Scotland, and that, if the witness was brought before a Court of justice there for execution upon the foundation of this Act, he could never avail himself of this record. My lords, I deny that, and I take it to be clearly otherwise, for what would be the consequence if he could not? Much more than the gentlemen are aware of. For, by the same rule that this record could not avail him there, no verdict, no acquittal, in England could protect a man from another prosecution in Scotland for the same offence, and the prisoners who have already had, or hereafter shall receive, their trial either in England or Scotland for the late rebellion and been acquitted, may, by being sent into the other part of the kingdom, be tried a second time, and be put twice in hazard of their lives. As this is contrary to the laws of England, I believe it is equally so to the laws of Scotland as they stood originally, for I take it to be contrary to the first principles of all laws that, after a man is fairly tried for an offence by a Court that has full cognisance of the crime, he should be taken up and tried again for the same offence. No law will admit of it. But with respect to treason it is made clear by the statute of 7 Anne, which makes the law of treason and the manner of trying it in Scotland the same as in England. My lords, if the gentlemen ask how this record may be made use of there, the method is by producing the record or proving a true copy of it, as is done in case of the record of a judgment of any other Court. And the judges in Scotland will be bound by this record. My lords, the absurd consequences arising from the contrary doctrine appear at first sight, and are too many now to enumerate. The gentlemen say that a confession of an error in law will not be admitted in any Court. I do agree that it will not, because the Court must judge upon the whole of the record, and determine upon their own judgment and knowledge of the law, whether (supposing all the facts to be true) there is error or not. The reason is because that is their proper province, and they neither want nor can be bound by the confession of the Attorney-General. But it is quite otherwise as to matters of fact, which the Court do not *ex officio* examine into themselves; they must take them to be either as they are stated and admitted between the parties themselves or appear by the verdict of a jury. To apply this to the present case, Mr. Murray says that he did surrender and submit himself to justice according to the Act of Parliament. The Attorney-General, by command of His Majesty, admits that fact. As there is no issue joined, a jury can't be summoned to try it, and it is impossible the Court should try it themselves by examining witnesses. They have no commission for it, and the law gives them no such power. The fact, therefore, must

Attorney-General

Attorney-General be taken to be true, and, as it cannot be now controverted, your lordships must judge whether it don't clear him of any attainder.

Sir John Strange—My lords, I should not now have stood up to have taken up any more of your lordships' time, but in regard to what was mentioned by the gentlemen who are counsel for the prisoner, that this record cannot be made use of in Scotland, my lords, I will beg leave to put them in mind of the statute made in the seventh year of Queen Anne, which says that trials for high treason in that kingdom are to be the same as if they were here, and whatever benefit a person will be entitled to here they would be equally entitled to there. And therefore I would not have it now taken for granted that in such cases that should not be admitted as evidence in one part of the kingdom which is evidence in another part of it.

Lord Talbot—My lords, if the record is now to be read only to show that Mr. Murray surrendered himself within the time prescribed by the Act, I should have no objection to the reading of it, but, if it is to prove Mr. Murray to be a competent or an incompetent evidence, then I think it of that consequence that I hope some lord will move to adjourn to the Chamber of Parliament.

Lord High Steward—My lords, if any debate arises upon the point that has been argued at the bar, your lordships must adjourn to the Chamber of Parliament to debate and consider it.

Then the Earl Stanhope moved the House to adjourn to the Chamber of Parliament, and the House was adjourned accordingly, and, after about two hours, returned in the same order as before.[1] The House was resumed, and proclamation made for silence.

Lord High Steward—The lords adjourned to the Chamber of Parliament upon the question which had been argued before them, whether the record of the Court of King's Bench offered in evidence by the Managers ought to be read or not. And their lordships have come to the following resolution, with which I am ordered to acquaint the Managers for the House of Commons and you, my Lord Lovat. And it is this, that the Managers for the Commons be admitted to prove and give in evidence the record of the proceedings in the Court of King's Bench upon the *certiorari*, whereby the Act of the last session of Parliament for attainting John Murray of Broughton and

---

[1] The author of the pamphlet reprinted in the New Spalding Club's Historical Papers (above cited) states that during the proceedings in the chamber of Parliament Lord Talbot argued strongly against the admission of Murray as a witness, and was supported by the Earl of Bath.

others, unless they surrendered themselves by a certain day therein mentioned, was removed before that Court.[1]

ATTORNEY-GENERAL—My lords, we desire Mr. Tully may be called to prove the record.

LORD LOVAT—My lords, I told your lordships before that I would give you very little trouble, and now I am willing to give you still less. I acknowledge the record, and shall not give your lordships the trouble of hearing it proved.

LORD HIGH STEWARD—That will save the trouble of proving it, but it must be read. Does your lordship admit the record to be read without further proof?

LORD LOVAT—Yes, if your lordships please.

Then the record was read by the Clerk at the table, and was as follows:—

"Pleas before our Lord the King, at Westminster, of Hilary term, in the twentieth year of the reign of our Sovereign Lord, George the Second, by the grace of God, of Great Britain, France, and Ireland, King, Defender of the Faith—amongst the pleas of the King.

England.—"Our present Sovereign Lord the King hath transmitted to his beloved and faithful Sir William Lee, Knight, and his associates, justices of our said present Sovereign Lord the King, assigned to hold pleas before the King himself, his writ of *mittimus*, together with a writ directed to the clerk of his Parliaments, and the return made to the same, and also the record of a certain Act of Parliament of our said present Sovereign Lord the King, made at Westminster, closed in these words—

The Writ of Mittimus.—"To our beloved and faithful Sir William Lee, Knight, and others, his associates, our justices assigned to hold pleas before us, greeting. We send you enclosed in these presents, the tenour of a certain writ of *certiorari*, directed to our beloved Ashley Cowper, Esquire, Clerk of our Parliaments, together with the return endorsed upon the back of the said writ, and also the tenour of a certain Act whereof mention is made in the same writ, intituled an Act to attaint Alexander Earl of Kellie, William Viscount of Strathallan, Alexander Lord Pitsligo, David Wemyss, Esquire, commonly called Lord Elcho, eldest son and heir-apparent of James Earl of Wemyss; James Drummond, Esquire, eldest son and heir-apparent of William Viscount of Strathallan; Simon Fraser, Esquire, eldest son and heir-apparent of Simon Lord Lovat; George Murray, Esquire, commonly called Lord George Murray, brother to James Duke of Athol; Lewis Gordon, Esquire, com-

1 Mr. Justice Foster, in "Crown Cases," page 50, observes, after discussing the law on the matter, that Murray's evidence in the Lovat trial was properly admitted.

John Murray

monly called Lord Lewis Gordon, brother to Cosmo George Duke of Gordon; James Drummond, taking upon himself the title of Duke of Perth; James Graham, late of Duntroon, taking on himself the title of Viscount of Dundee; John Nairn, taking upon himself the title or style of Lord Nairn; David Ogilvie, taking upon himself the title of Lord Ogilvie; John Drummond, taking upon himself the style or title of Lord John Drummond, brother to James Drummond, taking on himself the title of Duke of Perth; Robert Mercer, Esquire, otherwise Nairn of Aldie; Sir William Gordon of Park, John Murray of Broughton, Esquire; John Gordon, the elder of Glenbucket; Donald Cameron, the younger of Lochiel; Dr. Archibald Cameron, brother to Donald Cameron, the younger of Lochiel; Ludovick Cameron of Tor Castle; Alexander Cameron of Dungallon; Donald MacDonald of Clanronald, jun., son to Rhonald MacDonald of Clanronald; Donald MacDonald of Lochgarie; Alexander MacDonald of Keppoch; Archibald MacDonald, son of Colonel MacDonald of Barisdale; Alexander MacDonald of Glencoe; Evan MacPherson of Clunie, Lauchlan MacLauchlan of Castle Lauchlan, John MacKinnon of MacKinnon, Charles Stewart of Ardshiel, George Lockhart, eldest son and heir-apparent of George Lockhart of Carnwath; Lawrence Oliphant, the elder of Gask; Lawrence Oliphant, the younger of Gask; James Graham, the younger of Airth; John Stewart, commonly called John Roy Stewart; Francis Farquharson of Monalterye, Alexander MacGilivrae of Drumaglash; Lauchlan MacIntosh, merchant at Inverness; Malcolm Ross, son of Alexander Ross of Pitcalny; Alexander MacLeod, son to Master John MacLeod, advocate; John Hay, portioner of Restalrig, Writer to the Signet; Andrew Lumsdale, otherwise Lumsdain, son to William Lumsdale, otherwise Lumsdain, writer in Edinburgh; and William Fidler, clerk in the Auditor's office in the Exchequer of Scotland, of high treason if they shall not render themselves to one of His Majesty's justices of the peace on or before the 12th day of July, in the year of our Lord 1746, and submit to justice. The tenour of which said Act we, for certain reasons, have caused to be brought before us into our Chancery. And we do hereby command you that, having inspected the tenour of the said Act, you do further cause to be done thereon that which of right, and according to the law and custom of England, you shall see fit to be done. Witness ourself at Westminster, the 10th day of February, in the twentieth year of our reign."

The tenour of the said writ of *certiorari*, and the return made to the same, and also the tenour of the said Act, in the said writ mentioned, follow in these words:—

The Writ of Certiorari.—"GEORGE the Second, by the grace of God, of Great Britain, France, and Ireland, King, Defender of the Faith, to our beloved Ashley Cowper, Esquire, Clerk of our Parliaments, greeting. We being willing (for certain reasons) to be certified concerning the tenour of a certain Act by us made and enacted, by and with the advice and consent of the Lords spiritual and temporal, and Commons in Parliament assembled at Westminster, the 17th day of October, in the nineteenth year of our reign, intituled An Act to attaint Alexander Earl of Kellie (*and others as above*) of high treason if they shall not render themselves to one of His Majesty's justices of the peace on or before the 12th day of July, in the year of our Lord 1746, and submit to justice, do command you that, immediately after the receipt of this writ, you do distinctly and openly send before us into our Chancery the tenour of the said Act, with all things touching the same, as fully and perfectly as the same now remains in your custody, together with this writ. Witness ourself at Westminster the 7th day of February, in the twentieth year of our reign."

The Return.—"The execution of this writ appeareth in a certain schedule to this writ annexed, as within I am commanded, Ashley Cowper, Esquire, *Cler' Parliamentor.*' In the Parliament held at Westminster, the 17th day of October, in the year of our Lord 1745, and in the nineteenth year of the reign of our Sovereign Lord George the Second, by the grace of God, of Great Britain, France, and Ireland, King, Defender of the Faith; and there continued by several adjournments until and unto Wednesday, the 4th day of June, 1746, by the consent of the Lords as well spiritual as temporal, and of the Commons, and by the assent of the King's Majesty then present, the following statute (amongst others) was ordained, enacted, and established, to wit, An Act to attaint Alexander Earl of Kellie (*and others as above*) of high treason if they shall not render themselves to one of His Majesty's justices of the peace on or before the 12th day of July, in the year of our Lord 1746, and submit to justice.

"WHEREAS Alexander Earl of Kellie (*and others as above*), on or before the 18th day of April, in the year of our Lord 1746, did, in a traitorous and hostile manner, take up arms and levy war against his present Most Gracious Majesty within this realm contrary to the duty of their allegiance, and are fled to avoid their being apprehended and prosecuted according to law for their said offences, be it therefore enacted by the King's Most Excellent Majesty, by and with the advice and consent of the Lords spiritual and temporal, and Commons in this present Parliament assembled, and by the authority of the same, that if the said Alexander Earl of Kellie (*and others as above*) shall not render themselves to one of His Majesty's justices of the peace on or before the 12th day of July, in the year of our Lord 1746, and submit to justice for the treasons aforesaid,

John Murray then every of them the said Alexander Earl of Kellie (*and others as above*), not rendering himself as aforesaid, and not submitting to justice as aforesaid, shall, from and after the said 18th day of April, in the year of our Lord 1746, stand and be adjudged attainted of the said high treason to all intents and purposes whatsoever, and shall suffer and forfeit, as a person attainted of high treason by the laws of the land, ought to suffer and forfeit. And every of the said justices of the peace are hereby required to commit every of them the said Alexander Earl of Kellie (*and others as above*) so surrendering himself, to prison for the said high treason, there to remain till he shall be discharged by due course of law, and thereof immediately to give notice to one of His Majesty's principal Secretaries of State.

"I, Ashley Cowper, Clerk of Parliaments, by virtue of the writ of our said lord the King of *certiorari* to me directed, and to these presents annexed, do certify that what is above written is the true tenour of the Act of Parliament abovesaid in that writ expressed. In witness whereof to this schedule I have set my seal and subscribed my name. Dated the 9th day of February, in the twentieth year of the reign of our said lord the King, and in the year of our Lord [1747].

"Ashley Cowper."

Plea of John Murray.—"And now (that is to say) upon Thursday next after the Octave of the Purification of the Blessed Virgin Mary, before our said present Sovereign Lord the King at Westminster, cometh the said John Murray in the said Act named, under the custody of the Lieutenant of the Tower of London, by virtue of His Majesty's writ of *habeas corpus ad subjiciendum*, &c., into whose custody he the said John Murray had been before committed upon the account aforesaid, being brought to the bar here in his own proper person, who is committed by the Court to the said Lieutenant of the said Tower of London, charged as a person attainted of high treason by virtue of the said Act, and being asked by the Court here, at the instance of Sir Dudley Ryder, Knight, Attorney-General of our said present Sovereign Lord the King, who, for our said present Sovereign Lord the King, in this behalf prosecuteth, if he the said John Murray hath or knoweth of anything to say for himself, why the Court here should not proceed to award execution against him thereupon, he the said John Murray, for plea, saith, that it is very true that he is one of the persons in the said Act named and intended, to wit, the person therein designed and described by the name, style, and addition of John Murray of Broughton, Esquire, against whom, with the rest of the persons therein named, designed, and described, the said Act was made, passed, and intended for, and on account of the high treason therein mentioned, and thereby supposed to have been committed against our said present Sovereign Lord the King, but for further plea he saith, that long before the 12th day of July in the said Act mentioned, to wit, upon the 28th day of June then last past, he the said John Murray, at the city of Edinburgh, in the shire of Edinburgh, did, in due manner and according to the directions, and agreeable to the true sense, intent, and meaning of the said Act, render himself to the Right Honourable Andrew Fletcher, Esquire, Lord Justice-Clerk of Scotland, being one of His Majesty's justices of the peace in the said Act mentioned and intended for that purpose (he the said Andrew Fletcher having then and there full power and authority, by virtue of the said Act, to admit him the said John Murray to make such render of himself to him the said Andrew Fletcher, as aforesaid), and that he the said John Murray was, upon the said 28th day of June, in consequence of such render, as aforesaid, committed by him the said Andrew Fletcher to prison for and on account of the said high treason, according to the directions, and agreeable to the true sense, intent, and meaning of the said Act, and that he the said John Murray hath, ever since his said render and commitment, as aforesaid, until now, remained and continued, and still doth remain and continue, a close prisoner upon the account aforesaid, and this he is ready to verify and prove, as the Court shall award. With this further, that at the time of his said render and commitment, as aforesaid, he the said John Murray was, and ever since hath been, and yet is, willing and desirous to take his trial and submit himself to justice, pursuant to the directions and agreeable to the true sense, intent, and meaning of the said Act."

Confession of the Attorney-General—"And the said Sir Dudley Ryder, Knight, Attorney-General of our said present Sovereign Lord the King, who, for our said present Sovereign Lord the King, in this behalf prosecuteth, having heard and considered the said plea of him the said John Murray, by him now pleaded in form aforesaid, he the said Attorney-General for our said present Sovereign Lord the King saith that he doth not in any wise deny any of the matters of the said plea alleged, but doth now here in Court for and on behalf of our said present Sovereign Lord the King, and by the special order and command of our said present Sovereign Lord the King, admit and confess the same to be in all respects true. Whereupon it is considered and adjudged by the said Court here that the said plea of him the said John Murray, for him so above pleaded, as aforesaid, and also the said confession of the said Attorney-General by him so made of the said plea, as aforesaid, be recorded, and that he the said John Murray be remanded to the said Tower of London, under the custody of

John Murray the said Lieutenant, to be by him there kept in safe custody until he shall be from thence discharged by due course of law."

ATTORNEY-GENERAL—My lords, we desire that Mr. Murray may now be sworn.

LORD LOVAT—My lords, I desire leave to falsify the record, and to prove, by witnesses, that Mr. Murray did not surrender himself within the time prescribed by the Act of Parliament.

ATTORNEY-GENERAL—My lords, what the noble lord at the bar now insists upon is that he shall be at liberty to falsify the record, by showing, by witnesses, that Mr. Murray did not surrender himself according to the Act of Parliament, but I must submit it to your lordships that there is no ground whotsoever to admit the prisoner to go into that kind of evidence, because this is a record which, according to the known rules of proceeding, cannot be falsified, since it is a proof of a thing transacted in a Court of justice, before whom it was properly cognisable, and who alone in this part of the United Kingdom could hear it and had power to record it, and I therefore must insist that it is out of the power of any person whatsoever to contradict that record.

LORD HIGH STEWARD—My Lord Lovat, the Managers insist that it appearing by matter of record that Mr. Murray did surrender himself according to the Act of Parliament that matter cannot now be falsified.

LORD LOVAT—My lords, I must beg that since it is a point of law your lordships will be pleased to hear my counsel to it.

ATTORNEY-GENERAL—My lords, as to its being a question of law, whether the noble lord at the bar shall be at liberty to produce witnesses to falsify that record, to be sure, my lords, it is a question of law, because it cannot be said to be a question of fact, but it does not follow as a consequence, because the noble lord at the bar says that he has a point of law to submit to your lordships, that therefore your lordships should permit his counsel to argue it, for it is still in your lordships' judgment whether you have any doubt concerning it, and it is apprehended that this is too plain a case to admit of any doubt with your lordships, and therefore that you will not permit counsel to argue it, as the consequence can only be delay, and an indulgence of this kind in matters of no doubt would put it in the power of a prisoner to protract his trial and keep your lordships sitting as long as he pleased.

SIR JOHN STRANGE—My lords, I beg leave to have it clearly understood what it is that the noble lord at the bar insists upon, whether it be to prove by witnesses that Mr. Murray was not in custody within the time prescribed by this Act of Parliament, or that Mr. Murray did not surrender himself and submit to justice within that time.

A Reproduction of the Official Admission Pass for the Trial of Lord Lovat.

Lord Lovat—I put it upon that strict word that he did not surrender himself. John Murray

Lord High Steward—Lord Lovat, does your lordship desire to be heard by your counsel to that point?

Lord Lovat—Yes.

Mr. Forrester—My lords, it would ill become me in the station of counsel for the noble lord at the bar to decline arguing any point which he thinks may be of service to him. The question now made by the noble lord is singly this, whether he shall be at liberty to adduce witnesses, *viva voce*, to falsify the contents of this record, that is, to prove that Mr. Murray did not surrender himself within the time prescribed by the Act, which being closely connected to the former objection, I can at present, and until I have time to consider the question, do little else but what would be extremely indecent in me, repeat a great part of what I troubled your lordships with in the morning, and which is now over-ruled. But, my lords, the debating this point may lead to the consideration of another, and, indeed, a very material one, which is whether evidence of his being taken prisoner by the King's forces will make it a surrender within the legal construction of the Act of Parliament so as to warrant his plea and the Attorney-General's confession contained in the record, and this I shall, in point of law, beg leave to deny upon the authority of Lord Duffus' case and several other cases. Your lordships are to determine whether we shall be heard to these points or not, but, if I am at liberty to speak to them, as they are both questions of great difficulty, I must beg some further time for preparing myself and laying my thoughts together, since at this hour of the night, and unprepared as I am, it is impossible to argue them so fully as my duty requires, as the noble lord has a right to expect from me, and as your lordships have a right to expect matters to be debated at your bar.

Lord Lovat—My lords, I am so very weak and infirm, and have been obliged, in order to attend in obedience to your lordships' commands, for two days together to be up by three o'clock in the morning, I must therefore beg that your lordships will indulge me with a later hour and some respite, otherwise I shall die at your bar.[1]

Attorney-General—My lords, I did apprehend from what the noble lord at the bar said, that the point he wanted to submit to your lordships was whether he should not be at

[1] In the words of Horace Walpole, "It hurt everybody at old Lovat's tryal, all guilty as he was, to see an old wretch worried by the first lawyers in England, without any assistance but his own unpracticed defence."

John Murray liberty to bring witnesses to prove that Mr. Murray did not surrender himself within the meaning of the Act, but something has dropped since from the prisoner's counsel as if they meant to show that Mr. Murray did not in fact surrender, but was taken prisoner before the time given by the Act to surrender, and that this would not in point of law be a surrender within the Act. My lords, that is a question totally different from the former. It is one question whether he may be admitted to prove that he did not surrender according to the Act of Parliament, and another what would be the legal effect of his being apprehended previous to the time appointed. They are two entirely distinct questions, and whether they shall be admitted to argue the former is now for your lordships' consideration, but as to the latter it is a matter subsequent, and not now to be considered.

Then the Duke of Newcastle moved to adjourn to the Chamber of Parliament, and the Lord High Steward went back to his chair, and the House was adjourned accordingly.

The lords and others went back in the same order as before, and the House being resumed in the Chamber of Parliament, after debate

Ordered that this House will proceed further in the trial of the said Lord Lovat to-morrow at eleven of the clock in the forenoon, and a message was sent to the House of Commons by Mr. Eld and Mr. Thurston to acquaint them therewith. *Ordered* that the Lieutenant of the Tower of London, or his deputy, do take back the said Lord Lovat, and bring him again to the bar of this House in Westminster Hall, at eleven of the clock in the forenoon to-morrow.

Third Day—Wednesday, 11th March [1747].

About eleven of the clock in the forenoon the lords and others came from the Chamber of Parliament, in the same order as on Monday last, into Westminster Hall, where the Commons and their Managers were in the seats prepared for them respectively as before, and the lords took their places in the Court, and the Lord High Steward in his chair.

LORD HIGH STEWARD—The House is resumed. Is it your lordships' pleasure that the judges have leave to be covered?

LORDS—Ay, ay.

Then the Sergeant-at-Arms made proclamation for silence, and afterwards the following proclamation:—

SERGEANT-AT-ARMS—Oyes! Oyes! Oyes! Lieutenant of the Tower of London, bring forth your prisoner Simon, Lord Lovat, to the bar, pursuant to the order of the House of Lords to you directed.

The Deputy Governor of the Tower brought the prisoner to the bar in the like manner as before, and then he kneeled down.

LORD HIGH STEWARD—Your lordship may rise.

LORD HIGH STEWARD—My Lord Lovat, your lordship thought fit yesterday to insist upon it that, notwithstanding the record produced by the Managers for the House of Commons of Mr. John Murray of Broughton's having surrendered himself within the time and according to the terms prescribed by an Act of Parliament made in the nineteenth year of His Majesty's reign, your lordship should be permitted to give evidence by witnesses *viva voce* that Mr. Murray did not surrender himself within the time prescribed by that Act. To this kind of evidence the Managers for the House of Commons objected, because, as they alleged, it was giving evidence to contradict a fact which was verified by a record of the highest nature, and that therefore you should not be permitted to enter into such proof, whereupon you desired that your counsel might be heard to that matter as a point or question of law. Against this the Managers thought fit to object that it was no doubt or question of law at all, that the law of the land was full and clear and settled in this point, and that therefore your lordship ought not to be heard by your counsel to it. The House has taken all these matters into consideration in the Chamber of Parliament, and hath come to the following resolution, with which they have directed me to acquaint you, and it is this, that the counsel for the Lord Lovat be not permitted to argue that parole evidence should be received to prove that John Murray of

John Murray Broughton did not surrender himself according to the Act made in the last session of Parliament in that behalf, in contradiction to the record of the Court of King's Bench, produced by the Managers for the Commons.

The Lord High Steward asked leave to go down to the table, which was granted.

Lord High Steward—Gentlemen of the House of Commons, you may proceed.

Mr. Noel—My lords, we now desire that Mr. Murray of Broughton may be sworn.

Lord Lovat—My lords, I did object against Mr. Murray's being examined as a witness. Your lordships have been pleased to over-rule that objection, and I now submit that Mr. Murray may be examined, if you please.

John Murray called in and sworn.

Lord Talbot—My lords, I desire to ask Mr. Murray some questions for the sake of forming my own judgment in the matter, but, if it is improper that they should be asked, I submit it to your lordships.

Lord High Steward—My lords, the ordinary method of proceeding in these cases is that, where a witness is produced, he is to be sworn in chief, unless there be some objection to his competency, and then he is to be sworn upon a *voire dire.* After he is sworn in chief, the party who produces him asks him such questions as he thinks proper, after which the other party is at liberty to cross-examine him either to the matter of fact concerning which he has been examined, or any other matter whatsoever that shall tend to impeach his credit or weaken his testimony, provided the questions that are asked him are such as the law allows. So in this Court, after the Managers have produced any witness and have finished their examination of him, the prisoner has liberty to ask him whatever questions are proper, and it is most regular that, after both sides have gone through with their examinations of the witness, any of your lordships should ask him what questions you shall judge proper.

Mr. Noel—Mr. Murray, you will be pleased to attend to the questions that shall be asked you. Give your answers distinctly, and raise your voice as much as you can, that my lords may hear you. My lords, the first thing I desire of this witness is that he may give your lordships an account when was the first time that he heard of any invitation to the son of the Pretender to come into Scotland, and from whom he heard it.

Witness—My lords, to the best of my remembrance, in the month of February, 1741-2, when I was at Edinburgh, I had there occasion to see my Lord Traquair, who told me that there were several gentlemen, to the best of my memory the prisoner at your lordships bar, my Lord Perth, my Lord John Drummond, Sir James Campbell of Achenbreck, and Mr. John Stuart, brother to Lord Traquair, had employed one Drummond of Bochaldie to go from Scotland to Rome to assure the Pretender of their zeal for his service, and that they would be ready and willing, as soon as sufficient assistance could be had from France, to appear publicly in arms for him. And at the same time, he said that he had given Drummond a memorial signed by those persons—I think seven of them in number—to Cardinal Fleury, expressing their attachment to the Pretender and desiring him to procure assistance from the Court of France, and at the same time this Drummond carried with him a list of all the people that by those gentlemen were supposed to be ready and willing to join in the Pretender's service. John Murray

Lord Lovat (interrupting)—My lords, your lordships will be pleased to consider that what this gentleman says is only hearsay evidence, which should not be admitted before your lordships, as it gives you a bad impression of a man. I am now trying for my life and fortune, and hope your lordships will consider it.

Mr. Noel—My lords, I am so far from differing from the noble lord at the bar in this respect, that I did understand the witness was speaking only what he had heard from my Lord Traquair.

Attorney-General—My lords, the Managers do know and desire that your lordships will distinguish between evidence that does, and evidence that does not, affect the prisoner at the bar. The witness was giving an account by way of introduction, which will be material for your lordships' consideration. I beg leave to say it is impossible for a witness, in his giving an account of a transaction, to speak nothing but words that alone will affect the prisoner, and therefore this, though it does not affect the prisoner, may be proper to introduce that which he has to say that may affect him. What he now says is only giving an account of a plot or conspiracy entered into by several persons which did afterwards bring on the rebellion.

Lord High Steward—My Lord Lovat, the Managers do admit that what has been hitherto said by the witness under examination does not affect you, and they desire now to offer it only as evidence of a conspiracy in general, which, if they do not apply to your lordship by particular evidence, will not affect you.

Lord Lovat—My lords, as I said before, it gives a bad impression.

Lord Coke—My lords, I apprehend that we are right in going into this kind of evidence, because in the preamble to our Articles of Impeachment we set forth the general conspiracy.

John Murray SOLICITOR-GENERAL—My lords, what has hitherto been said is not evidence against the noble lord at the bar, and, God forbid, that he should be affected by anything that is not strictly evidence against him. And therefore it is fit that the view with which the evidence is offered should be fully understood. The preamble to the Articles of Impeachment asserts that ever since the breaking out of the war, and particularly in 1743, many persons have plotted and conspired with the enemy to procure an invasion of this kingdom by a foreign force, and to raise a rebellion at home. The first Article charges Lord Lovat to have been one of those conspirators. It is necessary, therefore, by general evidence to show that there have been such plots and conspiracies as the Commons assert, and then to affect the noble lord at the bar by proper evidence with being concerned in those plots. This method of proceeding is not new, but the established course. Upon the impeachment of the Lord Viscount Stafford a general evidence was given of the conspiracy, which was declared not to affect him, but as introductory only. The like was done upon the trials at law of the persons accused of having been in the same plot. The same method was allowed as proper, and liable to no just objection in many trials after the Revolution. In the reign of the late King, upon the trial of Layer, the like method was pursued. General evidence was given of a plot which did not directly affect him. I dare answer for the gentlemen who manage this prosecution that no one of us will urge against the noble lord anything which is not brought home to him by strict and legal proof. If we should he is safe in your lordships' judgment, which will distinguish general from particular evidence.

Then the witness was directed to go on with his narrative.

WITNESS—My lords, I mentioned to your lordships that at the same time that Drummond went over to Paris he carried with him a list of all the gentlemen in Scotland who it was supposed by those who signed this memorial were ready and willing to join them. But this list I take rather to be a general list of the Highlands of Scotland, nor do I imagine there could be any reason to think that the great number of people there mentioned could appear in favour of the Pretender. My Lord Traquair at the time of his informing me of this told me that Drummond was then in Edinburgh, and proposed that I should have a meeting with him. Accordingly, I had a meeting with him, and he repeated to me much the same thing that I have repeated to your lordships, said he had been extremely well received by the Cardinal, to whom he had delivered the memorial given him at Edinburgh; that he expressed much satisfaction, and was very sanguine, and had the Pretender's interest very much at heart, and, provided he could get sufficient assistance and assurance from those who are called the Pretender's friends in England, that then he would send over the troops required—the number was 3000 men—to be landed in Scotland, 1500 at or near Inverness, so as immediately to join with the clan of the Frasers; the other 1500 were to be landed on the west coast, near Cameron's of Lochiel, who was to take the command of them upon him, and to raise the people of Argyllshire. At the same time a body of 10,000 or 12,000 men were to be landed as near London as they possibly could. That at the same time Drummond was in Edinburgh he sent for Cameron, and when they met he repeated what had passed and the success he had at Rome and Paris, and assured them that, provided he could have assistance in England, the scheme might be put in execution in autumn following. After a week's stay in Edinburgh, Drummond went to London. I do not remember to have heard anything more concerning this matter till the August following. This was, to the best of my memory, the end of March or beginning of April that he left Edinburgh. John Murray

LORD HIGH STEWARD—What year was it in?—1742. We call it so in Edinburgh.

You begin the year in Scotland on the 1st of January?—Yes.

WITNESS—My lords, in the autumn following, when I was at my Lord Traquair's house in the country, he told me he understood by Drummond that Cardinal Fleury proposed sending a body of Swedish troops into Scotland, thinking they might be more agreeable to the people there, as they were Protestants, than French or Irish brigades would be, but, at the same time, said he thought it would be necessary that a person should be sent from Scotland to be deputed to solicit those troops from Sweden in conjunction with the person whom the Cardinal should employ. My Lord Traquair thought that I should go on that account. But I think it was rather Drummond's than my Lord Traquair's proposition.

When was this?—In August, 1742. I refused to comply with this. From which time I do not remember to have heard anything for six months, and about that time my Lord Traquair and Cameron of Lochiel,[1] at Cameron's house, did show me a letter written by Drummond from Paris wherein he said that upon his return to France he had represented the thing to the Cardinal in such a light as engaged him to promise that in a short time he would land the troops in Scotland as proposed. There were several other circumstances in the letter which I cannot now remember. So far as I can say that letter, in general, when it was read to me seemed very extra-

---

1 See Biographical Notes, p. 301.

John Murray ordinary, to think that an affair of such consequence as the invading these kingdoms and raising a civil war in the country was to be undertaken by a few people and by such kind of management. I said I apprehended it was a scheme of Drummond's to keep up a spirit of party in this country, and to make himself useful to the gentlemen who employed him, and that there was no such thing intended by Cardinal Fleury. My Lord Traquair determined that it was then necessary to know the real state of the case, and he desired I would go to Paris for that purpose. I at first did not comply with it. I did not care to execute it, nor did I agree to it till several weeks afterwards. I was then coming to London, and in January I came up, but upon the road I understood that Cardinal Fleury was dead.

When was this?—In January, 1743, by the Scotch style. I stayed some short time in London, and from thence I went over privately to Paris, and by means of one MacDonald, the banker, I found out Drummond. He carried me that evening to one Mr. Sempill, who is there called my Lord Sempill, and was the person employed by the Pretender to manage his affairs in France. They both joined in lamenting the death of the Cardinal, and said that had he lived in all probability the scheme would have been executed that spring, that the reason why it was not was owing to the Marshal Maillebois having orders from France to march his army towards Hanover instead of the coast of Flanders, as the Cardinal intended, but that the Cardinal had been so extremely sanguine in the Pretender's interest that he had given all his papers, memorials, and the like to M. Amelot, the then Secretary for Foreign Affairs. I proposed to see M. Amelot, and accordingly I went to Versailles, where I stayed two or three weeks. I was first presented by Drummond to Sempill, and had an audience of M. Amelot, whom I told I had been sent from Scotland by the persons who had signed the memorial which I mentioned to your lordships, and who were concerned in it, to know whether the King of France, his master, was willing to put the scheme in execution. He told me that Mr. Sempill had acquainted him with the reason of my coming. And thereupon he went to the King of France, and told him of it, and upon that I desired to know what answer he had from the King of France. The answer he gave me was that the King told him that I might assure those gentlemen that he had the interest of their master as much at heart as they, and that as soon as he had an opportunity he would put the scheme they proposed in execution. With this answer I returned to Paris, where I only stayed two nights. At first I observed that M. Amelot seemed very desirous to have such assurances from England as the Cardinal had required, and he applied to Drummond and Sempill on that head. When I left Paris Mr. Drummond determined to come over. I set out from Paris, and came privately to London. The reason of Mr. Drummond's coming over was to collect those assurances which had been expected from England. John Murray

What time was this?—It must have been the end of March or beginning of April.

In what year was it?—In 1743. I stayed but a few days in London after my return, and Mr. Drummond desired me that as soon as I arrived in Scotland I would acquaint my Lord Traquair of his being come to London, and the reason of it, and desired that he would come and assist in procuring the assurances from the Pretender's friends. Upon my return to Edinburgh I stopped at York, where I met with the late Lord Perth, who then was at York, and I acquainted him with what had been done, who seemed extremely dissatisfied at it. I soon afterwards came to Edinburgh, and soon after my arrival there I met Lord Traquair, whom I acquainted with Drummond's being come over, and that he desired his lordship to go to London to assist him in his intended purpose. His lordship went with that intent (as he said) in about two weeks after, about the beginning of April, to the best of my remembrance. On Lord Traquair's return to Scotland in autumn he acquainted me that he had several meetings with Drummond, and that he had endeavoured to get as many assurances as he could from the Pretender's friends, at least such as he thought so, (the persons he named were Lord Barrymore, Sir John Hinde Cotton,[1] and Sir Watkin Williams Wynne); that he had several meetings with these several persons, and that Sir John Hinde Cotton seemed extremely shy and unwilling to converse or meet on the Pretender's affairs, and none of them were willing to give any such assurances under their hands and seals as were given by the seven in Scotland. The same summer one Butler was sent from France to know the state of the Jacobite party in England.

Lord Talbot—My lords, I object to the witness's proceeding to give evidence which does not relate to the point in question. He has mentioned the names of several honourable gentlemen on a very extraordinary occasion which does not at all relate to the trial of the noble lord at the bar. He is calumniating the characters of several gentlemen who are my worthy friends. And therefore, if it is insisted that he should proceed, I think it will be worth our while to adjourn to the Chamber of Parliament to consider how far it shall be permitted.

1 A Jacobite and a protegé of the Duke of Argyll, whose patronage to him caused suspicion of his (Argyll's) loyalty to the House of Hanover.

LORD HIGH STEWARD—Gentlemen of the House of Commons, you hear what is said by the noble lord. It is objected that the witness is going on to give evidence of a fact not relating to the noble lord at the bar, but to other persons, and that this is an improper kind of evidence, and ought not to be given.

ATTORNEY-GENERAL—My lords, we did not examine the witness to those particular facts which he has mentioned that do not relate to the noble lord at the bar, but, in giving an account of the facts inquired into, he has himself entered into that kind of narrative, but, as it is only what he heard my Lord Traquair say concerning other particular persons, we do not insist on his proceeding in his hearsay account of what concerns those gentlemen.

MR. NOEL—My lords, what the witness has dropped in respect of the honourable gentlemen he has named does not affect them at all. It is nothing more than a relation which he had from my Lord Traquair, and not from any matter arising within his own knowledge. And, my lords, I may venture to assure your lordships, for myself and all the gentlemen concerned in this prosecution, that we will not ask the name of one person immaterial to the present trial. And therefore I must submit it to your lordships whether the witness should not be suffered now to go on, and that for the future, when he comes to any transaction of that kind, he should not name any persons till he comes to the noble lord at the bar.

LORD HIGH STEWARD—Your lordships hear what is mentioned by the Managers, that they agree that the witness, in mentioning these transactions in general, should not name any persons till he comes to the noble lord at the bar.

WITNESS—I was directed that when I came to be examined here I was to give a narrative of the springs, the rise, and progress of the late rebellion, as well as what related to the noble lord at the bar, but if I have committed an error I readily submit to your lordships' correction.

EARL OF CHOLMONDELEY—As the witness says he was directed to give a narrative with regard to the whole rise and progress of the rebellion, I beg he may be asked by whom he was directed?

LORD HIGH STEWARD—My lords, I did not, at this distance, hear the witness use the word "directed," but understood him only that he was brought here to give an account of the rise and progress of the rebellion. Possibly it might escape me.

EARL OF CHESTERFIELD—I did not hear the word "directed," but I should be glad to have it cleared up.

LORD HIGH STEWARD—Mr. Murray, when you spoke last of your giving a narrative of the rise and progress of the rebellion did you make use of the word "directed" or not?—

WITNESS—My lords, this is the first time I ever spoke in

public. I may have committed an error. I cannot say whether I made use of the word "directed" or no.

Earl of Cholmondeley—My lords, I had no other intention in the question but to know the meaning of the person who spoke the words, whether he apprehended that the general question asked him by the Managers was a direction to him, and whether that was what he meant.

Witness—My lords, some days after my examination in the Tower by the Honourable Committee of the House of Commons, a gentleman, who I believed was their secretary, came to me to take a further examination, and to ask me as to any other matter that had occurred since my last examination. Some days after that he told me that I should be called here before your lordships upon the trial of my Lord Lovat, and that at the same time it would be expected that I should give an account of the rise and progress of the rebellion in general.

Sir William Yonge—My lords, now the witness at the bar has explained what he meant by the word "directed," I hope your lordships will have no ill impression of the Managers from anything that may have dropped from the evidence. And, my lords, I beg leave to assert that no direction has been given to Mr. Murray by the Managers, and that they neither have given, nor will give, any direction to any witness whatsoever. My lords, we well know that it does not become us to do anything of that kind, nor have we done it. So far from it that when we first examined the witness at the bar we examined him solely to the point of the conduct of the noble lord at the bar. My lords, we did afterwards determine among ourselves that, as it was our duty to lay before your lordships that conspiracy wherein the noble lord at the bar appeared to have acted a part, we did therefore give Mr. Murray notice that he would be examined before your lordships to that point. My lords, we never had any information from him on that subject, and this is the first time I ever heard him give an account of this general conspiracy. My lords, we were so careful in our examination of the witness in the Committee that I well remember the question being asked him by the worthy Manager who sits near me, and it was in the most general terms that we could conceive, in order to let your lordships into the knowledge of this matter. And your lordships will observe, through the whole course of this proceeding, that the utmost candour will be made use of by the Managers in their examination of the witnesses, and that they will put no leading questions to them, but general questions, and such as they are to answer upon oath, and according to the truth.

Earl of Cholmondeley—My lords, I beg leave to say that I did not conceive that the Managers, in their examination of witnesses, made use of the least direction or authority whatso-

John Murray ever. I have the greatest sense of their candour and fairness. It is my opinion of them, and of the whole body by whom they are deputed, and it was upon that principle I proposed my question to the witness.

LORD TALBOT—My lords, I pray that the witness may be asked whether he is upon this occasion a voluntary or an involuntary evidence.

ATTORNEY-GENERAL—My lords, the Managers are now prosecuting for the whole Commons of Great Britain. They are prosecuting upon the foundation of evidence for a treason of the greatest magnitude. There is now a witness at your lordships' bar, whom they are examining to prove that treason, and, while they are so, I hope they shall not be interrupted. There is no doubt but when they have done with the examination of the witness, if my lords think proper to ask him any questions, your lordships have a right to do it, but we are now examining the witness on behalf of the prosecution, and we hope we shall have liberty to go through with it, and then your lordships will permit him to be examined by anybody else. But, my lords, at present we are in possession of the witness, and we beg we may have liberty to go on.

EARL STANHOPE—My lords, I beg the question proposed may be asked, or that we may adjourn to the Chamber of Parliament.

LORD HIGH STEWARD—My lords, the rule for the examination of witnesses in this Court, in either House of Parliament, and everywhere else, is that, if a witness is produced by a prosecutor or plaintiff, they have a right to examine him first, but, if any objection is made to the questions asked by the prosecutors, whether they are Managers of the House of Commons upon an impeachment or counsel upon an indictment, the objection is first to be considered, and if the objection prevails, and is allowed, then the question is not to be asked. But all questions that are asked, whether touching the matter of fact to be tried or the credibility of the witness, are to be asked at the proper time. The party who produces the witness has a right to go through the examination first, and then the other side cross-examines him, and after that is over the judge asks him such questions as he thinks proper, unless, as I said before, there be any objection to the questions or any doubtful matter arises that wants immediately to be cleared up. The same method is to be observed here, and the reason of it, my lords, is that, unless your lordships observe this method, you will be in perpetual confusion.

EARL STANHOPE—My lords, the question now proposed arose from an expression that just now dropped from the witness.

The witness proceeded in his evidence.

WITNESS—My lords, this Butler, whom I mentioned to your

lordships, was for some time in England during that summer that my Lord Traquair was in London, when, to cover his intention, he bought up a number of horses for the King of France's use, and expressed himself so well pleased with the encouragement he had from the Pretender's friends in England that he said that, as soon as he went over, he would represent it in such a light to the King of France, his master, as he imagined would induce him to send the succours desired. Upon his return to Versailles, where Drummond went with him, Drummond went to Rome, as he said, at the desire of the French Court, to persuade the Pretender to send his son to France. Accordingly, he did persuade him to do it, but Drummond returned to France before the Pretender's son left Rome. After Drummond went to Paris he came to London, to acquaint the friends of the Pretender in England that the King of France was determined to send over a body of troops in the spring. This came to my knowledge by two letters from Drummond, the one written from Paris in December and the other written from London. The first letter he sent over was not forwarded in time to my Lord Traquair, but when Drummond returned, he found it lying there. He enclosed it in another letter, and they both came to my Lord Traquair's hands at Edinburgh. In the first letter he mentioned his intended journey to Rome. In the second he mentioned his return to Paris, and the reason of his coming to London, and that he found the Pretender's friends there very backward; that with difficulty he had persuaded them to agree to the French's landing. In this letter there were a great many contradictions and absurdities in regard to the landing a body of troops in Scotland and England at the same time. It particularly mentioned that Earl Marischal was to command the 3000 men that were to come from Dunkirk to Scotland, and at the end of the same letter he says, "but I do not know how my Lord Marischal is to be equipped"; which, with other circumstances, determined us to write a letter to Drummond, to desire him to explain himself. My Lord Perth and my Lord Traquair showed me the letter and desired I would prepare a letter to Drummond, desiring him to explain himself. Accordingly, I wrote a letter in their presence, which they both signed, and I believe—I cannot say positively—that I signed it myself. This letter, as my Lord Traquair said, was sent to London, to be forwarded to Drummond at Paris, but the person to whom the letter was delivered in London, wrote to Drummond, and told him that such a letter was in his hands, and desiring to know whether he should send it to him at Paris or not. Drummond said in answer that he should not send the letter lest it should be intercepted, but desired he would burn it.

John Murray

Mr. Noel—What time was this?—In the month of January, 1743.

According to what style?—It was in the year 1743, not long before the intended embarkation at Dunkirk.

When was that?—To the best of my memory, in 1743.

Be pleased to recollect the time, because it is very material. —It was about two months before the intended invasion.

Lord High Steward—You may possibly recollect the time from the other circumstances. Do you remember the year of the battle of Dettingen?—I believe it was in the year 1743.

Mr. Noel—How long was this after the battle of Dettingen that you speak of, or was it in the January before, or after the battle?—I believe it was the January following.

Mr. Noel—It would be proper for you to recollect from these circumstances, if you can, whether it was in January, 1743, or 1744, according to the Scotch style?—January, 1744, by the Scotch style.[1] In two weeks after there was another letter came from Drummond, consisting of a few lines only, wherein he said that in all probability before that letter came to hand the Pretender's son would be landed in England, with the troops under the command of Marshal Saxe. From this time to July following, so far as came to my knowledge, there were no accounts from abroad. It was proposed to me, as I had then an intention that summer of going to Flanders to see the army, that I should go the length of Paris, to know in what situation their affairs then stood. The first time I declined it, but was afterwards brought to agree to it, upon being showed a letter of Mr. Sempill, wherein he made a number of excuses for the intended invasion's not taking effect, and desired fresh assurances from Scotland, and that endeavours should be used in England, upon which I was pressed to go. We then thought it extremely necessary that we should know upon what footing things really were. I accordingly came to London, and from thence I went to the army in Flanders, stayed only a few days there, and then I went to Holland, and from thence, in a private manner, to Paris. When I went to Paris I was introduced to the Pretender's son by Drummond and Sempill. The first time I saw him, so far as I can remember, there was nothing essential passed. I desired to see him in private, which I accordingly did the next day. My design was to represent to him that I thought the persons employed by him at Paris were imposing upon him, and that they had no other intention but to serve themselves, to keep up the spirits of the party in Britain, and thereby make themselves necessary to the party. With this intent I explained the letter written by Drummond, endeavoured to show the contradictions in it, and that Drummond

[1] See footnote on p. 6.

endeavoured to serve himself, and not him. He said at that **John Murray** time he was determined to come to Scotland.

Whom are you speaking of?—The Pretender's son. He mentioned the association, and said he was determined to come into Scotland, and did not doubt but the King of France intended an invasion in the spring, but that he was then preparing for it, and intended to execute it as soon as the campaign was over, and that, if he did not do it before, he was determined to come into Scotland. I endeavoured to show him that the undertaking was desperate, and that he could not propose having above 4000 or 5000 men, supposing all the friends he could expect should be ready to join him, and it was seen afterwards that he had not so many; notwithstanding which he insisted upon coming. I was so much against it that I spoke to Sir Thomas Sheridan, a person who lived with him for many years, and told him of the danger of such an attempt, and that it would be the ruin of many families, and the destruction of the country. Sir Thomas Sheridan said he would endeavour to persuade him against it, and, upon his arrival in Scotland, told me he had, but to no purpose. After staying a few days in Paris, I returned to Scotland, where I gave an account, not to all, but to some of the persons concerned in the memorial, of what had passed, and everybody but my Lord Perth declared against the Pretender's son coming into Scotland, upon which I wrote a letter to him, representing the opinion of his friends in Scotland, and setting forth the bad consequences of such an undertaking. This letter I committed to the care of a gentleman who was going to London, in the month of January, 1745 (Scotch style). This was neglected to be forwarded, and was returned to me in the month of April following. I, notwithstanding, endeavoured to forward that letter several times, and there having been occasion to send from the west of Scotland, by my Lord Perth's means, the packet was sent to France, but could not arrive in time before the young Pretender set out. In June I received a letter from the young Pretender, wherein he said he was fully resolved and determined to come into Scotland, and that he was to set out in June, and proposed to come to the west of Scotland, and appointed signals for his landing. Upon the receipt of this I sent it by an express to my Lord Perth, desiring him to forward the letter, or the contents of it, to Cameron of Lochiel's house, because I began to reflect that it would be necessary some methods should be taken to inform the gentlemen in the Highlands, who were supposed to be ready, and to see if they approved of it. Upon that I went to Cameron's house of Lochiel, who told me that he had sent his brother, Doctor Cameron,[1] with a copy of that letter to the noble lord at the bar. Doctor Cameron returned the next

[1] See Biographical Notes, p. 301.

John Murray day and said he had accordingly gone to the noble lord's house, that he had told him he had business of consequence to impart to him, and that he had taken his promise to mention nothing of what was to pass between them, upon which he showed my Lord Lovat a copy of the letter. I cannot say these were the very express words, but it was to this effect, upon which the noble lord at the bar declared that it was a foolish and rash undertaking, and that he should not land, and, if he did, that none of the men would join him. And this is what Dr. Cameron told me, and it was the opinion of all those of the Highlands that he should not land, but return. They desired I would write a letter of the opinion of those gentlemen to the Pretender, and of the bad situation the country lay under, and to desire as their utmost wishes that he would return to France, which letter I did write. I wrote two of them, and committed them to the care of a gentleman, and which letters he received upon the island.

Who received them?—The Pretender's son. The first notice I had of his landing was by an anonymous letter that I received about a week after. It did not say expressly that the Pretender was landed, but, by the words of it, I judged it was so. I was desired to come to the house of Lord John Drummond. There I understood that he was landed, and, in a little time after, joined him at the house of MacDonald of ,[1] upon the west coast. About ten days after that he erected a standard in a place called Glengarry, where he was joined by the Camerons, the MacDonalds of Keppoch,[2] and a few of the MacDonalds of .[3] With those he marched to the house of Macdonald of Glengarry. There was a gentleman of the name of Fraser of Gortuleg, whom he there applied to, and the laird of Lochiel, as being persons acquainted with the noble lord at the bar. Lochiel told me there was such a person there, that there were two commissions granted by the old Pretender in favour of the noble prisoner, which he desired the young Pretender to send. Accordingly, I asked him for those commissions. He said they were in a trunk with other papers which he had left up the country by reason of the approach of General Cope, who was then expected in the country, but desired, at the same time, that Mr. Kelly might write a commission, whether it was of lieutenant-general or no I cannot say, but I saw the commission written by Mr. Kelly. I was also to make an apology to my Lord Lovat why the original commissions had not been sent.[4] Whether

1 Kinlochmoidart.
2 Under Alexander MacDonald of Keppoch, who was killed at Culloden after showing great heroism. See interesting notes in Mr. Andrew Lang's "History of Scotland," vol. iv. (Appendix).
3 Clanranald.
4 Murray makes similar statements in his "Memorials" (p. 333).

Third Day.

I made the apology verbally to Mr. Fraser of Gortuleg, or **John Murray**
whether I did it by letter I cannot say. I did not see it put into the packet or sent, and I did not inquire whether he had received it, because I did not doubt of the thing. After the arrival of the Pretender's son at Edinburgh nothing material relating to the noble lord at the bar happened between the last time I spoke of and the time of his arrival there. Some time after the battle of Prestonpans, Cameron of Lochiel came to me and told me that one Hugh Fraser, who had been clerk or servant in some capacity to my lord at the bar, but was then an attorney at Edinburgh, was a fit person to send to my Lord Lovat to desire him to send out his clan. I agreed that he should go, and he had instructions so to do. Whether I wrote to my Lord Lovat by Hugh Fraser or no I cannot recollect; very probably I did, but cannot say positively I did. The next thing in regard to the noble lord at the bar that happened was upon the return of the Highland army from Derby to Glasgow. There this Hugh Fraser came to Glasgow, and this was the first time I ever saw him after he left Edinburgh. He came at that time, as he said, from Perth, and was sent by the Master of Lovat to procure arms for a few men which he had under his command, and to know where he should join the army. It was then proposed to write to my lord the prisoner at the bar to endeavour to persuade him to appear publicly in favour of the Pretender. This was agreed to, and the letter was written by Cameron of Lochiel, and signed by him, Cluny MacPherson,[1] and myself. This letter was delivered to Hugh Fraser with one that was written by the Pretender's son himself, a letter of compliment. I do not remember that there was any commission, or anything sent, save these two letters and a letter which I wrote to the Master of Lovat, which was sent by Hugh Fraser. If there were any more sent, it is more than I can remember. Hugh Fraser at the same time asked if there had not been a patent granted by the old Pretender to create my Lord Lovat a duke, to which Lochiel answered that if there had been any such granted it was in the hands of his father, John Cameron, who was then at Dunblane. It was for this reason that I did not address this letter or packet to my Lord Lovat, but left that to the management of Hugh Fraser, if he should find the patent creating my Lord Lovat a duke when he should come to Dunblane. Hugh Fraser, at the same time, answered that my Lord Lovat had made a proposal that Lord John Drummond (it was either he or my Lord Strathallan, who then commanded at Perth, or perhaps both of them) should march with

1 See Biographical Notes, p. 303.

John Murray the troops under his command to Inverness, and bring with him some more people of his own. The proposal, if it came from my Lord Lovat, as Hugh Fraser said it did, was a very judicious one, and my Lord Lovat must have desired it to cover his country from the troops then under Lord Loudoun's command, as my Lord Lovat had left Inverness some little time before that. And the next thing that occurs to me with respect to the noble lord at the bar is, that, while I was at Inverness, I received a letter from the hands of Fraser of Gortuleg. This, he said, came from my Lord Lovat, but was written, to me seemingly, in some clerk's hand. This letter was produced, but, one paragraph of it being very remarkable, I asked Gortuleg the meaning of it, and he said that my Lord Lovat was desirous of having that patent creating him a duke, which he expected some time before. I said that I had no such patent, and told him that he ought to put my Lord Lovat off from any such expectation.

You said that this letter came to you at Inverness. Pray, when did it come to you?—It was in the end of February, or beginning of March.

In what year?—In the year 1746.

According to the Scotch style?—Yes. I had no occasion either to see or hear from the lord at the bar from that time for some weeks after the battle of Culloden, and, when in company with Lochiel, I was informed that my Lord Lovat was in that country, and that he lay at the place called Glenmely, and there was a boat sent to bring Lord Lovat to the other side of the lake, where a meeting had been proposed by Lochiel. I believe that meeting was accidental in regard to the noble lord at the bar, because Lochiel expressed great satisfaction that they should have Lord Lovat's advice and assistance. Another reason which induced me to think so was that Cameron sent a servant with two horses to procure wine and spirits from Beaufort, Lord Lovat's seat, there being neither in that part of the country. Cameron of Lochiel, with some others and I, came to the place where Lord Lovat was. He was then upon the side of a lake.

What is the name of that place?—I heard it is called Morell, or Morlaig, but whether that is the real place I cannot say. The first night we were together, or rather the only night that I was there, I do not remember that anything material passed, but, in general, we told my Lord Lovat that there was a meeting to be the next day, and that we should be very proud of his advice. Accordingly, the next day there was a meeting of about twelve or thirteen gentlemen, where we did desire the noble prisoner at the bar to give his opinion. There were present Cameron of Lochiel, Barisdale, John Roy Stewart, old

Glenbucket, Dr. Cameron, and a nephew of Keppoch's, and some few others. I cannot particularly remember them all. John Murray

You have not said whether the noble lord at the bar was there?—Yes; he was at that meeting.

Did you see him there?—Yes; I proposed in that meeting that my Lord Lovat should give his opinion. My Lord Lovat said that in his opinion the only thing for the gentlemen there to do was to raise a competent number of men to protect their country, families, and cattle, and endeavour to defend themselves.

To protect their country from what?—To protect or defend their country from the King's forces, who were then at Inverness. There were no other forces. The number of men then proposed to be raised was 3000 or 3500; a compact body, whom it was easy to find provisions for. This proposal was agreed upon, and the particular number of men that each gentleman should bring was agreed upon. Among the others, the clan of the Frasers was named for 400, to be commanded by the Master of Lovat, but my Lord Lovat himself would not answer for his son, but required Lochiel to answer for him. My Lord Lovat said that he was an old man, and not able to do anything himself, and that he would not answer for his son's abilities, but desired they would let Lochiel answer for him, and that he did not doubt but he would do it. Lochiel accordingly answered for him. There was a sum of money distributed there, and, I think, about seventy louis d'or given to the servant of my Lord Lovat to carry to his son as ten days' pay for the 400 men which he was to bring out.

Was my Lord Lovat present or not at the time you speak of when that money was given to his servant?—I cannot say positively whether my Lord Lovat saw the servant get the money, but it was distributed by a person who was my clerk, and my Lord Lovat was at the other end of the room.

Was it in the same room?—Yes; my Lord Lovat was in the same room that the money was distributed in. There were several persons there to whom money was paid.

Can you name the servant who received it for Lord Lovat?—No. I think he was called the steward of my Lord Lovat.

From whence came the money?—From France.

What was the sum that came from France?—Thirty-five thousand louis d'or at that time. [Proclamation was made for silence.] After this meeting was over, so far as I can remember, I, with Lochiel, crossed over to the opposite side of the lake, and my Lord Lovat, as I understood and he himself proposed, remained there all that night. Four or five days after I had occasion to be at a place called Glendesherrie,[1]

[1] Glen Dessary.

John Murray when my Lord Lovat was on the opposite side, at a house formerly belonging to the brother of Lochiel. I went there to my Lord Lovat the next day, with no intention to speak to him of business, but upon seeing his servant to whom the money was given I asked him when he intended to send the servant away with it. He said he should go that day or the next, and then called a person who was called his secretary, and desired him to write a letter to the Master of Lovat in my name, but what were the contents of the letter, or that I saw it, I cannot remember, but I took it, in general, that the contents of the letter were to give the Master of Lovat the reason why the money was sent. I did not then stay above an hour or two with my Lord Lovat, but returned to Lochiel. What was agreed upon at the meeting and proposed to be done did not take effect so soon as was expected; neither, indeed, was there above 400 or 500 men on the whole that met about ten days after the time first proposed. That handful of men were two days at Lochiel's house before the King's troops marched northwards in pursuit of them. Upon intelligence that the King's troops were on their march two men were ordered out to see what number of men there were, and if we could make any head. They saw a great number of men, upon which we retired to the head of the lake, when it was determined that we should disperse, and every one do the best he could for himself. From thence I went into the country that belongs to the Clan Ranald, where I received a few lines by a young man who said he was servant to my lord at the bar, wherein he said it was necessary for him to have a watch or guard to attend him of twenty-two men and a lieutenant, and desired that I might send him money to pay those men twenty days' pay, I think it was. I do not remember that I wrote any answer to this letter, because I had no pen, ink, or paper, but I gave the servant fifteen louis d'or, having then not much money, and desired him to give it to my Lord Lovat. After that I had a message from the noble lord at the bar, by one Bishop MacDonald,[1] desiring that I would see him before I left the country, but, so far as I remember, it was nothing farther than compliments. Since that time till yesterday I never had the honour to see the noble lord at the bar, nor had any letters from him, nor corresponded with him.

Were the fifteen louis d'or that you sent to my Lord Lovat part of the French money that was landed there?—Yes; it was part of the French money.

---

[1] Lovat's companion in the island on Loch Morror. See Father MacDonald's "Moidart."

Third Day.

My lords, he has told your lordships already that the men that were to be raised were to defend the country against the King's forces. Now, I beg to know whether it was mentioned at that meeting where these men were to march or where to rendezvous?—It was proposed that the general rendezvous should be near the house of Keppoch. Lochiel's people, Barisdale, and Clanranald's were to have rendezvoused upon the lake, about two miles above Lochiel's house, and then to proceed to the general rendezvous by Lochiel's. John Murray

Attorney-General—Pray, had you any blank letters from the young Pretender after he came to England or that were sent to you?—I had letters that were sent to me, and were not directed, but left with me to deliver to such persons as I thought willing to support the cause.

Please to give an account to my lords what those letters were and the import of them.—I do not remember the exact number of letters, but I did receive a number of letters. They were not directed, but left to be directed to such people in Scotland as were thought the best friends to the Pretender and proper to cultivate a party for him in the country.

Please to give an account to my lords at what time these letters were delivered to you and by whom.—There were some of the letters, either two or three of them, that I brought with me from Paris, and others were sent to me, but who delivered them to me I cannot particularly remember.

Please to mention to my lords who delivered you the letters you received at Paris.—The young Pretender himself.

What were the directions he gave then?—There was a credential attached to every letter, and they were to be delivered to such persons as were disposed to promote his interest in the country.

And what was the meaning of the credential? Was it signed by the young Pretender or by anybody?—Yes, by him.

Please to give an account to my lords to whom you delivered those letters.—One of those letters, together with the credentials, I delivered at Edinburgh to the laird of MacLeod.

Please to give an account to my lords to whom you delivered any other of those letters.—There was another of those letters sent to Sir Alexander MacDonald.[1]

You say it was sent. Then you did not deliver it yourself? —No.

Do you know whether it was received or no?—No; I never heard it was.

Please to give an account to my lords of any other of these letters which you delivered.—The other letters, so far as I

1 Of Sleat, who declined to join the Prince.

John Murray can remember, were put into the custody of Lochiel, who was the proper person to send them to the people who were to have them. As to those who had them I cannot distinctly name them all, but my Lord Perth had one, I am sure.

What time was it that those several and respective letters were delivered?—They were delivered in the months of November and December, 1744.

Was that after the time you came from Paris?—Yes, it was.

Were they delivered in order to forward the intended invasion from France, which you gave an account of before?—They were designed by the Pretender as letters to be given to people who were most his friends to know whether or no they were ready to join him, and the credential annexed was for them to forward his interest in the country.

Mr. Noel—You have told us that a computation was made at that meeting of the number of men that could be raised. Please to give an account to my lords whether any particular person, and who, mentioned the number of troops that might be raised?—It was the general opinion that 3000 men should be raised, and my Lord Lovat said that such a number would be sufficient.

Did he mention any proportion of men that were to be raised by the Master of Lovat?—He mentioned 400 Frasers to be raised by the Master of Lovat.

Lord High Steward—Gentlemen of the House of Commons, have you done with the examination of this witness?

Attorney-General—My lords, we have done with this witness at present.

Lord High Steward—My Lord Lovat, the Managers for the House of Commons declare that they have done with this witness at present. Will your lordship ask him any questions?

Lord Lovat—My lords, I beg leave to tell your lordships that I am the most incapable man of the three kingdoms to make my defence, because, as I mentioned to your lordships before, I want both my sight and my hearing, and I therefore begged of your lordships to allow my counsel to examine my own witnesses and counter-examine the witnesses against me, but your lordships were not pleased to allow that. Your lordships are much more capable of examining the witnesses than I am, and therefore I shall refer it to your lordships, and beg leave to sit down. I will ask this witness no questions now.

Lord Talbot—My lords, I beg leave to ask this question. (To witness)—Did you voluntarily surrender yourself to the King's forces, or were you taken by the King's forces?—I did not intend at that particular time to surrender myself, and I presume it is not necessary for me to say now whether I ever did intend it or not, but at the time that the party of dragoons came to the house where I then was, the doors were shut, and I was in such a position as that I could have killed two of them myself, but I rather chose to submit myself and throw down my arms.[1]

My lords, the question that I ask is, whether he did or did not voluntarily surrender himself, and whether his intention was then to submit to the King's forces?—I did say that it was not my intention then particularly to submit myself. It was not my intention till I saw the dragoons.

Did you use any means to make your escape afterwards?—I never did.

Have you ever taken the oaths of allegiance and fidelity to the King?—I never did.

Did you never take those oaths, or oaths of the same nature, to anybody else?—No.

Sir William Yonge—My lords, we hope the witness shall not be obliged to answer questions of this nature. It is a question that tends to accuse himself of high treason.

Lord Talbot—My lords, I did not ask him any question to accuse himself of any crime which he had not himself before confessed, and, as he had before accused himself of that crime, this may be said to be a continuation of it, but cannot be said to be a fresh accusation. I should not have asked him the question if he had not before accused himself.

Lord High Steward—My lords, there is no reason to spend your lordships' time upon this point, for the gentleman has already answered the question.

Lord Talbot (to witness)—Are you at present a prisoner, or under confinement? (Murray)—Yes, I am, and have been ever since I came to the Tower.

Are you, upon this occasion, a voluntary evidence?—I should be glad to have the meaning of that question explained, and to know what is meant by a voluntary evidence.

Lord Talbot—My lords, the meaning of the question is, whether the witness is not an evidence, in hopes of a pardon, and whether, if he himself was pardoned, he would be an evidence at all.

Attorney-General—My lords, on behalf of this prosecution I must oppose that question being asked. The question, as I understand it, is whether the gentleman under examination is a witness in hopes of a pardon, and whether he would be a witness if his pardon had been obtained. My lords, this is a question, as I apprehend, not proper to be asked, because it

[1] The *London Gazette* of 5th July, 1746, contains an account of Murray's arrest at Polmood, Peeblesshire.

John Murray is no question as to any matter of fact at all, but only a question concerning what the witness would do upon supposition of a fact which has not happened. I do not apprehend that any question can be asked of a witness but what concerns a matter of fact, not what a witness would or would not do upon a future contingency. The question must tend to a fact, and the witness either is, or is not, capable of giving evidence; but, my lords, to ask questions of this kind is entering into the recesses of a man's heart, which nobody has a right to inquire into, and it is such a sort of question as I do not remember ever to have heard asked in a Court of justice, and perhaps it is what the witness is incapable of answering, for, till the event happens, he cannot say what he would or would not do. We therefore hope your lordships will think that this is an improper question, and that the thoughts, inclinations, or wishes of a witness ought not to be inquired into here, where matters of fact only are to be tried.

Lord Talbot—My lords, I asked the question for this reason, that I might know with what view his evidence was given, and so judge of the credibility of it. (To Murray)—Do you believe your life depends upon the conformity of the evidence that you shall give on this trial to former examinations which you have undergone?

Sir William Yonge—My lords, I presume, without troubling your lordships with any argument, that all that has been said by the worthy Manager who spoke last, to oppose the former question is much more applicable to the question now proposed to be asked, and therefore, without adding anything more why this question should not be asked, I shall submit it to your lordships, and humbly apprehend it is our duty to oppose the asking of this question.

Lord High Steward—Gentlemen of the House of Commons, do you oppose this last question being asked?

Attorney-General—I should beg that the question might be a little more fully explained; I do not remember to have ever heard the like.

Lord Talbot—My lords, the question to me seems extremely clear and plain, and I beg leave to repeat it to your lordships, and if you have any difficulty about it, I will readily submit. My lords, the question is whether you (the witness under examination) believe your life depends upon the conformity of the evidence you shall give upon this trial to your former examinations. I suppose the gentleman was examined as well by the Managers for the House of Commons as their Clerk.

Lord Halifax—My lords, all that the noble lord who asked this question means by it, is comprehended in the former question that he asked, and that is—whether the witness is a voluntary witness or not.

Third Day.

Lord High Steward—The witness said he did not know what was meant by the word "voluntary," and desired it might be explained. John Murray

Lord Talbot—My lords, I urged the other question only as explanatory to that, and all that I meant by it was to know whether the witness at the bar is governed by hope or fear?

Witness—My lords, if your lordships please, I will answer the question. I am upon my oath, and obliged to tell the truth, and I say that possibly, and very probably, had I been in another situation in life, I should not have appeared before your lordships as a witness against the noble lord at the bar.

Lord Talbot—My lords, I am extremely well satisfied with the gentleman's answer to the question, and it gives me a much better opinion of his evidence than I had before.

Lord Barrington—My lords, I beg leave to ask this witness a question explanatory to the last question. If you had a full pardon, and were at this bar, and were obliged to answer upon oath, would you not give the same evidence that you now have given?

Lord Talbot—My lords, I apprehend that is only asking the witness whether he would come here voluntarily and perjure himself.

Lord Barrington—My lords, the question I proposed is not whether the witness would come voluntarily to this bar, but whether, if he had a full pardon, and was brought to this bar (as every man may, whether free or not free), if he had a free pardon, and was compelled to give evidence, whether he would give the same evidence upon oath as he has now given?

Lord Talbot—My lords, this is a question that no man alive, in this gentleman's circumstances, can possibly answer.

Witness—My lords, I beg leave to answer the question. If I was in such a situation as has been now stated to your lordships, and brought here with a pardon in my pocket, but brought here to give evidence against the noble lord at the bar, I would not add to, or impair a syllable of, or vary in the least from, what I have now said.

Lord High Steward—Is the evidence you have here given upon your oath true?—Yes, it is.

Sir John Strange—My lords, I beg leave to ask this gentleman a question relating to a transaction which has been lately mentioned. He was asked whether he did or did not surrender himself voluntarily to the King's forces. His answer was that he could, he believed, have despatched two of the dragoons, but that he did not make any resistance. Now, I desire he may acquaint your lordships whether that was, or was not, before the 12th day of July last?—It was upon the 28th day of June last.

My lords, I desire to know whether or not, from that time till now, he has not been in custody, and amenable to justice.

John Murray

WITNESS—I have been in custody ever since that time.

ATTORNEY-GENERAL—My lords, I desire to know whether he was then brought before any judge or justice of the peace, and whom.—I was carried to my Lord Justice-Clerk in Edinburgh the day I was taken into custody.

Were you then committed, or no, by the Justice-Clerk?—I was that night committed by the Justice-Clerk to the castle of Edinburgh.

On the 28th of June?—Yes.

Did you continue in the castle of Edinburgh from that time till you were sent for from thence to London?—I did continue there till I came to London.

Did you ever make, or endeavour to make, any escape all that time?—I never did.

A LORD—Did you, at any time since you have been in custody, receive any hopes or promise of a pardon?

WITNESS—I have never, since I have been in custody, been promised a pardon, nor have heard a word of pardon mentioned to me since I was in custody.

Then the witness, by the direction of the Lord High Steward, withdrew.[1]

Hugh Fraser

SIR RICHARD LLOYD—My lords, the next witness we beg leave to produce is Hugh Fraser of Dumballoch (who was called in and sworn).

Proclamation for silence.

SIR RICHARD LLOYD—Do you know the noble lord at the bar?

HUGH FRASER—Yes, I do.

How long have you known him?—I have known him many years ago.

Do you remember whether you were sent for at any time, and when, to the house of my Lord Lovat?—I got a message from Peter Fraser of Belladrum. It was he that brought me the message.

From whom was that message brought?—From Lord Lovat, as he told me.

When was that?—I think it was about the end of September, 1745.

Were you sent for at any other time about this part of the year?—I did not go upon the first message.

Did you go upon the second?—Yes, I did.

What distance of time was there between the first and second message?—I believe there might be a day or two thereabouts, to the best of my memory.

When you came to my Lord Lovat's house, pray, what

1 Prince Charles wrote to his father from Paris on 28th April, 1747—"Poor Ld. Lovat is executed by ye Rascality of Jn. Murray."

passed between my Lord Lovat and you?—Upon my word, I cannot remember particularly. Hugh Fraser

Do you remember whether any particular paper was shown you at that time, and what it was?—No; I don't remember seeing any particular paper at that time.

Was there any paper read or talked of by anybody at that time relating to the Pretender's son?—There was a conversation there about that time, and, to the best of my remembrance, it was about the troubles in the country.

Did you ever see or read a paper said to be a manifesto from the Pretender's son, or did you ever hear it read?—Yes, I did.

Where did you hear it read?—I read that paper in a back room at my Lord Lovat's.

Who gave it you to read?—I cannot remember who gave it me to read.

Do you remember who first showed it you?—My Lord Lovat directed some person in the room to give it me. Whether it was Robert Fraser or not I cannot say.

Do you remember to have heard my Lord Lovat say anything of that paper?—I have heard him say it was a pretty well written paper.

I beg you'll inform their lordships whether at that time you heard any conversation about the clan of the Frasers.—Upon my word, I cannot remember whether I did or not at that particular time.

Did you about that time hear anything about the clan of the Frasers?—I heard them spoken of several times.

Did you hear it spoken of at any of those times who was to command them?—Yes; I heard that the Master of Lovat was to command them.

Who did you hear say that?—I heard my Lord Lovat say it.

To what purpose did my Lord Lovat say he was to command them?—It was to go south.

To join whom?—To join the Pretender.

What did he call the Pretender, by what name?—He called him "the Prince."

Were there any other of the clans expected at that time to join the Frasers to march southwards?—I heard my Lord Lovat say that he was uneasy about an answer to a letter which he or his son had written to the Isle of Skye.

From whom was that answer expected?—From the laird of Macleod.

Did you hear my Lord Lovat say what sort of answer he expected or hoped for?—By all that I could learn of the letter it was a letter desiring that Laird Macleod's men should come and join them.[1]

---

[1] Macleod of Macleod declined to join the Pretender.

O

Hugh Fraser A letter from whom desiring that Macleod's men might come and join them?—I cannot be positive whether it was from my Lord Lovat or his son.

From whom did you learn the contents of the letter?—I heard my Lord Lovat speak of it.

Was any application made to you concerning the raising of the men or their joining?—My Lord Lovat asked me what number of men I could raise.

Of what clan were you to raise them?

Sir William Yonge desired that the last question might be repeated, which was done, and the witness made the same answer as before.

Sir Richard Lloyd—What men did he speak of and what clan?—The Frasers. There are no other men in that part of the country.

With what view were these men to be raised?—To join the rest of the clan of the Frasers, which were to be commanded by the Master.

Did you tell my Lord Lovat what number of men you thought you could raise?—No; upon my word, I did not.

Did you hear my Lord Lovat say anything about the raising of his clan, and who was to raise them, or did raise them?—I heard my Lord Lovat say that the Master was the man that was to raise the clan and to head them.

Was he to do that by his own power or inclination, or by advice from anybody else?—That is a thing I can give but an opinion upon.

What is your opinion upon it?—That the Master could not have raised the men except my Lord Lovat had countenanced the thing, and it had been done by his permission.

Have you heard my Lord Lovat say anything in regard to his son's being active or not in raising the men?—I have heard my Lord Lovat say more than once that his son was very slow in raising of the men.

And did he say so as praising him for his slowness in raising the men or as in dispraising him?—I thought it was to dispraise it.

Did you hear my Lord Lovat say anything of his own abilities or inabilities to raise men and head them?—I have heard my Lord Lovat say that he was a tender, infirm man, and not able to go about those things himself.

Have you heard him wish himself younger?—I have heard him say he wished himself younger that he might go and command the men himself.

Command them in whose service?—In the Pretender's service that he was talking of.

Do you know what they mean by the fiery cross in that country?—I remember the fiery cross when it went about my father's ground. It was a long pole, with two cross stricks burnt at the fore-end, and the design of it was to raise the men and to threaten them with fire and sword that their houses should be burnt if they did not rise. Hugh Fraser

Was the fiery cross carried through the clan that you know of or have heard?—I have heard that it was carried through the clan. I did not go about all the country.

You say you saw it at your father's?—Yes, I did.

By whose order is it that those crosses are usually carried about to raise men in the several clans?—Order is given by the person that wants the men.

Is it not always ordered by the chief of the clan? Does anybody but the chief of the clan take upon them to order it?—I am an entire stranger to that. I never saw the thing before.

When you were at Lord Lovat's house at the time you speak of did you observe any tents there?—Yes; I observed some bell tents there.

What number of them?—I cannot be positive whether two or three.

Were they new or old ones?—They were new. They seemed to me to be new.

What arms were upon them?—My Lord Lovat's crest was upon them.

Did you see any colours?—I saw colours at the house of Castle Downie.

What arms were upon them?—There was upon one large pair of colours my Lord Lovat's arms, to the best of my memory.

Do you know if my Lord Lovat saw them?—I can't tell.

Was anything said to you, and by whom, to induce you to join the Pretender more than you have given an account of already?—There were several things dropped in conversation, but it is such a distance of time that I cannot remember what they were.

Was any person present there besides yourself and my Lord Lovat when you were at his house?—There were several persons there.

Did any conversation then pass or not about throwing off the mask?—Yes. Mr. Alexander Macleod, and several others of the country there, were speaking about the Pretender, and Mr. Alexander Macleod said that much depended upon my Lord Lovat's throwing off the mask, or words to that purpose.

To whom did he say these words?—To my Lord Lovat.

What answer did my Lord Lovat make to that?—My Lord Lovat I saw take off his hat and put it upon the ground, and heard him say, "There it is then."

Do you remember any particular healths that were drunk then?—I have heard the Prince's health drunk several times there at the table at Castle Downie.

Hugh Fraser Was my Lord Lovat present or not, or did he drink it?—My Lord Lovat was present at the table.

Do you know of any force that was made use of in that clan to make them rise?—I know there went parties about.

Did you heard my Lord Lovat say anything about his expectation which side would prevail?—I heard my Lord Lovat say he was sure the Prince would prevail.

Whom did he mean? Whom did he call the Prince? Whom was he speaking of?—Of the young Pretender.

Do you know of any subsistence that was given by Lord Lovat to anybody?—I have heard my Lord Lovat say that he had ordered his factor to give an allowance, monthly or weekly, to the wives and children of the men.

Of whom?—Of those that went with his clan.

Upon what occasion did they go?—Those men that were to go south with the young Pretender.

Was it all, or only those that were to be in his clan?—There were a great many in the country that perhaps had nothing to support their families in their absence when they were gone south.

Do you know of any letter that was shown you from the young Pretender dispensing with my Lord Lovat's personal presence?—Yes; I remember to have read the letter.

Who gave it you to read?—My Lord Lovat.

From whom was that letter?—He said it was from the Marquis of Tullibardine.

How was the letter signed?—The letter was signed "Athol," in large letters.

What were the contents of it?—I don't remember the particular contents of it. To the best of my memory, it appeared to be in return to another letter which had been sent by my Lord Lovat, and it was to excuse his personal attendance.

Whose personal attendance?—My Lord Lovat's.

His attendance where?—To go south in the Pretender's service.

Lord High Steward—Where is that letter?—I don't know.

You say my Lord Lovat gave it you?—Yes.

What did you do with it?—I returned it again.

To whom did you return it?—To my Lord Lovat or his secretary. I don't know which.

Sir Richard Lloyd—Do you know whether there was any reward given to the clans when they were raised for their subsistence?—I know there was meal, cows, and mutton given them.

For what was it given them?—To maintain those men.

Where were they then?—There were several of them about Castle Downie.

By whose order were those things given?—That I don't know, indeed. Hugh Fraser

Did you ever hear my Lord Lovat say anything about their being maintained by his or anybody else's order?—I don't remember, indeed.

Mr. Noel—My lords, the witness has already told your lordships what the noble prisoner at the bar declared about the person's success whom he called the Prince. I beg he may inform your lordships whether my Lord Lovat when he spoke about that success did or did not say anything about his sending for men, and for what purpose?—I don't remember what he said at that particular time.

Do you at any other time?—Yes, indeed! I heard my Lord Lovat say he would send his son and men.

For what?—To serve the Prince.

Who did you understand he meant by the Prince?—The Pretender's son.

You mentioned the particulars about pulling off the mask. You said that Mr. Alexander Macleod said that much depended on Lord Lovat's throwing off the mask, that my Lord Lovat, upon that, threw his hat upon the floor and said, "Then there it is." Pray, what was the subject-matter of the conversation when that was done?—The subject-matter of the conversation was the young Pretender's cause; and it was about that they were speaking at that time.

Attorney-General—My lords, the Managers have done with their examination of this witness.

Lord High Steward—My Lord Lovat, has your lordship any questions to ask this witness?

Lord Lovat—My lords, there have been such proceedings against me since I was ordered to be tried as never was heard of in Scotland or England.

Lord High Steward—In what respect does your lordship mean?

Lord Lovat—I mean that after I was brought up to be tried before your lordships the Impeachment had been read against me, my Answer put in to it, and the Commons had replied to it, and after I had leave to summon witnesses in my defence, I had summoned a great many witnesses out of Scotland to come here in my defence, I did not imagine there would be the least difficulty in their coming up. But, my lords, I find there was a person there, who was a kind of a Deputy-Sheriff, but never was known as an officer of justice, went to several private meetings, and endeavoured to prevent my witnesses coming up.

Lord High Steward—My Lord Lovat, I would not interrupt

Hugh Fraser you if it were not for your own sake. If your lordship has any matter of complaint, my lords will be ready to hear you at a proper time, upon a proper application, but this is not a proper time for such an application. You have counsel to advise you as to the proper method and time of doing it, with whom you must advise.

LORD LOVAT—My lords, I was going to object to this witness before he was sworn, because he had been called in by that Deputy-Sheriff, who threatened the men, if they offered to come up to give evidence for me, and some were put in prison, and driven from their houses, particularly those they thought would favour me, after I had your lordships' order to summon my witnesses. And therefore I shall object to any witness that shall come from that little Court. I beg this witness may be asked whether he was examined at Inverness before he came here?

WITNESS—Yes, I was.

LORD LOVAT—My lords, I thought, as I was to be judged in a Court of the Supreme Judicature, and was innocent, that I was safe in such hands, but I cannot think myself safe when such officers as those shall manage the witnesses, and threaten those who will not say as they say.

LORD HIGH STEWARD—I have already told your lordship that if you have any complaint to make, you must make it at a proper time, and in a proper manner, and my lords will hear it. You may go on to ask this witness any questions concerning any practices that he knows of.

LORD LOVAT—My lords, I beg this witness may be asked if he was examined upon oath in December or January last, and by whom?

WITNESS—Yes, I was examined at Inverness by one Kilravock.

What is Kilravock?—He is a gentleman that lives about four miles from Inverness.

What is he?—He had substitution from the Sheriff-depute.[1]

Did you see Chevis of Muirtown? What part did he act there?—This gentleman had got a copy of the charge sent into the country, and he came, in obedience to that charge, among the rest.

What is a charge?—A kind of summons.

Were you threatened by any person, to give evidence against me, and by whom?—I was not, indeed.

Were you promised any favour or reward for being evidence against me?—No, indeed.

---

1 This means that he was an Honorary Sheriff-Substitute—a gentleman appointed to act as Sheriff or County Court judge in the absence of the regular Sheriff or Sheriff-Substitute.

By whom have you been maintained since you came to London?—I have been, since I came to London, in the custody of a messenger. Hugh Fraser

By whom were you maintained?—I do not know at whose expense it was. I have had victuals and drink, and a bed, and never was asked for anything.

Have you been in custody by any order, force, or compulsion?—No, not at all. I have not been under any order, force, or compulsion.

Since you have been at the house of the messenger, have you been at liberty to go where you pleased?—I have gone abroad, walked in the park, and about Kensington, and I go out at night to take a glass.

When you went out did not a messenger attend you?—Yes; he went to take a walk with me.

A Lord (to witness)—When was it that you were at Lord Lovat's house that he said he would send his son and clan into the Pretender's service?—I think it was the beginning of October, 1745. It was after the rebellion broke out.

A Lord—Where was it, and what persons were then present?—It was in my Lord Lovat's room, at Castle Downie.

Sir John Strange—My lords, I would beg leave to ask this witness one question for form's sake. (To witness)—Pray, what county is Castle Downie in?—It is in the county of Inverness.

A Lord—Pray, which of the prisoner's servants was present then?—Upon my word, I can't remember that.

Lord Lovat—Did you receive any money, or were you promised any money, for your expenses in coming to London to be a witness against me?—There was money given to bear our expenses.

A Lord (to witness)—Pray, who was present when my Lord Lovat said that he would send his son, with his men, into the Pretender's service?—I think there were several present, but I cannot condescend upon who they were.

A Lord—Name any one of them. Was Alexander Macleod there?—I don't remember.

Lord High Steward—My Lord Lovat, have you any more questions to ask this witness?

Lord Lovat—Not till I make my defence, and then I hope your lordships will give me liberty.

Lord High Steward—Does your lordship mean that when you come to your defence you would ask this witness any questions?

Lord Lovat—No, I don't mean that.

Lord High Steward—Your lordship will be at liberty to ask any other witness what questions you please.

Hugh Fraser

SOLICITOR-GENERAL—Was the proposal of my Lord Lovat to send his son and clan into the Pretender's service, as you have mentioned, before or after the news of the battle of Prestonpans came into that country?—It was after.

Did you observe any difference in the behaviour of my Lord Lovat in regard to his raising his clan, or taking any steps towards it, after the news of that battle, from what his behaviour was before?—I did not see my Lord Lovat before the battle of Prestonpans.

How long was it after the battle of Prestonpans that you saw him?—I don't remember.

Was it before the news came to Castle Downie of the troops from France being landed?—Upon my word, I don't remember.

Then the witness, by order of the Lord High Steward, withdrew.

LORD LOVAT—My lords, I beg your lordships' leave to withdraw for a little time.

The prisoner was removed from the bar accordingly.

SERGEANT-AT-ARMS—Our Sovereign Lord the King strictly charges and commands all manner of persons to be uncovered, on pain of imprisonment.

In about a quarter of an hour the prisoner was again brought to the bar.

John Riddell

ATTORNEY-GENERAL—My lords, the next witness we shall beg leave to produce is John Riddell (who was called in and sworn).

LORD HIGH STEWARD—My Lord Lovat, have you any objections against this witness, John Riddell?

LORD LOVAT—No.

ATTORNEY-GENERAL—My lords, I beg this witness may give your lordships an account whether he knows the noble lord at the bar.

WITNESS—Yes, I do.

Do you remember if you were at Castle Downie soon after the battle of Prestonpans?—Yes, it was.

Did you, before that time, see Barisdale or any other person there?—Yes.

Did he come there first by himself or not?—I saw Kinlochmoidart there.

At that time?—I cannot remember whether it was the same time or not.

How long was Barisdale there?—Two nights.

Did he bring any horses with him?—Four dragoon horses.

Whose arms were upon the furniture?—The King's arms were upon them, an R and G, or a G and an R.

Did you see any of the clan of the Frasers there?—At the same time some of them were there. John Riddell

Was my Lord Lovat there at that time?—Yes.

Did you ever see any of the chiefs of the clans dine at my Lord Lovat's table?—Yes.

Did you hear any healths drunk there?—Yes.

Whose health did you hear drunk?—Prince Charles's health.

Was my Lord Lovat present at that time or not?—Yes.

Did you ever hear my Lord Lovat drink any of those healths?—I cannot say that. I'm not sure; it is so long since.

Did you ever hear my Lord Lovat drink any other healths relating to the rebel army?—Never, to the best of my knowledge.

Did you ever hear him say anything relating to his countenancing the rebel army?—No; I do not remember.

Pray, give my lords an account whether you ever saw any meal delivered out at my Lord Lovat's.—My Lord Lovat has given precepts for meal several times.

What do you mean by precepts?—Precepts for so much oats for the horses or meal.

Do you mean by that an order?—Yes.

Pray, what was done with the meal that was ordered to you?—I got a precept for two bolls of meal in part of my wages.

Do you know of any precept that was given to Thomas Fraser?—Yes, for four bolls.

For what?—It is more than I can tell.

Do you know anything of bell tents being made?—Yes, I saw them made.

Where were they made?—At Castle Downie.

Was my Lord Lovat there?—Yes.

What were they made for?—I can't tell.

By whose order were they made?—I can't tell.

What became of them?—I heard they were sent to Perth.

For whose use, for what purpose, were they sent there?—They went there with a company of men. I don't know for whose use they were.

Who were the company of men?—They were the Frasers.

What were they collected together for?—They marched southward with a design to go to Perth, as I heard.

Whose people were at Perth then?—The rebel army.

Did they march to join them?—It is more than I can tell.

Had you any orders from my Lord Lovat concerning the preparing yourself and horses to go with my Lord Lovat or his son?—Yes; he ordered me to get myself ready to go.

Where were you to go to?—With the Master.

Did not my Lord Lovat tell you where he was to go to?—No; he did not, to the best of my knowledge.

John Riddell

Where did you understand he was to go to?—To Perth.

For what purpose?—To join that army.

What army do you mean—the King's army or the rebel army?—I can't tell that.

How did you understand it? As you were to go to Perth, don't you know what army you were to join?—There was no army at Perth but the rebel army.

Do you remember any number of men passing by Lord Lovat's house?—Yes, very well.

Did you see my Lord Cromartie or his officers there?—Yes.

How long did they continue there?—One night.

What time of the year was it?—Hallowmas,[1] or thereabouts.

Did you hear my Lord Lovat say anything to these gentlemen concerning his men being or not being ready?—I did not hear from my Lord Lovat; I heard it from some of his servants.

What did you hear?—I heard the servants say that my Lord Lovat mentioned something about the men not being ready.

Did you hear my Lord Lovat say anything about it in the chamber?—No; if it was spoken it was in the Erse language, and I did not understand it.

Was my Lord Lovat present in the house when Lord Cromartie was there?—Yes.

Did you see them together at table?—Yes.

Did you hear any of the conversation that passed betwixt them?—No.

Did you hear nothing concerning the drinking of any healths?—No; not at that time. I did not.

At what time did you hear it?—A good while before.

What healths were drunk, and by whom?—The chieftains of the clans drank Prince Charles's health.

Was my Lord Lovat present?—Yes.

Did he contradict the health?—I did not hear he did.

Were you present or near when a number of Frasers were drawn up?—I saw 700 men together once.

Where were they?—In the Aird.

Is that place near my Lord Lovat's house?—It is within half a mile.

Was my Lord Lovat there at that time?—No; I never saw my Lord Lovat there.

Was he at home then?—Yes.

By whom were they drawn up?—By my Lord Lovat's chamberlain.

Were there any officers among them?—Yes.

Where did the officers lodge?—They went through into the country, to farmers' houses, change-houses, and ale-houses.

---

1 1st November.

Did any of them ever dine at my Lord Lovat's house?—Sometimes they did. John Riddell

Did they dine with my Lord Lovat himself?—Yes.

Did he know that there were 700 men drawn up there, or near that place?—I cannot tell whether he knew that there were 700 of them, but I believe he knew they were there.

Do you know what kind of mark they had upon their bonnets?—They had a cockade and sprigs of yew.

What kind of cockades had they?—White cockades.

Was not that the distinguishing mark of the rebel army?—Yes.

Did they make use of the sprigs of yew as a distinguishing mark?—Yes.

Did you see any companies of those men there?—Yes; three or four companies.

Where did they march to?—To the southward.

Did you at any time see any of the officers take leave of my Lord Lovat?—Yes, I did.

What passed upon that occasion? Which way did they take leave of one another?—My Lord Lovat shook hands with them, kissed them, and bid them farewell.

Did my Lord Lovat wish them anything?—I cannot say I heard that.

Do you remember that at any time after, one Fraser of Byerly was with my Lord Lovat?—Yes. That man was always with my Lord Lovat.

Did you hear my Lord Lovat ask him any questions about the Pretender's son?—No, I never did.

Recollect yourself, whether you did or no?—I cannot mind indeed; if I did, it is out of my memory.

Did you ever hear my Lord Lovat ask any other person concerning the Pretender's son?—I heard my Lord Lovat once ask what sort of a man he was.

Of whom did he ask that question?—Some of the chieftains. Some of them that had been at Falkirk. I do not know who they were.

Do you remember what answer was given my Lord Lovat to that question?—I do not.

Do you remember whether my Lord Lovat mentioned anything to him concerning the Pretender's son's preservation?—I do not.

Duke of Bedford (to witness)—You say that my Lord Cromartie's men were at Castle Downie, my Lord Lovat's house. Pray, were they received there as friends, or did they come there by force?—The men did not come to Castle Downie—only Lord Cromartie, his son, and the officers.

Did they come there by force, or were they received as friends?—They were in the house all night.

John Riddell

Were they entertained as friends?—I did not hear anything to the contrary. They were lodged there all night.

Attorney-General (to witness)—You say you heard my Lord Lovat ask what sort of a man the Pretender's son was. Pray, when was it that he asked that?—I cannot name the time certainly.

Attorney-General—My lords, we have done with this witness.

Lord High Steward—My Lord Lovat, the gentlemen of the House of Commons have done with this witness. Will you ask him any questions?

Lord Lovat—When were you brought to town, and by whose orders were you sent to town?

Witness—I have been brought to town since the 24th of August, and was sent up by the Judge Advocate.

What is the Judge Advocate's name?—David Bruce.

Were you examined at Inverness, after the battle of Culloden, and by whom?—I was examined by the Judge Advocate, in the Duke of Cumberland's lodgings.

When were you so examined?—It was the 24th of April last.

Were you threatened by any person to give evidence against me, and by whom, and what was the expression used on that occasion?—I was threatened to deliver up my money, but not about my being an evidence.

What were the threatenings?—That they would put me in prison, and hang me next morning.

Sir John Strange—My lords, I would not interrupt the noble lord at the bar, but I would be glad to know whom the witness speaks of.

Witness—After I was examined, they heard I had some money. Brigadier Mordaunt demanded the money, and Mr. Bruce threatened that if I did not give up the money to the brigadier I must go to prison.

Lord Lovat—Were you a servant of mine?—I served you for five years.

In what capacity?—As a groom.

Were you taken prisoner?—I delivered myself up to the Duke of Cumberland, at Inverness, eight days after the battle of Culloden.

Who was it that threatened to hang you?—The Judge Advocate.

Did any person come to you, since you came to London, with a pretended letter, said to be signed by me?—Yes; there was a man whose name is Lesly, who came to see if I knew my Lord Lovat's hand.

What was desired of you by that person, and what answer did you give him?—I said that I did not know whether it was my Lord Lovat's hand or not, but that it did not look like it. John Riddell

Sir William Yonge—My lords, I beg to know of this witness whether he did or did not surrender himself a prisoner to the Duke at Inverness?

Witness—Yes, I did. I delivered up myself to the Duke, to get a pass to go to Edinburgh, but never was in the rebellion in my life.

Did you come to Inverness on horseback?—Yes; there were two of us.

Whose horses had you?—My Lord Lovat's.

You say there were two of you, and that you were both on my Lord Lovat's horses, and that you were threatened to have your money taken from you?—Yes.

Pray, how came you by that money?—By selling the horses.

Do you know, or were you informed of the contents of the letter which Mr. Lesly asked you whether it was Lord Lovat's hand?—I never saw the letter, but the subscription, and he showed me that, to see if I knew it.

Did not Lesly inform you what were the contents of the letter?—No. To the best of my remembrance he said it was signed by my Lord Lovat in 1738.

Then the witness, by direction of the Lord High Steward, withdrew.

Sir William Yonge—My lords, the next witness we beg leave to produce is William Walker (who was called in and sworn). Wm. Walker

Lord High Steward—My Lord Lovat, has your lordship any objection to this witness?

Lord Lovat—No, I have none.

Sir William Yonge—My lords, I beg leave to ask this witness if he lived in my Lord Lovat's family, and how long?

Witness—Yes; for three years and a half.

Do you remember any persons coming to him after the battle of Prestonpans, and who were they?—Yes; there was Alexander Macleod and MacDonald of Barisdale.

Was Kinlochmoidart there?—Yes.

Was young Glengarry there?—Yes; he was there one day, I think on a Sunday.

Did they dine at my Lord Lovat's table?—Yes; all except Glengarry.

Do you remember any healths that were drank?—Yes; I heard Barisdale drink the young Pretender's health.

By what name?—By the name of "the Prince."

Was my Lord Lovat present then?—Yes.

Wm. Walker

Do you know one Thomas Fraser, a baker?—Yes.

During the time that those persons were at my Lord Lovat's house did he give them any advice, and what was it?—I never heard it. It was always in my lord's room, and I never went in but at dinner.

Did you hear them say anything about the young Pretender and the clan of the Frasers?—I heard my Lord Lovat say that they must take care not to let the young Pretender run into an engagement.

Do you know Thomas Fraser, the baker?—Yes.

Was he at my Lord Lovat's then?—He came to Castle Downie with some colours they were to make at Inverness.

What colours were they?—Two standard colours, four bell tents, and two painted flags.

What were they painted with?—My Lord Lovat's arms were upon the flags.

What became of those things?—Cameron sent them away after my Lord Lovat was taken.

Do you remember the marching of two companies to Perth?—Yes.

Do you remember soon after the Master of Lovat's coming into the room where you were?—Yes.

Was my Lord Lovat there?—Yes.

What passed there between them?—When the Master came into the room my Lord Lovat was speaking to him. I don't know what it was about.

What did the Master do then?—The Master rose up, and took his bonnet and threw it upon the floor, and threw the white cockade in the fire, and damned the cockade.

What did the father do upon that occasion?—He rose up in a passion, and said what could he do, and was forcing his son out.

I beg you'll inform their lordships upon what occasion it was that the Master of Lovat threw his cockade into the fire, and what his father had said to him to occasion it.—I don't know that, indeed.

Did you hear his father say anything to him?—His father spoke to him in Erse.

Do you understand Erse?—No, I do not. The Master of Lovat went to the door, and Mr. Fraser, the minister, stood up in the Master of Lovat's behalf, upon which Mr. Fraser of Byerfield rose up and said, "What have you to do with it? You have no estate to forfeit."

What said my Lord Lovat upon that?—I do not know what he said upon that.

Did they say nothing in English after that?—They spoke in a language I did not understand.

Did my Lord Lovat say nothing in English?—Not that I

know of. Only he said what could he do more. He was forcing his son out, the very life of him. Wm. Walker

Pray, do you know upon what account that was said?—It was an answer he gave to Byerfield.

To whom did Byerfield speak when he said he had no estate to forfeit?—To Donald Fraser, the minister.[1]

Do you remember anything about a smith and a tinker repairing any arms?—Yes; there was one Hugh Monro and another.

How long was it that they were at Castle Downie?—About a fortnight, I think.

Were there any arms where they were?—Yes, in the wardroom.

Where was the key kept of that room?—The key was very often in my Lord Lovat's room, in his custody.

Did my Lord Lovat usually give out that key to anybody that went into the wardroom, or did he use to go there himself?—My lord always gave the key out to anybody that wanted it to get shoes for the horses or the like. My lord never went there himself.

Do you know anything of the smith and the tinker's going into my lord's room?—Yes.

What passed there? Did my lord give them anything?—A dram.

Have you ever been in the wardroom?—Yes.

What was usually kept there?—Several sorts of things. It is more than I can tell how many.

Did you see any number of men rendezvoused in that neighbourhood?—Yes.

What number? How many companies did you see?—I don't know how many companies. The first of the rendezvous we reckoned there were 700 or 800 men.

Were they armed?—Some of them were armed and some not.

How far from Castle Downie did you see those men?—About a mile from it.

Did you ever see them afterwards?—Yes; I saw a company of them drawn up on the green.

Was my Lord Lovat at home then? Did he see them drawn up?—He was at home, but I believe did not see them.

How near is that green to my Lord Lovat's house?—About 100 or 200 yards.

Do you know of any violence or force that was used to make the men rise?—The chamberlain forced them, and young Inverallachy.

---

1 Of Killearnan. He had a serious quarrel with the Presbytery of Tain. (See Transactions of the Gaelic Society of Inverness, vol. xiii., p. 136, &c.) Lord Lovat writes to the Rev. Donald Fraser of the members of Presbytery as "those wicked Crockadales who would go to the gates of hell to devoure you."

Wm. Walker

In what manner did they force them?—They threatened to burn their houses after the battle of Culloden if they did not rise.

But before that how did they threaten them?—That they would take their cattle and plaids from them if they did not rise. Lord Lovat was then a prisoner to my Lord Loudoun, and was then in his custody.

Do you remember when my Lord Cromartie marched by my Lord Lovat's?—Yes.

Was Lord Cromartie or his son or any of the officers at my Lord Lovat's?—Yes; my Lord Cromartie and Lord MacLeod were there all night.

Did you hear my Lord Lovat make use of any expressions or excuse that his men were not ready?—My Lord Lovat said it was a shame to see Lord Cromartie's men go by his nose. But what it was for I can't tell.

Sir William Yonge—My lords, we have done with our examination of this witness.

Lord High Steward—My Lord Lovat, would your lordship ask this witness any questions?

Lord Lovat (to witness)—Were you threatened by any one to give evidence against me and by whom, and what were the expressions used on that occasion?—No, I was not.

Were you examined at Inverness, and by whom?—I was examined at Inverness by Mr. Bruce and Brigadier Mordaunt.

What passed between you and Mr. Bruce?—I was examined. Nothing passed between me and Mr. Bruce at that time.

Or at any time afterwards?—Nor afterwards.

Was any force used to get out the men while I was a prisoner, or while I was at home, or after my return from Inverness?

Lord High Steward (to witness)—First, was there any force used to get out the men while my Lord Lovat was at home?—I cannot truly tell that. It is more than I can tell.

Was any such force used while he was a prisoner at Inverness?—Lord Lovat was with Lord Loudoun when the force was used to raise the men.

Did you say that the dispute between Lord Lovat and his son happened after the Frasers had marched southwards or not?—It was the Frasers of Stratherick that had marched. There was not a man marched out of the Aird at that time.

Lord Lovat—Did I know of the marching of the men?—My Lord Lovat knew nothing of it. It was Fraser of Byerfield that took as many of the Frasers as he could get to the castle of Culloden in order to take the Lord President prisoner. But my Lord Lovat knew nothing of that, for when he heard of it he was like to go mad. He cursed for a matter of two hours, and we had no peace with him. Wm. Walker

Was that the occasion of my quarrel with my son?—No, my Lord Lovat, nor the Master of Lovat, knew nothing of it, for this Byerfield, as I heard, was designed to raise the men without my Lord Lovat's authority, and if he had got the command of the house of Culloden he would have kept them there. It was he that marched with the Stratherick men to Perth.

A Lord—Did my Lord Lovat or his son know nothing of this?—No; they were 24 miles off.

What was the occasion of the quarrel between Lord Lovat and his son?—I cannot tell.

Were you present in the room when the dispute began between my Lord Lovat and his son?—No; I was not in the room. I came in with a dish in the meantime, and there was this little John Fraser of Byerfield speaking to my lord. My Lord Lovat fell foul of the Master, who rose up and took his cockade off the 'scriptore[1] and threw the cockade into the fire, and damned it.

What language did they talk in?—They talked in Erse when I heard it first.

You say that Fraser, the minister, took part with the Master?—Yes.

Did he talk in Erse?—Yes.

Then how do you know he spoke in favour of the Master?—The reason why I knew it was that little John Fraser flew up to Donald Fraser and said he had no estate to forfeit, and that if he had got a stipend it was all he had to take care of.

Lord Lovat—Do you know whether I used my endeavours to get my men home after they were taken out by Fraser of Byerfield or any other person?—MacDonald of Barisdale would have my Lord Lovat's men out, and was never away from the house, and there came on a great snow that my Lord Lovat's men did not go out at that time, but about two days after that some of them went up to a hill with Barisdale's men, and they would take cattle to maintain them upon the road, when my Lord Lovat sent for them from Urquhart and brought them all back again. When there were any of them risen at all then my lord was prisoner with Lord Loudoun.

A Lord—Pray, what kind of servant is a chamberlain?—The steward who gathers in the rents.

Did you ever hear of the cross being carried about the country?—I never either saw it or heard of it.

---

1 Escritoir.

Wm. Walker LORD LOVAT—Do you know whether Fraser of Dumballoch that was here to-day went out in arms at the head of a company to Urquhart till I brought him home?—I saw him that day at Lord Lovat's table, but whether he got to Urquhart or no I cannot tell.

A LORD—Did the men that went to Urquhart dine with my Lord Lovat?

WITNESS—Yes.

Then the witness, by the direction of the Lord High Steward, withdrew.

Hugh Munro MR. YORKE—My lords, the next witness we shall produce is Hugh Monro.

Hugh Monro was called in.

LORD HIGH STEWARD—My Lord Lovat, has your lordship any objection against Hugh Monro's being examined as a witness?

LORD LOVAT—Yes. He is my tenant.

LORD HIGH STEWARD—Would your lordship have him examined upon that point?

LORD LOVAT—Yes.

The witness was sworn upon a *voire dire*.

LORD HIGH STEWARD—My Lord Lovat, what questions would you ask him?

LORD LOVAT—Have you any lands, houses, or yard that you hold of me?

WITNESS—Yes.

LORD HIGH STEWARD—What lands do you hold of my Lord Lovat?

WITNESS—Six bolls a year.

How do you hold it of my Lord Lovat, as vassal or by lease or tack?—While I was a servant I had it from him.

Do you hold it of my Lord Lovat now?—Another man hath taken possession there.

Have you the same tenure under my Lord Lovat as you had before?—Yes.

ATTORNEY-GENERAL—My lords, I beg this witness may be asked if he holds any lands of my Lord Lovat at this time.

WITNESS—I have the same land that I had before, but another man hath it in possession ever since Whitsunday.

What is that other man's name?—Kilbocky.[1]

How does he hold it of my lord?—I don't know.

LORD LOVAT—Do you think you have any right to hold this land though another man is in possession of it?

[1] Mr. Fraser, younger of Culbokie, Kiltarlity, was a captain in the Fraser company under Inverallachy.

Witness—No; I have no right to hold it. Hugh Munro

Lord Sandys—Why do you say you have no right to hold it?

Witness—Because the superior lord may turn me out of the land at any time.

Has the superior lord turned you out of the land?—No.

Lord High Steward—Who do you take to be your superior lord?

Witness—My Lord Lovat.

Sir William Yonge—Had you any wages from my Lord Lovat while you were his servant?

Witness—Yes, I had.

What were the wages you had?—£5 a year.

Was it paid in money or in lands of any rent?—It was paid in land.

Was that the land you now speak of which you hold of my Lord Lovat?—Yes.

Have you any title to that land now you are not his servant?—I don't know what way it is.

Do you think you have any claim to the land now you are not his servant?—No, I have none.

How long have you left my Lord Lovat's service?—I was always his servant. I did not leave his service.

Lord Lovat—The person that now is in possession of that land, has he it by my consent?

Witness—I don't know. The man that is in possession says he must have the rent this year.

Attorney-General—Did you ever hold this land by any writing?

Witness—No.

Did you ever hold it by any contract for any certain term?—I had the land from my Lord Lovat for what I worked for him in the year.

Lord Lovat—Were you turned out of this land by force or against your will?

Witness—No; I was not.

A Lord—By what means were you dispossessed of this land?

Witness—I have the same land yet.

Mr. Grenville—In what capacity were you a servant to my Lord Lovat?

Witness—I was his blacksmith.

Do you know the person who you say is now in possession of that land?—Indeed, do I.

What is he? Is he a servant to my Lord Lovat?—No; he is a gentleman.

Lord Halifax—My lords, I submit it to your lordships, as this witness has already contradicted himself several times, whether he should not be ordered to withdraw.

Sir John Strange—I stood up to acquaint your lordships

Hugh Munro that we should not insist on the examination of this witness, but desire it may be understood that we only do that from the manner of his answering the questions which have been asked him, and do not thereby submit to the objection that has been made against him by the noble lord at the bar.

Then the witness, by direction of the Lord High Steward, withdrew.

The Duke of Newcastle moved to adjourn to the Chamber of Parliament.

Lord Lovat—My lords, I have most humbly represented to your lordships every day of my trial that I am so weak and feeble that I am not able to attend your lordships. I fainted away thrice this morning before I came up to your lordships' bar, but yet was determined to show my respect to your lordships, or die upon the road. My lords, it is impossible for me to come up in the manner I have done for these three days past. I am every day obliged to get up by three or four o'clock in the morning, and therefore I beg your lordships to have compassion on me, and to give me a later hour and a day's respite that I may try to recover myself.

The Lord High Steward went back to his chair, and then the House adjourned to the Chamber of Parliament, and the lords and others returned in the same order as before.

The House being there resumed.

Ordered that this House will proceed further in the trial of Simon, Lord Lovat, in Westminster Hall on Friday next at eleven of the clock in the forenoon. A message was sent to the House of Commons by Mr. Eld and Mr. Thurston to acquaint them therewith;

Ordered that the Lieutenant of the Tower of London or his deputy do take back the said Lord Lovat and bring him again to the bar of this House in Westminster Hall on Friday next at eleven of the clock in the forenoon.

Fourth Day—Friday, 13th March [1747].

About eleven of the clock in the forenoon the lords and others came from the Chamber of Parliament in the same order as on Monday last into Westminster Hall, where the Commons and their Managers were in the seats prepared for them respectively as before; and the lords took their places in the Court, and the Lord High Steward in his chair.

Lord High Steward—The House is resumed. Is it your lordships' pleasure that the judges have leave to be covered?

Lords—Ay, ay.

Then the Sergeant-at-Arms made proclamation for silence, and afterwards the following proclamation:—Oyes! Oyes! Oyes! Lieutenant of the Tower of London, bring forth your prisoner Simon, Lord Lovat, to the bar pursuant to the order of the House of Lords to you directed.

The Deputy-Governor of the Tower brought the prisoner to the bar in the like form as before, and then he kneeled down.

Lord High Steward—Your lordship may rise.

The Lord High Steward desired leave to go down to the tables, and went down accordingly.

Lord High Steward—Gentlemen of the House of Commons, you may proceed.

Mr. Yorke—My lords, the next witness we shall produce to your lordships is Thomas Fraser. T. Fraser

Thomas Fraser was called into Court.

Mr. Yorke—My lords, we desire this witness Thomas Fraser may be sworn.

Lord High Steward—My Lord Lovat, has your lordship any objection against Thomas Fraser being sworn as a witness?

Lord Lovat—My lords, I have no objection to him, but, my lords, I am not able to rise up and sit down, having been ill all night, and am very ill now. I hope your lordships will excuse my rising up and down.

Thomas Fraser was sworn.

Mr. Yorke—My lords, I would ask this witness if he knows my Lord Lovat, and I desire he would speak out?

Witness—Yes, my lords, as well as I do myself.

How long have you known him?—Ever since I was a child.

Have you been employed to work for my Lord Lovat at any time about September, 1745, and upon what occasion were you so employed? Answer the question distinctly.—No; I never was employed by him.

Were you employed at Castle Downie about that time?—

T. Fraser Yes; I was at Castle Downie, and was employed by my lord's chamberlain.

About what business?—About mending some old colours.

And what else were you employed in?—About some camp colours.

Were you employed in anything else?—Yes; there were some bells for arms that I was employed about.

Who gave you directions about making these things?—John Fraser, my Lord Lovat's chamberlain or steward, and he paid me for my pains when I had done.

At what house was this work done?—Most of it was done at my own house at Inverness.

Was none of the work done at Castle Downie?—There was a camp colour and some other things done at Castle Downie.

Whose arms were put upon these colours, or bells for arms? —There was no arms upon them but the crest of Lord Lovat's family, the deer's head.[1]

Was that crest put both upon the bell tents and colours?—It was upon the camp colours and bells of arms.

Were the arms upon the colours?—They were a stand of old colours that were done by Fraser.

Where were these colours set up afterwards, or were they set up at all?—Yes; I stuck them up on the green of Castle Downie.

Did my Lord Lovat ever see them there?—To my knowledge, he never did.

What were those bell tents and colours which you painted intended for? What was to be the use of them?—I cannot tell that, upon my faith.

Did my Lord Lovat know of your being employed about these things?—No; he did not, to my knowledge, as I shall answer.

Who paid you for them?—The chamberlain or steward.

Do you think the chamberlain would have paid you for them without my Lord Lovat's order?—I can't tell that; let the judges determine that.

Pray, who used to pay you for work that you had done for my Lord Lovat before that?—The chamberlain.

Was my Lord Lovat in the house at the same time?—Yes; he was in the house. He was very sick.

Did you observe my Lord Lovat ever look at these colours that you set up?—I saw him one fair morning take a walk upon the green and take an old colour in his hand.

Did he see there the colours which you set up?—Yes; the bells of arms and colours.

Did he say anything to you about them?—Yes; he seemed to be very ill-pleased.

1 "A stag's head erased or attired argent."

Fourth Day.

What was he ill-pleased with?—I don't know whether it was with the manner of doing the work or because it was done at all. T. Fraser

When his lordship expressed himself ill-pleased did he direct you to take them away or not?—No; they were to stay there till they were dried by the wind.

When he expressed himself to be ill-pleased did he order them to be taken away?—He did not speak a word to me afterwards about them.

Do you know what become of those colours?—No; I went home to Inverness, which is the place of my residence. But when I am employed by any man I must answer and obey.

Mr. Yorke—My lords, we have done with this witness.

Lord High Steward—My Lord Lovat, will your lordship ask this witness any questions?

Lord Lovat—No, my lords.

Then the witness, by direction of the Lord High Steward, withdrew.

Attorney-General—My lords, the next witness we shall produce is Hugh Fraser,[1] who was secretary to my Lord Lovat from 1741 to 1744, when Robert Fraser, who was before examined, became secretary in his room. Hugh Fraser

Hugh Fraser was called in.

Lord High Steward—My Lord Lovat, have you any objection to this witness?

Lord Lovat—No, my lords.

Lord Halifax—My lords, as the noble lord at the bar has complained that he is sick and faint I move that your lordships may dispense with his rising up.

Lords—Ay, ay.

Hugh Fraser was sworn.

Attorney-General—Do you know the noble lord at the bar?

Witness—Yes.

How long have you known him? And raise your voice.—I've known my Lord Lovat for about five years.

Did you ever serve my Lord Lovat, and in what capacity?—

Lord High Steward—Raise your voice, Mr. Fraser.

Attorney-General—In what capacity did you serve Lord Lovat?—I served my Lord Lovat in the capacity of a secretary.

---

1 This witness had been a prisoner in Edinburgh Castle. Murray of Broughton in his "Memorials" (p. 415) says—"Yesterday was brought hither by a party of Kingstone's who were sent in search for him, Hugh Fraser, who was the secretary and confident of Lord Lovat." The author of the "Account" reprinted by the New Spalding Club says (p. 335) Hugh Fraser had originally refused to give evidence against Lord Lovat.

Hugh Fraser

When did you first come into his service, and when did you quit it?—I came into Lord Lovat's service in April or May, 1741, and left it towards the end of December, 1744.

Give an account to my lords whether you were at Edinburgh in the month of September, 1745.—I was.

Do you know one William Fraser of Belnain? Was he then at Edinburgh?—Yes.

Had you and he any, and what, conversation together? And did you come to any resolution upon it in order to your going to my Lord Lovat's?—I had a conversation with Mr. Fraser.

Did you two come to any resolution together concerning your going to my Lord Lovat's in relation to his son the Master of Lovat?—We did.

Please to tell my lords what that resolution or agreement between you was?—The resolution between Mr. Fraser and me was this, that, as there had at that time a rebellion broke out in the north of Scotland, it was agreed between us to be proper that I should go into the north country in order to converse with my Lord Lovat upon the subject of his son's going out of Scotland to avoid any censure or wrong interpretation that might be put upon his conduct, as he was then in that country.

Had you and this Fraser at that time any apprehensions that he might be prevailed upon to go into the rebellion?—We had no grounds for any apprehensions, further than the spreading contagion there was at that time.

Was there any proposal made by William Fraser or you to prevent his being infected with that contagion?—The proposal made by Mr. Fraser and agreed to by me was that he should be removed and go abroad.

Did you or did you not propose that he should go abroad?—The thing was unanimous. I don't know which of us proposed it.

To what place was he to go?—We intended that he should go to Leyden.

At whose expense was he to go to Leyden?—The expense in the end was to fall on my Lord Lovat, but it was to be defrayed by Mr. Fraser for a year, to be advanced by him.

What was agreed upon with respect to making any proposals of this kind to my Lord Lovat?—It was agreed that it should be proposed to my Lord Lovat and his son, and was not to be done without my lord's consent.

Was it agreed upon that you should go to my Lord Lovat upon this proposal?—Yes, it was.

And did you go to him?—Yes.

And did you deliver the message to him?—I did.

And what answer did he give you?—He approved very much of the proposal, and agreed to the thing.

"A perspective view of Westminster Hall, with both Houses of Parliament assembled, on the Tryal of Simon, Lord Lovat."

(From a contemporary print.)

(For description, see Appendix V.)

How long did he continue in that agreement to this proposal? **Hugh Fraser**
—Some days after he said he did not think it quite so convenient a thing, and that he had altered his mind in regard to that.

Pray, did he say anything concerning his intention about the Master his son's going into the rebellion?—He communicated his design to me when he talked to me on the subject, which was that the Master should.

Should do what?—Should go into the rebellion; that is, to head the clan of the Frasers.

Did you hear my Lord Lovat say anything or no concerning his own intentions originally to head the clan in the rebellion?—My Lord Lovat told me then that he had intended to head them himself, but that he had altered his resolution.

For what purpose or with what view did he alter his resolution?—In order to stay himself at home, I suppose.

And who was intended to go in his room?—I said before that the Master was to head the Frasers.

Do you mean by saying he altered his resolution that he had resolved the Master should go?—Yes.

Did you hear my Lord Lovat say anything concerning the number of men that he had thought might have been raised or that would rise?—My Lord Lovat did talk to me of a greater number of men he thought might be raised than was likely to rise.

What number did he mention?—If I remember right, he talked of 4000 or 5000.

Did he give any reason in relation to his resolution concerning the Master's going out instead of himself?—He told me that he had once intended to have headed them himself in expectation that there would be a rising of 4000 or 5000 men, but, as that was not then likely to happen, he intended that the Master of Lovat should go with the clan to head them.

Please to give an account to my lords if he at that time told you of any disappointment he met with from other people.—He talked in general that some people had not acted up to their engagements, or to that purpose.

Please to give an account to my lords if you remember the time when the battle of Prestonpans happened.—Yes; I remember the time very well.

Was you at Castle Downie after or before that?—After that battle.

How long were you there after that battle?—It may be about eight days after.

Did anybody come to Castle Downie when you were there and give an account to my Lord Lovat of that battle, and who was it?—There were several gentlemen came to Castle Downie while I was there who said they had been in that action.

What did they say concerning it?—What they said of it was giving a history of the matter of fact.

Hugh Fraser

Who did they give the history to?—To the company, where I was present. I don't know to whom in particular.

Was Lord Lovat present at any conversation of that kind? —I do not doubt but he was.

Do you remember whether he was or not?—I believe he was.

Did you hear Lord Lovat say anything, and what, concerning that battle?—I remember to have heard my Lord Lovat say that it was a victory obtained not to be parallelled in history.

I beg you will give an account to their lordships who the persons were that came to my Lord Lovat's with this account of the battle. Please to name them.—That they came with an account of the battle is more than I can say.

Who were the persons that told it, and who were there?—MacDonald of Barisdale was there.

Was any other person there?—There were with him servants, and one gentleman, I think, that was in company.

Was young Glengarry[1] there?—Yes; the son of Glengarry was there.

Were Barisdale and Glengarry in the rebellion or no?—So they said themselves.

Are these the persons that said they had been in the battle? —They said they had been there, and gave an account of their own conduct in it.

What did they say they came northward for?—That they told their real business I cannot affirm. What they gave out was that they intended to levy more men in order to prosecute the affair they had undertaken.

What affair do you understand that to have been?—The rebellion, sure enough.

Was my Lord Lovat present or no at the time when they declared what they came into the north for?—He must have been present, because where I heard them speak of it was in his room.

Do you remember if my Lord Lovat said anything, and what, upon his being told of the views of Barisdale and Glengarry's coming into the north?—He said they might raise 5000 men, and I don't remember I heard him say any more upon this subject.

How long did you continue at Castle Downie this time that you went there?—For a matter of twelve or fourteen days, I believe, at first.

Whither did you go to when you went from Castle Downie? —I returned to Edinburgh.

[1] This refers to Angus MacDonell of Glengarry, the chief's second son. The eldest son, Alastair (Mr. Lang's "Pickle the Spy") was then a prisoner in the Tower. See Biographical Notes, p. 304.

Fourth Day.

Did my Lord Lovat charge you with anything to be communicated at Edinburgh as from him?—I am sorry to say he did. Hugh Fraser

What was that charge my Lord Lovat gave you to communicate, and to whom were you to communicate it?—What my Lord Lovat gave me in charge to communicate was in import the conversation I before mentioned to have passed at Castle Downie, that he had once intended to have raised and headed such a number of men as I mentioned.

What number was that?—4000 or 5000, the number I have mentioned already.

Pray, give an account to my lords of the remainder of the messages which my Lord Lovat sent by you to Edinburgh.—It was this, that he intended to have headed such a number of men, but that his age and infirmities would not allow him to do that, and that he had resolved his son should head the Frasers and go into the rebellion.

Did my Lord Lovat add anything to what you have now mentioned? Did he give any reason why he chose to send his son rather than go himself?—I have given the reason already. To the best of my remembrance that was the principal reason.

Did he give any other? Did he mention anything relating to his mark of affection for the cause?—He said the Master of Lovat's going, for whom he had such a regard, was a greater mark of his attachment and affection than if he had gone himself.

Did he at that time mention anything of the danger there might be of his going himself personally, and what danger was it?—He talked much of the inconvenience and danger that would attend it, and mentioned the inconvenience of crossing the Forth, and that it could be done no other way than by the Bridge of Stirling.

A Lord—I desire to know to whom the message was sent.

Attorney-General—I intended to ask the question the noble lord mentions. You were giving an account of some inconveniences that Lord Lovat had mentioned; go on with it.

Witness—I have given the reason why he did not go himself. I mentioned Stirling Bridge, and that he said it was impossible for him to cross the Forth elsewhere, and that might be very dangerous to him.

To whom did he charge you with that message, or to whom was it to be delivered?—To the Pretender's son.

Did you, or did you not, deliver that message to the Pretender's son?—I did deliver it to him.

What answer did the Pretender's son give you to it?—The answer he gave was no more than that it was very well, or to that purpose.

Hugh Fraser

Who was it gave that answer to you?—The Pretender's son.

How long did you continue at Edinburgh after this before you went from thence?—I continued at Edinburgh from that time, which was the time of my arrival from the north, in the beginning of October, till the beginning of November after.

Before you left Edinburgh, did any person, in behalf of the Pretender's son, come to you, and who, in order to employ you upon any message to my Lord Lovat?—I left Edinburgh twice. Which of the times is meant?

When you left Edinburgh at the beginning of November.—Before I left Edinburgh in November I was called upon by one who appeared to me to be in the service of the Pretender, and by him carried to Holyrood House.

Who was at Holyrood House then?—The Pretender's son was the principal tenant.

When you came to Holyrood House, who was the person you were brought before, and what conversation passed between you?—I was brought before Mr. Murray.

Who is he?—John Murray of Broughton, who then took upon him the name of secretary to the Pretender's son.

Was anybody with Mr. Murray at the time you had this meeting with him when you went to Holyrood House?—There were two or three gentlemen in the house.

Can you name them?—Some of them I can.

Who were they?—Cameron of Lochiel was one.

Who was there else?—MacDonald, and Stewart of Ardshiel.[1] These three were in the room with Mr. Murray.

Was MacDonald of Keppoch there?—Yes.

What did Mr. Murray say to you upon that occasion?—He told me that there had been a letter intercepted from the north which was directed to me, and that he understood from that letter that it was owing to me that the Frasers had not already marched.

Marched whither?—Marched, and gone into the rebellion, and that the letter bore that none of them would march till I should go into the north country.

Was anything said concerning my Lord Lovat upon that occasion?—I believe Mr. Murray told me that he had heard from a gentleman who was one of their own party that my Lord Lovat was very well disposed towards supporting the cause.

Did he say anything concerning my Lord Lovat's intention to raise men or no?—I can't tell.

In the letter was anything of it mentioned?—The letter I

---

[1] Leader of the Appin Stewarts during the '45.

never saw. It was not given to me. I asked for a sight of the letter, and asked from whom it was written, and they told me it was from one of the Frasers. **Hugh Fraser**

Did you give any answer to this or no?—The answer I gave was that it was a misrepresentation of me, and a falsehood.

In what respect was it a misrepresentation?—Because the moving or not moving of the Frasers no way depended on me.

Please to give an account, and go on with what passed between Mr. Murray and you.—Mr. Murray said that it was possible it might be so, but that it was necessary, for the vindication of my character, that I should go into the north country.

Go on.—I told him that my business would not allow me to do it.

What was agreed upon then?—That I should write such an account of the situation of the rebel army at Edinburgh as he then gave me, and they would be satisfied with such account.

Did you, or did you not, agree to this?—I did agree to it.

What was the consequence of that agreement?—I agreed to it, and obtained a pass for the bearer of it, and, in consequence of that pass, I meant to send what I took to be the real state of the matter on both sides.

Did you or did you not write, according to this proposal?—I went to write, and was about doing it, when I was called upon a second time by the same person who had called upon me before, and was brought by him to the same place.

What passed when you were thus brought back to the same place?—I was told that writing would not do, but I must go myself.

Lord High Steward—Who told you so?

Witness—Mr. Murray.

Attorney-General—Be pleased to inform their lordships what was done upon that. Did you or did you not agree to go?

Witness—In the end I did agree to it, because I understood, if I had not, I must have expected a worse service.

What was the message you were to go upon?—The message I was charged with was to give such an account of their own situation as they had given me.

Were you charged with any letter for my Lord Lovat, and from whom?—There was a letter from Mr. John Murray delivered to me, and directed to my Lord Lovat.

Was it delivered to you open or sealed?—The letter was open when it was delivered to me.

Did you or did you not read it?—I did read it.

Who delivered it to you?—Mr. Murray.

Pray, give an account to my lords of the contents of that letter that was thus delivered to you by Mr. Murray.—The

Hugh Fraser import or contents of the letter was, to the best of my remembrance, that Mr. Murray was extremely glad of the accounts he had received with respect to my Lord Lovat's intentions, and that he begged of him to persevere in them, and that he earnestly desired that the Frasers should march forthwith; and, I think, to the best of my remembrance, there was a route directed for them.

Was there any place mentioned where they were to meet the army?—The place where it was intended, according to that route, they should join the rebel army was about Moffat or Carlisle.

Did you go with that letter or not to my Lord Lovat?—I went into the north country, and some time after my arrival at that place I delivered that letter.

To whom did you deliver that letter?—To my Lord Lovat.

When you delivered Lord Lovat that letter, did you give him any account of the situation either of the rebels or the King's Army, or of the affairs relating to the rebellion?—I gave him the account, which I intended to have written, of the situation on both sides of the question so far as I knew of it.

What was that representation that you made, and did, in fact, deliver or give to my Lord Lovat?—The representation I delivered to my Lord Lovat at that time was this, that, with respect to the Government, there were above twenty-one battalions of forces arrived from Flanders; that there were two regiments arrived from Ireland; that the Dutch auxiliaries were expected; and that the rebels did not seem to be a party sufficient, according to their number, to engage with such a number of regular and well-disciplined forces.

What did my Lord Lovat say to this representation of yours that you thus made to him?—My Lord Lovat said that he conceived what I had said with respect to the situation of affairs on both sides of the question to be very true.

What did he say as the consequence of that belief of his?—He further said but[1] that he thought himself too far engaged to look back.

Did he say anything else relating to that matter?—Yes; I believe it was part of the conversation that he forbid me to mention or intimate anything of the conversation that had thus passed between us to his son.

Can you tell the reason why he was unwilling that his son should know of it?—As for the reason, that must depend upon my own conjecture, since Lord Lovat expressed none.

Did you continue at my Lord Lovat's house after this for any, and what, time?—I continued from my arrival there, which was the beginning of November till the middle or towards the end of December.

---

1 Only.

Fourth Day.

You had by that an opportunity of seeing some of my Lord Lovat's conduct and hearing his conversation. Please to give an account to my lords whether there was any rendezvous of the Frasers, my Lord Lovat's clan, during the time you were there.—I heard there was a rendezvous before I came into the country, but I was present at none, nor saw any while I was there. I suppose by the word "rendezvous" you mean a gathering of men? **Hugh Fraser**

Have you ever seen any of them?—I never saw a universal one or general one. Perhaps I might see forty or fifty men together at a time.

Have you seen forty or fifty men at a time gather together there as a body of men in arms?—No; I cannot say I did see or was present at any gathering of men in arms.

Did you ever see a list of the officers appointed out of my Lord Lovat's clan?—I have seen such a list.

By whom was that list shown to you?—It was shown to me by the Master of Lovat.

Do you know whether my Lord Lovat saw that list?—I do not know that, indeed.

Were you yourself appointed or named as one of the officers in that list?—I was.

What was the office or post you had there?—I was named there a captain-lieutenant.

Did my Lord Lovat call you by that name or title or by any other after this time?—My Lord Lovat has called me by that name after this.

Was it or was it not the usual name he called you by?—Yes, very often.

Did he ever call you by the name of captain before that time?—No.

What did you understand by your being called by that name by my Lord Lovat? Did you understand by that that he looked upon you as a captain or officer in his son's regiment? —I understood by that that my Lord Lovat apprehended it was so written in that list.

Did my Lord Lovat understand by it and so express himself that you were actually a captain, as well as wrote so in that list?—Actually a captain I was not; he could not understand what was not, because, as I had not undertaken or done anything, all the foundation he had for calling me captain was owing to my name being in that list.

Have you had any conversation with my Lord Lovat concerning his dissatisfaction at his son's backwardness in raising the Frasers?—I have heard my Lord Lovat complain sometimes of his son's backwardness to raise the clan and sometimes of his too much forwardness.

Did you ever hear him say anything concerning the conse-

Hugh Fraser quence of this engagement of his in the rebellion in respect to himself?—I have heard him say that he apprehended the conduct of his clan upon this occasion would be his ruin, and very probably cost him his life.

I beg you will inform their lordships whether the officers of this clan or of the Master of Lovat's regiment did or did not use to live or dine with my Lord Lovat.—I have dined at my Lord Lovat's table several times with the officers who were named in that list.

Did you ever hear the Pretender's son spoken of at dinner or at any other time in my Lord Lovat's house?—Any particular conversation with respect to the Pretender's son I cannot recollect, but that he has been spoken of there is little reason to doubt, because it was the topic of conversation in all the country.

By what name or title was the Pretender's son usually called in the conversation between my Lord Lovat and those officers?—To the conversation between my Lord Lovat and those officers I cannot answer, but in the conversation upon that subject in my Lord Lovat's presence I can say he was called Prince Charles.

Now, my lords, I will beg leave to ask the witness concerning another matter of fact. Did you ever hear my Lord Lovat say anything concerning a patent to create him Duke of Fraser by the Pretender?—I have heard him say there was such a thing in being.

Did he ever say whether he had or had not seen the original patent or any copy of it?—He did not say that he had seen the patent. I think he said he had never seen it.

Did you ever hear him say anything concerning any copy of it which he had?—He showed me half a sheet of paper whereon was written what had been shown or given to him as a copy of such a patent.

What patent do you mean?—The patent to create him a duke.

By whom was that patent said to be granted?—The copy that I saw was in the name of one whom I took to be the old Pretender, who called himself James the Eighth.

How was that subscribed, do you recollect?—I don't remember it was subscribed or superscribed.

Was there any name at the top of it?—I really cannot say.

That copy which you saw, by whom was it shown to you?—It was shown me by my Lord Lovat.

You were saying that you continued with my Lord Lovat from the second time you came to Castle Downie to the latter end of December. Please to inform their lordships if during that interval of time any of the men of the Frasers did actually march in order to go to the Pretender's army or to join them?

—Yes; there were men that marched. About six or seven companies of men marched about six or seven miles from their own country to an adjacent country. Hugh Fraser

What place was that they went to?—It was a place called Urquhart.

What became of those men? How far did they march?—I said before, about six or seven miles.

Were they afterwards recalled?—They were.

Who were they recalled by?—They were recalled by a letter from my Lord Lovat, directed to his son, the Master of Lovat.

Did or did not they comply with that letter which recalled them?—The son complied, and they, in consequence, I suppose, complied with the son's orders.

Did the whole clan comply?—All except about twenty-five of them.

Did they return to their own habitations?—They returned.

At or about what time was this?—I believe it was in the month of November.

Now, sir, I would ask you, did you take it that the Master of Lovat marched with them by order of my Lord Lovat, or was it out of his own head that he thus marched?—The men had marched, and were in that country before the Master of Lovat went from Castle Downie. When he went from Castle Downie it was not with a view to proceed upon that march, in case he should be able to prevail on the men to return. I went along with the Master, and, after we came where the men were, we called the officers together and proposed to them that they should return. The only reason we gave them for this advice was a storm of snow which then fell, and which would probably render their march very troublesome, but, by the influence of MacDonald of Barisdale, it was carried against the Master's sentiments that they should march. Upon that resolution, I returned to Castle Downie, and, a few hours after my return, my Lord Lovat wrote the letter I mentioned himself, which occasioned their coming back.

Please to inform their lordships whether you were sent at any time by my Lord Lovat to the Lord President of the Session of Scotland, or mention first if my Lord President was at Inverness.—He then was at his own house at Culloden.

Was my Lord Loudoun there?—He was at Inverness.

Were you sent by my Lord Lovat to the Lord President, or to my Lord Loudoun, with any, and what message?—I was sent by my Lord Lovat to my Lord President and my Lord Loudoun both.

What was the message that you were sent with?—The intention of the message was to see to discover from those gentlemen what would be the result of the Frasers marching, and going into the rebellion.

Hugh Fraser

Was that the intention of the message?—Yes; it was.

Did you carry any letter, or letters, from my Lord Lovat to the Lord President or my Lord Loudoun?—There was a letter I carried from my Lord Lovat to the Lord President.

Did you know what were the contents of that letter? Did you read it?—I did.

What were the contents of it?—The contents of it were informing my Lord President that the Master of Lovat had gone off in a headstrong way, and carried the Frasers into the rebellion.

What did my Lord Lovat mean by the word "headstrong"?—I suppose he meant that it was contrary to his advice.

When you came to my Lord President, did you deliver that letter?—Yes, I did.

What answer did my Lord President give to it?—He told me by word of mouth that the consequence that would arise to my Lord Lovat from such a step taken by his clan would, in all probability, be the seizing of his person and making an inquiry into his conduct.

Did you or did you not return with that answer of my Lord President, and deliver it to my Lord Lovat?—I returned with that answer of my Lord President, and with an answer to the same purpose from my Lord Loudoun, and delivered them both to my Lord Lovat.

Were you likewise charged with a letter from my Lord President to Lord Lovat?—My Lord President did write to my Lord Lovat, in return to his letter.

Did you see that letter?—I saw it.

Can you give my lords an account of the contents of it?—The import of it was what I already told their lordships.

Did you or did you not go to my Lord Lovat with those messages and this letter?—I did.

Before you delivered this letter, or these messages, had you any meeting with the Master of Lovat?—I had a meeting with the Master of Lovat upon the way. It was concerted between him and me before I set out upon that message that he should meet me privately by the way, in my return, in order to know what passed between my Lord President and me, and my Lord Loudoun and me.

Had you that meeting before your return?—Yes, I had.

What passed between you two at that meeting?—I made a report to the Master of Lovat of all the conversation I had with those two gentlemen.

Was there anything concerted or agreed between you two upon that occasion?—The result of our comparing our sentiments on that meeting was that the Master of Lovat, if it was possible, should be got immediately sent over to Holland, and that the scheme which we had proposed some months before should then be put in execution with respect to the Master of Lovat's following his education at Leyden, or some other University in the Low Countries. Hugh Fraser

What answer did you return to my Lord Lovat in regard to these messages?—I reported what was agreed upon between the Master and me, and agreeable to my Lord President's letter, and to my Lord Loudoun's verbal message by me. I say we had agreed that there was a report to be made agreeable to this resolution between the Master and me, to my Lord Lovat.

Please to inform their lordships, in the first place, whether you delivered my Lord President's letter to my Lord Lovat.—I did.

And did you make a report to my Lord Lovat, according to what was agreed upon between his son and you?—I did.

Please to repeat them again to my lords, and state what was the message you delivered to my Lord Lovat besides the letter?—The report I delivered to my Lord Lovat besides delivering the letter was this, that it was my Lord President's belief that an order would be immediately sent down from London for the seizing of his person, and inquiring into his conduct, and that it was my Lord Loudoun's determination to put that order in execution as soon as ever it came into his hands.

Do you recollect anything more concerning it? Do you remember whether it was to be put in execution in case the Frasers did, or in case they did not march?—In case the Frasers did march.

Is this the whole substance of the report that you made to Lord Lovat?—Yes, so far as I remember.

What answer did my Lord Lovat make you upon that occasion?—When I made the report I do not remember any particular conversation that passed upon it.

Did he give you any answer to it at any other time, and when?—There was a conversation between us soon after about it. I believe it was the next day after my return to Castle Downie.

What did my Lord Lovat then say to you relating to those messages, or to that report which you made?—I believe my Lord Lovat said that he thought the report of securing his person and inquiring into his conduct was to be considered rather as a bugbear.

Was the Master of Lovat present at that time?—Yes, he was.

What did my Lord Lovat say to his son upon that occasion?—My Lord Lovat told his son what I have already said, that he looked upon it to be rather a bugbear, and that it was his opinion he should proceed in the undertaking he was engaged in.

Did he upon that occasion give or make any orders concerning what was to be done?—Yes; that the men should march immediately.

Hugh Fraser

Did he give any orders for it?—Not in the way of an order.

What did he say upon the occasion?—That it was his opinion that the men should march immediately.

What men did you understand by that were to march immediately?—The clan of the Frasers.

What march did you understand it was to be, or whither were they to march?—To join the rebel army.

Was there any other company present at this conversation besides my Lord Lovat and the Master and you?—Yes; there were two other gentlemen.

Did Lord Lovat then say anything to them concerning it by way of asking their opinion or their agreement to it?—He asked the opinion of all the gentlemen present after he had given his own by saying that it was his opinion, and that he hoped all the gentlemen present agreed to it.

What did you understand by that?—That he hoped all present agreed to the opinion which he had delivered himself.

Did you give any answer to that or any opinion concerning it?—Yes, I did.

What was it?—So far as I remember, the answer I made was that my opinion had not been asked, but that, notwithstanding that, I thought myself obliged to give it, and it was this, that if the affair could not be entirely dropped, that it should be put off for some time.

Did my Lord Lovat give any answer to that?—When I said that my opinion had not been asked, he told me that some people's opinion might be easily read in their countenances, or words to that purpose.

What answer did you make upon that?—The answer I have already given.

What answer did Lord Lovat give as to the putting off the march for a while?—No answer at all, so far as I remember. The Master of Lovat upon that burst out into tears, and said he had been made a fool of, and a tool from first to last.

Did he say anything more?—Yes; he said that he had been one day doing and another day undoing, but that now he was determined that whatsoever resolution Lord Lovat should come to, that he would execute it, let the consequence be what it would with respect to himself and other people.

Was there anything more passed? Did Lord Lovat say anything upon this occasion?—My Lord Lovat said that he had given his opinion already, and that he would not alter it, or to that effect.

You have seen my Lord Lovat and his son pretty often together, and were at his house for two or three months together. Pray, what was your opinion as to the backwardness of the Master of Lovat or as to his obedience or disobedience to his father in respect to his going into the rebellion? Do you think that the Master was guilty of obstinacy and disobedience to his father in going into the rebellion, or that by so doing he complied with his father's orders and inclinations?—If I am to form my opinion with respect to the Master of Lovat upon his own good sense and understanding or his avowed principles I should apprehend that he would not have gone into the rebellion had he been left to himself. And if I am to form my opinion upon the private conversations I had with him, and particularly one which I remember I had in Urquhart, I say, if I am to form my opinion upon what he, with respect to his intentions and sentiments, declared to me, it is my belief that he would not have had any concern in this rebellion had he been entirely left to himself. **Hugh Fraser**

I desire to ask you, sir, whether, from your own knowledge of the situation of the clan of the Frasers and of the power and influence which either my Lord Lovat or the Master had over them, do you think that the Master of Lovat could have raised the clan without the concurrence and order of my Lord Lovat?—I believe had the Lord Lovat and the Master acted in direct opposition the one to the other that the clan would have been divided, and part would have gone with one and part with the other, but what part to either of them is what I cannot determine.

About what time was it that the news came first to Castle Downie of the landing of Lord John Drummond with soldiers from France?—It was about a day before I went to my Lord President, or that day.

I desire to know whether, in your opinion, that news had any influence to determine my Lord Lovat's conduct at that time.—I cannot take upon me to say what it was that determined my Lord Lovat's conduct.

Did you hear my Lord Lovat say anything about that particular event of Lord John Drummond's landing then?—I've heard my Lord Lovat report what intelligence had been returned to him on account of that landing.

Please to give an account to my lords when the Master of Lovat and the Frasers did march, and where they marched to.—Some part of the Frasers marched at one time and some at another. Some of them marched a short time after this conversation passed between my Lord Lovat and the Master, at which I was present.

Where did they march first?—They marched first to Perth, but the Master of Lovat did not go along with them.

Did my Lord Lovat know or not know of their marching?—That I don't know of my own knowledge, but that my Lord Lovat must have heard of their march is certain.

Did they or did they not march against his orders?—Truly, that is what I cannot easily answer. He certainly gave orders

Hugh Fraser for them not to march sometimes, and it was sometimes given out that he gave orders for their marching, but I did not see either of these orders.

Please to give my lords an account when the Frasers did march to Perth, and be as correct as you can.—The times that they marched were different.

Did they march in large numbers?—They marched in very small numbers, not, I believe, above fifty at a time, and the number that marched in all was but very small.

What number do you suppose might march?—When they were strongest at Perth they were between 200 and 300 at most.

Please to give an account to my lords whether my Lord Lovat was apprehended by Lord Loudoun's or my Lord President's order, and when.—The next morning after the conversation passed between the Lord Lovat and the Master, as I mentioned already, I left Castle Downie.

Were the Frasers then gone, or were they going to Perth?—I believe there were none of them gone at that time, but I cannot say that I remember positively, but their march was then resolved on.

Do you remember when it was precisely that you came from my Lord President's to my Lord Lovat?—I do not remember the precise day of the month.

About what time of the month was it?—I dare say it must be about the beginning of December.

You say that you went to Perth with the Master of Lovat. Pray, who was with you?—The Master and I went to Perth by ourselves alone.

When you came there where was the body of the rebel army?—I believe it was in England.

How soon after that did they come into Scotland again?—About two or three weeks at most. After the Master and I had got to Perth there came an account that the rebel army had returned to Glasgow.

Had you any orders from the Pretender's son about marching?—There were orders given by Mr. Murray that the rebel forces should march to Stirling to join those coming from Glasgow.

Did the Frasers go thither?—They did.

How far did they go?—To Stirling.

Was there any message sent to Glasgow or any place thereabouts by the Master of Lovat relating to the Frasers?—Yes, there was. It was sent from Perth to Glasgow.

For what purpose was it sent?—In order to procure firelocks for the Frasers.

Did you yourself go to Glasgow?—I did.

To whom did you apply there?—To Mr. John Murray.

Fourth Day.

Please to give an account to my lords what was the effect of the application of yours.—The effect of it was that an order was sent to Lord John Drummond, in the name of one that called himself the French Ambassador, that Lord John Drummond should deliver arms for the Frasers out of the arms that he had in charge that were the King of France's arms, as he himself said. Hugh Fraser

How long did you stay at Glasgow?—About twenty-four hours.

Before your return from thence had you any conversation or meeting with Mr. Murray of Broughton, the Pretender's secretary?—I called upon him there, and saw him in his own room.

What was the import of your conversation at that meeting?—The business that brought me there was to desire him to send the arms I mentioned.

Was that the only subject of your conversation?—No; we talked with respect to the situation of matters in the north country and with respect to the imprisonment of my Lord Lovat and his escape from Inverness, which I had then heard of.

Was there any proposal then made concerning the army's going into the north country to take Inverness?—There was a proposal then made that a detachment should be sent from the army in order to make themselves masters of Inverness.

What more passed between you relating to this proposal?—That proposal was agreed to, and a resolution formed upon it, in a council that was called in the afternoon.

Did you at that time hear anything or receive anything from my Lord Lovat?—No; I had no charge from my Lord Lovat when I went to Glasgow.

But when you were there did you receive any order from Lord Lovat?—I received no order or letter from my Lord Lovat while I was at Glasgow.

Had you any orders or letters from Lord Lovat at all relating to the sending any men northward? I do not mean while you were at Glasgow, but in Stratherick, or any other place.—Before I went to Perth there was a letter delivered to me.

You say it was concerted to send a detachment to Inverness, or that a detachment of the army should go thither. What was done in pursuance of that resolution?—Nothing at all.

You say that you received a letter from my Lord Lovat at Stratherick. Pray, what were the contents of it?—I did say so. There was a letter delivered to me. It was not signed, but it appeared to me to be the handwriting of Robert Fraser, who then acted as secretary to my Lord Lovat, but it had no name subscribed to it.

What was the import of that letter?—The request of the letter was that I should have gone to Perth in order to have

Hugh Fraser prevailed with the gentlemen who commanded at that place to send a number of forces to Inverness in order to make themselves masters of that place by dislodging my Lord Loudoun and to rescue my Lord Lovat.

Was anything done upon this?—Nothing. I refused to do it.

Before you went from Glasgow, and returned with the answer to the message you had delivered there, did you receive any message from Mr. Murray, the secretary, or any packet, and what was it?—Mr. Murray proposed to me to carry a packet from Glasgow to Perth.

Did he deliver you any packet?—I refused to take it, because I told him that very probably his packet would require despatch, and that I rid my own horses, and did not incline to abuse them.

Did you or did you not receive the packet?—When he told me afterwards that he had no other person to carry it, and that it did not require despatch, I accepted of the packet.

Do you know what that packet contained?—I came to know it afterwards.

And what were the contents of it?—There was a separate letter directed to the Master of Lovat only with respect to the army, and there was a large packet of papers not directed to any person, but which, Mr. Murray told me, I was to deliver to the Master of Lovat.

Do you know what that letter or packet did contain?—Upon my return to Perth, as the Master of Lovat happened not to be there at that time, another gentleman and I took the freedom to open the large packet.

What did you find in it?—There was in it a commission of lieutenant-general to my Lord Lovat, that is, in my Lord Lovat's name, and it was granted in the name of James the Eighth.

What was there in it else?—There was another commission in it to my Lord Lovat of lieutenant of some northern county granted in the same manner.

Did that appear to be signed and sealed by the Pretender?—It had a subscription and superscription and a seal.

Was there anything else contained in that packet?—There was another commission to a gentleman of the name of Fraser.

What did that commission import to be?—It was a colonel's commission.

Do you recollect to whom it was made?—The gentleman was named Fraser, one who was called Inverlacky; and a gentleman of that name was then acting in that capacity among the Frasers.

Did that commission appear, upon the face of it, to be signed, and sealed, and by whom?—Yes: it was signed and sealed in the same manner as the other commissions were.

Fourth Day.

Was there anything else in the packet?—There was a letter under the hand of the Pretender's son. Hugh Fraser

To whom was that directed?—It was directed to my Lord Lovat.

Was there any other paper there?—Yes; there was a letter from Mr. Murray, Cameron of Lochiel, and MacPherson of Cluny.

To whom was that letter directed?—That letter had no direction or cover; it was in the large cover.

Were those all that were in the large cover?—All that I remember.

Was the large cover addressed to anybody?—No.

What was the reason of that?—The reason give me by Mr. Murray was that it was intended for my Lord Lovat, but could not be directed, because he could not ascertain by what title to write it.

What was the doubted title?—The doubted title was that of a duke.

Duke of what?—Duke of Fraser or Beaufort—Fraser, I believe.

Does not my Lord Lovat's house go by two names?—Yes, by the name of Castle Downie and Beaufort.

Do you know whether that letter that was signed by Cluny MacPherson, Lochiel, and Mr. Murray was referred to in the letter that was sent by the Pretender's son?—I do not know that it was.

Do you recollect the substance of the letter from the Pretender's son to my Lord Lovat?—The substance of the letter, as far as I can recollect, was requesting my Lord Lovat to come and join with him in person.

My lords, these are all the questions we have to ask of this witness.

Lord High Steward—My Lord Lovat, the gentlemen of the House of Commons have done with this witness. Would your lordship ask him any questions?

Lord Lovat—My lords, I have told your lordships already that I am so ill that I am not able to speak, or to get up or sit down, and therefore hope your lordships will indulge me to retire a little and refresh myself.

Lord High Steward—My lords, my Lord Lovat desires leave to withdraw for a little while.

Lords—Ay, ay.

Upon which Lord Lovat withdrew for a little while, and being returned,

Lord Lovat—I desire that your lordships will indulge me in permitting your Clerk to read the questions I would ask.

Hugh Fraser

LORDS—Ay, ay.

LORD LOVAT's questions were as follows:—

Were not you taken prisoner by the King's forces after the battle of Culloden?

WITNESS—I was.

Have you not been in custody ever since, and are you not so now?—I have been, and I am.

Have you as yet obtained any pardon?—I know of none.

Are you in expectation of a pardon from what you shall depose against me?—I will answer that question very readily. I do not expect punishment will be inflicted, but I assure your lordship it is no condition or paction made with me.

Have you ever had any offer made to you of a pardon upon this or any other condition, and what was that condition?—I have had no offers made to me of a pardon upon any condition whatever.

LORD TALBOT—My lords, I have taken a particular account of the evidence of this witness, which I beg leave to repeat to your lordships in the presence of the witness, that in case I misrepresent any part he may correct it, I having been already accused of unfairness in the manner of stating my questions. My lords, the witness says that the men marched before the Master of Lovat went from Castle Downie, that he and the Master of Lovat followed the men and endeavoured to prevail upon them to return, but that Barisdale prevailed upon them to advance, contrary to the desire and advice of the Master of Lovat, that my Lord Lovat afterwards wrote a letter to them to return, and that they did return, that my Lord Lovat certainly gave orders sometimes that they should not march. (To witness)—Am I right in this state of the evidence?

WITNESS—Yes, my Lord Lovat certainly gave orders for them sometimes not to march, and, I believe, he gave orders at other times for them to march.

LORD TALBOT—My lords, he says that he believes that at other times my Lord Lovat ordered them to march, but, my lords, this might be only a general report, without any foundation, as it might be the report of Barisdale, in order to prevail on them to march.

LORD HIGH STEWARD—My lords, the noble lord is in the right to state the evidence to the witness in order to introduce questions by way of explanation, but to observe upon that evidence now is not regular.

LORD TALBOT—My lords, all that I mean is to come at the truth, which I cannot do from my own knowledge. (To witness)—You have said that you have heard my Lord Lovat say that the conduct of his clan might cost him his life.

WITNESS—I did.

Now, my lords, the question I would ask him from all this put together is whether he did understand by these expressions of my Lord Lovat that he disapproved of the conduct of his clan?—That my Lord Lovat disapproved to me in private, and that I have heard him disapprove and condemn in public the conduct of his clan is truth, that I affirm before Almighty God.

Have you been examined by anybody relating to this trial since you were a prisoner before you came to this place?—I have.

My lords, I will beg leave to ask him whether the confessions he made upon that examination, or the answers he gave there, proceeded from the hope of a pardon?

WITNESS—I cannot say that I would have done it had I been convinced that I should meet with no mercy, though, at the same time, I had no assurance given me of mercy, neither had I any promise of pardon.

Do you believe that your pardon may depend upon the consistency of the evidence you shall give here with what you have said upon those former examinations?

DUKE OF BEDFORD—My lords, I do not think that is a proper question to be asked of any witness, and, if it is insisted upon to be asked, I shall beg your lordships may adjourn to the Chamber of Parliament to determine that question, and I will there give my reasons against it.

LORD TALBOT—My lords, I have no partiality for the noble lord at the bar, but what I have said proceeded from a principle of humanity, a principle of honour, and a principle of justice.

LORD HIGH STEWARD (to witness)—You have spoken of different orders that were given at different times. Sometimes my Lord Lovat ordered the men to march, and at other times not to march. Do you know, of your own knowledge, of any of these orders being given?

WITNESS—I have already said that I saw an order under his hand for the returning of seven companies of men from Urquhart, whither they had marched.

Whither were they to return?—To their own houses.

When was that order given?—In the month of November.

What orders did you ever see or hear from my Lord Lovat for the men to march?—I never saw any order of my Lord Lovat for the men to march.

They why did you speak of those orders?—I have given my reason for that, that I heard such orders talked of, but that I heard them given I never did say, and never will.

LORD ORFORD—When my Lord Lovat declared himself dis-

Hugh Fraser satisfied with the conduct of his clan was it for their being too forward or too backward in going into rebellion?

WITNESS—I have already said that I have heard him dissatisfied for their too great forwardness, and I have likewise heard him dissatisfied for their too great backwardness.

ATTORNEY-GENERAL—My lords, in consequence of some questions that have been asked, I beg leave to know of this witness whether what he has said in evidence before your lordships, notwithstanding his having said it under the circumstances of his being now a prisoner, is or is not true.

WITNESS—I say that what I have said is literally fact.

Then I beg he may inform your lordships whether, supposing he had been called on to be a witness, and had not been a prisoner, but had been, by virtue of your lordships' summons obliged to come before you to give evidence upon this trial, would he have given any other evidence than what he hath given before your lordships?—If I would give evidence in any case it should be the truth, and if the truth were such as I did not choose to disclose I would declare positively that I would give no evidence at all.

Were not you in so dangerous a condition in point of health when you were at Fort Augustus that your life was not expected?—At Fort Augustus I was past all hopes of recovery, and at Inverness.

During that time did not you give, in substance, the same account of these transactions as you have given now?—There were questions asked me then, and the answers I gave to them were the real truth. Matters were not then so fully explicated as they have been since, so that those declarations were not so complete as the account I have given now, but the answers that I made there were still the real genuine truth as to those questions that I was asked, and so is the account I have now given.

I beg he may inform your lordships if, so far as his examination then went, it was not the same as his examination is now.—So far as the examination was then extended it was the same as now. Truth is always the same; it will never vary from itself.

Did you not then expect to die?—I expected not to live, sure enough.

Was it from the condition you were in by your distempter that you expected not to live?—It was from my wounds and the ailments that I laboured under.

My lords, we have done with this witness.

A LORD—I beg this witness may inform your lordships if the packet which he carried from Mr. Murray containing the papers that he has mentioned was ever delivered, and to whom.

Fourth Day.

WITNESS—That packet was never delivered to my Lord Lovat. Hugh Fraser

A LORD—I beg he may inform your lordships to whom that packet was delivered.—When I came to Perth a gentleman, who then commanded among the Frasers, and I, opened the packet to see what it contained, and while I was intending to shut it up again and to forward it to the Master of Lovat, the Master himself came into the room, and I told him the freedom we had used with those letters and packets. He said that we might always use that freedom, and were welcome. All those papers which I have mentioned to have been contained in that packet were then lying upon the table where we stayed. I told the Master, in general, what they were, and he threw them from him, and there they continued to lie till I went from Perth to Stirling, and as that march was made a little precipitately, those papers and everything else that belonged to me that were in the room were thrown into my cloak-bag, and they and my cloak-bag continued in my possession till some few days before the battle of Culloden, when I lodged them in a house at Inverness, and went myself to the field of battle.

Then the witness, by the direction of the Lord High Steward, withdrew.

SIR WILLIAM YONGE—My lords, the next gentleman we beg leave to call is Lieutenant Alexander Campbell.[1] A. Campbell

Lieutenant Campbell was called into Court.

LORD HIGH STEWARD—My Lord Lovat, have you any objection to Lieutenant Campbell being a witness.

LORD LOVAT—I don't know him. I never heard of him.

Alexander Campbell was sworn.

SIR WILLIAM YONGE—My lords, we beg leave to ask this witness whether at any time in the year 1745 he went to Castle Downie.

WITNESS—Yes, I did.

About what time was it that you went?—I don't remember particularly. It was some time in October.

Upon what account did you go there?—To require some cattle that were carried off from some people in the shire of Ross.

By whom were these cattle carried off?—By some of my Lord Lovat's people. I don't know whether it was done by his orders or not.

When you came near Castle Downie did you see any number of armed men?—Yes, I did.

How were you received by those armed men, with acclamations or in what manner, and how many were there of them?—I cannot condescend upon the number of men.

---

[1] The author of the tract in the New Spalding Club Historical Papers describes this gentleman as "Factor to Lord Fortrose."

A. Campbell How were you received by them, with acclamations or how?—Yes.

How were you received; in what manner?—They were all out with their arms, some of the Macleod's deserters that came from Inverness.

How were you received there by those men; in what manner?—Some of them took off their bonnets.

Were there any shouts or huzzas made use of?—Yes; some of them did.

Upon what account?—I can't tell.

Did not they say anything to you of the reason of it?—No; they spoke nothing to me.

Did you go to dine with my Lord Lovat at Castle Downie?—No, I did not.

Were you at Castle Downie with him?—Yes.

Had you any conversation with my Lord Lovat there?—Yes.

What conversation had you with him?—I told him I came to require the cattle, and he told me the cattle were not brought there by his order, but his son's.

My lords, the witness had better go on with the rest of the conversation. I know he can, without being asked particular questions, for I would not lead him.

Witness—I do not remember what passed.

Lord Talbot—My lords, I must take notice to your lordships that I think it is a very odd expression to make use of to a witness, that "He had better answer the questions for I know he can." It is a kind of threatening the witness.

Sir William Yonge—My lords, I stand here as a Manager on this trial for the Commons of Great Britain, and I hope I say nothing that is offensive to your lordships, and that the manner in which I asked the witness the question showed that it proceeded from a fairness in stating of it. My lords, I think, as a Manager, I ought to know what a witness can say, and the whole tendency of what I said was advising the witness, without giving your lordships unnecessary trouble, to tell all he knew, fairly and impartially, without my being obliged to put any leading questions to him. And I hope I shall have your lordships' liberty to go on.

Lord High Steward—My lords, everybody knows that it is the constant course and usage of Parliament that when a Committee of Managers is appointed by the House of Commons upon an impeachment it is their duty to examine—and they always do examine—the witnesses beforehand; and the same method is used by prosecutors for the Crown upon indictments. If this was not done, it would be impossible to know whether a witness could speak materially to the facts in questions or not.

Lord Talbot—My lords, though they are Managers, I am

a judge. I have as high a veneration for the representatives of this kingdom as any man in the world. I sat some time among them myself. But, I am sure, my lords, the representatives of England do not desire a language may be used to a witness that may seem threatening. And, my lords, I took the expression used by the Manager in this light. The expression was that he had better speak, which, I apprehend, was as much as to say that if he hoped for mercy he must tell it. My lords, I desire a fair examination, that I may form a true judgment. My honour depends upon it. A. Campbell

LORD HIGH STEWARD—My lords, I desire this may be forborne. It is my duty to acquaint your lordships that it is irregular and contrary to all rules of proceeding. The honourable Manager explained his words in a very proper and candid manner, that he thought it was fairer in him to ask the witness general questions, to declare what he knew of the fact, than any particular questions which might tend to lead him, and he was in the right.

ATTORNEY-GENERAL—My lords, in order to clear up this matter, I beg leave to ask the witness whether he is now a prisoner.

WITNESS—No.

Were you ever a prisoner?—Yes; I was a prisoner with the rebels.

Had you then the King's commission?—Yes; when I was a prisoner.

Were you engaged in the King's behalf against the rebels when you were taken?—Yes.

SIR WILLIAM YONGE—Your lordships now see that the witness is no prisoner nor under any terror of apprehension, but has now the King's commission in his pocket, and therefore I beg leave to ask him what the conversation was that passed between my Lord Lovat and him about the cattle?

WITNESS—As I did not expect to be called here as a witness, so I do not remember what passed upon that occasion.

Did my Lord Lovat persuade you to join the rebels or not?—He did not.

Did he say nothing to induce you to it?—He said nothing at all to induce me to join them.

Or his son?—No.

My lords, I don't know whether it be so proper, but have you never said so?—No; I never did say so.

MR. NOEL—My lords, I beg leave to ask him whether any discourse passed between my Lord Lovat and him touching the rebellion?

WITNESS—Yes.

A. Campbell Pray, tell my lords what that was.—He said his son was engaged in the rebellion, not him, and that he was a very loyal person.

My lords, we have done with this witness.

Lord High Steward—My Lord Lovat, would you ask this witness any questions?

Lord Lovat—No; I have no questions, my lord, to ask this witness. I never saw him before in my life.

Then the witness, by the direction of the Lord High Steward, withdrew.

Peter Fraser Mr. Lyttleton—My lords, the next witness we shall produce is Peter Fraser, tutor of Belladrum.

Peter Fraser was called into Court.

Lord Lovat—My lords, I have a material objection to this witness. He is my tenant in all that he professes.

Lord High Steward—Would your lordship ask him that question, or would you prove it upon him by witnesses?

Lord Lovat—I humbly think he will not deny it. If he does, I have witnesses to prove it.

Attorney-General—My lords, I beg the noble lord at the bar may explain what he means by saying if he denies it that he has witnesses to prove it, for if the noble lord puts it to the oath of the witness and he denies it then he cannot, without the consent of the Commons, call a witness to prove it.

Lord High Steward—My lords, the rule is, that upon an objection made to the competency of a witness the party objecting may either put it to the oath of the witness produced, or call witnesses to prove it. If he puts it to the oath of the witness produced, then he is concluded as to the point of competency by the answer he gives to it, unless the other side consents to waive that. My Lord Lovat, do you choose to put this to the oath of Peter Fraser or to call a witness to prove it?

Lord Talbot—My lords, I desire to know if this witness should deny it, whether my Lord Lovat may not give evidence of this man's being his tenant when he comes upon his defence.

Lord High Steward—Gentlemen of the House of Commons, you hear what the noble lord says. What do you say to it?

Attorney-General—My lords, to be sure my Lord Lovat may give such proof by way of objection to the credit of the witness, but not to his competency.

Lord High Steward—My Lord Lovat, do you choose now to put this question to the oath of the witness himself or to call a witness to prove it?

Lord Lovat—I will put it to his own oath.

Then the witness was sworn upon a *voire dire*.

Fourth Day.

Lord Lovat—My lords, I desire to ask him whether or no the lands he possesses are not my lands? Peter Fraser

Witness—Yes, they are. I possess them in virtue of my nephews' right, who hold a tack under my Lord Lovat.

Lord High Steward—How do you hold them in virtue of your nephews? Is it as their manager or tutor?

A Lord—My lords, I will beg leave to ask a question to explain that, which is, whether or no the witness pays the rents of those lands to my Lord Lovat's chamberlain or steward?

Witness—I do.

Lord Lovat—Do you pay any part of that rent in your own right?

Witness—No; I do not. I only pay it in virtue of my nephews, as taking care of them.

Attorney-General—My lords, the question which the noble lord at the bar has now put to the witness is that which I intended to have put to him, which is whether he holds any lands in his own right or only as tutor? He has told your lordships that he holds none in his own right, but only as tutor to his nephews.

Mr. Lyttelton—My lords, we pray the witness may be sworn in chief.

Peter Fraser was sworn in chief.

Lord Lovat—My lords, I beg to ask him whether he does not hold a tack of land within the lordship of Lovat, of Aird, or Stratherick.

Witness—I do not.

Mr. Lyttelton—I beg this witness may inform your lordships whether in the year 1745 he was at my Lord Lovat's house at Castle Downie.

Witness—Yes, I was.

And whether he remembers to have seen any of my Lord Lovat's men rendezvous there about that time.—Yes, I did.

Did you see any of the officers that headed those men go to my Lord Lovat's house and converse with him there?—Yes, I did.

Whom did you see there?—Simon Fraser of Macleod.

Did he talk to my Lord Lovat about the regiment, or ask any orders from him?—I never heard him say anything, only that my Lord Lovat desired him to go to their colonel. That is all I heard.

Whom did he call their colonel?—His son, the Master of Lovat.

How came he to be their colonel? Had not the Lord Lovat the absolute power over his clan?—Yes; he had.

Do you imagine or believe that the Master of Lovat could have carried the Frasers into the rebellion if his father had been against it?—No; he could not. I am sure he could not.

Peter Fraser

Had the Master of Lovat any manner of foundation to think he could raise the men himself, or did he at his own charge or cost pay those men when they went into the rebellion, or had he money to do it?—I suppose he had no money of his own.

Who do you think furnished him with the money necessary for that purpose?—Really I know nothing of the money. I saw no money given.

Do you know anything of Barisdale's keeping a party of men upon my Lord Lovat's ground?—Yes.

What were they there to do?—To overawe the country.

To do what?—To rise in arms.

In arms for whom?—For the Pretender.

Had he got any of them to rise in arms then?—Yes.

Did he make any of my Lord Lovat's vassals rise in arms at that time?—They stayed in the country till they saw some of the men did convene.

Do you know of anybody's giving the men any cattle or meal?—Yes, my Lord Lovat gave them some cows.

To whose men? To Barisdale's men?—No, to my Lord Lovat's men.

Those that joined with Barisdale?—Yes.

Did you see Barisdale converse with my Lord Lovat then?—Yes, I did.

Did my Lord Lovat know that he was then in the rebellion?—No doubt of it.

Did he wear any mark of distinction to show it?—He wore a white cockade.

Do you remember any part of the conversation between Barisdale, Macleod, and my Lord Lovat concerning my lord's declaring openly for the Pretender?—I remember one day that Alexander Macleod said that all would be well if my lord would pull off the mask, upon which my Lord Lovat, by way of reply, pulled off his hat and said, "There it is, then."

What did that conversation relate to?—I heard no more of it.

What were they talking about?—I only heard that he said all would be well if my Lord Lovat would pull off the mask.

What did that conversation mean? What meant "all would be well"?—I cannot tell.

What did my Lord Lovat mean by pulling off his hat?—All that they said was that all would be well, if my lord would pull off the mask, upon which my Lord Lovat pulled off his hat and said, "There it is, then."

Did he throw his hat down?—I did not see that.

Did my Lord Lovat offer you to be an officer?—No, he never did.

My lords, we have done with this witness.

Fourth Day.

LORD HIGH STEWARD—My Lord Lovat, would you ask this witness any questions? Peter Fraser

LORD LOVAT—Were you examined at Inverness, and by whom, and who were the persons you saw there?

WITNESS—I was examined at Inverness before one Kilravock. He was a depute. And I was examined before my Lord Loudoun.

Were you examined upon oath?—Yes, I was summoned and strictly deponed.

Upon oath?—Upon oath.

Who were the persons you saw at Inverness when you were examined?—We were examined but one by one. As soon as one was examined another was called in, and no other person heard what the examinations were.

Who were present at the examinations?—Lord Loudoun, Kilravock, and a clerk.

At what time was you examined at Inverness?—I do not remember the day of the month, indeed.

What month was it?—It was in January; the latter end of January.

In January last?—Yes, in January last.

LORD HIGH STEWARD—You say you were at Castle Downie in 1745, and saw all the men rendezvous there. In what month was that?

WITNESS—In November.

Then the prisoner begged leave to withdraw a little, which was granted, and he soon after returned to the bar again.

MR. LEGGE—The next witness we shall call is John Farquhar. J. Farquhar

At the prisoner's request, he was sworn upon a *voire dire*.

LORD LOVAT—Are you tenant to me?

WITNESS—No.

What is your name?—John Farquhar.

What employment are you of?—I was servant to Mr. Murray.

John Farquhar was sworn in chief.

MR. LEGGE—My lords, we propose to examine this witness as to the steps taken by my Lord Lovat subsequent to the battle of Culloden, in order to revive and restore the Pretender's cause in Scotland. (To witness)—Were not you servant to Mr. Murray of Broughton?

WITNESS—Yes.

In what capacity did you serve him?—I was his groom.

J. Farquhar For what space of time did you serve him? From what time and to what time?—From Michaelmas till the 9th of June last.

In what year?—In 1745.

Was there a meeting of the chieftains in the rebel army after the battle of Culloden?—Yes.

When was that meeting?—On the 10th of May last.

Who were the persons that met on that occasion?—Mr. Murray of Broughton, Lochiel, young Clanranald,[1] Cameron of Dungallon, Dr. Cameron, and several others that I did not know, and my Lord Lovat. They met at the island of Mortlaig.[2]

Did you hear of any French ships having landed any money in Scotland then?—Yes.

Upon what day did you hear that they landed that money?—Upon the 4th of May.

What did you imagine was the subject-matter of the meeting you mentioned?—In order to have a second gathering of the rebel army.

Did you hear any, and what orders given to anybody, and to whom, upon that occasion?—There was an order for the men to be gathered together at a place called Glenmany.

Who were the persons that gave those orders?—There was Lochiel, and the several other persons that were present at the meeting.

How did Lord Lovat behave on that occasion? Did he express any satisfaction on that head?—He was present during all the time I was there.

Did he say anything about the number of men that were to be raised?—The next morning, when the parties were going away, my Lord Lovat said they had no need to fear, and he did not doubt raising eight or ten thousand men presently.

Some lords desired the last answer to be repeated, which was accordingly done by the witness as follows:—

Witness—The next morning, when the parties were going away, Lord Lovat said that there was no need to fear, for that he did not doubt to raise eight or ten thousand men presently, and that those, with the Highland men, would be able to fight the Elector of Hanover's troops. He said this to Lochiel's officers, when they embraced each other.

Had my Lord Lovat any of his own clan there?—Yes, he had some of them to wait upon him.

Were they armed?—Yes, with swords, dirks, and pistols.

Did they wear any mark of distinction in their hats?—Some of them had sprigs of yew, and such like things, in their hats, by which they were known to be of that party.

---

[1] Ranald MacDonald of Clanranald, son of the fifteenth chief. See Biographical Notes, p. 304.

[2] The witness confuses Mortlaig (Muirlaggan) and Morar. The former, where the meeting took place, is not an island.

Did you hear my Lord Lovat express any wishes that he had joined their army?—He said he wished to God he had joined the Prince, as he called him, at first when he came over. J. Farquhar

While you were there did you hear the Pretender's health drunk?—Yes.

By what style or title?—By the title of Prince Charles, to the young one.

And what title did they give to the old one?—The title of James the Eighth.

Who were the persons that drank it? Did you hear my Lord Lovat drink it?—Yes.

Pray, how long did this council last?—From night till next morning. I was there from two o'clock till ten in the morning.

You mentioned the French money as being landed on the 4th of May. Do you know anything of the disposition of any part of that money?—Yes.

To whom was it given?—To the officers of the rebel army.

For what purpose was it given them?—For a second gathering of the men.

Do you know what was the general resolution that that council came to, or what was their determination?—That they would assemble a body of the several clans to march south, so far as I could conjecture.

Why do you conjecture that?—I heard it.

Did you hear of any expectation of further assistance from France?—Yes.

What number of men did you expect?—I did not hear any particular number mentioned, but we expected a reinforcement every day.

Where was the rendezvous to have been?—At Glenmany.

Did they meet there?—Yes, several of them.

What do you think prevented the rest of them from meeting there?—The King's troops.

Mr. Legge—My lords, we have done with this witness.

Lord High Steward—My Lord Lovat, will you ask this witness any questions?

Lord Lovat—Was you taken prisoner by the King's forces?

Witness—No.

Do you know whether the money that came over from France in the ship was given to Mr. Murray?—I cannot tell. Mr. Murray was there when the money came.

A Lord—Do you know of any more meetings than one between Lochiel and Lord Lovat?

Witness—No.

Then the witness, by the direction of the Lord High Steward, withdrew.

C. Stuart MR. GRENVILLE—My lords, the next witness we beg leave to call is Charles Stuart.

Charles Stuart was called into Court.

LORD HIGH STEWARD—My Lord Lovat, have you any objection to this witness?

LORD LOVAT—No.

Charles Stuart was sworn.

MR. GRENVILLE—My lords, we beg this witness may inform your lordships whether he remembers the battle of Culloden.

WITNESS—Yes.

Did you go with Mr. Murray, the Pretender's son's secretary, after that battle to Mortlaig?—Yes.

Was there a meeting there of any of the rebel officers?—Yes.

Who were present?—There were Lochiel, Clanranald, Barisdale, and several others.

Was my Lord Lovat there?—Yes, he was there.

Where were they?—In a little hut.

Were you in the room with them?—Yes, I was.

Did you hear what passed in the room? If you did, please to give my lords an account of what passed there.—Lochiel and Mr. Murray of Broughton came there, where they met with my Lord Lovat and several other of the Highland chieftains. They wanted to create an association for re-assembling the men together in order to procure a peace or terms of surrender with the Duke of Cumberland, or to stand it out to the last. Mr. Murray ordered me to draw up the articles, which I wrote, and it was signed by every chief that was there.

Did my Lord Lovat sign it?—No, all but he.

Was it proposed to him to sign it?—Yes, it was, and he would not.

What was the purport of it?—That they were to assemble again in ten days in order to procure terms of peace from the Duke, or stand it out to the last.

What number of Frasers was proposed to be raised?—I think three or four hundred.

Did anybody undertake for the Frasers?—I think Lochiel did.

At whose request did he undertake for the Frasers?—When it was proposed to my Lord Lovat to sign the paper he said he would not, and desired Lochiel to answer for his son.

What did he say about Lochiel?—He desired Lochiel to answer for his son.

Did he or did he not answer for him?—I cannot tell.

What reason did my Lord Lovat give why he would not

sign the paper himself?—I do not remember he gave any reason. C. Stuart

Do you remember any expressions made use of by my Lord Lovat then?—No.

Was there any money given then to any of the chiefs of the clans?—Yes, to all of them.

Who delivered it to them?—I did.

Was there any delivered to Lord Lovat?—No, not to him, but it was given to some of the persons about him. I do not know whether it was his servant or not.

Was he my Lord Lovat's servant?—I do not know. He was a person about him.

For what was it delivered? For what purpose?—For the Master to raise the men against the time.

You saw the money given, and were the person that delivered it?—I did.

How much was there of it?—Seventy or eighty pounds.

How came you by the money?—I got it from Mr. Murray.

What money was it?—Part of 35,000 louis d'or that was landed some days before from France.

Was my Lord Lovat present when the money was delivered?—Yes, he was.

Did he object to anything that was done, but to the signing of the paper?—I do not remember he did.

Was the money that was given in guineas or in louis d'ors?—It was all in louis d'ors.

Was there anything said about a neutrality then?—I think my Lord Lovat said that he was a neutral person, so would have no concern in it.

Do you remember Mr. Murray's being at Arisaig?—Yes.

Did he receive any letter there from a captain of any guard that my Lord Lovat had?—I saw a man come from the house where my lord was, and said he came from the captain of my lord's guards with a letter for Mr. Murray, and asked some money of him.

Did you send any money to my lord?—Yes.

How much did you send?—I believe it was about fifteen guineas.

By whose order did you send it?—It was by Mr. Murray's orders I delivered the money.

Sir John Strange—My lords, I will beg leave to ask this witness whether he was ever abroad on any occasion.

Witness—I was, but 'tis long ago.

How long ago is it?—It was in the year 1736.

Do you remember to have met with a person called Roy Stuart whilst you were abroad?—Yes.

Where did you meet with him?—At Boulogne, in France.

C. Stuart Where was he going when you saw him there?—He said he was going to Rome.

Please to recollect as near as you can the time when it was you saw Roy Stuart at Boulogne, and give my lords an account thereof?—I think it was in 1736, as near as I can remember.

When Roy Stuart told you he was going to Rome, did he say upon what errand he was going?—He said he was going with letters of recommendation from my Lord Lovat.

My lords, I should not trouble your lordships with asking the witness any questions of this kind if we had not laid a foundation for it already by having proved that a message was sent by this Roy Stuart from my Lord Lovat to the Pretender at Rome, and therefore what I now inquire of him is not matter of hearsay, but it is in corroboration of the circumstance which has been proved to your lordships that my Lord Lovat did give such a message to this Roy Stuart, and, therefore, I will beg leave to ask this witness what message did Roy Stuart say he was going upon?—Nothing else.

Lord Lovat—My lords, I submit it to your lordships if this or any other witness shall be examined upon hearsay evidence.

Lord High Steward—My Lord Lovat, you hear in what manner the Managers offer this evidence. They say that they have proved by one witness that you sent a message by Roy Stuart to the Pretender at Rome. Now, to corroborate that evidence, they offer to prove that Roy Stuart, about the same time, declared to this witness that he had such a message to carry.

Lord Lovat—What the other witness said was hearsay.

Sir John Strange—My lords, I will set the noble lord at the bar right. It was such hearsay as he had from my Lord Lovat's own mouth, for Chevis, the witness, said, on his examination, that after Roy Stuart had made his escape out of Inverness gaol, when he was going away to Rome, he heard my Lord Lovat charge him with a message to the Pretender at Rome, to assure him of his fidelity, and to prosecute the affair of his patent for a duke, so that was not hearsay, but positive evidence.

Lord Lovat—That positive evidence would say that I was a natural idiot!

Lord High Steward—Chevis did swear either that he heard my Lord Lovat charge Roy Stuart with a message to the Pretender to assure him of his fidelity and to expedite his commission of lieutenant-general of the Highlands and his patent of a duke, or else that Lord Lovat told him that he had charged Roy Stuart with such a message, but I am not certain which it was.

Sir John Strange—My lords, I beg leave to ask the witness,

when he met with Roy Stuart, and he said he was going to Rome, what he said he was going upon. C. Stuart

WITNESS—All that Roy Stuart said was that he depended on letters of recommendation he had from my Lord Lovat, and was in expectation of getting the post that Colonel Allan Cameron had.

What letters were these he mentioned?—Letters he said he had from my Lord Lovat.

SOLICITOR-GENERAL—My lords, in order to explain a little more particularly the affair of the meeting, as this witness says that my Lord Lovat refused to sign the paper, I desire to ask him what part my Lord Lovat took in the deliberations about raising the men, before he had an opportunity of making that refusal?

WITNESS—I was busy at that time in distributing the money, and do not remember.

SOLICITOR-GENERAL—My lords, we have done with our examination of this witness.

LORD HIGH STEWARD—My Lord Lovat, would you ask this witness any questions?

LORD LOVAT—No.

Then the witness, by direction of the Lord High Steward, withdrew.

LORD COKE—My lords, the next witness we beg leave to produce is Lieutenant John Dalrymple. J. Dalrymple

Lieutenant Dalrymple was called into Court.

LORD HIGH STEWARD—My Lord Lovat, have you any objections to Lieutenant Dalrymple?

LORD LOVAT—My lords, I do not know him, but have no objections to any Dalrymple.

Lieutenant Dalrymple was sworn.

LORD COKE—My lords, I beg leave to ask this witness where he was when my Lord Lovat was taken.

WITNESS—I was on board the "Furnace" sloop.

Where was she?—At Loch Morar.

Had you any conversation with my Lord Lovat after he was taken prisoner?—I had frequent opportunities of discoursing with him, as I dined and supped with his lordship on board the sloop.

What did he say upon those discourses? What was the purport of them?—On the 8th of June I heard him say that if his advice had been taken the rebel army might have laughed at the King's troops and tired them out all summer. He said it was not their business to fight the King's troops,

J. Dalrymple but that, as summer was coming on, they might have taken themselves to the mountains, and could have lived on butter, cheese, and milk, for that the Duke of Cumberland's horse could be of no service to him in that country. At another time I was asking his lordship how he came to be engaged in this affair, after having received so many favours from the Government. He said he did it more in revenge to the Ministry for having taken away his independent company than anything else. And, in talking of the Pretender's son, he called him Prince, and, when he came on board, there was one Fraser taken, from whom we took about twenty-two guineas, and my Lord Lovat complained that the money had been taken from his servant, which he had given him to pay his men with.

Had my Lord Lovat any men in arms with him when he was taken?—That I am no judge of, because I was on board.

Lord Coke—My lords, we have done with this witness.

Lord High Steward—My Lord Lovat, would you ask this witness any questions?

Lord Lovat—Were you in Captain Fergusson's ship?[1]

Witness—Yes, your lordship may remember me very well.

Then I hope you parted my money amongst you. Did you see him take my strong box, in which were seven hundred guineas—I did not see him take the box.

Did you see it in his cabin?—I saw the outside of it. I never saw the inside.

Sir John Strange—My lords, he says he saw the outside, but did not see the inside of the strong box. He will inform your lordships whether he was present when the papers were taken out of that box afterwards.

Witness—No, I was not present at the opening of it.

Then the witness, by direction of the Lord High Steward, withdrew.

D. Campbell Mr. Noel—My lords, the next witness we beg leave to produce is David Campbell.

He was called into Court.

Lord High Steward—My Lord Lovat, have you any objection to David Campbell?

Lord Lovat—No, I have no objection to any of the Campbells.

David Campbell was sworn.

---

[1] In Flora MacDonald's narrative to Home she speaks of being detained for twenty-two days "on board Captain Fergusson's ship" after her apprehension by a body of Militia. *Vide* Home's "History of the Rebellion."

Fourth Day.

Mr. Noel—Please to tell my lords whether you were with Captain Fergusson upon any occasion, and in what capacity. D. Campbell

Witness—I was a volunteer with General Campbell when we went to search the islands. Our officers and forces that served with General Campbell in the Western Highlands were divided. A good many went by land and a good many by sea, and it fell to my share to go with Captain Fergusson. I was on board and on shore with Captain Fergusson for about six weeks.

What islands did you go to search, and for what purpose?—We went into several islands to search.

Do you remember your going into the island of Morar?—The coast of Morar is on the continent.

Where did you search?—All along the continent, and in all the islands that lie there.

Whom did you find there?—We found a good many rebel gentlemen in the islands and upon the continent.

Did you find any of the MacDonalds there?—We apprehended several of that name.

Do you remember one called the Bishop or Vicar-General?—We had intelligence of his being in Morar, but the day we expected to have taken him he escaped with some others.

Were you present when my Lord Lovat was taken?—I was not present when he was taken, because it was ashore.

Did you see him after he was taken, and where?—I saw him that morning when he was taken and brought on board the "Furnace" sloop. I was then on board that ship.

Did you search for any letters belonging to my Lord Lovat, on his being brought on board, and where did you search?—Captain Duff, who was the captain of the "Terror" man-of-war, was the oldest officer, and, as such, was the commanding officer of all those vessels, and when my Lord Lovat was brought on board, Captain Duff and Captain Fergusson determined to open his box and search it.

Did they find any letters there?—My Lord Lovat and the two captains desired me to be present at the opening and examining of the box, and accordingly I came off the deck and was present, and was desired to take down a particular of everything in the box, which I did write down accordingly, and there was a bundle of papers, which seemed to be letters, that was the last thing we came to in the box; and when we went to examine those letters I undertook to examine and read them, which I was desired to do, and I read them all.

Do you remember any particular letter that you took notice of to my Lord Lovat? If you do, pray tell my lords what Lord Lovat said upon it.—I remember that the purport of all the letters except the last, or the last but one, was about my Lord Lovat's domestic affairs. I cannot be positive whether it was the last or the last but one, but that was a letter directed to my lord from his son.

D. Campbell Did you say anything, and what, to my lord upon that letter? —I read over that letter. My Lord Lovat at first had said to us that we should not find, among those papers that we were examining, any matters of disloyalty or correspondence with the rebels, and I expected it was so; but this letter, seeming to be a correspondence with the rebels, I said to my Lord Lovat, after I had read the letter, "I think your lordship had better not have this letter here." My lord said I was right, and he thought so too, or to that purpose.

Did you say anything to my Lord Lovat concerning his engaging or not engaging in the rebellion?—Yes.

What did you say to him?—I cannot be positive whether I said it in the manner of a question or in the way of conversation, but I took notice to him the one way or the other that I wondered his lordship should be along with the rebels, and be concerned in bringing his country into confusion. I remember I either asked him, or had conversation with him, to this effect.

What answers did you receive from my lord?—What I remember of the purport and effect of it was that he had been disobliged by the Government, and angry ever since he had his independent company taken from him.

Did he give that as an answer to the question that you asked him?—He answered that immediately upon that question, or this part of the conversation, as far as I can recollect.

Did you hear my Lord Lovat say anything about his opinion of fighting the battle of Culloden?—Yes, I have heard my Lord Lovat say that the rebels and the Pretender's son did not behave soldierlike in fighting the Duke of Cumberland at that time.

Did he say that as the opinion of others or as his own opinion? —To the best of my remembrance, the purport of the conversation seemed to be that he thought it was an unsoldierlike and a bad manner of carrying on their affairs.

Did he say anything about any opinion of his having been or not been taken?—I don't remember I heard anything of that.

Recollect yourself whether he did or no.—It is so long since that happened, and I never expected to be questioned about that conversation, that I do not recollect any particular circumstances about my Lord Lovat's giving any particular reasons.

Did he speak anything of his own advice or opinion not being followed, and what was it, or to what purport or effect?—I cannot recollect whether he did or not.

Did he say anything about continuing in the Highlands, or for what purpose?—I cannot charge my memory with that circumstance.

Did you hear my Lord Lovat say anything about his coming to London after he was taken?—Yes.

What did he say upon that occasion?—In the course of conversation sometimes my lord said he was in hopes that he might get friends that would befriend him, and he observed that his being dealt mildly with might be of more service to the Government than rigorous methods, and that it would be of more service if they would spare him than treating him with rigour could possibly be. D. Campbell

Did he say in what respect it might be of more service?—I do not remember that.

Did he mention particularly in what he could be of service or no?—I do not remember any particulars farther than that the general tenour of his conversation seemed to imply that he could be of service to the Government by letting them into the politics of the rebels, or some of their counsels, or to that purpose. I cannot be positive to any particular thing.

My lords, the witness says that he was sent for down from the deck on board the "Furnace," as he understood, at the request of my Lord Lovat, to be present when the box was opened, and that accordingly he went down for that purpose. Now, I desire he may inform your lordships whether there were or were not many papers in that strong box.—It seemed to be a bundle containing from about twenty-five to thirty letters.

After you had read a number of them, before you came to the letter from his son that you have mentioned, did my Lord Lovat say anything about the contents of the papers?—He said, either before or after I had the letters, directing his discourse to the company, that we should find nothing in those letters that would show any correspondence of his with the rebels.

Did he drop anything to that purpose during your reading the papers?—I cannot say whether he did or not.

Was the paper you have spoken of at the bottom?—I took them all up in course as they lay, and that was the last, or last but one.

What did you say upon having read that paper?—I said that he had better not have had that paper there, and he said I was right.

What did my Lord Lovat say or do upon that occasion?—I remember nothing further than what I have expressed.

Lord Halifax—My lords, this witness has told your lordships that among the letters which were in this box there was a letter found from my Lord Lovat's son to him, which makes me imagine there was some treasonable correspondence in that letter. I therefore pray he may acquaint your lordships what the purport and tenour of that letter was.

Sir John Strange—My lords, we shall produce the letter in the course of our written evidence[1]; and therefore we do not ask him any questions about it now. (To witness)—When you said that you believed the letter had better not have been there, did my Lord Lovat say anything to his servant how such a mistake

[1] P. 223 *inf.*

D. Campbell happened?—I do not recollect any such circumstance. It might have been, but I do not remember any such thing.

Do you recollect that he said anything to his secretary, or any of his people, about him?—No.

Sir John Strange—My lords, we have done with this witness.

Lord High Steward—My Lord Lovat, would you ask this witness any questions?

Lord Lovat—Were you present when I surrendered my sword in the desert of Morar?

Witness—I was not present. I was not ashore all day. I came on board the night before, and therefore could not see my Lord Lovat surrender his sword.

Do you know whether it was to Captain Dugal Campbell, of the Argyllshire Militia, that I surrendered my sword?—Captain Campbell was upon the command. He is a relation of mine. When he came on board he said he had taken my Lord Lovat prisoner. I heard Captain Fergusson's boatswain mention how they came up with Lord Lovat.

Did Captain Fergusson threaten Captain Campbell for not delivering up my strong box, and did they not fall to loggerhead about it?—Captain Fergusson never said anything about it. Captain Campbell did, but I do not apprehend they were at loggerheads. Captain Campbell told me that, when he had got Lord Lovat and the box, he did not know where Captain Fergusson was. He went a different route, and afterwards Captain Campbell's servant gave Captain Fergusson the box, and desired him not to part with it.

Did you see my brother-in-law, Major-General Campbell, in Captain Fergusson's ship when it lay there?—I did not see him, because I went just before to another ship.

Do you know that I delivered up my strong box to General Campbell, and said it would be as safe as in my own hands?—No, I was not there.

Do you know whether General Campbell and Captain Fergusson went themselves into the cabin to examine my strong box, and stayed there two hours?—I don't know it, but I had an inventory of the things in the box, and whoever had the box, the things contained in it were in the inventory.

Attorney-General—I desire to know if the strong box was not opened by a key delivered by my Lord Lovat just at the time it was opened.

Witness—Yes, it was; and the things put in the same order they were before, and the key delivered back to my Lord Lovat.

Had it ever been opened before that time?—This was the first opening of it.

Fourth Day.

D. Campbell

At the time you took the inventory, was not that the first opening of the box, and was not the key delivered by my Lord Lovat?—Yes.

Then the witness, by direction of the Lord High Steward, withdrew.

Sir Everard Fawkener

Attorney-General—My lords, we will now call Sir Everard Fawkener.[1]

Lord High Steward—My Lord Lovat, have you any objection to Sir Everard Fawkener?

Lord Lovat—Not any.

Sir Everard Fawkener was sworn.

Attorney-General—I desire, Sir Everard Fawkener, that you will please to give an account to my lords of the conversation you had with Lord Lovat after he was taken prisoner.

Witness—After Lord Lovat was taken and brought prisoner to Fort Augustus, and lodged in an apartment of the fort there, His Royal Highness the Duke ordered me to go and visit him, not with any design to examine him particularly, for His Highness said he intended to send him to London, there to receive what the laws of his country should order, but that as, in all appearance, he had been a great cause of the mischiefs brought upon his country, this visit was designed to see whether he would discover anything that might tend to bring those mischiefs to a more speedy end. When I went to him, I thought it would be the most candid way of proceeding to inform him who I was, and accordingly I told him that I had the honour to be secretary to His Royal Highness the Duke. My Lord Lovat said that, notwithstanding the circumstances he then appeared in, he had formerly rendered great services to the Government, and the present Royal Family, and that he had received several marks of the late King's favour. And my lord imputed to Marshal Wade the cause of his present misfortunes, which was the taking away his company, which he expressed his resentment at by saying that if Kouli Khan had landed in Britain, he should have thought that would have justified his lordship to have joined him with his clan, and he would have done it. He said further that he had been in a condition to render service to the Government, and that he might be of future service to the Government, and that mercy as well as justice belonged to sovereigns, and that if His Majesty would extend mercy towards him he would show his loyalty, and deserve more than twenty such heads as his were worth. I would have entered more particularly into the services that he would render the Government but that I found, by his own discourse, that the service he meant was no more than to bring

[1] See Biographical Notes, p. 301.

his clan for the future into the service of the Government instead of employing them against it. He said the world allowed him some abilities, and he would apply them to that service, and concluded with this, saying he was

> . . . *in utrumque paratus*
> *Seu versare dolos, seu certæ occumbere morti.*

Can you charge your memory with any particular expressions he made use of?—I cannot say whether what I have said was the subject of one or two conversations, but he used to send for me frequently, and I remember there was one thing he would seem to make reconcilable, which was his principle of loyalty to the family of the Stuarts, and the services done for the late King and the Royal Family.

What were the services he said he could render the Government?—Only that he would employ the Frasers in the service of the Government, instead of employing them against it, and employ his talents in the support of it.

Did my Lord Lovat confess or deny that he had been concerned in the rebellion?—He did not seem to me to take the trouble to deny it, but rather acquiesced in it that he had.

Did he ever say he was not concerned in it?—I cannot say he ever did.

Attorney-General—My lords, we have done with this witness.

Lord High Steward—My Lord Lovat, would you ask Sir Everard Fawkener any questions?

Lord Lovat—No; only that I am Sir Everard's humble servant, and wish him joy of his young lady.

Attorney-General—My lords, we have now done with calling our *viva voce* evidence, any further than what will be necessary to prove the written evidence which we shall produce, and therefore what we propose now is to call a witness to prove some letters, some of them of the signature and handwriting, and all of the dictating, of the noble lord at the bar.

Sir William Yonge—My lords, I submit it to your lordships if it would not be better to have the whole of the written evidence together, rather than to go on to-night with part of it only. We submit it entirely to your lordships whether we shall go on now or not.

Lord Lovat—And I hope your lordships will remember poor Lovat, who cannot stand, and that you will give a little respite till Monday, or order his funeral.

Lord High Steward—Gentlemen of the House of Commons, is your written evidence likely to be long?

Attorney-General—My lords, it will be very long.

Fourth Day.

LORD HIGH STEWARD—Will it take up more than one day?

ATTORNEY-GENERAL—My lords, it is difficult to say with certainty how long it will take up. There is a great deal of written evidence to lay before your lordships, and there must be the summing up of the whole evidence by one of the Managers.

LORDS—Go on, go on.

SIR WILLIAM YONGE—My lords, then we will beg leave to call Robert Fraser. He was sworn and examined on this trial before, and was my Lord Lovat's secretary.

Robert Fraser was called into Court. **Robert Fraser**

SIR WILLIAM YONGE—Look upon that letter (showing the witness a letter) and tell my lords of whose handwriting it is.

WITNESS—'Tis my own.

By whose order did you write that letter?—By order of my Lord Lovat.

Did my Lord Lovat dictate it to you or not?—My Lord Lovat dictated every word of it.

Look upon the signature of the letter, and tell my lords of whose handwriting it is?—'Tis my Lord Lovat's.

Did you or did you not see him sign it?—I saw him sign it.

As the letter is not addressed to anybody, please to inform their lordships to whom it was intended to be sent.—It was intended to be sent to John Murray of Broughton, the Pretender's secretary.

Was it sent from Castle Downie?—No, not from Castle Downie.

LORD HIGH STEWARD—How do you know this letter was intended to be sent to Mr. Murray?—My Lord Lovat told me so.

SIR WILLIAM YONGE—Was the letter sent at any time?—Yes, it was sent from Gortuleg.

When was it sent?—After my Lord Lovat had made his escape from Lord Loudoun.

How long was that after the letter was writ?—It was written in December, and sent in January.

Then the letter (marked No. 3), signed "Lovat," was delivered in, and read by the Clerk at the table, as follows:—

PRODUCTION No 3.

Honoble and Dear Sir,

I received with vast pleasure the honour of your letter of the 31st October, by the bearer, who has the honour to be known to you. He is my relation, and was my secretary for several years, and he is now Captain-lieutenant in the first battalion of my son's regiment. He gave me great joy in letting me know at this time, as well as when he came from Edinburgh some weeks ago, that you were in perfect health, notwithstanding of the extream fatigue and

Robert Fraser constant hurry that the essential affairs of the Royal Prince keeps you in day and night.

I do assure you, dear sir, that no man in Scotland is better pleased to hear of the continuation of your health, and the prosperity of your person in every shape, than I am, as I always found you a worthy gentleman, full of good sense and politeness, full of true loyalty and valour, and faithfully zealous for the interest of the Royal Family, and, in the meantime, mighty civill and oblidging to me, when I had the honour to see on the subject of the King's affairs, which never were so well taken care of as since they were in your hands. I wou'd be therefore a most stupid, worthless animal if I had not a most grateful sense of your goodness and friendship towards me. So, dear sir, you may believe me when I assure you that my heart and soul is full of thanks and gratitude for the great marks of freindship that I had the honour to receive from you, and I have laid my positive commands upon my son to love, honour, and respect you as my best freind, and to make you his patron at the Prince's Court, and to do nothing that is essentiall without your advice, and he will find it his own interest to observe exactly my instructions on that head.

I solemnly protest, dear sir, that it was the greatest greif of my life that my indisposition and severe sickness keept me from going south to my dear brave Prince, and never parting with him while I was able to stand, but venture my old bones with pleasure in his service, and before his eyes, while I had the least breath within me. But when I found that by pains and weakness in my knees I lost the use of my limbs, I resolved to give a proof of my singular zeal for my dear master the King, and for my brave, glorious Prince, that I truly beleive few or none in Scotland wou'd do but myself. I send my eldest son, the hopes of my family and the darling of my life, a youth about nineteen year old, who was just going abroad to finish his studys and education, after having learned with applause what is taught in our Scots Universitys, and was graduate Master of Arts. But, instead of sending him abroad to compleat his education, I have sent him to venture the last drop of his blood in the glorious Prince's service, and, as he is extreamly beloved, and the darling of the clan, all the gentlemen of my name and clan (which, I thank God, are numerous and look well, and always beleived to be as stout as their neighbours) are gone with him.

There is not the head of ane old family or trybe of my name and clan in this country that have staid at home. Only a few old gentlemen, infirm like myself, that were not able to travell. And, as my son is adored by the common people of my clan, he has brought along with him a considerable number of the best of them, in two handsome battalions, and if they were as well armed and equipped as I could wish, they would look as well as any clan that went south this year, for, as I possess the largest and best estate in the shire, I have a great number of commons on my property, about 1500 good and bad, and that which is very singular is that, in that 1500 there is not thirty but what are Frasers, which no chief in the Highlands can say of his clan but myself, for most of them are mixed with men of all the other clans.

I flatter myself that my son will behave well at the head of my people, and I am sure every one of them will be ready to live and dye with him, and, if he lives, I hope he will be ane useful servant to the King and Prince and ane honour to his family, for he has very good parts and learning for his age. And since I am like to make my exit very soon out of this troublesome world, and that,

I thank God, I have served my King faithfully from my infancy till now, and that it is well known by all the gentlemen in the King's interest in the north that for many years past I was the life and spirit of the King's affairs in these countrys; and as I made it my only business to encourage and keep up the hearts of the King's freinds, it was very fatigueing and troublesome to me, and vastly expensive by my extravagant housekeeping, and giving away often a little money to the King's freinds that wanted it much, and from whom I never expect any payment, and now I give the last prooff of my uncommon and unalterable zeal for my dear master the King, in sending what is dearest to me in the world, my eldest son, and my clan, to venture their lives with the glorious Prince Royal, and under his eyes. Robert Fraser

As it would be ill manners to trouble you in a letter with some essentiall things that concerns my own person and family, I have entrusted my cousin, the bearer, to give you a true account of what I have to say, which I hope you will receive with your ordinary goodness and freindship for me. And I earnestly entreat, after you consider what I have to say, that you represent it to the Prince in the kindly and freindly manner you always behaved to me. And, as I ask nothing of His Royal Highness that is either expensive, dishonourable, or disadvantageous to His Royal Highness and to his interest, I am convinced that His Royal Highness will give me a just and gracious answer, which will for ever fix me, my posterity, and all concerned in me, to His Royal Highness's person and family. And I can say without vanity that there is not one family in the north of Scotland more capable to serve him and his Royal Family than mine, nor none that has deserved it more of the Royal Family of Stuarts since their accession to the throne than the Frasers and the Lords of Lovat. They likewise signalised themselves with honor and valour for King Robert Bruce and his offspring; and it is likewise singular that no Lord Lovat, of twenty-four that have been of my family, ever fought or voted against their King.

I beg you ten thousand pardons for this digression, but, as I look upon you as my best freind, I thought proper to let you know this under my own hand, which I hope you will forgive, and the tediousness of this letter, and beleive that I am, as much as any man alive, with the outmost esteem and respect and with a most sincere and constant gratitude while there is life in me, honoble and dear Sir,

Your most obedient, most oblidged, and most affectionate,

faithful, humble servant,

Lovat.

Attorney-General—This letter will be proved to have been received by John Murray of Broughton. My lords, he is not now here, and therefore we do not call him to that particular. But the next letter we shall produce is a letter written by my Lord Lovat to the Pretender's son. The letter itself will appear to be torn in some parts, which will, in a small degree, mangle the sense, but that will be supplied by a copy of the same letter, written at the same time, by the same hand, and by the order of my Lord Lovat, which we shall produce to your lordships.

Sir William Yonge (producing the letter to the witness) asked—Of whose handwriting is that?

Witness—It is mine.

Robert Fraser

By whose order did you write it?—By my Lord Lovat's order.

Was it dictated to you by him?—Every word of it.

Was the letter signed by my lord?—It was.

Is the signature there or is it torn off?—It is torn off.

Look upon that copy of a letter and tell my lords whom that was written by?—By me.

By whose order?—By my Lord Lovat's order.

For what end or purpose was it made?—It was made for a copy to keep.

Is that a copy of the other letter which you were just now shown?—That is a copy, that was drawn from the principal.

Was the original sent at any time?—Yes; it was.

When was it sent?—It was sent from Gortuleg at the same time the letter to Mr. Murray was sent.

Can you give an account how the signature of the original letter came to be torn off?—I cannot.

Attorney-General—My lords, there is some part of the signature remaining. The top of the L and the top of the T remain. My lords, we desire the letter may be read.

Sir William Yonge—Deliver both the letter and the copy, to explain it.

Lord High Steward—Was the signature originally there?

Witness—Yes.

You say my Lord Lovat dictated it?—Yes.

Did he sign it?—Yes.

Was the name entire upon it when it was sent away from Gortuleg?—Yes, it was.

When was it sent away from Gortuleg?—At the same time with the former letter that has been read.

When was that sent?—In January.

By whom was it sent?—By a tenant of my Lord Lovat's, one of his Stratherick men.

Lord High Steward—My lords, as both the letter and the copy have been proved, it will be proper for your lordships first to hear the original read, imperfect as it is, and then the copy.

The Clerk read the letter (No. 1), dated Beaufort, November, 1745, and then read the copy of the same letter (No. 2).

PRODUCTION No. 1.

N.B.—The words and parts of words in brackets are supplied from the copy letter (production No. 2).

Most Royal Prince,

*I reckon it the greatest misfortune of my life, and which has occasioned me more greif and sorrow than any cross accident that ever happened to me, that my long indisposition, and severe pains and tortures [that I] suffered for a long time deprived me of the vast [joy and] honour I would have had in kissing your [Royal High]ness's hands, and in ventureing my old [person] before your eyes. And, as my dear master's and [Sov]ereigns, your Royal father and grandfather [never ha]d a more faithful and zealous subject than [I have b]een to their Royal persons and interests, since I [ha]d the use my reason, so nothing in this world could give me so much pleasure as to signalize myself and end my days in the service of your Royal Highness, where I would not be useless, having been bred to the war by the best masters in Europe these fifty years past. But now, finding myself a perfect invalid, not able to mount a horseback, nor to walk half a mile, and consequently not able to exert myself either as a soldier or as a General Officer, which my dear master, your Royal father, was pleased to make me above forty years ago.

Finding myself in this unhappy, cruell situation of not being able to pay my duty to your Royal Highness in every respect, I did resolve to give your Royal Highness the next mark of my greatest zeal that I am capable of, if it was to gain your Royal Highness ten kingdoms; and that is, to send my eldest son, the bearer of this letter, and the great hopes of my family, and the darling of my soul, to venture his life [and] his young person, in your Royal High[ness service]. And I hope that his great zeal and for[wardness to serve] your Royal Highness in every shape y[ou please to command] him will be a proof that he is my [true son].

I have sent along with him all [the principal] gentlemen and heads of families of my [clan, with] eight hundred of my common people of hi[s own choice]; and it is singular in my clan that, of [thirteen] or fourteen hundred men that are on my proper[ty], they are all Frasers; and there is not twenty of them of any other clan. Both history and tradition tell us that the clan of the Frasers always behaved well, and now, when they have a most glorious and brave Prince at their head, I truely rather hear of my son's death, and of all my clan that went along with him, than to hear of their misbehaviour, which wou'd soon put my gray head with sorrow to the grave; but I do not in the least fear it. I therefore deliver my son and my clan most heartily and frankly to your Royal Highness, to do with them what in your Royal Highness's goodness and pleasure you think fit.

I hope there is none of your Royal Highness's freinds or servants that has come to this country but will do me the justice to declare that I am, and always have been, the most zealous and most active partisan that [your Roya]l Highness has in the north of Scotland; and [in that I o]wn I did but my duty.

This letter is already longer than in good [manners] I ought to have troubled your Royal Highness [with, but] as I have a great many essential things to lay [before] your Royal Highness, I will make a memorial [of them] and give them in to my good friend Mr. [Murray], your Royal Highness' Secretary of State, that he [ma]y represent to your Royal Highness what is in [it], when you are at leasure.

I pray God preserve your Royal Highness' person, and give you success and glory in all your enterprizes, as you have had hitherto, and I am, while I live, ready to loose the last drop of my blood, and with as great zeal as any man on earth.

Most glorious and most Royal Prince

Your Royal Highness' most constant and faithful slave,

. . . .

Beaufort, Nov., 1745.

Robert Fraser

Lord High Steward—By whom was this letter intended to have been sent to the young Pretender?

Witness—It was intended to have been sent by the Master of Lovat.

How long had you this copy in your hands?—I had it in my hands for some time after it was written. It lay in my desk.

How long had you it in your hands?—I cannot be positive.

To whom did you deliver the copy?—I do not know to whom I delivered the copy.

Attorney-General—My lords, though it is impossible for your lordships to doubt who is meant by the words "Most glorious Prince" and "Your Royal Highness" in the letter, yet, if your lordships please, this witness may be asked, as he wrote the letter by my lord's dictating, who was meant by these words.

Witness—I took it to mean the Pretender's son.

Sir William Yonge—My lords, the next letter we beg leave to produce is another letter that was intended to be sent to the Master of Lovat. Look upon that letter (showing the letter to the witness), and tell my lords of whose handwriting it is?

Witness—It is mine.

By whose order did you write it?—By my Lord Lovat's.

Was it dictated by Lord Lovat to you?—Every word of it.

Was it signed by my Lord Lovat when it was written?—I cannot be positive whether it was signed or not.

Recollect, if you can, whether it was signed or not?—To the best of my remembrance, it was signed. It was intended to be sent with the other letters to the laird of Lochiel, who was then at Perth. It was written by me, and dictated by my Lord Lovat, every word.

Can you take upon you to say that it was signed or not?—To the best of my knowledge, it was.

Was that letter sent at the same time with the others?—Yes, it was.

At the same time and by the same person?—Yes.

By whose orders were they sent?—By my Lord Lovat's.

What were you ordered to do with these four letters?—To put them up in a packet, which I did, and directed them to the Master of Lovat.

By whom were you ordered to do it?—By my Lord Lovat.

Were there three or four letters in all?—There were four letters.

Lord High Steward—Was this letter sent in the same packet with the others?

Fourth Day.

WITNESS—Yes; it was.

Then the letter (No. 4) was delivered in at the table and read by the Clerk as follows:—

PRODUCTION No. 4.

My dear Laird of Locheil,

I could hardly beleive ane angell from heaven if he had told me that Donald Laird of Locheil wou'd forget Simon Lord Lovat, as you have done. And this is the more surprizeing that you cannot say, nor justly think, that in one article of my life I fail'd to show my singular affection and respect for my dear cousin Locheil, but, on the contrary, gave you all the marks of freindship in my power, or that I was capable off; and yet, my dear cousin, since ever you join'd the Prince you never did me the honour to write me one scrape of a pen, notwithstanding of the strict union and freindship that we always lived in, and our constant correspondence. I solemnly protest, that I know not what to attribute this sillence to, since I cannot accuse myself of anything that deserves it at your hands: for you never saw me fail in my loyalty to the King, or in my affection and freindship towards you, nor never will, tho' you should continue as unkind as you are. I therefore beg of you, my dear cousin, to let me hear from you, and be so good as to comfort my languishing soul and drooping spirits by assuring me that you are the same affectionate Laird of Locheil to me that ever you was. I truely never had so much need of your comfort and assistance as at this time, for I am in vast distress of body and mind.

The base and treacherous behaviour of our wretched cousin, the Laird of MacLeod, has almost cost me my life already. The night before he took his journey to the Isle of Sky from this house, sitting by me, he looked up serriously and swore to me that as he should answer to God, and wished that God might never have mercy on him and that he might never enter into the kingdom of Heaven, but that his bones might rott on earth, be burnt, and his ashes blown up in the air, if he did not come with all speed imaginable, and with all his men that was already prepared, and come and join my son and the clan Fraser, and march south with them to the Prince's service, wherever he was. He swore the same terrible oaths and imprecations next day to my son, and to your faithful servant Gortuleg. And if he had keept his oaths and word, I had so mannaged this part of the north that about 6000 men had march'd south to the Prince's assistance, which I thought wou'd much encourage his own loyal party, and frighten the English to his obedience. But when I got MacLeod's letter about twelve days after, in which he told me that, after deliberating fully with his neighbour, Sir Alexander, and weighing the arguments on both sides, he and his neighbour had resolved to stay at home and not to trouble the Government.

In reading this line I had almost fainted, and my body swell'd with anger and vexation, so that I could not sleep nor eat for several days; and I am yet far from being recovered, for I have a severe stich and pain in my left side, which keeps me from my night's rest and has intirely taken away my appetite, so that I beleive the treachery of that unnatural, ungrateful, and wicked man will be the occasion of my death very soon. But before I die I resolved, if possible, to give such a mark of my zeal for my good master the King, and for the glorious, brave Royal Prince, his son, that I beleive few in Scotland would do but myself.

I send my eldest son, who is the great hopes of my family, and the darling of my life and soul, to venture his life and blood in the brave Royal Prince's service, and he has all the gentlemen of my

Robert Fraser clan with him, except a few old gentlemen that are not able to travell. He has Stray, Killbokie, and Religg, the principal heads of families of the Frasers this side of Lochness, and he has Foyers, Ferraline, and Leale-Garth, as the principal heads of the familys in Stratherrick and Abertorff, and he has certainly taken with him the flour of my clan. I pray God preserve him and them, and influence them to fight gallantly before the brave Prince's eyes, for I had much rather hear of my son's death, and of my clans, than that they should misbehave, since history cannot shew ane occasion in which the Frasers misbehaved, for, I thank God, they were always known to be brave.

Now, my dear cousin Locheil, you cannot but think it just and reasonable that I deliver my son to your care, in every respect, and that your clan, Cluny's, and mine, should be most unite, and live together like brethren; and that the quarrell of the one should be the quarrell of the other, according to our mutual engagements by word and write, in which, I hope, we will never fail. The treacherous behaviour of the monstrous Laird of MacLeod should put all relations and intimate freinds on their guard not to fail to one another, for he has, by his treachery and unnatural behaviour, fixed upon himself the most infamous character of any man on earth. That traitor, instead of coming to this house, where he was always Mr., to join my son, according to his promise, has marched the other side of Kessock this day with 400 of his chosen men and gentlemen. I beleive that, hearing that my son's regiment was in arms in this country, he was afraid to pass through it, though it's the best way to Inverness. His fears was groundless, for I woud not hurt my mother's kin though it was in my power. But if my son saw the laird, I believe he would shott him, or bring him prisoner to the Prince, because of his abominable breach of oath and promises to him.

When he sent a little sneaking gentleman here with his treacherous letters, my son and Gortulegg made two bitter answers to them. When the little gentleman sought my answer, I told him to tell his cheif that he was a traitor to the King, and a murderer of my son and me, which he might be sure I would resent if I was able; but that I would never black paper to a man that had so basely betray'd me; that since he went to the devill, I would leave him there and have no more to do with him.

Honest Gortuleg, who made up a company to go with my son, and who would be most usefull to him, fell very ill eight days ago of his old distemper, ane inflammation in the kidneys, of which he had almost dyd some years ago in Lochaber, and many times since. He lies in the next room to me; we are both much indisposed, and invalids. He joins me in assuring you and my dear cousin Lady Locheil, and all your lovely family, of our most affectionate, humble duty and best respects.

Since you are justly the Royal Prince's great favourite, I hope you'll be so kind, dear cousin, as make my court to His Royal Highness; for tho' it is my misfortune not to be able to follow him wherever he goes (which would be the delight and honor of my life), yet you can freely assure His Royal Highness that he has not a more faithfull and zealous partizan in Scotland. And tho' I am not able to mount a horseback or travell afoot, yet I have done His Royal Highness more service than any one of my own rank in Brittain, for I keep life and spirits in his affairs more than any man in the north. And tho' the President tells me plainly that I have forfeit life and fortune, and that my person is not safe in this house, yet I am resolved to live and die with courage and resolution in my King and Royal Prince's service, but no death that they can invent can lessen my zeal or fright me from my duty.

I beg, my dear cousin, you may acquaint me what you know of our dear cousin, Mr. William Drummond of Bochaldy, for I can get no certain accounts of him, which vexes my soul and heart, for he was one of the men in the world that I loved most, and that loved me most. Robert Fraser

I beg you ten thousand pardons for this very long letter; but it is to punish you for your sillence, and to convince that I am always the same man towards you and yours.

I entreat you make my most affectionate compliments to my dear son-in-law, Cluny. I am persuaded he will do honor to all concerned in him. I am convinced that you will easily beleive that I am, as much as any man alive, with unalterable esteem, attachment, and respect,

My dear Laird of Locheil,

Beaufort, Novr. . . .

(The signature of this letter was torn.)

ATTORNEY-GENERAL—My lords, there was another letter, which we take to be one of the four which was sent in that packet. It is not a very material one, and we shall produce it to your lordships rather to connect the evidence of this witness than for anything contained in it. It is a letter to the late Marquis of Tullibardine, by the name of Duke of Atholl.

SIR WILLIAM YONGE (producing the letter, the signature to which and part of the date is torn off)—Of whose handwriting is that letter?

WITNESS—My own.

By whose directions did you write it?—By my Lord Lovat's.

Did he dictate it to you?—Every word of it.

Was the letter signed by Lord Lovat?—Yes; it was.

Did you see my Lord Lovat sign it?—Yes; I did.

Is the signature torn off?—Yes.

Was that letter sent with the others?—It was sent with the former that have been read.

In the same packet?—Yes.

Which was directed to the Master of Lovat?—Yes.

For whom did my Lord Lovat say that letter was designed?—For the Duke of Atholl.

Whom did he mean by that?—The Marquis of Tullibardine (the Duke of Atholl that was abroad.)

By whose order did you send that letter?—By my Lord Lovat's orders.

Then the letter (No. 5), dated 5th December, 1745, was delivered at the table and read by the Clerk as follows:—

PRODUCTION No. 5.

My good Lord Duke,

I had the honour to receive two very ob . . . from your Grace, for which I give you . . . nks; and I can freely assure your Grace . . . ness and civility towards me have had

Robert Fraser . . . pression upon me that I will remember . . . ays of my life with gratitude and thankf . . . . And your Grace shall always find me most ready to serve your person and family.

I had the honour to return answers to both your Grace's letters, one by Mr. MacDonell and the other by Mr. MacPherson, both of the Army; but as the bearer has the honour to be your Grace and is my relation, and one whom I trust as much as any of my family, I have put it upon him to acquaint your Grace of everything that happens in this country worth your while to hear, since I had the honour to receive your Grace's letters, which I am sure he will do very exactly and very faithfully, for he knows everything that is done in this country, and does not want understanding.

I humbly beg the continuance of your Grace's goodness and civilitys towards me, and be so just as to beleive that I will remain while I live, with the utmost esteem, attachment, and respect,

My good Lord Duke,

Your Grace's most obedient, most oblidged,
and most affectionate, faithful, humble servant,

Beaufort, December 5, 1745.

(The signature of this letter was torn.)

Attorney-General—My lords, the next letter we beg leave to produce is a letter from my Lord Lovat to his son. My lords, your lordships have heard already of a letter which was found in the box from the son to the father, to which this will appear to be an answer. The father's letter we shall prove in the same manner as we have done the others, and the son's will be proved to be of his handwriting, and to have been in the box at the time it was examined and opened in the manner your lordships have heard. (To witness)—Of whose handwriting is that letter (showing the letter to the witness)?—It is of my own handwriting.

By whose orders did you write it?—By my Lord Lovat's.

Was it signed by my Lord Lovat?—It was not signed.

Was it ever sent by my Lord Lovat's order?—Yes.

To whom?—To the Master of Lovat.

Did my Lord Lovat dictate it to you?—Yes; every word of it.

Did he order you to send it to the Master of Lovat?—Yes; he did.

Did Lord Lovat frequently order letters to be written and order his secretary to send them without signing them?—Yes, my lords, he did.

Was not that generally to people the most intimate with him?—Yes; only to his intimates.

Lord High Steward—Do you know anything of the sending of this letter?

Witness—Yes.

By whom was it sent?—By one of my Lord Lovat's tenants. Robert Fraser

Was it sent at the same time with the packet?—Yes; I believe it was, but I am not positive as to the precise time it was sent. It was either then or a little after. If I was to read the letter I could tell. (The witness looked upon the letter.)

Does that enable you to recollect when the letter was sent?—Yes, my lords, it does. It was sent at the same time with the other letters that I spoke of.

With that packet which has been mentioned?—Yes.

Attorney-General—My lords, this letter consists of two pieces. One is a postscript, and therefore we beg leave to ask this witness whether the postscript was written by him and dictated by my lord and sent at the same time with the other?

Witness—Yes; it was.

Then the Clerk read the letter (No. 10) at the table, which was as follows:—

PRODUCTION No. 10.

My dearest Child,

I received the pleasure of your letter by the two expresses that I sent to you the first of this month, which you forgot to mark the date of. It gave me great joy, my dear Simon, to know that you are in perfect health and to see such a handsome letter of your own write and diction. But I must tell you, my dear child, that you advance severall things in it that are not just, and that you cannot support in reason. In the first place your reason for your not writing to me before since I made my escape (though I accept of your excuse) was neither just nor relevant, for it was not to be supposed that either Loudoun or the President would be in terms with me so soon, after having so signally affronted them. But, in the second place, it is impossible there could be any terms 'twixt Lord Loudoun, the President, and me that should keep you from writeing to me; no, if I should be attainted. So your reason for not writeing to me was ill-founded. As to your advice, that comes in immediately after it, in representing to me that if I could make my peace with Loudoun and the President, and save my person and estate, that you would content yourself with a thin regiment. This thought, my dear child, was not at all digested, and intirely ignorant to my circumstances; for, in the first place, Loudoun can no more save my person and estate than any of your subaltern officers can. Nay, they cannot as much engage to make me free from prison for any time. So that it would be madness for me to make any terms with them, but to speak civilly, and to keep myself out of their way. But the fact is, my dear child, which you forgot, or perhaps that I did not take pains to inform you of it, that above seven years ago I was one of those that entered into a formal association to venture our lives and fortunes to restore the King and his offspring, and we signed our mutuall engagements for this purpose with our hands and seals, and sent it to France to the Cardinall de Fleury, then First Minister of France, by the hands of Mr. William Drummond of Bochaldy. The Cardinall was so pleased with it that he showed our engagements and subscriptions to the King, his master, and begged of His Majesty to support us. And the King desired the Cardinall to assure us of

Robert Fraser his protection, and that he would us his assistance and succours to restore our King. When Mr. Drummond acquainted my own King of this prooff of my loyalty, and of my constant zeal for his person and interest, from my younger years till now, he gave me evident prooffs of his goodness and favours towards me since, as much as to any subject. He gave Mr. Drummond a commission to carry to me of Generall of the Highlanders, which I have, and severall letters writt with the King's own hand, that His Majesty would pay all the money I paid Fraserdale and his creditors for the estate of Lovat, and, last of all, the King was so good as to give such a singular mark of his favour to me and to my family that he created me Duke of Fraser, &c., and sent me that patent by William Drummond, of which I have ane authentick copy, signed and countersigned by the King. I would be a monster of ingratitude if this did not attach me to His Majesty more than ever. Bochaldy, not thinking it safe to bring the patent to Britain, left it with his uncle, old Locheil, at Bullen, in France, who is now come over with Lord John Drummond, his Colonel; and I hope he has taken my patent along with him. I beg you may assure him of my most affectionate respects. He and I always lived like two brothers, and loved one another most dearly. I am sure he still retains affectionate sentiments for me, as I do for him. I hope he will deliver you my patent. or a good account of it. So, my dear child, since that association I made it my business, wherever I was, to promote the King's interest, and to gain and engage faithfull subjects to serve him, so that I have done more against this Government than would hang fifty Lords and forfeit fifty estates. I have therefore nothing for it now but to promote everything that is for my dear Prince's honour and interest. And nothing made me ever speak as much as a fair word to Lord Loudoun, or the President, but to endeavour to save my person from prison, since I was not able to go to the feild and fight for my King; but, since that is over, and that I have no safety from prison but by being in hills and woods and inaccessible places, my greatest desire under the sun is that you should make a good and handsome figure in the Prince's army, which I wish, and I am as anxious to see done as yourself, and would do as much for it as I would do to save my life or keep myself from prison, which would be soon death for me: and, as Loudoun told me the day before I made my escape that he had as much to say against me as would hang all the Frasers of my clan, I have no reason to hedge or dissemble with any man of the Government. So you may assure yourself that I will put all irons in the fire to send you South all the men that's engaged with you, and as many more as I can get.

You are quite mistaken, my dear child, when you think that your comeing North would not engage them to go South. I am sure it would do much more than my orders; for the tenth man would not go this day at my desire that would go first when you began this work. However, I will be working at them all I can.

I am makeing up, with all the heast possible, a habitation for myself in the house of Muily, for that country is the strongest hold in Scotland, for I will make a hundred good men defend it against all forces that King George can have in Scotland. Besides, I ordered a boat to be made to carry me out and in to the Isle of Muily when I please, so that it is morally impracticable to attack me in that country, where I am resolved to go, if possible, next week, if my accommodation be finish'd. I keep Farraline till I go out of the country, for if he went away just now, when the people of the Aird are going south, and Simon, with some men, out of this country, I would be hunted like a fox, by Loudoun, up and down the country, which perhaps would cost me my life by cold and fatigue, so that I am resolved to stay at my dear Gortuleg's house, which I reckon my home as much as if I was at Castle Douny, till my accommodation is made up at Glinstrafarer.

I shall send you my fine pistols and furniture after I cause put them up in a new portmantua, for it would be a pity to spoil them, for they will be few so good in the army. I wonder that you are so long without writeing to me, for you may be sure that it's a comfort for me to hear often from you, and when I am a week without hearing, in the situation that you are in now, you may believe that I most be very uneasie. Therefore, my dear Simon, for Christ's sake, don't be a week without writeing to me, and let me know how all matters goes with you, and what situation the Prince's army is in, and write encourageing news that may be shown to your people.

I shall long much for the return of this express, and I ever am, with great affection,

My dearest Simon,

Your dutyfull Father.

January 14th, 1746.

P.S.—I send you enclosed the four letters that you should have carry'd with you from Castle Douny, which, I hope, you will have occasion to deliver out of your own hand. You may tell the P. when you deliver the letter to him out of your own hand that your father thought it the greatest misfortune of his life that his sickness and infirmitys deprived him of the honour of attending His Royal Highness wherever he went, and that his only comfort now is that he is capable to give his R.H. such a mark of his zeal as to send you and his kindred to venture your lives for him, and that he himself is every day exposed to be made a prisoner and be sent to London to have his head struck off, since it can be easily proven against him that he has done more against the Government than any one of his rank in Brittain, and hopes that since, by God's help, he has made what may be called a miraculous escape out of the hands of his cruell enemy, he will yet expose his person, with his sword in his hand, to serve His R.H. and to do his duty before his eyes. You will make your court and mine to Mr. Murray as much as you can; he is a very pretty honest fellow, and, I am very sure, wou'd be ready to serve us. And tell young Locheil and John Roy that I expect that they will make my court and yours to His R.H. in every shape, and that they both know the entire trust and confidence I put in them.

I hope your Captain-leivt. is come home by this time, and it was very right to send him, for he is certainly one of the prettiest fellows of your clan. Give my service to him, and tell him that I beg of him to remember all that I spoke to him about my patent, and when you talk seriously with him about it, I entreat that you both put all the irons in fire you can, to make the thing succeed. I ask nothing of His Royal Highness but to give his countenance, and own publickly what his father has done for me, which if he refuse, I most keep to the oath that I gave before the Duke of Perth, the Earl of Traquair, Locheil, and other gentlemen that first engaged in the present project with me, that I would never draw my sword till that was done. And I cannot suppose or imagin that His R.H. will make the least scruple about it, since it is for his own honour and interest, as well as for that of my family. I beg over and over again, my dear child, to let me hear more often from you. I give you my affectionate blessing. I pray God and His angells that you may be preserved in life and health till you come to my age. Adieu, my dearest Simon.

I need not tell you who the bearer is. He is a very honest pretty

Robert Fraser fellow, the natural head of the M'Tavishes. One of the deserters goes in company with the bearer, and the rest of them will be up with you in a day or two, in company with John, Dunchea's son, and John, Thomas Gortmore's son. They came all to me here, and were insinuateing complaints against their officers, but I would not hear them, as the settleing the matters of your regiment is your province, not mine. But I promised them that you would use them well, and that they would meet not only with all manner of justice, but with clemency, as this was the first fault. So, I hope, they won't fare the worse that I recommend them to you. I beg you may dispatch the bearer, and send a man with him here.

To the Honble the Master of Lovat, commanding a regiment of Frasers at Perth, or Stirling.

Attorney-General—My lords, it will now be necessary that we should give your lordships an account of the son's letter, and likewise of his handwriting, and therefore beg leave to ask the witness whether he was acquainted with the handwriting of the Master of Lovat?

Witness—Yes; I have seen him write frequently.

Is that his handwriting, as you believe or recollect?—Yes.

Have you seen him write?—Yes.

Lord High Steward—Have you often seen him write?

Witness—Yes.

Sir William Yonge—My lords, we shall now beg leave to call a witness to prove where this letter was found.

Captain Robert Duff was called into Court.

Lord High Steward—My Lord Lovat, has your lordship any objection to Captain Duff being sworn as a witness?

Lord Lovat—No, none at all.

Capt. Duff Captain Duff was sworn.

Sir William Yonge—My lords, we beg leave to ask this witness whether he was present on board the "Furnace" when my Lord Lovat's strong box was opened.

Witness—Yes, I was present.

The letter was produced to the witness.

Sir William Yonge—Look upon that paper, and acquaint my lords if that paper was taken out of my Lord Lovat's strong box at that time. Look it all over, and be positive, if you can. (Captain Duff looks over the letter.)

Witness—I saw this letter taken out of Lord Lovat's strong box.

Was that letter taken out in the presence of the Lord Lovat?—Yes, it was.

Did my Lord Lovat say anything about that letter at that time, or did anybody else say anything about it?—I spoke to my Lord Lovat then, and told him that I believed that letter was not designed to fall into my hands.

Fourth Day.

Did Lord Lovat make any answer to you?—My Lord Lovat made no answer that I can remember. Capt. Duff

Sir John Strange—My lords, one witness is enough to prove this fact, but Campbell has also told your lordships that he took this letter out of the box.

Then the letter (No. 9) was delivered in at the table, and read by the Clerk as follows:—

PRODUCTION No. 9.*

This letter is directed, To the Right Honourable Simon Lord Fraser of Lovat.

Stratherick.

My dr. Papa,

I received this day the pleasure of your lop's letter of the 1st. I'm very glad you have no complaints of your health, notwithstanding the fatigue you have of late undergone in your escape from Inverness, which gave everybody here great joy. The reason of my not writing your lop. by the express I sent last was that I did not know but you might be on terms with Lord Loudon and the President, after makeing your escape.

I'm as sorry at my bad success with the commanders here as your lop. can be, but there is no help for it. Nor were they altogether to blame, as the Prince's sudden return to Scotland made it dangerous for them to take any step of consequence without his particular orders, and these they had in a very few days after I came to Perth, and the orders were that they should all march directly to Sterling. This, your lop. sees, put it out of their power to march northward. But, as I saw your lop's. safety and the King's interest required an expedition to the north, I left no stone unturned to bring it about. I therefore, immediatly upon hearing of the Prince's being at Glasgow, dispatched my Captain-lieutenant (who was of great use in urgeing this matter to the people at Perth) to Glasgow to negotiate the affair there. He is not as yet returned; but I make no doubt, how soon the affair at Sterling is ended, but a proper body of troops . . . lordered to clear the North, and sooner the Art . . . are cannot bring it about.

As to your lop's conduct in the meantime, if I might give an advice, it would be, not to lose on both sides. I am far from meaning by this that you should come to Perth; so far from it that, provided your lop. could make conditions for your own person and estate with Ld. Loudon and the President, I should be content with a thin regiment, but, in case they have neither authority or inclination to give this, I humbly think you should immediatly come to a resolution and put it in execution, for, if your lop's clan do not all immediatly join the Prince, the cause will soon be found out. I would not much care if your lop's. person and estate were preserved by their stay, but it will be hard if it does not better your condition with the Government, when it must evidently make it worse with the Prince. I'm sorry for the opinion your lop has of the two Charles's. I realy think you wrong them, but tho' they had all the inclination in the world, your lop knows, you always accusd me of not being very subject to advice. As to what Sir Archibald

* The letter was torn where blanks are shown.

Capt. Duff Grant writes of Inveralachie, I have all the reason in the world to believe it is a very great falshood, and I am surprized your lop should give any notice to it. As to my going to Sterling, if it was the people at Perth that were to command in that expedition, your lop . . . ry right, and I would be quite a conver . . . your argument, but the Prince's positive orders to us all, his comeing there himself to command us, and venture his person with us, in my opinion, quite alters the case. As to my going north, I know your lops influence over your clan too well to think that when your orders fail my presence will have any weight. I'm certain your commands, though only intimate by your officers, will do in a day more than my presence wou'd in a week, and I'm persuaded that your people will come up to a man, if you order them, and, if you do not, that they will stay at home, so that their comeing or not entirely depends on your lop. Besides, my going north at this time . . . u'd look a little odd, when the Prince is co . . . Scotland, has sent us his positive orders, let us know, that he himself is to come and command us in person, that I should at such a critical time run home would look ill, and the pretext (as it would be called) of r . . . ing men wou'd not screen me from an imputation your lop, I'm sure, wou'd alwise wish me to shun. These reasons, I dare say, convince your lop that my going north is not only unnecessary but very improper at this time.

All your lop's fr . . . ds here join me in wishing that your lop. may live for many years to serve your king and country. * . . . great affection,

Your lop's

Dutifull . . .

. . . Fraser.

Then the Lord Sandys moved to adjourn to the Chamber of Parliament, and the Lord High Steward going back to his chair, the House was adjourned accordingly, and then the lords and others returned in the same order as before.

The House being resumed in the Chamber of Parliament,

Ordered that this House will proceed further in the trial of Simon, Lord Lovat, on Monday next in Westminster Hall at eleven of the clock in the forenoon, and a message was sent to the House of Commons by Mr. Spicer and Mr. Edwards to acquaint them therewith;

Ordered that the Lieutenant of the Tower of London or his deputy do take back the said Lord Lovat, and bring him again to the bar of the House in Westminster Hall on Monday next at eleven of the clock in the forenoon.

Fifth Day—Monday, 16th March [1747].

About eleven of the clock in the forenoon the lords and others came from the Chamber of Parliament in the same order as on Monday last into Westminster Hall, where the Commons and their Managers were in the seats prepared for them respectively as before. And the lords took their places in the Court and the Lord High Steward in his chair.

Lord High Steward—The House is resumed. Is it your lordships' pleasure that the judges have leave to be covered?

Lords—Ay, ay.

Then the Sergeant-at-Arms made proclamation for silence, and afterwards the following proclamation:—Oyes! Oyes! Oyes! Lieutenant of the Tower of London, bring forth your prisoner Simon, Lord Lovat, to the bar, pursuant to the order of the House of Lords to you directed.

The Deputy-Governor of the Tower brought the prisoner to the bar in the like form as before, and then he kneeled down.

Lord High Steward—Your lordship may rise.

The Lord High Steward asked leave to go down to the table, and went accordingly.

Lord High Steward—Gentlemen of the House of Commons, you may proceed in your evidence.

Sir William Yonge—My lords, we beg leave to call Robert Fraser again. **Robert Fraser**

Robert Fraser was called into Court.

Sir William Yonge—My lords, he has been already sworn, and (showing the witness a letter) look upon that letter and acquaint their lordships of whose handwriting it is.

Witness—It is mine; it was written by me.

By whose order did you write it?—By my Lord Lovat's order.

Was it dictated by my Lord Lovat?—Every word of it.

Is it signed?—It is not signed.

Did you send that letter to anybody?—Yes; it was sent from Gortuleg to the Master of Lovat at Inverness.

By whose order did you send that letter?—By my Lord Lovat's order.

Then the letter (No. 11) was delivered in, and read by the Clerk at the table as follows:—

PRODUCTION No. 11.

My dearest Child,

Gortulegg came home last night, with Inveralachy's brother and the two Sandy's, Fairfield's son, and mine. And I am glad to

Robert Fraser know that you are in perfect health, which, you may be sure, I wish the continuance of. I am sure, for all Sandy's reluctancy to come to this country, he will be better pleased with it than anywhere else, for he has his comrade, Gortuleg's son, to travell up and down with him, and I shall not desire him stay ane hour in the house but when he pleases.

My cousin, Mr. William Fraser, tells me that the Prince sent notice to Sir Alexander Bennerman, by Sir John M'Donnell, that he would go some of these days and veiw my country of the Aird, and fish salmon upon my river of Beauly. I do not much covet that great honour at this time, as my house is quite out of order, and that I am not at home myself, nor you. However, if the Prince takes the fancy to go, you must offer to go along with him, and offer him a glass of wine and any cold meat you can get there. I shall send Sandy Doan over immediately, if you think that the Prince is to go, so I have ordered the glyd post to be here precisely this night.

Mr. William Fraser says that Sir Alexander Bennerman will not give his answer to Sir John M'Donnell till he return, about the Prince's going to Beaufort, and that cannot be before Saturday morning. So I beg, my dearest child, you may consider serriously of this, not to let us be affronted, for, after Sir Alexander and other gentlemen were entertain'd at your house, if the Prince should go, and meet with no reception, it will be ane affront and a stain upon you and me while we breathe. So, my dearest child, don't neglect this, for it is truly of greater consequence to our honour than you can imagine, though in itself it's but a maggot. But, I fancy, since Cumberland is comeing so near, that those fancys will be out of his head. However, I beg you may not neglect to acquaint me (if it was by an express) when you are rightly informed that the Prince is going there. I have been extreamly bad these four days past with a fever and a cough, but, I thank God, I am better since yesterday afternoon. I shall be glad to see you here, if you think it proper, for as short or as long a time as you please. All in this family offer you their compliments. And I ever am, more than I can express,

My dearest child,

Your most affectte and dutifull Father.

March 20th. 1746.

P.S.—The Prince's reason for going to my house is to see a salmon kill'd with the rod, which he never saw before, and if proposes that fancy, he must not be disappointed. I long to hear from you by the glyd post some time this night. I beg, my dear child, you may send me any news you have from the east, and from the north, and from the south.

Lord Halifax—My lords, I should be sorry to ask any questions that might interrupt the Managers of the House of Commons in their proceedings. I should likewise be sorry that any questions should be asked by me that should in any degree preclude the noble lord at the bar from any defence he should think proper to make. But, my lords, as the answer, in consequence of my question, will thoroughly establish or else greatly diminish the credit which your lordships may give to this evidence, therefore I think it my duty to ask whether, after the writing of this letter, my Lord Lovat did himself read the letter and approve of it; and I look upon it this would be a necessary question to ask in regard to all the other letters which have been or shall be produced. Robert Fraser

WITNESS—I never did write a letter from my Lord Lovat, but I first made a scrawl or a draft of it, and whenever it was transcribed upon clean paper it was always read to my Lord Lovat.

LORD HIGH STEWARD—Repeat what you said just now aloud.

WITNESS—I first made a scrawl or draft of all the letters that I wrote for his lordship, and afterwards transcribed them upon gilt paper, and then read them every word to his lordship. Sometimes my lord read them himself and sometimes I read them to him.

Upon your oath, when you read any letter to my Lord Lovat, after it had been written over fair, did you read it truly as it was written, word for word?—Yes, word for word.

SIR WILLIAM YONGE (producing another letter to the witness)—Look upon that letter and tell my lords of whose handwriting it is?

WITNESS—It was written by my own hand.

SIR WILLIAM YONGE—My lords, we have done with this witness for the present.

LORD HIGH STEWARD—My Lord Lovat, would you now ask this witness any further questions?

LORD LOVAT—No; I hope to convince these gentlemen that no footman should give credit to his evidence.

Then the witness withdrew.

ATTORNEY-GENERAL—My lords, we beg that Mr. John Murray of Broughton may be called in again. John Murray

Mr. Murray was called into Court.

ATTORNEY-GENERAL—My lords, he has been already sworn. We pray, my lords, that this witness may be shown the letter (No. 3)[1] that was read to your lordships before, and that was proved to have been written by my Lord Lovat to Mr. Murray.

The letter (No. 3) was shown to the witness.

ATTORNEY-GENERAL—Do you remember ever to have seen that letter before?

WITNESS—I am sorry to say that I received this letter at Inverness in the end of February or beginning of March by the hands of Mr. Fraser of Gortuleg.

Mr. Murray says he is sorry to have received it, but I desire to ask him if he did in fact receive it.—I did receive it at Inverness.

My lords, we pray that the letter written by the Pretender's son to my Lord Lovat may be shown to Mr. Murray. The use

1 See p. 209.

John Murray which we shall make of it we shall explain to your lordships by and by. (The letter (No. 6)[1] was accordingly shown to Mr. Murray.) (To witness)—Of whose handwriting is the name at the bottom of that letter? The whole letter is written by the Pretender's son himself.

The whole letter?—Yes.

Both the body and the subscription?—Yes.

Is it directed to anybody?—For the Lord Lovat.

Is that direction also of the same handwriting?—The same hand.

Do you know if that letter was ever sent?—This letter was delivered, together with the other letters, to Hugh Fraser at Glasgow.

By whom was it delivered to him?—By me, to the best of my remembrance.

Was it or was it not sent and delivered by the direction of the young Pretender?—It was by his direction.

What was it delivered to Hugh Fraser for?—It was delivered to him to forward to my Lord Lovat.

Lord High Steward—Have you ever seen the Pretender's eldest son write?

Witness—Very often.

Upon that knowledge you have of his handwriting, do you, upon your oath, believe that letter to be of his handwriting?—Yes, I was present in the room when he wrote it.

Then the witness was shown by Sir William Yonge another letter (No. 7).[1]

Sir William Yonge—Whom was that letter written by?

Witness—This letter was written by Cameron of Lochiel.

By whose order was it written?—It was written by the direction of the young Pretender himself.

Was that letter signed, and by whom?—The letter was signed by Cameron of Lochiel, MacPherson of Cluny, and by myself.

To whom was that letter directed, or is there any direction or address to it?—No, there is none.

To whom was it intended to be sent?—To my Lord Lovat.

Was it or was it not delivered to anybody to be sent to my lord?—Yes, it was delivered to Hugh Fraser.

At the same time with the letter from the Pretender's son?—Yes, at the same time and in the same packet.

Sir John Strange—What is the reason why it was not addressed?

Witness—The reason why it was not addressed was that Hugh Fraser asked if there was a patent granted by the

1 See p. 230.

Pretender to create my Lord Lovat a Duke. To which Lochiel answered that, if there was any such patent, it was in the hands of his father, John Cameron, who was then at Dunblane, and therefore that packet was not addressed, because it was not then known whether there was such a patent or no, and it was left without any direction till Hugh Fraser should inquire whether there was any patent of duke or not. John Murray

Are you acquainted with Cameron of Lochiel's handwriting or not?—Perfectly well.

Were you present when that letter was written or no?—There were none present but Cameron of Lochiel, MacPherson of Cluny, and I.

Did you see them sign that letter?—Yes, I did.

Attorney-General—My lords, I mentioned to your lordships that I would explain the use intended to be made of these two letters. Your lordships have observed that among the several species of treason charged by the Articles upon the prisoner at the bar one of them is his corresponding with the Pretender's son, and likewise with persons employed by him. My lords, in order to show a correspondence between the prisoner and the Pretender's son and the persons named in that letter we have shown in evidence that the prisoner at the bar had an interview with Cameron of Lochiel, MacPherson of Cluny, and Mr. Murray, which is one kind of correspondence. And, my lords, it is material to show that those persons with whom the noble lord at the bar thus corresponded were persons employed by the Pretender's son, it being, by an Act of the 17th of His present Majesty, made expressly high treason to correspond with any persons employed by the Pretender's son. My lords, the first letter now mentioned is a letter written by the Pretender's son to my Lord Lovat, in which your lordships will find he refers to another letter, which is the second letter produced to your lordships as a letter written by his order and containing his sense. Your lordships have heard from Mr. Murray that the first letter was written by the Pretender's son, and that the second was written by his order, and that proves expressly that the persons by whom they were written were persons employed by the Pretender, and, consequently, any persons corresponding with them were guilty of high treason within the meaning of the Act. We therefore pray that the letters may be read. We do not offer them as letters received by my Lord Lovat, but as letters written by persons employed by the Pretender's son. The first is proved to be written by the Pretender's son himself, and the second by his direction.

Then the letter, dated the 2nd of January, 1746, signed "Charles, P.R.," was delivered in and read by the Clerk at the table, as was also the other letter of the same date from

John Murray Cameron of Lochiel, MacPherson of Cluny, and Mr. Murray, which said letters are as follows:—

PRODUCTION No. 6.

Glasgow, Jan. ye 2d, 1746.

I have just now read a letter written to you by Lochiel, Clunie, and Murray; and you may depend on its containing my true sentiments, as much as if it was all writ with my own hand. I shall only add to it that you cannot do me either more pleasure or more service than by coming to join me out of hand, and then you need doubt as little as I do of our being perfectly satisfied with one another.

CHARLES, P.R.

For the Lord Lovat.

PRODUCTION 7.

My dear Lord,

You need not be surprised, from the situation we have been in for some time past, that we have faln out of the way of writeing, notwithstanding of which our particular love and affection for your Lordship and family, as well as our sincere attachment to our King and countrey, seems to render itt absolutely necessary to give your lordship the trouble of this letter.

We are no strangers to the great pain and trouble your Lordship had taken to persuade MacLeod and Sir Alexander[1] to act that part, which was so consistent with their honour and interest, and, if we may venture to say so, the very being of their familys, for your Lordship well knows that, upon the falling or standing of the several Highland familys now engaged in this affair theirs equally depends. For did we faill in our attempt, and the conqueror prove either so weak or wicked as to endeavour the extirpation of our familys (which perhaps would not prove so easy as they imagine), these two gentlemen wou'd probably be taken (upon some false pretext) into the general corps of disaffected, with a view to make a clean stage of the whole. Or allowing that, from the scandalous activity of one, and shamefull indolence of the other, they were spared, yet their distant and small influence, in proportion to the body of the clans, wou'd necessarily render them insignificant to any party that might, from unforeseen causes, afterwards appear.

Your Lordship's firm and steady behaviour, in spite of all the under-hand dealings, as well as open threats, of the Lord Loudoun, and your neighbour the President (who has rendered himself a scandall to all Scotsmen and a nauseance to all society), together with the early noble and generous appearance of the Master of Lovat in the cause of his King and countrey, has not only gain'd your lordship the admiration of this island, but has settled the affection and friendship of the Prince for your family upon a more firm and solide foundation than, we dare venture to say, it was ever on with any of the Royal family of Steuart, notwithstanding your lordship's many heavy sufferings in that cause. And this, my lord, we don't assure you from our-selves alone, but by His Royall Highness speciall and repeated orders.

Now, my lord, allow us to congratulate you upon your happy escape from Inverness. Had it been any other, we could not possibly have given credite to it, from the circumstances of the story, but knowing with what address Lord Lovat has so often extricate himself from difficulties unsurmountable by the rest of mankind, we cou'd not

[1] MacDonald of Sleat.

allow ourselves to form the leaste doubt of the truth of it, and are now only in pain to think of the fatigue you must have undergone, and the danger your health must have run, in so sudden a change of your usuall way of liveing. John Murray

The glorious retreat His Royall Highness made from within four score miles of London, upon intelligence of the French being landed in Scotland, haveing an enemy within twenty miles in front, and Mr. Wade within three days' march of Lancoster in his rear, plainly shows what a great and enterpriseing mind is able to perform. The unactivity of the enemy in not harassing the Royal army when so much in their power, with the feeble and weak attack they made upon our rear near to Penrith, where they were most severely handled, makes it evident how easy a game we wou'd have did Scotsmen act with that unanimity and vigour that made their ancestors so famous over all Europe. From the present situation of the Prince's army on this syde of Forth, who are all in the highest spirits, the numbers in the north already in arms, the victory Lord Louis Gordon has obtained over MacLeod and his adherents, the landing of a body of French troops, with a fine train of artillery, the Kings of France and Spain declareing the Prince their ally, and taking him under their speciall protection, the French Ambassador haveing taken on his publick character, and, in fine, ane absolute promise from the Court of France of a descent of 15.000 men in England, as by letters received eight-and-forty hours agoe from his Royal Highness the Duke of Albany and York, and from Cardinal Tencin, makes it plain that it now depends on us alone to restore the Royall Family to the throne of their ancestors, the rights and liberties of the subject, and Scotland to that honour and indépendency your Lordship has so long and ardently wish'd for, which last article we are absolutely sure of, as Scotland, in the worst of events, must be ours.

And now, my Lord, the only proper means that appears to us, in common with all the Prince's wellwishers, to bring this to the wished-for issue is your Lordship's openly appearing in arms, and joining the Royall standard, in which case we are certain that there is not a man beyond the Forth, however timorous or cautious (except some few who have already destined themselves to perdition), but will appear with the greatest alacrity and chearfulness. But, not to take up too much of your lordship's time, what His Royall Highness above all things wishes and desires is, to have your Lordship with him to take upon you the command of the army, for though the Prince knows that your Lordship's age makes it impossible for you to undergo the drudgery part of a Generall yett he is sensible that your advice and council will be of greater value than the addition of several thousand men. Though your Lordship has your own equipage, yett we are apt to believe the Prince's coach and six (of which he himself makes no use) will be as convenient a *voyture* for your Lordship, and the French Ambassador, with Lord Pitsligo, who has been in itt all along, won't prove disagreeable company.

In short, it is impossible for us to give the hundred part of the reasons that makes us so sensible of the absolute necessity of haveing your Lordship about the Prince's person, which you will be fully satisfy'd of at meetting.

This moment Hugh Fraser is come here, and has given the Prince a detail of your Lordship's situation, and that of the country, with the proposal your Lordship sent to the army at Perth, of which he approves exceedingly, and will to-morrow send orders, by express, to Lord John Drummond to meett him at Bannockburn, Saturday first, there to concert in what shape it shall be putt in execution, and to move four or six piece of cannon towards Blair Castle without delay; but of this your Lordship is most earnestly entreated not to

John Murray mention one word to anybody, leaste the makeing it publick should procure the escape of some folks, who may otherwise be catch'd napping, and your Lordship is begg'd to cutt off all intelligence from that quarter.

We shall now only beg that your lordship give no ear to any of the storys spread in the north, as the gazettes have not contained one word of truth in relation to us since we left Edinr., and do us the justice to believe that we are, with most sincere regard, attachment, and esteem, wishing you many happy and prosperous New Years,

My dear Lord,

Your lordship's most obedient, most faithful,
and most sincerely affectionate, humble serva . . .

Glasgow, January 2nd, 1746.

The signature of this letter was torn off.

Attorney-General—My lords, we have done with Mr. Murray.

Lord High Steward—My Lord Lovat, would you ask any questions of Mr. Murray?

Lord Lovat—My lords, I did ask your lordships before if I might have liberty to cross-examine the witnesses brought against me, and your lordship told me I might have an opportunity of doing it when I came to make my defence.

Lord High Steward—Your lordship misunderstood me. I did not say that you would have an opportunity of cross-examining any of the witnesses produced against you when you came to make your defence, but that you were at liberty when the witnesses were produced to ask them such questions as you should think proper, and that when you came to your defence you might make such observations upon their evidence as you should think fit. But, if your lordship has a mind to call any of those witnesses in your defence which have been produced against you, I do not doubt but the Managers of the House of Commons will take care that they shall attend.

Sir John Strange—My lords, if the noble lord at the bar will give notice overnight of any of our witnesses that he thinks necessary to call in his defence, we will take care that they shall be in the way.

Lord High Steward—My Lord Lovat, would you now ask any questions of Mr. Murray?

Lord Lovat—My lords, I shall say nothing till I come to make my defence, and then I shall hope to have an opportunity to say what is just against these witnesses.

Robert Fraser Sir William Yonge—My lords, we now beg leave to call Robert Fraser again.

Robert Fraser called into Court again.

Fifth Day.

SIR WILLIAM YONGE (showing the witness a letter (No. 21))—Look upon that letter and tell my lords of whose handwriting it is? Robert Fraser

WITNESS—It is mine.

By whose order did you write it?—By my Lord Lovat's.

Did he dictate it to you?—Every word.

Who is the letter signed by?—By my Lord Lovat.

Did you see him sign it?—Yes.

To whom did he order it to be sent?—To the Duke of Cumberland.

LORD HIGH STEWARD—Was that letter read over by my Lord Lovat, or was it read over by you to him, before it was sent?

WITNESS—It was read over both by my Lord Lovat and by me to him.

Then a letter, signed "Lovat," without any date, was delivered in and read by the Clerk at the table, and was as follows:—

PRODUCTION No. 21.

Sir,

This letter is most humbly address'd to your Royal Highness by the very unfortunate Simon Lord Fraser of Lovat.

I durst not presume to sollicit or petition your Royal Highness for any favour, if it was not very well known to the best people in this country attached to the Government, such as Lord President, &c., and by those that frequented the Court at that time, that I did more essentiall service to your Royal Family in suppressing the great Rebellion in the year 1715, with the hazard of my life, and the loss of my only brother, than any of my own rank in Scotland, for which I had three letters of thanks from my Royal master, by the hands of the Earl of Stanhope, then Secretary of State, in which His Majesty strongly promises to give me such marks of his favour as would oblidge all the country to be faithfull to him thereafter. Indeed, the gracious King was as good as his word to me, for, as soon as I arrived at Court, and was introduced to the King by the late Duke of Argyll, I became, by degrees, to be as great a favourite as was about Court, of a Scotsman; and I often carried your Royal Highness in my arms in the parks of Kensingtown and Hamptown Court, to hold you up to your Royal grandfather that he might embrace you, for he was then very fond of you and of the young princesses.

Now, sir, all I have to say in my present circumstances is that if your Royal Highness will be pleased to extend your goodness towards me, in the generous and compassionate manner, in my present deplorable situation, if I have the honour to kiss your Royal Highness's hands, I would easily demonstrate to you that I can do more service to the King and Government than the destroying a hundred such old and very infirm men like me, past seventy (without the least use of my legs or knees), can be of advantage, in any shape, to the Government.

Your Royal father, our present Sovereigne, was very kind to me. In the year 1715 I presented, on my knee, to His Majestie a Petn in favours of the laird of M'Intosh, to obtain a *noli prosequi* for him, which he most graciously granted, and he gave it to Charles Cathcart, then Groom of his Bed Chamber, and ordered him to deliver it into my hands, that I might give it to the laird of M'Intosh. This was but one testimony of severall marks of goodness His Majesty was

Robert Fraser pleased to bestow on me while the King was at Hanover, so I hope I shall feell that the same compassionate blood runs in your Royal Highness veins.

Major-General Campbell told me that he had the honour to acquaint your Royal Highness that he was sending me to Fort William, and that he beg'd of your Royal Highness to order a litter to be made for me to carry me to Fort Augustus, as I am in such a condition that I am not able to stand, walk, or ride. I am, with the outmost submission and most profound respect, sir,

Your Royal Highness most obedient
and most faithfull humble servant,

LOVAT.

SIR WILLIAM YONGE—My lords, we have done with this witness.

LORD HIGH STEWARD—Lord Lovat, would your lordship ask him any questions?

LORD LOVAT—No.

Then the witness, by the direction of the Lord High Steward, withdrew.

LORD HIGH STEWARD—Gentlemen of the House of Commons, have you any other witnesses to produce?

SIR WILLIAM YONGE—No, my lords, we have no more witnesses to produce.

Address for the Prosecution.

Sir J. Strange SIR JOHN STRANGE—My lords, the Commons have now gone through all the evidence they propose to lay before your lordships in support of their Impeachment, and as that has unavoidably run this cause into a great length of examination, they think it may not be improper to have the whole that relates to the impeached lord collected together and presented to your lordships' view, in as concise a manner as the great variety of circumstances that have attended this case will admit of. This province is assigned to me. And we choose to enter upon it now, at the close of our evidence, as the most fair and candid way of proceeding with regard to the impeached lord, for, should the Commons reserve the summing up, and observing upon their evidence to make a part of the reply (as they might do), the noble lord at the bar (his defence being then closed) might perhaps be under some disadvantage; whereas, in this way of proceeding, if any mistake shall be committed in stating of the evidence, or any observations made upon it that the case will not bear, an opportunity is hereby given to the party accused to set it right.

My lords, the Articles that have been read to your lordships contain four distinct charges of high treason. The First is—

Sir J. Strange

the compassing and imagining the death of the King; the Second is the levying war against the King in his realm; the Third is corresponding with the Pretender to His Majesty's crown; and the Fourth is, corresponding with the Pretender's son, and others employed by him, knowing them to be so employed.

The two first of these are declared to be treason by the express words of the statute of 25th Edward III. The third is made treason by the 13th and 14th William III. cap. 3, the words of which extend to the corresponding with the Pretender by letters, messages. or otherwise. The fourth species of treason is against the statute of 17th George II. cap. 39, which makes it treason to correspond with the Pretender's son, or others employed by him, knowing them to be so employed.

As I have no imagination that any doubt can arise whether, when the matters of fact are proved to your lordships' satisfaction, the case will not come within the provisions of these laws, I shall forbear entering into any argument upon them, and shall only say that, although the Articles have charged the first sort of treason, in the precise words of the statute of 25 Edward III., which are, "Compassing and imagining the death of the King," yet the law does not require evidence of actually accomplishing so horrid a crime, for that sacred life is so guarded that the bare going about, or contriving so flagitious a scheme, is sufficient to constitute this great offence, provided those purposes are manifested by overt acts; and that, although levying of war is a distinct branch of high treason, yet it is also an overt act of the former species, "that of compassing and imagining the death of the King."

My lords, in stating this evidence to your lordships, I can in no way do it so intelligibly as by following the example of the learned Manager who opened the nature of the case, and divided it into three distinct periods of time.

The first period contains the behaviour of the impeached lord before the landing of the Pretender's son in Scotland, in the month of July, 1745; the second period includes the facts proved to have been committed by the noble lord at the bar from the time of the Pretender's son's landing to the battle of Culloden; and the third period relates to what happened afterwards, to the time of my Lord Lovat's being sent up and committed to the Tower.

As to the first period of time, your lordships are pleased to observe that our evidence goes so far back as the year 1719. And, my lords, we chose to take it up there because, in the noble lord's Answer, he values himself much upon "having given, in the year 1715, the strongest proofs of his zeal for and attachment to His late Majesty, and the succession of the crown in his illustrious family, against such as had undertaken

Sir J. Strange the destruction of both, and now laments his misfortune to have his fidelity questioned at the end of his days, when near worn out with age and infirmities, and to be charged with intending the subversion of a Government he had in the strength and vigour of his age exerted his utmost power and address to support."

My lords, I have faithfully rehearsed the words of this Answer, which, I think, made it necessary for the Commons to show that the noble lord's engaging in the late rebellion was not the effect of dotage, or through the constraint or by the imposition of others, but proceeded from a long and deep-rooted principle of disaffection to the Protestant succession and of attachment to the cause of the Pretender.

To begin then at the year 1719—Mr. Chevis, a near neighbour of the impeached lord, has sworn that the noble lord told him that, in the year 1719, when an invasion was attempted by Spain upon Scotland, and Lord Seaforth was raising his men in favour of the Pretender, he (Lord Lovat) wrote a letter to Lord Seaforth to acquaint him that Lord Lovat would join him with his clan, and that this letter was delivered to Lord Seaforth after it had been first shown to one Chisholm of Knockford. This Chisholm, it appears, informed the late Duke of Atholl of the contents of the letter, and his Grace sent up notice of it to the Government. This came to my Lord Lovat's ears, who was greatly alarmed at it, but your lordships find he had soon the dexterity to get up his letter upon terms he had an opportunity of making with Lady Seaforth; after which he showed it in confidence to a trusty friend of his, who declared it to be a treasonable letter, and, as such, it was thrown into the fire.

My lords, I cannot help observing to your lordships that it appears from this transaction that the noble lord was then contriving to commit treason, and yet screen himself from punishment, for he declared he had not signed the letter, and therefore, if it had been forthcoming, it could not be fixed upon him.

In the year 1737 your lordships find him sending a message by Roy Stuart to the Pretender at Rome, to assure him of his fidelity, and to hasten his patent that had been promised him for a dukedom. It has likewise appeared in evidence that he afterwards sent another message of the same nature by Drummond. In the year 1739 he appears to have proposed an invasion to Drummond of Bochaldie, in favour of the Pretender, his lawful Sovereign (as he called him), and in whose cause he then declared he was determined to live and die, an expression your lordships cannot but have observed occurs also in his letters; and the same proposal Mr. Chevis has proved was afterwards made by my Lord Lovat to Lochiel and Cluny M'Pherson. My lords, I pass over the poetical performance between Roy Stuart and the noble lord, and go on to the year 1740. About this time it was he declared to Mr. Chevis that he had signed and sealed an association of the Highland chiefs in favour of the Pretender, and which Lord Lovat declared was sent over to Cardinal Fleury. Sir J. Strange

My lords, this material part of our evidence is so far confirmed that Mr. Murray (the Pretender's son's secretary) has proved his hearing of it at Paris, and that it was also mentioned to him at a private audience he had of the Pretender's eldest son, in France.

He has likewise proved what passed between M. Amelot and him, upon the footing of such an association and the assurances given by that Court of encouragement and support. But, above all, your lordships have heard it confirmed by a passage in a letter of the noble lord's to his son that was read at the table, wherein he tells him "that, above seven years ago, he was one of those that entered into a formal association to venture their lives and fortunes to restore the Pretender (by him called King) and his offspring, which engagement (he says) was signed with their hands and seals, and sent to France to Cardinal de Fleury, then First Minister at that Court, and was by him shown to the King, his master, who promised them his assistance and succours to restore their king. Since which (says he) "I have made it my business to promote the King's interest, and to gain and engage faithful subjects to serve him." And, in his letter to the Pretender's son, he appeals to all who have come into that country who (he says) will do him the justice to declare that "he has always been the most zealous and most active partisan they had in the north of Scotland, and in that, he owns, he did but his duty." This he repeats in his letter to Lochiel, and boasts himself to be "the person who kept life and spirits in the Pretender's affairs, more than any man in the north."

In the year 1742 your lordships find him declaring he had got a commission to be lieutenant-general of the Highlands, and a patent of duke from the Pretender, and which he said he had merited by his services to that family. This declaration is proved by Mr. Chevis. The talk of it, and seeing a copy in a desk, supposed to be signed by the Pretender, is proved by Robert Fraser, and Hugh Fraser says my Lord Lovat showed it him.

Mr. Murray told your lordships he found my Lord Lovat expected the original patent had been brought over, but Mr. Murray not being certain that such a patent had ever passed, he sent his letters to Lord Lovat without an address, but enclosed in a packet with other papers, and this, he has told your lordships to-day, was done for fear of committing a

Sir J. Strange mistake, either by directing them to His Grace or only to Lord Lovat. This affair of the commission and patent is also confirmed by a passage in the letter to his son that I appealed to before, wherein he tells him that, "in proof of the sense his own King had of his loyalty and zeal, he had sent him such a commission and patent, besides a number of letters under his own hand, the original of which patent, he tells his son, was in Drummond's hands, but he, Lord Lovat, had an authentic copy of it, signed and countersigned by his King." These favours, he adds, had more than ever attached him to that interest, and he "should be a monster of ingratitude if they had not." And in the postscript he charges his son to inquire for the patent, adding that "he asked nothing of His Royal Highness" (as he calls the Pretender's son) "but to give his countenance, and own publicly what his father had done for him."

Your lordships have likewise heard it proved that during all this time the whole turn of his conversation was in favour of the Pretender. He declared he had made an alliance, by the marriage of his daughter, which added to his strength and would enable him to humble his neighbours. The healths drank at his table have been mentioned by the witnesses, particularly that execrable one proposed by himself, of "confusion to the White Horse and all their generation."

The next thing your lordships heard of were his encomiums on the Pretender, whose countenance, he said, proclaimed him to all beholders the rightful King. There are likewise in proof his exultations on the taking of Ostend, as laying open all the coast of Flanders and exposing us to an invasion in the compass of one night from the French, who, he declared, would carry all before them. And this we rely upon as a circumstance of great malignity when it is considered what numbers of our troops were then abroad in the cause of liberty and Europe, and what a situation our power at home was in at that time.

Your lordships have likewise heard his declarations about the Reformation and the Revolution, and of the noble lord's scheme to get rid of both, which was to bring in the Pretender; and as to religion, his declaration to Mr. Chevis was that he believed there was no true religion in the world but one, and that was the Church of Rome—a very extraordinary declaration this to be made by one who, by having had an independent company in the King's service, and, upon other accounts, must have seemed at least to have been of a different opinion.

Thus circumstanced, my lords, and this temper of mind, was Lord Lovat in at the breaking out of the rebellion in the summer of 1745, which is the second period of our evidence. And this part of our evidence, your lordships will be pleased to remember, began with the early notice it appeared my Lord

Lovat had of the Pretender's son's being landed in Scotland. Sir J. Strange
Upon the news of this, my lords, he prepares immediately to support him. His son, a youth of about nineteen years old, either newly come home or sent for from the University on purpose, is appointed to head the clan. The design of sending him to travel is laid aside. A proposal made by those who were willing to have kept the son out of rebellion is (upon consideration) rejected by Lord Lovat, who, at the same time, declared that his first intention was to have headed the clan himself, but that now his son should go, since others had disappointed him who, he expected, would have joined forces with him. And, in consequence of this, orders are proved to have been given by my Lord Lovat for all military preparations.

My lords, this proposal for the son's travelling is proved by Hugh Fraser to have been made to and rejected by the noble lord, who also, in his letter to Murray, makes use of these words—"I have sent," says he, "my eldest son, the hopes of my family and the darling of my life, a youth about nineteen years old, who was just going abroad for his studies and education. I have sent him," says he, "instead of this, to venture the last drop of his blood in the glorious Prince's service." Hugh Fraser has also proved his being charged with a verbal message to the Pretender's son to the same effect, and his being sent back by Murray with a letter to Lord Lovat. He has also proved that, when he delivered the letter and told my Lord Lovat the true state of the Pretender's affairs, which, he said, were not very inviting, after so many regular forces were come from Flanders, which the rebels would not be able to encounter, my lord's declaration upon that occasion was that "he had gone too far to go back"; and, for fear this news should dishearten his son, he ordered Fraser not to say a word of it to him. Before or about this time likewise it was that he received the Pretender's manifesto. He orders his son to read it out aloud to the company. And when Mr. Chevis (who never went near him afterwards) was offering some objection to it, my Lord Lovat told him that he talked treason, or it was treason in him to object to the reading the manifesto.

Soon after this, your lordships may recollect, it has appeared that great preparations were made for supporting the cause of the Pretender. Arms, colours, tents, powder, and ball are prepared and laid in by Lord Lovat's order. His arms and crest are painted, supervised, and approved by himself. So eager is he, that his son is upbraided for his backwardness, and the retainers of the family are spoken to to hasten him. He thunders out his anathemas against a gentleman who, he thinks, had disappointed him, which, if he had not done, he

Sir J. Strange says in his letter to Lochiel, "he had so managed that part of the north that above 6000 men had marched south to the Prince's assistance, which he (Lord Lovat) thought would much encourage his (the Pretender's son's) own loyal party and fright the English to his obedience." At this time likewise it was that he wrote those letters to the Pretender's son and his secretary, which were so audibly and distinctly read to your lordships that they stand in no need of a repetition to make their impression.

In the next place, your lordships find him magnifying the skirmish at Prestonpans into a victory not to be parallelled in history, which, I may venture to say, was certainly calculated by my lord for the encouragement of his people. When the late Earl of Cromartie's men marched south and passed by Castle Downie, your lordships observe him repining that they should be first ready, and what a shame it was they should pass by his nose. He entertains the late Earl of Cromartie and his officers, then in arms for the Pretender, and declaring in my lord's hearing they were going to assist the Pretender's son. And this (as it came out upon a noble duke's question) was in a friendly, hospitable manner, and not as a person quartered on by compulsion. All this while his men are gathering together! There are two rendezvous of the clan, and seven hundred Frasers drawn up within half a mile of his house. He offers (as it has been proved) commissions to several persons, declares his son was to be their colonel; threats and promises are made use of by him, and the fiery cross is carried about.

The distinguishing mark of the rebels, the white cockade, is worn by the officers in his presence. He drinks to their success, and, in his letter to the Pretender's son, "begs of God to preserve him and give him success and glory in all his enterprises." He advises those he is sending forth not to let the Pretender's son hazard his person by going into engagements. He prophesies victory and success to him. Let us all be thankful that his prophesies were not fulfilled! All this while your lordships find him balancing between hopes and fears. He gives orders and contradicts them, either as our own forces arrive or there comes assistance to the rebels from France. Insomuch that his son is at last forced, with tears in his eyes, to beg he "may no longer be made a fool or a tool of," but may then have such orders as the father will stand by. And then it was, he directed the clan to march, and said "those were the orders he would stand to." And, to prove they marched by his direction, I appeal to his letter to the Pretender's son, wherein he says, "I have sent with my son all the principal gentlemen and heads of families of my clan, with eight hundred of my common people," and the words of his letter to Mr. Murray are, "I have sent my son." He also tells his son, in the letter that has been read, that " he will put all irons in the fire to send him men. I will be working at them," says he, " all I can." Sir J. Strange

His friends and dependants, however, were in doubt what to make of him, and whether it would be safe for them to exert themselves or not, suspecting (and not without cause) that he was keeping open a backdoor for himself, and therefore it was they also thought it necessary to call upon him to dissemble no longer, but to take off the mask, which he performed before them by pulling off his hat and laying it at his feet, telling them, " There it is then." And in the letter addressed to him from the Pretender's son your lordships must have observed a jealousy he had of him, for he is there pressed to come and join him in person, " and then " (says the letter-writer) " you need doubt as little as I do of our being perfectly satisfied with one another."

In the course of our evidence, my lords, it has appeared that he was taken prisoner by Lord Loudoun, as fomenting the rebellion, and his escaping afterwards has been proved. He corresponds with his son and Lochiel when in arms for and employed by the Pretender, knowing they were so employed, which is one of the overt acts of treason laid in the Impeachment. And what is the game he is all the while playing against his son? From first to last it is an endeavour to avoid being fixed himself, and to throw it all upon his son, that son whom he had in a manner forced into the rebellion. This appears by Robert Fraser's evidence relating to a draft of a letter to the Lord President, charging the young man with obstinacy, and forcing out the clan against the father's inclination, or power to control him, which, when the Master had discovered, by accidentally going into the secretary's room and insisting to see the draft, which the father had ordered he should not, he declares (in great resentment of such usage from his father), " that he would go himself to the President and put the saddle upon the right horse. Good God ! " (says the Master) " how can he use me so ! " And the disposition of the son is further proved by the circumstance of pulling the white cockade out of his hat in the father's presence and throwing it into the fire. And this likewise was confirmed by the evidence of Hugh Fraser, who has told your lordships that, both from the public and private discourse and behaviour of the Master, he is satisfied he was better disposed than to have gone of his own accord into the rebellion. To this I may add what fell from Chevis on his cross-examination, who, when he was asked by the noble lord about a plot to hang the old one and save the son, declared to your lordships he never heard of any other than directly the reverse. A behaviour this from a father to a son, which I the less wonder at in the noble lord, when I consider he was at the same

Sir J. Strange time forgetting that natural allegiance which he owed to the "father of his people."

There is one circumstance more upon this head, which is that, when he began to find His Majesty's forces were likely to be an overmatch for the rebels, he privately sent out Hugh Fraser to find what terms he could get from Lord Loudoun and the President, and what might probably be the consequence to himself if his clan continued in arms. And this, my lords, brings me to the glorious action at Culloden, a battle which, the noble lord declared, was rashly entered upon, contrary to his opinion, which was that the rebels should have retired to the mountains, where, he thought, the Duke's horse could not follow them, and where they might easily have subsisted themselves till they had received a reinforcement of troops and money. Upon this occasion he pointed out the distress such a conduct must have brought upon the King's troops and upon that great commander, who, under the wise precautions of His Majesty, and by the good providence of Almighty God, has proved to be the deliverer of his country. Surely, my lords, there is no need for me to dwell any longer on that period of time which includes the rebellion.

The third and last period is what happened afterwards, and this, my lords, consists of a great number of particulars which have been proved at your lordships' bar. The first thing your lordships have heard of is his personal conference with the Pretender's son on the night of the battle of Culloden. The excuses made by the noble lord to that person for not coming himself to join him, on account of his age and infirmities, have appeared in evidence, and are to the same effect with those which have been read out of his letters. They are proved to have been to outward appearance satisfactory to the person to whom these excuses were made, and your lordships find the parting between them was with mutual embraces.

The next thing your lordships have heard of in the course of our evidence is the flight of the noble lord in order to avoid being taken by the King's troops. To this end he retires into a part of the country, where he imagined it would be impossible for them to find him out or harass him. In such a place it is he had that meeting with the rebel chiefs, on which occasion his behaviour is very remarkable, for it has appeared that at that consultation he continued to be, what at other times he boasted to have been, the life and spirit of the party. Who so forward to reassemble their scattered forces as he? It was he that declared they had no need to be afraid, for he did not doubt but eight or ten thousand Highlanders might yet be raised to defend themselves, either to get terms from the Duke or fight the Elector of Hanover's troops, which was the expression he made use of. In consequence of this, it was then agreed to raise men, and a paper is drawn up for that purpose. The noble lord, indeed, avoided signing it himself by desiring Lochiel to vouch for his son, the Master's, proportion. But it is very observable that, when his cunning suggested to him the declaration, that he was a neutral person, it presently forsook him, or else he had not accompanied it with another declaration that denoted his repining at his not having joined the Pretender's son on his first landing. This agreement to raise men is immediately followed by a distribution of French money for that purpose, which money, to the amount of 35,000 louis d'or, had been just received to support the rebels. Sir J. Strange

The money, indeed, that was intended to raise the Frasers with was not paid into the noble lord's own hands, but (the Master being absent) it was delivered to a servant that attended upon the noble lord, and part of it was by himself soon after sent to his son, which brings it home to my Lord Lovat as his own act. It shows him privy to the design for which it was advanced (which was treasonable), and his own hand is in the transaction. As this money has appeared to have been sent over to support the rebellion, and those who joined in it, the noble lord thought he had a right to a share of it, and therefore sends to Murray for some of it, which he demanded and received for twenty days' pay of a guard to attend his own person and defend him against the King's troops, who were in search of rebels at that time. And when soon after his son came to desire he might be permitted to surrender himself to the Duke, he calls him "a person of a mean spirit,"[1] and advises him against it, that son, who would have been "contented with a thin regiment," so the father had been safe.

When taken, his guilt is immediately suggested to him, and he declares openly that he expected to lose his head. He comforted himself, however, that his estate was so settled that it would be preserved to his family. Your lordships have likewise heard the circumstances that attended the search of his strong box. When papers were found in it he declares in a jocular way that they would find no treason in them. He continues in this strain whilst many private and immaterial papers were reading, but, when the letter from his son (which has been read in evidence) appeared, and he is asked whether that came within his description, or was designed to be found there, he changes his note, is surprised at its being found there, and agrees it was not in a proper place. After all this, I need only barely mention the offers he made to merit his life by discoveries, and appeal to the letter written by him to the Duke of Cumberland, just now read at the table. Those must have proceeded from a consciousness that he had forfeited his life before.

How the noble lord will be able to reconcile all his softening

[1] See p. 78 *supra*.

Sir J. Strange insinuations in his letter to the Duke with what he before said to Lochiel, wherein he declares, "he is resolved to live and die in his King and Royal Prince's service, and that no death the Government can invent can lessen his zeal or fright him from his duty," I must leave to his lordship; for I own it is past my skill.

My lords, I am very ready to acknowledge that in the course of our evidence one of the witnesses has said that, by what he could observe, the noble lord did not seem to be averse to His present Majesty, but his resentment, he said, was against the Ministry that had taken away his company. But how far that is agreeable to his actions, healths, and declarations, that he was ready to join Kouli Khan if he had come over, your lordships will consider. And, as to his objection to Mr. Murray's evidence as remaining an attainted person, I will only say (that it may appear in this trial when it comes abroad into the world) that, although Sir Thomas Armstrong suffered upon the notion that a compulsory taking within the year was not strictly a surrender, yet in the second year of His present Majesty's reign, in the case of one Roger Johnson, who had been outlawed for treason, and was taken within the year allowed by the statute, the then Attorney-General, like a true friend to the liberty of the subject, disdained to insist upon Armstrong's case, and the Court of King's Bench held it was immaterial whether he came before them on a voluntary surrender or a compulsory caption, so long as it appeared the man was there and amenable to justice within the times, and, in consequence of this, the man had his trial, and was acquitted. To apply this to our witness I need only observe that it has appeared in evidence that his time was not out till 12th July, 1746, and he was committed prisoner by the Lord Justice-Clerk fourteen days before, and has ever since remained in custody amenable to the law. The precedent, therefore, I have cited is directly in the point, and founded in the justice and equity of the case, for a man who has a fixed time given him to come in ought not to be prejudiced by being taken up before.

Some questions, my lords, have been asked our witnesses upon their cross-examinations, and some objections thrown out about expectations of mercy, which I do not see it is necessary to take notice of at this time. If they are relied upon by the noble lord, in his defence, the reply will be the most proper time to answer them, and to that I shall leave it. All that now remains for me to do in discharge of the commands I have been honoured with by the Commons would be to take particular notice of the letters that have been read and the strength they communicate to the evidence of the witnesses. But, as I have attempted something of this nature as I went along, and they are also fresh in your lordships' memory, it does not seem necessary to be making a separate head of them. Sir J. Strange

In gratitude, therefore, to your lordships who have thus honoured me with your attention, I forbear to descant any farther upon these letters, and if in this I shall be thought by those who sent me hither to have been remiss in my duty to them (to whom I own myself accountable), I shall humbly implore their forgiveness for any omissions I may have been guilty of in this service. This only I will say upon the letters, that whatever bodily infirmities the noble lord may labour under, yet whoever reads or hears those letters and considers the strength and energy of the expressions, dictated by himself, must agree with him in what he intimated to Sir Everard Fawkener, that the faculties of his mind were yet entire.

I have now done, my lords, with stating the evidence that has been given in proof of the high treason charged in the Impeachment; and I should abuse your lordships' patience if, after this, I should attempt to apply it particularly to the several statutes I took notice of in the outset. Surely, my lords, I may venture to say that these facts (if not answered by the noble lord) must, in your lordships' judgment, amount to a full proof of all the high treason with which he is charged, and will abundantly justify me in alluding to that expression contained in the noble lord's own letter to his son, wherein he boasts "to have done more against this Government than would hang fifty lords and forfeit fifty estates."

Thus, my lords, have the Commons maintained their Impeachment, and supported it (as they think) with a weight of evidence suitable to the dignity of their interposition. They think they have sufficiently shown your lordships that this unfortunate lord was not fit to be trusted to bring his clan about again, *et versare dolos*, as he offered to do. On the contrary, they think it appears that they have properly singled him out and brought him to this bar on their own prosecution, here to receive your lordships' judgment for the other part of the alternative pointed out by himself.[1]

---

[1] The Editor is indebted to Mr. William Mackay, Solicitor, Inverness, for the right to reproduce the following letter by the Lord High Steward to Sir John Strange bearing on this case, and also Sir John Strange's acknowledgment. The last paragraph in each letter contains the reference to the Lovat Trial.

Powis-House, Mar: 17, 1746.

Sir,—I beg the favour of You to send me a copy of Your Notes of Roger Johnson's case. I remember'd the Case, but thought it had passed entirely upon the consent or acquiescence of the Attorney General, witht any opinion given by the Court.

Permit me to take this opportunity of returning You my Share of

Trial of Lord Lovat.

LORD HIGH STEWARD—Gentlemen of the House of Commons, have you anything further to offer in support of your Impeachment?

SIR WILLIAM YONGE—No, my lords.

LORD HIGH STEWARD—My Lord Lovat, the gentlemen of the House of Commons have closed what they have to offer by way of evidence and in support of the charge against you, and now is the time for you to make your defence by making such observations as you shall think fit upon the evidence which has been given against you, and upon what they have offered by way of argument to enforce it. Your lordship may likewise open your own evidence which you have to offer and call your witnesses and pursue your own method as you shall think fit, provided it be agreeable to law and the course of proceeding in such cases.

LORD LOVAT—My lords, I have already told your lordships several times since I came here that I was very weak and feeble, and really afflicted with a distemper that made me almost incapable to appear here, if it had not been to show my obedience and respect to your lordships, and I now humbly beg that since you are so good as to indulge me to say something for myself, that you will give me four or five days at least to recover my health a little and to prepare my evidence. And, my lords, I have another thing humbly to propose to your lordships. There is an evidence, a very material evidence for me, who is a member of the House of Commons.[1] I would humbly beg that your lordships would be pleased to take such methods

---

Thanks for your excellent performance yesterday, & to assure you that I am, with great Esteem & truth,—Dear Sir, Your most faithfull humble Servant, HARDWICKE.

Any time this day will be time enough for the Notes.

[Addressed on cover:—To Sir John Strange.]

REPLY OF SIR JOHN STRANGE (Undated).

MY LORD,—I took ye opportunity of yesterday's Recess to see Mrs. S. whom I Left Indisposed on Sunday night, & that is ye true Reason of my not sooner obeying yr. Gr. Commands.

As I am but just now returned and there is no time to copy ye Case *Johnson*, I have sent the original wch. I hope may be more satisfactory, as I find it has undergone yr. G'. perusal, and is corrected with your own Hand; & this I Hope will justify me in the Manner of Citing it.

I acknowledge the gr. Honour you do me in taking such Notice of my mean appearance, & am with the Greatest Duty —Your Grace's most obedient and most hmbls. Servent, J. S.

[1] The eye-witness of the trial, whose "Account" is reprinted in the New Spalding Club's Historical Papers (above cited), says that this unnamed member of Parliament "prov'd to be Macleod," but that Lord Lovat decided not to call him when he learned that his witnesses could be cross-examined (p. 337).

as you shall think proper to make him appear at the bar and give his evidence, which is but two or three words, whatever day your lordships please.

LORD HIGH STEWARD—My Lord Lovat, as to what you have mentioned, first, in asking for four or five days to make your defence and prepare your evidence, that is an interruption of a trial I have not known, but it is in the judgment of the lords what time they will be pleased to give you. As to what your lordship hath said in regard to a member of the House of Commons being a material evidence for you, you must be advised by your counsel (who are to advise you as to matters of law and the proper methods of application) in what manner you are to make your application for that purpose.

LORD LOVAT—My lord, I will take your lordship's advice and will do so, but it will be impossible for me to appear before you except I am better in health.

LORD HIGH STEWARD—Gentlemen of the House of Commons, have you anything to offer in relation to what my Lord Lovat has now said?

SIR WILLIAM YONGE—My lords, nothing, but to submit it to your lordships, when you will be pleased to proceed. My lords, the time that the prisoner at the bar has desired is very extraordinary, and will be very inconvenient; but, my lords, a reasonable time the Commons will have no objection to.

LORD LOVAT—My lords, I am at your lordships' disposal. I am a prisoner here, and submit entirely to your lordships' determination, be it what it will.

The Lord President moved to adjourn to the Chamber of Parliament, and the Lord High Steward going back to his chair, the House was adjourned accordingly; and then the lords and others returned in the same order as before.

And the House being resumed in the Chamber of Parliament,

Ordered that a message be sent to the House of Commons, by Mr. Sawyer and Mr. Mountague, to acquaint them that the Lord Lovat having requested that Normand M'Leod, Esquire, a Member of their House, might be examined as a witness at his trial, the lords do desire that they will give leave to the said Normand M'Leod to be so examined at the said trial; and that their lordships will proceed further thereupon in Westminster Hall on Wednesday next at eleven of the clock in the forenoon;

Ordered, that the Lieutenant of the Tower of London, or his deputy, do take back the said Lord Lovat, and bring him again to the bar of this House in Westminster Hall on Wednesday next at eleven of the clock in the forenoon.

Sixth Day—Wednesday, 18th March, [1747].

About eleven of the clock in the forenoon the lords and others came from the Chamber of Parliament in the same order as on the first day into Westminster Hall, where the Commons and their Managers were in the seats prepared for them respectively as before. And the lords took their places in the Court, and the Lord High Steward in his chair.

Lord High Steward—The House is resumed. Is it your lordships' pleasure that the judges have leave to be covered?

Lords—Ay, ay.

Then the Sergeant-at-Arms made proclamation for silence, and afterwards the following proclamation:—Oyes! Oyes! Oyes! Lieutenant of the Tower of London, bring forth your prisoner, Simon, Lord Lovat, to the bar, pursuant to the order of the House of Lords to you directed.

The Deputy-Governor of the Tower brought the prisoner to the bar in the like form as before, and then he knelt down.

Lord High Steward—Your lordship may rise.

The Lord High Steward asked leave to go down to the table, and went accordingly.

Lord High Steward—My Lord Lovat, your lordship may now proceed to make your defence.

The Prisoner then acquainted their lordships with his great age and infirmities, which rendered him, as he alleged, incapable of speaking what he had to offer, and that therefore he had put into writing what he had conceived and was advised to say on this occasion, and which he desired their lordships would be pleased to permit their Clerk to read at the bar; and their lordships permitting it, the same was read by the Clerk, as follows, viz.:—

Lord Lovat

My lords,—In my unhappy situation it is with the highest pleasure and gratitude that I return my acknowledgments to your lordships for the indulgence you have shown me during the course of my long trial, and had I, my lords, met with any degree of justice from those who have appeared as witnesses against me it would have been unnecessary for me to have troubled your lordships with anything in my own defence, but as there can be no security against the oaths of persons who are swayed by malice, or interested by the hopes of life and fears of punishment, it becomes necessary for me to trouble your lordships with a few observations—first, as arising from the particular circumstances of my case; and, secondly, upon the nature of the evidence that has been produced against me, and the degree of credibility which such sort of evidence deserves. Lord Lovat

With respect to the first, my lords, upon being served with a copy of the Articles of Impeachment, I immediately applied to your lordships for an order to bring up those witnesses whom I thought necessary for my defence, and, considering the complicated nature of the treasons charged upon me, and the great period of time they were intended to comprehend, it cannot surprise your lordships that my list contained sixty or thereabouts. But, to my very great misfortune, uncommon methods have been used against me to prevent their attendance. The ordinary judges have been divested of their offices and obliged to appoint others, who were recommended by the King's officers to officiate for them. Nay, the ordinary seats of justice have been, in my particular case, forsaken, and new Courts erected, to which numbers have been forced, under the severest menaces, to attend as witnesses against me, whilst all whom those new judges and rulers, upon their inquisition, found might be serviceable to me in my defence, have been overawed and intimidated, so that they durst not attend my trial. These, my lords, are facts as notorious in themselves, as unprecedented in these kingdoms, and facts which I can instantly prove to your lordships' satisfaction, partly by affidavits now in my hands, and partly by witnesses of undoubted credit, who have been brought 500 miles from the Highlands of Scotland, with a view to be examined against me, and who, it is probable, have been laid aside, lest what I now take the liberty to affirm to your lordships should, upon their examinations, have been made to appear.

My lords, by these and such like methods have my witnesses been terrified from appearing, at least so very few have had the resolution to venture that they scarcely deserve to be named, and cannot be material for my defence without the assistance of the others. I am therefore under the hard necessity to forget yet a little longer the inconveniences of a close and tedious imprisonment, and to stifle that desire of liberty which is so natural to me for some longer time till, by your lordships' effectual interposition, I can command the attendance of my witnesses, and, of consequence, justify my innocence. For if your lordships consider that my very words and actions have been made the subject of a critical examination from the year 1719, my case must appear extremely hard, and necessarily requires a very circumstantial proof, by examination of those persons with whom I have had any intercourse from that period till now. But if your lordships should instantly oblige me to proceed upon my defence, unprepared as I am, I must submit. Locked up a prisoner in the Tower, I cannot make your lordships' order effectual against the several persons in the list I

Lord Lovat gave into this Honourable House, and to proceed to trial, whilst I am under these circumstances, has the appearance of so much hardship that I flatter myself it will move your lordships effectually to interpose and order some proper method by which my witnesses can be forced to attend, and not suffer a peer of the realm to be destroyed because he cannot work impossibilities, or oblige me, like the Israelites of old, to make bricks without straw.

I must therefore humbly move, and insist with your lordships, not to introduce a precedent in my case, which may be attended with the worst of consequences to any lord who shall hereafter be brought to your lordships' bar. And, indeed, my lords, I say this not altogether out of a regard to myself. I am now fourscore years of age,[1] have suffered many changes, and, thank my God, have no unbecoming fear for anything I can yet suffer. I know, by the quick advances and frailties of old age, that, in the course of nature, I am hastening to my end, and, by the favour of the Almighty, I have been long preparing for the great and solemn change. But this, my lords, may produce a precedent that shall prove fatal to many of younger years. And, surely, your lordships must be convinced I have the greater reason to insist on this demand, upon considering what I propose to lay before your lordships, in the second place, namely, a few observations upon the nature of the evidence and the credit that those witnesses deserve who have sworn against me.

In general, your lordships have undoubtedly perceived the high improbability that runs through the whole of Chevis's oath. He, my lords, takes upon him to swear to conversations as far back as the year 1719, and mentions as if I was then engaged in plots against His late Majesty, at the very time many of your lordships know, and that it is notorious, I was highly in his favour. It might, my lords, carry the air of vanity for me to mention to your lordships the many particular services I was thought to have done His Majesty in the year 1715. But, allow me, my lords, to say they were services of such a nature as made His Majesty think me entitled to very distinguishing marks of his favour, as will appear by several letters which, by His Majesty's orders, I had the honour to receive from the late Lord Stanhope, my great and very worthy friend.

[1] This seems to be inaccurate, and is contradicted by Lord Lovat's own statement in his letter to Lord Loudoun, dated 23rd November, 1745 ("Inverness Gaelic Society's Transactions," vol. xiv., p. 12). See also his letter to Earl of Stair on 18th August, 1745, where he says he is then sixty-eight ("Inverness Gaelic Society's Transactions," vol. xiv., p. 8), and his letter to the Duke of Cumberland after his arrest, where he says he is "past seventy" ("Anderson's Family of Frasers," p. 123).

So that, my lords, Chevis's accounts are even more than improbable; besides, that the minute and particular manner in which he swears to circumstances that have happened so long ago must render his testimony too suspicious to be believed. And allow me to observe a very remarkable circumstance, that he has carefully avoided to name any one man who was present at any one of those conversations, and could possibly have been brought to confront him, lest the same Providence which detected the elder, in the case of Susanna, might have detected Chevis. **Lord Lovat**

A further circumstance your lordships will also allow me to observe, that it is not to be supposed that I, or any man of common sense, should have talked so often and so freely upon a subject of that delicate nature to a person who, if your lordships can possibly believe himself, was always so openly and zealously affected to the present establishment. But can your lordships yet conceive any good opinion of a person who voluntarily offers himself as an evidence to little trifling conversations which the only opportunity he had of hearing was his eating at my table, when he must have starved at his own and perished for cold unless my money had furnished him with clothes? In evidence of this I was till very lately possessed of many of his accepted notes for greater sums than I am afraid he is yet able to pay, I having prevailed with a friend to let me have money upon them to supply my present wants, and I should be sorry if he shall suffer by his friendship to me.

The next three evidences who have appeared at your lordships' bar against me are those infamous fellows who call themselves secretaries, the one (and on this occasion I name Murray) the most abandoned of mankind, who, forgetting his allegiance to his King and country, has, according to his own confession, endeavoured to destroy both, like another Catiline, to patch up a broken fortune upon the ruin and distress of his native country, to-day stealing into France to enter into engagements upon, your lordships may believe, the most sacred oaths of fidelity, soon after, like a sanguinary monster, putting his hand and seal to a bloody proclamation, full of rewards for the apprehending the sacred person of His Majesty, and, lest the cup of his iniquity had not been filled, to sum up all in one, impudently appears at your lordships' bar to betray those very secrets which he confessed he had drawn from the person he called his lord, his prince, and master, under the strongest confidence.[1] Your lordships will perceive I have yet forborn to mention the other circumstances of his having received,

---

1 The Library of the British Museum contains a copy of a pamphlet, "Lord Lovat's Last Legacy to his Particular Friend, Secretary Murray," a satire in verse (author unknown).

Lord Lovat since the battle of Culloden, 35,000 louis d'or, which he yet expects to live and riot on; but, my lords, who can consider the price of blood and treachery and not bestow that sort of pity which Murray, the greatest criminal, the true disciple of his master, Iscariot, calls for?

One thing more, my lords, I cannot omit, and that is to take some notice of the indecent and scandalous liberty the wretch has attempted to take by aspersing a number of very noble, worthy, and honourable persons, of whose innocence your lordships were so fully persuaded as to stop him in his career lest, like one of Samson's foxes, he should destroy some of the very worthiest members of the commonwealth. But if, after all that I have said, your lordships can pay the most distant regard to this secretary's evidence, it is hard to determine how many of His Majesty's other faithful subjects may escape the licentious liberty of his impeachments, for let him once think that upon the multiplicity of his accusations his worthless life depends, and there is no reason to apprehend any of the most faithful subjects can boast of a long security. I will not, my lords, trouble your lordships much upon the objections to which my counsel have spoken against the competence of this witness; but, if a desire of life to so wicked a person, who must be afraid to die, can be any inducement to swear falsely, it is apprehended impossible any of your lordships can give the least degree of credit to the oath of the villain, secretary Murray.

My lords, the next secretary I choose to trouble your lordships with is Robert Fraser, a person who never had the good fortune to be worth a shilling, and whose veracity and truth never exceeded his riches. He, my lords, has taken upon him to swear to letters written by himself, and many of them not pretended to have been signed by me. Others, my lords, have neither date nor direction, and no sort of proof has been attempted to be brought by the Managers, where or in whose custody they were said to have been found. How weak an evidence, therefore, this is to fix so heavy a charge as high treason upon a peer of this realm is humbly submitted. But, my lords, this witness has also, to go through the whole drudgery of swearing, framed a very improbable and awkward tale to your lordships of his having found, in a writing desk in my house, a copy of a pretended patent creating me Duke of Fraser, which, by the by, the Managers have not offered to produce, and I must leave it with your lordships whether it is at all likely that, if I had been possessed of such a patent, I should have left it so carelessly loose, or that, if I had, this witness should have been the only person in my numerous family to have seen it, for I am not now speaking of the testimony of the other witness, Hugh Fraser. My lords, is it, or can your lordships think it possible I could have had the copy and not have had the original? The one was quite as easily sent as the other, and your lordships all know that it is a mighty unusual thing to send copies of patents when dignities are intended to be conferred. As to the other part of Robert Fraser's testimony that relates to his writing for arms, powder, and ball, I am persuaded it cannot make the least impression upon your lordships. First, because he has not deposed to express quantities; and, secondly, that it might have been so easy for the Managers to have brought a positive proof, had the fact been true, by the persons from whom these things were said to have been bought, or, at least, by those who carried them to my house, though, indeed, I can make no manner of doubt that had this gentleman, Robert Fraser, thought it material he would have gone a little farther and sworn to that, as he is one of those honest gentlemen whose mouths seldom open but for their tongues to lie. Lord Lovat

My lords, I must next trouble your lordships with Hugh Fraser, and again repeat a general observation that a person himself in the rebellion, and who did, upon his oath, declare at your lordships' bar that he would give no evidence except in expectation of life, cannot be reckoned an unsuspected witness, for, according to the value which he shall set upon his own life must his evidence be less or more hurtful to me, since, my lords, life is the purchase, and his giving evidence the only price. He says that I showed him a copy of the patent, and yet, long after this pretended time of showing, he, my lords, was the very person to whom Murray declared he knew nothing of such a patent. He was also the person who received those treasonable letters that have been read against me, and it is not pretended that after this interview with Murray at Glasgow I ever saw him or had any intercourse with him till I was brought to your lordships' bar. Nor is it laid to my charge that I ever received any of those letters or commissions which Fraser is said to have brought from Glasgow. And here, my lords, I must repeat the same observation against Fraser of Dumballoch, who was himself in the rebellion, and therefore, in like manner, swearing away my life to preserve his own.

Many other particulars, my lords, I purposely omit, reserving my observations till I shall have your lordships' order to bring up my witnesses, and then, my lords, I shall be able to falsify those particulars, and, indeed, the whole substance of this heavy charge against me.

I must, my lords, beg your lordships' pardon for taking up so much of your time. I labour under so many disadvantages from old age and the decay of the faculties of the mind that it is no wonder I should make a bad defence for myself,

Lord Lovat unassisted either by counsel or solicitor, and that so many great and eminent persons, skilled in the laws, and masters of Ciceronian eloquence, have appeared to manage the prosecution against me. But I hope in your lordships' hands my old life is safe, and that your lordships, whose noble blood is like so many fountains from whence issue streams of humanity, justice, and honour, will not, nay, cannot find me guilty upon the evidence of such witnesses as have defiled your bar, and have no other method left to expiate their own crimes but by laying them upon me. For your lordships must allow me to observe that all the witnesses, except Sir Everard Fawkener, have both their lives and estates depending upon their giving such evidence as may convict me. And even as to Sir Everard, he has judgment enough to know that, should I be acquitted, he would find it difficult to defend an action at my instance for reparation of uncommon wrongs and acts of violence done by his order upon my estate, in cutting very valuable woods, and appointing receivers of my rents, and, consequently, he has too great an interest in my conviction to be considered or received by your lordships as an unexceptionable witness.

My lords, to me, who am no lawyer, it appears extremely strange and unreasonable that *socii criminis* should be admitted witnesses before they are pardoned; but if it is true that the law of England differs in this respect from the law and usage of all other nations, I should be glad to know how that difference has been introduced. I take it, my lords, for granted that it is not by the force of any statute, for I am sure the great learning and ingenuity of the Managers have omitted to mention none that concerns the case of treason, and, if it is by the common law, my objection is entire, and can only be determined by your lordships, as in this case my jury.

In some sort of felonies, my lords, I remember to have often heard of statutes which authorise a proof of that nature, but in treason I never heard of one; and, indeed, the necessity does by no means appear to me to be the same, first, because the one is not so common as the other, and, secondly, because there can be no room to plead a penury of witnesses in treason, which is laid to my charge, whereas there may in felonies. Another strong consideration will naturally occur to your lordships, that the revenge or malice of power cannot operate in felonies, but may in treason.

If, my lords, I should be told it has been established by custom, I must beg leave to say that, as it seems contrary to justice and reason to trust to the evidence which an accomplice unpardoned is to give, it is incapable of being hallowed by custom, since I am assured that it is an established rule that unless a custom is reasonable and according to justice, it is void. But, allow me, my lords, to ask what reason can be given why these confessed rebels have not been honoured with a pardon previous to my trial? If it is that the Government believe in that case they would not swear the truth, can the wit of man invent a stronger argument why your lordships, in equal diffidence, should not believe them when they have no pardon, for, if they are such abandoned villains (and, in truth, my lords, I believe them such) as to perjure themselves after a pardon, when they can neither gain nor lose by the evidence they are to give, surely your lordships ought not to trust them when their lives depend upon giving such evidence as may convict me who have yet the honour to be a brother peer. Lord Lovat

One thing more, my lords, and I have done, and that is, should this sort of proof be once established, I may venture to say that *delatores* would become greater nuisances here than ever they were at Rome, and that all our noble and ancient families will be by degrees cut off, upon pretence of Jacobite or Republican plots, since the history, my lords, of all ages shows that power can make plots, and fatal experience proves that in every age are villains ready, like my three secretaries, to prove what power shall hereafter dictate or expect.

Thus far I thought it my duty, in vindication of myself, to trouble your lordships, and, without further trespassing upon your patience, freely submit my life, my fortune, my honours, and, what is dearest of all, my posterity to your lordships.

Lord High Steward—My Lord Lovat, do you think fit to call any witnesses?

Lord Lovat—No, my lords.

Solicitor-General—My lords, though the noble lord perseveres in denying the charge, yet, as he has called no witnesses, but rests his defence altogether upon complaints, observations, and objections to the force and credibility of the evidence against him, if I was to follow my own inclination and judgment I should think it unnecessary to say anything upon a matter already sufficiently understood. But I am told by the opinion of those whose opinion is to me a law that I shall not do my duty, nor perform the part assigned me, unless I close this solemn trial by calling back your lordships' memory and attention to the principal grounds upon which we have proceeded, especially as they have now been objected to as insufficient and complained of as setting an example which may be dangerous to innocence hereafter. Solicitor-General

The gentlemen who manage this prosecution have in the course of it meant to do justice to their trust in such a manner that the noble lord at the bar should feel the weight of truth, but not of his accusers; and it is not to aggravate guilt or

Solicitor-General

to press down the load heavier upon him that I am at this time commanded to speak, but to satisfy your lordships now, and the world hereafter, from the nature of the evidence by which this accusation has been supported why no part is attempted to be answered.

He has put your lordships in mind that the law requires you, as his judges, to be his counsel, which is certainly true. And I am persuaded compassion, inseparable from noble minds, has been ingenious to suggest to your thoughts doubts and objections in favour of one standing in that place, who certainly labours under some infirmities, and is allowed to defend himself by no other tongue than his own.

If scruples have arisen in the minds of any of your lordships, they will gain strength from that consideration, and the honest prejudice which you must feel from his want of assistance may be of more advantage to him than the ablest assistance he could have had. It is proper, therefore, it may even be necessary, to endeavour to set the whole in such a view as may tend to obviate every possibility of doubt.

There are but two things for your lordships' consideration upon this occasion. First, whether the evidence given is a convincing and legal proof of the charge, if it be believed; and next, whether there be any reason to induce your lordships not to believe it. The only thing in the course of this proceeding which has not yet been done to satisfy your lordships with regard to both these points is to apply the particular evidence that has been given to the principal overt acts laid in the Articles of Impeachment. As this is the only thing which has not yet been done, it is the only thing which I shall attempt to do.

There are three kinds or species of treason of which the noble lord at the bar stands accused by these Articles—compassing and imagining the death of the King; levying war against His Majesty within the realm; and corresponding, contrary to a late Act of Parliament.

The two first are treasons, declared to be so by the statute of the 25th of Edward the Third. Compassing or imagining the death of the King is an inward thought or operation of the mind, and therefore, as God alone can judge of thoughts, because He alone can know them, so for this kind of treason no man can be convicted unless he does some open act which proves the secret intention of his mind. It is not necessary that the open act should have an immediate tendency to take away the natural life of the King, but any design to subvert his government, or to raise war against him, which may in consequence draw on his death, has been long settled to be an overt act of this species of treason.

In high treason, for greater security, the law requires a

Solicitor-General

formal as well as a convincing proof, and therefore no man can be found guilty of high treason which is not proved by the testimony of two witnesses. One, let his credit be never so good, let him be supported by never so many circumstances, is not sufficient. But it is not necessary that two witnesses should give proof of the same overt acts. If they give evidence in proof of distinct overt acts it is enough, provided they are overt acts of the same species of treason.

Having mentioned what legal proof is required (for this was the law before the 7th of King William, and is therefore applicable to the present occasion), I will state the overt acts of each species of treason whereof the noble lord stands impeached and apply the evidence to them.

Of "compassing and imagining the death of the King," the principal overt acts laid in the Articles are three—First, that he conspired, with several of the King's subjects, to induce a foreign power (the French) to invade this kingdom; Second, that he corresponded with the Pretender in order to dethrone the King, and with that view solicited and accepted a commission from him to be lieutenant-general of the Highlands, and also solicited and obtained from him a patent creating him duke, as a reward of his engaging in that design; Third, that he conspired to raise war and rebellion against His Majesty within this realm. That conspiring with a foreign power to invade the kingdom is an overt act of compassing the death of the King cannot now be doubted.

As to the proof: Robert Chevis proves that in June, 1739, he heard Lord Lovat propose to William Drummond of Bochaldie the project of an invasion; that in 1740 he heard him say there was an association and drank success to it.

Robert Fraser proves a letter of the 14th of January, 1746, from the noble lord to his son, to have been dictated by him, afterwards read over to him, approved of, and sent, in which are these words—"I was one of those that entered into a formal association to venture our lives and fortunes to restore the King and his offspring, and we signed our mutual engagements for this purpose with our hands and seals, and sent it to France to the Cardinal de Fleury, then First Minister of France, by the hand of Mr. William Drummond of Bochaldie. The Cardinal was so pleased with it that he showed our engagements and subscriptions to the King, his master, and begged of His Majesty to support us, and the King desired the Cardinal to assure us of his protection and assistance and succours to restore our King."

Here are two witnesses who give evidence of that, which is direct proof against the noble lord of this overt act. But this direct proof is strengthened by general evidence. John Murray of Broughton proves that such an association and

Solicitor-General

memorial was sent to the Court of France, and that William Drummond of Bochaldie was the person who carried it. He names all who signed it. He was himself carried by this Drummond of Bochaldie to Monsieur Amelot and introduced as coming fom those who signed and sent the association and memorial. He was received by Monsieur Amelot upon that footing. He had an answer from the French King to carry to those from whom he came.

This general evidence is again corroborated by that which is positive proof against the noble lord. In his postscript to the letter I mentioned before, he says if his patent of duke was refused he would keep to the oath that he gave to the gentlemen who first engaged in the project with him, that he would never draw his sword till that was done. He mentions three of the persons by name who first engaged with him, so that the general evidence is supported by this postscript as to some of those who signed the association, and particularly as to Lord Lovat himself. The authenticity of this letter and postscript do not rest upon the positive testimony of Robert Fraser only, but is supported by the letter from my lord's son, to which this is an answer, proved to be the handwriting of the son, and to have been found in my lord's custody.

There are other circumstances which give credit to the proof of his having entered into the association which was sent to France by William Drummond of Bochaldie. In his letter to Lochiel he inquires after Mr. William Drummond as the man whom he loved, and who loved him best. Robert Fraser says Lord Lovat told him that his patent was in the hands of one Drummond, in France. And in his letter of the 14th of January to his son he says the patent was sent by William Drummond as a reward of his having joined in the association.

The second overt act of this species of treason which I mentioned was that he corresponded with the Pretender in order to dethrone the King, and, with that view, solicited and accepted a commission from him to be lieutenant-general of the Highlands, and also solicited and obtained from him a patent creating him duke, as a reward of his engaging in that design. Though corresponding with the Pretender be made treason by Act of Parliament, yet corresponding in order to disturb the King's government is an overt act of compassing the death of the King, and so it is laid in the Articles. As to the proof of this overt act: Robert Chevis heard him, in 1736, send a message by Roy Stuart to the Pretender with assurances of his fidelity, and that he would live and die in his cause, and charged Roy Stuart to expedite the sending over his commission of lieutenant-general and patent of duke. This is corroborated by Charles Stewart, who met Roy Stuart in 1736 at Boulogne, and was told by him that he was going to Rome, and hoped for a place under the Pretender through letters of recommendation which he carried from Lord Lovat. Solicitor-General

Robert Chevis was told by Lord Lovat in 1742 that he had got a commission of lieutenant-general, and obtained a patent. Robert Fraser saw at Gortuleg, among Lord Lovat's papers, a commission from the Pretender appointing him lieutenant-general. He saw the copy of a patent creating him duke. He was told by Lord Lovat, after his escape from Lord Loudoun, that his patent of duke was in the hands of one Drummond in France. Hugh Fraser was told by Lord Lovat that his patent of duke was in Lochiel's hands, and in November, 1745, my lord showed him a copy of the patent. In his letter to John Murray of Broughton he refers to his cousin the bearer (who was this Hugh Fraser) about a suit he had to make. John Murray of Broughton says Gortuleg explained this to relate to his patent. In his letter to his son, speaking of the Pretender, he says, "When he was acquainted with the association he gave Mr. Drummond a commission to me of general of the Highlanders, which I have. Last of all, the King was so good as to give such a singular mark of his favour to me and my family that he created me Duke of Fraser, and sent me that patent by William Drummond, of which I have a copy." The original, he says, was left with old Lochiel. In the postscript to this letter he says, "Tell your captain-lieutenant (Hugh Fraser) I beg of him to remember what I spoke to him about my patent. Put all irons in the fire. I ask nothing of His Royal Highness but to give his countenance and own publicly what his father has done for me, which, if he refuse, I must keep to the oath, &c., never to draw my sword till it was done." This is corroborated by general evidence given by Broughton and Hugh Fraser. They talked at Glasgow about it. The packet was not directed till Hugh Fraser should learn from old Lochiel whether he had such a patent. Of this overt act there is direct positive evidence by the testimony of three witnesses, Hugh Fraser, Robert Chevis, and Robert Fraser, supported by two more, Charles Stuart and John Murray of Broughton, and all the circumstances which confirm the authenticity of the letters.

The third overt act which I mentioned of this species of treason was that he conspired to raise war and rebellion against His Majesty within this realm. In his letter to the Pretender's son he says, "None of your servants but will do me the justice to declare that I am, and always have been, the most zealous and active partisan your Royal Highness has in the north of Scotland." In his letter to John Murray, "For many years past I was the life and spirit of the King's affairs in these countries," &c. "I made it my only business to encourage and keep up the hearts of the King's friends." In his letter to his

Solicitor-General

son he says, "Since that association I made it my business, wherever I was, to promote the King's interest and to gain and encourage faithful subjects to serve him. So that I have done more against this Government than would hang fifty lords and forfeit fifty estates." In the postscript, "It can be easily proved against him (your father) that he has done more against the Government than any one of his rank in Britain." Hugh Fraser proves that he said he thought of heading the Frasers himself, as he believed 4000 or 5000 men would have risen, but that he was disappointed. He sent a message to the young Pretender by the witness that he had intended to have gone at the head of 4000 or 5000 men to support his interest. When the witness gave him the true state on both sides, he said he had gone too far to go back.

In his letter to Lochiel he says he had so managed the north that 6000 men would have marched south to join the Pretender had not the design been frustrated. Robert Fraser proves that he made excuses to Lochiel, Keppoch, and others for not having joined them publicly; that he made excuses after the battle to the young Pretender, and they both embraced. This is strengthened by general evidence given by John Murray of Broughton that, when the young Pretender landed, a message was sent to Lord Lovat by Dr. Cameron, and Gortuleg came from him. And also by general evidence given by Robert Fraser that, soon after the Pretender landed, one Cameron came to Lord Lovat, and Gortuleg went to the young Pretender. This is strengthened too by most of his letters, which imply a previous concert, and assurances given; they are full of apologies for his not acting up to that which he seems conscious was expected from him. His wavering and irresolution speak a mind divided between former engagements and present fear. At first, when he thought 4000 or 5000 men would be raised, he intended to have headed them himself. When that scheme was disappointed he neither would join the rebels himself nor send his men. Upon the news of the battle of Prestonpans he resolved his son should go. When an account came of the landing of the Dutch forces in England he resolves his son should stay, so as to give occasion to that expression of his, that one day undid what another did. At last, when Lord John Drummond landed in Scotland with a body of French forces, and assurances of powerful succours from France, he returns to the design of sending his son. This conduct and fluctuation of counsel show he equally dreaded either breaking former engagements when the attempt wore a face of success or keeping them when it looked desperate, and gives credit and strength to all the direct and positive evidence that the case was so. Thus this overt act is proved by the testimony of two witnesses, Robert and Hugh Fraser, and supported by all the circumstances which confirm the authenticity of the letters.

The second species of treason whereof the noble lord stands accused by the Articles is "levying war against the King within the realm."

My lords, levying war, properly speaking, and in the nature of the thing, is itself an open act, and may be laid as an open act, of compassing the death of the King. It is impossible to consider a man as levying war without having done some act. In treason there are no accessories; all who assist are principals. Though a man should not himself appear in arms, nor commit any hostilities with his own hands, yet, if he voluntarily aids in any manner those who are in arms, and commit hostilities, he is guilty of levying war. But, though levying war be really an act itself, to be proved by the hostilities committed or assistance given, yet, as the letter of the statute of Edward III. requires the four kinds of treason first mentioned in that Act to be made out by open deed, overt acts are always laid of this species of treason, though generally they are only descriptions of the manner of levying war.

In the present case the Articles have pointed out particularly the manner in which the noble lord is charged with having levied war. And of this species of treason there are three overt acts laid—First, that he encouraged, by messages and letters, the Pretender's son and his adherents, then in arms, waging war against His Majesty within this realm. Hugh Fraser proves that he carried a message from Lord Lovat to the young Pretender, the purport of which your lordships have heard. Robert Fraser proves his letters to the Pretender, Lochiel, and John Murray of Broughton. His evidence as to the letter I last mentioned is supported by its appearing to be written in answer to a letter of the 31st of October from Broughton, and Hugh Fraser swears he brought such a letter from John Murray of Broughton to Lord Lovat, was privy to the contents, and gives an account of them. And John Murray of Broughton proves that he received this letter from Gortuleg. All these letters are established by the postscript to his letter to his son of the 14th of January, 1746, in which he says—"I send you enclosed the four letters which you should have carried with you from Castle Downie. You may tell the Prince when you deliver the letter to him." The authenticity of this is supported by his son's letter, to which this is an answer. So that to this overt act there are two positive witnesses, Hugh and Robert Fraser, besides all the circumstances which give them credit.

The second overt act of this kind of treason laid in the Articles is that he sent his son, at the head of an armed force, to join the young Pretender and his adherents and assist them in

Solicitor-General

the war they were then carrying on against His Majesty within the realm. Robert Fraser proves that Lord Lovat sent letters early to two heads of different tribes of the name to prepare their men in order to join the Master of Lovat; that he ordered colours and bell tents to be got ready; that his men were twice rendezvoused just by his house, with his privity; that he ordered the witness to give them gunpowder and delivered him the key of the place where it was for that purpose; that he furnished them with bonnets, shoes, and shot. His letters to the young Pretender, Lochiel, Broughton, and the son himself show that he sent his son and the men he led. Hugh Fraser says, after his return from the President, Lord Lovat gave his opinion that his son should march with all despatch, that this was his final opinion, and should not be countermanded. Robert Chevis proves that my lord offered him a captain's commission. Hugh Fraser of Dumballoch says Lord Lovat asked him what number of men he could raise, and said the Master was to head and raise them, declared he would send his son and clan, wished himself younger that he might go and command the men himself, blamed his son's slowness in raising the men, promised gratuities to the wives and children of those who went south to the Pretender, and engaged to support their families in their absence. W. Walker was present at part of a dispute between Lord Lovat and his son, who threw his cockade into the fire. He heard Lord Lovat say to Fraser of Byerfield, "What would you have me do? I am forcing my son out, the life of me." Peter Fraser of Belladrum proves that when the men were rendezvoused the officers used to go to Lord Lovat, and he bade them go to his son, their colonel. There are more, but I have already named six witnesses to this overt act, whose evidence is confirmed by a variety of circumstances.

The third and only other overt act of this kind of treason which I shall mention is that he conspired with many persons in arms how to renew the rebellion when it was almost suppressed, and to raise forces to keep it alive. John Murray of Broughton proves that Lord Lovat met at Mortleg, in Morar, fifteen of the chiefs of the rebels; that he said three thousand men would be sufficient, and mentioned four hundred Frasers as the quota of his son, and desired Lochiel to answer for his son. John Farquhar proves that he embraced Lochiel's officers, and said he did not doubt their getting seven or eight thousand real honest men to fight the Elector of Hanover's troops. Charles Stuart proves that three or four hundred Frasers were proposed as his son's quota, and that he desired Lochiel to answer for his son. All agree French money was distributed for the purpose of raising men, and that 70 or

80 louis d'ors were given to a man belonging to Lord Lovat for the Frasers. John Murray of Broughton says that four or five days after my lord talked of sending the servant who had received the money to his son with it, so that to this overt act there are three concurring witnesses.

The third head of treason laid in the Articles, which is "knowingly corresponding with the eldest son of the Pretender and persons employed by him, contrary to the late Act of Parliament," I pass over, because the evidence to support that part of the charge is also evidence upon the two other kinds of treason, and, as such, it has already been taken notice of.

All this particular proof is strongly corroborated, if it wanted any support, by a general evidence of guilt. Lieutenant Dalrymple proves that Lord Lovat, after he was taken, being asked how he came to be engaged, said it was in revenge for the loss of his company. David Campbell asking how he came to be engaged in a thing of this kind at his years, Lord Lovat said he had been disobliged by taking away his company. Sir Everard Fawkener has told your lordships that he did not take pains to deny his guilt, that he put the part he had acted upon resentment to the Ministry for having taken away his company, that he said for the sake of revenge he would have joined Kouli Khan had he come.

His escaping after he was first apprehended, the condition and place in which he was taken, show that he thought his only safety lay in flight. After he was taken, his declarations to those who took him, his conversations with Sir Everard Fawkener, well knowing who he was, show an absolute conviction that the part he had acted was too notorious to be dissembled.

My lords, this being the nature and strength of the evidence upon which the case now in judgment depends, from the precedent which may be made upon this occasion, I little thought to have heard of danger to innocence hereafter. If this were a doubtful matter, if it were a measuring cast, the Commons had rather the guilty should escape than run a risk of the innocent being condemned. When they accuse, they desire the person accused may be convicted upon clear, satisfactory, and unanswerable proof, or not at all. The noble lord at the bar has complained of many hardships. Few are the trials in which such a complaint would be so little founded. He had full time to prepare for his defence. At his own request he has been indulged with adjournments during the trial. He has had all the advantages of assistance which could be given or connived at.

I wish the inflexible rule of law, as it still stands in prosecutions of this kind, could have allowed him to make his full defence by others. The appearance of a hardship would have

Solicitor-General

been removed; but, as this case is circumstanced, the removing that appearance would have helped the prosecution much more than the prisoner. I speak it feelingly I had rather reply to the ablest advocate than do what my duty now requires of me. It is painful to the last degree to observe upon anything which has dropped from himself, but some notice must be taken.

He has laboured to prove that no credit ought to be given to the witnesses against him, because many of them are accomplices, and speak from the danger of their situation. I will allow that the hopes of life or the fear of death may have induced some of them to give evidence upon this occasion, but not a false evidence. The same hope or fear is a security against that. When the Commons accuse, and your lordships sit as judges, what expectation can they have but from their ingenuity and veracity? Should they be caught prevaricating, should they be detected in a false accusation, desperate were their condition indeed. But the noble lord is misinformed when he says an accomplice ought not to be believed at all till he is pardoned. If so, he could not be examined. The utmost force of the objection is no more than a circumstance to weigh in the scale against his credit, but, then, it must be balanced with the matter of the evidence, the manner in which it is given, the proof by which it is supported, and that by which it is contradicted. The matter here is probable and consistent. Nothing of consequence rests upon a single testimony. They who support each other, first told their stories separately, have never since had an opportunity of conferring, and therefore could not agree in a fiction—one, perhaps, first examined in London, another at Inverness, neither knowing what the other had, could, or would say, kept in separate custodies ever since. It is impossible they should unite in the same falsehood. The manner, too, in which they gave their evidence carried with it a degree of conviction. To instance one, the behaviour of Hugh Fraser demonstrated what he told your lordships. He said if he had no hopes of mercy he would not have spoken at all, for if he submitted to be examined he must speak religiously the truth. The visible agonies and anguish of mind under which he laboured, the ingenuity with which he answered the precise question put to him, without ever going a syllable beyond it, could not but force belief to all he said, and showed he gave the answer because it was true, but wished not to have given it upon this occasion. When he first discovered what he knew he has told your lordships that he thought himself in the article of death, and from what he then said he never has varied since.

The proof by which their testimony is supported I have already laid together in one view. To contradict them nothing is offered. The noble lord says the witnesses who could clear him are not here. Though in the course of the trial we heard of his having witnesses and what they would prove, he has not had time enough to bring them! He complains of their having been prevented! As he has not witnesses enough, he won't call any! These are pretexts, but he let fall the true reason why he has no witnesses. There is no making bricks without straw. There is no calling witnesses without facts. There is no making a defence without innocence. There is no answering evidence which is true. He has not so much as suggested what these witnesses could prove if they were here. Solicitor-General

I will do him the justice to believe that if he could, with truth, he would not now throw the whole upon the stiff-necked, headstrong disobedience of his son. That unhappy boy is already attainted, and now actually in custody. Though he might have been made the scapegoat if he were out of reach, yet, in his present situation, I am sure the noble lord would not defend his own life by loading this unfortunate youth, much less would he attempt such a kind of defence contrary to truth, for so it must be if either the prisoner himself or our evidence is believed.

Would he call witnesses to prove the letters which have been read to be forged? Consider how they are authenticated. To some his signature still remains. He does not controvert its being like his hand. The bodies are written by Robert Fraser. A letter, unquestionably signed and sent by the noble lord to His Royal Highness the Duke was produced. The body is written by the same Robert Fraser. The signature to this, and the signature which remains to the others, appear manifestly of the same hand. One of the most material letters is an answer to a letter written by his son. That, too, must be a forgery; yet it was found in his own custody. But the intrinsic evidence of authenticity is still stronger. If the letters are forged, how come they to give the same account of the association, and mention the same persons concerned, as your lordships have heard from the general evidence? If the general evidence is a fiction, how could the same story get into these letters? If Robert Fraser invented the letters, how came Hugh Fraser, and others, to give the same account of the patent and commission which is to be found in them? If the patent and commission never were seen or heard of, how could they be put into forged letters? But remarks are unnecessary where the case is so plain.

I have said thus much to show that the noble lord's alleging he wants assistance, or has not his witnesses may be of more service to him than any assistance or witnesses he could have, and to show that the Commons have not taken upon themselves this prosecution, to lay the noble lord at the bar under any dis-

Solicitor-General

advantages in his defence. From the witnesses who have been examined, the case must appear to your lordships such as no advantages could have enabled him to get the better of. There are many circumstances which induced them to single out this prosecution, many circumstances of a public, many of a peculiar nature. I am almost tempted to mention some of them, but, in part, they have occurred to your lordships in the course of the examination, and I refrain lest I should drop anything that might tend to inflame. Everything of that sort has by everybody been carefully avoided upon this occasion. That "Ciceronian eloquence," as he calls it, from principles of justice and humanity has not been used against him. Every gentleman who has spoke in this trial has made it a rule to himself to urge nothing against the prisoner but plain facts and positive evidence, without aggravation. They have addressed themselves to your judgment and not to your passions. I daresay your lordships have observed that, though the evidence given consists of a variety of facts, some more directly affecting the noble lord, others less, and some, perhaps, not affecting him at all, neither in the summing up the evidence nor in what I have now troubled your lordships with, has anything been mentioned as direct evidence against him which is not so. Circumstances which only tend to corroborate have been mentioned in that light, and evidence which in no way affects him has not been repeated or observed upon at all.

My lords, the whole is now before your lordships. It is your province to make the conclusion which ought to be drawn from the premises.

Lord Talbot—My lords, the abilities of the learned Manager who just now spoke never appeared with greater splendour than at this very hour, when his candour and humanity has been joined to those great abilities which have already made him so conspicuous, that I hope one day to see him add lustre to the dignity of the first civil employment in this nation. My lords, I observe one thing in the defence of the noble lord at the bar which, for the sake of the Managers for the representatives of Great Britain, and out of the regard that I have for their constituents who deputed them, I think myself obliged to take notice of.

My lords, the noble lord at the bar in his defence complains, I believe, very unjustly, of the hardships he has suffered in being deprived of his witnesses, and at the same time mentions that there are witnesses of indisputable credit who were brought up in order to be witnesses against him, but who have not been examined by the Managers, for fear they should, on their cross-examination, support those facts.

My lords, I therefore now desire, for the honour of the gentlemen who are Managers of this prosecution, that the noble lord at the bar may be asked whether he is now willing to have those witnesses produced, and to have them asked any questions concerning that matter?

Attorney-General

ATTORNEY-GENERAL—My lords, what has been taken notice of by the noble lord, and what is desired by him, is extremely irregular, after the Managers have closed and summed up their evidence, and the noble prisoner had liberty and time given him, in the most indulgent manner, to make his defence in such way as he should be advised. He was pleased to make a speech to your lordships containing a great variety of facts, but declined producing any witnesses, and, though called upon for that purpose, thought proper to acquaint your lordships that he should offer none to support those facts which he had alleged. Your lordships have, upon that declaration, been pleased to proceed to hear the Managers' reply.

My learned friend on my left hand hath executed that part with great justice to the commands of the Commons, and all that tenderness to the noble prisoner which was consistent with his duty. Your lordships have heard and felt the weight of it.

The proceedings are closed, and wait only for your lordships' opinion. The Managers therefore are surprised to find the noble lord now calling upon the prisoner to examine witnesses whom he did not think proper himself to examine, after the fullest opportunity of considering it. And it appears by his own speech he has had correspondence with his witnesses since they came up. The Managers therefore must insist that your lordships will proceed to give your opinion upon the whole of the evidence which is now fully before you.

My lords, I cannot but take notice of the method which the prisoner at the bar has taken, of reflecting upon this prosecution, in his speech. He has complained in a heavy manner, and endeavoured to induce your lordships to believe that those who have had the conduct of this prosecution have been using undue methods, either to get witnesses to support the charge or to prevent him from having any witnesses in his defence. If the prisoner at the bar could have made out anything of this kind, your lordships would certainly have heard it here, in evidence, for his not doing it could not be out of deference to the Commons, or to your lordships, or to His Majesty.

He has represented as if a new method was taken of erecting uncommon Courts of justice to compel some witnesses to

Attorney-General

give evidence on one side, and deter others from doing it on the other. My lords, it is indecent to lay reflections of this kind before your lordships in this manner. Is the noble lord at the bar now to say, "I could have evidence if I had an opportunity of producing it, and if your lordships will give me time I will prove all that I have said"? My lords, what has he been doing ever since the Articles were exhibited? Who are the persons he could now examine? Many of his witnesses, he has said himself, are come up. Has he made any use of them? Have they been examined at your lordships' bar? On the contrary, did not the prisoner say he would produce no witnesses? Yet, says he, "I will reflect upon the proceedings and say that I could have witnesses if I had leave and time to produce them."

My lords, a prisoner who is tried for his life may think he has a right to say anything, how false, how unjust soever, but it is incumbent on your lordships to prevent the effect of such reflections, to do justice to all parties, to the Government, the Commons of Great Britain, and the Managers. The prisoner seems to have hopes that your lordships may be prevailed upon, by this means, to believe that there is some truth in what he says. Your lordships' indulgence now of further time, on this pretence, would give some colour to that suggestion, and it will be imagined that it was believed by your lordships. I call upon the prisoner himself to declare whether your lordships did not indulge him with an opportunity of calling any witnesses, even those brought up on the part of the Managers, on his giving them notice for that purpose. If your lordships should now, upon what has been said by the noble lord, which I do not doubt but he said from the great regard he has to justice, and from his compassion for a person appearing in the circumstances of the prisoner, I say, my lords, if upon such a suggestion your lordships should now call again upon the prisoner to produce his witnesses, it will be giving credit to that false and injurious insinuation, and I hope your lordships will not give colour to imagine it was believed by you, by giving leave to the prisoner now to call witnesses for that purpose.

Lord High Steward—Have you done with your evidence on both sides?

Lord Lovat

Lord Lovat—My lords, I am an unfit person to say anything after that great man that has spoken last, but, since I am now upon my trial for my life and fortune, I must tell your lordships what is really fact, though perhaps it may not be pleasing to that great man, that there is not one syllable of what he has said true. My lords, it is certain that I got your lordships' order for bringing up sixty witnesses to this place; and it is certain that I sent a gentleman, who was once allowed to be my solicitor, and, though I was robbed of my whole money, and did not get a farthing out of my estate since I was taken prisoner, yet I had interest enough to get £500 from Mr. Ross, which was given to this man to bring up my witnesses. My lords, he came there to Inverness, and found all the witnesses that I had named to him were very ready to come up, but I was extremely surprised to find that there was a new Court, besides the Court of the House of Peers, a little depute of the Sheriff's, that took upon him to leave the common place of justice in the Tolbooth at Inverness, and to go to a private place in the suburbs, and there to erect such Courts as he thought fit, and there he examined what witnesses he pleased, and those which he thought friends to me were some of them put into prison, others overawed and terrified, and others chased out of their houses, their houses burnt and their cattle taken away, and most of the rest obliged to go to the Highlands, and threatened to be undone if they came to be evidence for me.

My lords, after my friend that was sent to bring up my witnesses used all his endeavours, and offered to bear their expenses and to keep them, he could not get them to come up, because there was an influence used by the general officers in His Majesty's service, and persons sent up and down the whole country to threaten part of the witnesses and to bribe others of them. So that, my lords, though I am no lawyer, nor orator, as the learned gentleman on my left hand is, yet I heard from a very great man that this was a precedent which never happened in Scotland, and, he believed, not in England, and he said to me that it was most certain the lords would take notice of it, because the affront had been done to themselves. My lords, after I was arraigned before your lordships, and that the House of Commons had brought up Articles against me, that your lordships would not allow any little Court of inquisition to go afterwards and to judge my cause, as it were, before your lordships. Therefore, my lords, it is simply impossible for me to make my defence while I am not allowed the witnesses that your lordships ordered for me. That what I say myself is true there are two affidavits here of it, if your lordships please to let them be read by the Clerk.

Lord High Steward—My Lord Lovat, by our law affidavits cannot be read as evidence upon a trial. You must call witnesses to prove the facts. But I would ask your lordship the name of that agent whom you sent down into Scotland to bring up the witnesses, and who gave you this information?

Lord Lovat—His name is Hugh Fraser.

Lord High Steward—My Lord Lovat, I must put your lordship in mind that you made three applications to the House of Lords

Lord Lovat by petition to put off your trial. The first was on the 19th of February, and the others on the 2nd or 3rd of March. One of those petitions was supported by an affidavit made by one Hugh Fraser. Was that the same Hugh Fraser whom you sent as your agent into Scotland?

LORD LOVAT—Yes, my lord, it was.

LORD HIGH STEWARD—Then, my lord, there is another affidavit annexed to your petition to put off the trial on the 3rd of March, which is the affidavit of George Ross. Now, in neither of these petitions, though one of them is supported by the affidavit of Hugh Fraser, whom you admit to be the person you sent into Scotland to summon your witnesses, is there any allegation of any undue practices or any restraint upon your witnesses. How comes it to pass, when this Hugh Fraser came back from Scotland and made an affidavit to support the petition to put off your trial, that this complaint was not made then?

LORD LOVAT—My lords, in the first place, it could not be done before, because they went upon these methods but just before Hugh Fraser came up. I have a minister of the Gospel, a very honest and worthy man, whom they designed to make an evidence against me, and, I believe, he will tell the truth upon the subject of the hardships done to my people to keep them from coming up here to be evidences, I mean my tenants.

Mr. Noel MR. NOEL—My lords, I did not intend to have troubled your lordships at all, not finding the noble lord at the bar had, in his defence, made it necessary for me to take any part in the reply, since what he has said (if it had been more material than the nature of it appears to be) he hath said unsupported by any evidence at all, and the noble lord very well knows that in every Court of justice a prisoner is not expected to make his defence by what he thinks fit to say himself, but he must support it by evidence, or it can have no weight in answer to the evidence produced to support the charge against him; and, my lords, it was for that reason that I did not trouble your lordships in that part of the case, which hath been so amply, minutely, and accurately gone through by my learned friend who has spoken to it. But, since the noble lord has irregularly mentioned several matters since the reply was closed, I shall take the liberty to make some observations upon what he has insisted upon.

My lords, the noble lord at the bar has made it matter of complaint to your lordships as if particular methods of practice had been used to prevent his witnesses coming up to appear in his behalf. Your lordships will give me leave to say that such allegations ought to be considered as the highest injustice, when his lordship has not called one single witness to the truth of them or to his own defence. My lords, this affectation of saying things without supporting them by any proof, after hearing the reply of the Commons and the summing up of the whole proceeding, is a method which was never known to be endured in any proceeding by way of legal trial. My lords, it is extremely easy for any noble peer upon this occasion, when he stands to be tried for his life, and has no defence to make nor no witnesses to produce—it is easy, I say, my lords, to throw in matters by way of calumny, but your lordships will not endure it unless it is made at a proper time and supported by proper evidence. Mr. Noel

My lords, I am the more surprised at this from the noble lord at the bar, because, whatever he may think of it, this I will say, that I know of no instance in any case where a prisoner has been more fairly dealt with, or used with more candour and humanity on the part of those whose business it is to make out the charge against him, nor on the part of those by whom he is to be tried. And it is the more extraordinary, because, if I am not mistaken, till this very day he has declared to your lordships that he had numbers of witnesses ready to produce who would falsify every fact which has been alleged against him.

My lords, I will take notice, now I am up, of another objection made by the noble lord to some of the witnesses that have been produced against him. My lords, it is a known objection. It has been often made, and as constantly overruled.

The noble lord says some of the witnesses are persons interested, that they are criminal, as accomplices in this rebellion, and therefore ought not to be believed. Your lordships will give me leave to suggest whether the laying down that as a rule would not be of very ill consequence, and in effect secure the most wicked offenders from all possibility of punishment and justice. My lords, it is from a principle of right reason, and absolutely necessary to the preservation of Government, that those who are concerned with them should have liberty to do justice to the public by their testimony. It is so in all cases of robbery, murder, and other felonies, and much more in cases of treason, where the whole is in danger. My lords, if this was not so, the very end of government would fail in every particular if those who are concerned and best able to discover the truth are not allowed to give testimony for the sake of preserving the nation. But, my lords, in the present case I do not recollect any material fact against the noble lord at the bar but what has been proved by every witness *viva voce*, and by every letter that has been read, wherein not only his corresponding and treasonable engagements have been made appear, but he has expressed himself almost in every letter

Mr. Noel as manifesting the glory he took and zeal he showed in that wicked service which he is proved to be engaged in to the last.

My lords, we have nothing now to do but to expect your lordships' opinions upon the evidence and facts that have been laid before you, and in contradiction to which there is not one single evidence produced by the noble lord.

Here the prisoner offered to speak.

Lord High Steward—My Lord Lovat, my lords will be ready to hear everything that you can offer which is material for your defence, but I must acquaint you that the Commons, by the constant rules of proceeding in cases of this kind, are entitled to the last word.

Lord Lovat—My lords, I am far from blaming the honourable Managers for the Commons, though they prosecute me with great warmness, and especially the man at their head, who was some time ago my friend and acquaintance. But, my lords, whatever they were pleased to object against me, as I was forced to speak for myself, I was obliged to answer, and, my lords, since I asked the favour of this House to force up my evidence in the manner they thought fit, your lordships saying that no affidavit was good upon the subject, my lords, I have two very good witnesses, one a very reverend minister of the Gospel, that will prove the most extreme hardships that ever were imposed in this country to hinder my witnesses from coming up to me, so that, if your lordships do not, in your great justice and goodness, think it proper to order, in the manner your lordships please, to have my witnesses come up, I must submit to your lordships. You may do what you please.

Lord High Steward—My Lord Lovat, I particularly asked your lordship whether you would call any witnesses to prove what you alleged in your defence, to which you answered that you would not.

Lord Lovat—My lords, I would call witnesses upon no other account than this that I have mentioned. I have witnesses to prove the falsity of what has been said by the witnesses against me, but, since I do not get time to do that, I give it up.

Lord High Steward—Your lordship does not attend to what I said, which was, that I asked you two or three times whether you would call any witnesses to prove any part of your defence, to which you said, "No." If you had any witnesses why did you not call them at that time?

Lord Lovat—This minister was brought up as one of the counter evidence. I told your lordship that I would call no witnesses that day.

Lord High Steward—Is that minister here?

Lord Lovat—He is here.

Lord High Steward—Gentlemen of the House of Commons, it is certainly an irregular method in which the noble lord at the bar would proceed to call witnesses after the reply, but I desire to know of you whether you oppose my Lord Lovat's calling witnesses now.

Attorney-General

Attorney-General—My lords, it is a difficulty upon us, who are appointed Managers, to carry on this prosecution, and would do it with all the candour and indulgence possible, to insist that the noble lord, who is trying for his life, should not now be admitted to produce witnesses, but it is perhaps as difficult to know how to dispense with that which is the known course and method of proceedings merely because the prisoner, in an irregular and improper manner, thinks fit to desire it. The Managers do not oppose their being produced from an imagination that they would say anything material for the noble lord at the bar, but, if your lordships are to break through all methods and rules of proceedings, your lordships will consider the consequence. The noble lord at the bar told your lordships that he did not intend to call any witnesses, and upon that footing the Managers replied. He has now told you that he would do it. But what is it that he would examine them to? Is it to make out any part of his defence to the treason charged on him? That is not pretended, but to prove the hardships he complains of in being hindered from having his witnesses, and the noble lord at the bar wants your lordships' order now for their coming. The tendency of this, if it means anything besides complaint, is to put off the cause after it is heard, and, unless I had a greater authority than I have at present, I cannot take upon myself, and I do not find that the rest of the gentlemen who are Managers can take upon them, to depart from the known established course of proceeding, and to introduce a precedent that may be of bad consequence. And, my lords, I can hardly think that the noble lord at the bar would insist upon doing it, but because he thought that the Managers must insist that he ought not. There is nothing that has occurred now that did not, must not, have occurred to him before, and when the prisoner thought fit to declare to your lordships, after having full time allowed him for the maturest consideration and counsel appointed for his assistance, that he would not call any witnesses, you cannot but think such determination of his was upon the advice that his counsel gave him, and your lordships will hardly think that the noble lord can at present thus unadvisedly determine to call any witnesses, which before, upon the footing of the advice he must be presumed to have taken, he determined not to do, from any expectation that they would be able to do him any real service, but from views of another kind. The Managers, therefore, doubt not that your lordships will proceed in this case, as you would in any other, to consider the evidence and give such judgment on the whole as your lordships shall think most right and just.

Trial of Lord Lovat.

Lord Lovat—My lords, I have often told your lordships of the infirmities that I labour under. I have often mentioned them to you, and the want of memory is the thing I regret most. I have been a cripple these four years, and therefore not very capable to go to head men in the rebellion, yet I am much surprised to hear that honourable person that is at the head of the law, and very deservedly placed there, that he should lose his memory in an hour's time. My lords, the reason is plain to your lordships why I did not adduce witnesses this morning. The reason was because I begged of your lordships time to bring my witnesses up from Scotland, that they might be produced to prove my innocence, and the only reason that I now desire to call these two witnesses, if your lordships please, is that they may prove before that great man such examples of extreme hardships as he will never find out in all his law books.

Lord High Steward—My Lord Lovat, you mentioned but one witness at first, and now you mention two. Who is the other?

Lord Lovat—The two are Donald Fraser and Alexander Fraser.

Lord High Steward—Gentlemen of the House of Commons, do you oppose my Lord Lovat's being admitted, though it is irregular, to call these two witnesses?

Attorney-General—My lords, I think we cannot consistently with our duty to the Commons give up this point, which would be attended with many dangerous consequences, the whole of which your lordships may not now be able to foresee, if a man, when he has closed his defence and says that he will examine no witnesses, and the Managers have replied, should afterwards be admitted on such a pretence as this to examine witnesses.

Earl of Cholmondeley—My lords, I am satisfied that the manner in which the noble lord at the bar desires now to call his witnesses is totally different from any proceeding that I ever saw, but, as the accused lord in his defence has alleged several hardships that he has undergone in having his witnesses prevented from attending his trial, and as that contains the highest reflection upon the Government and those who are employed under it, I would therefore desire to know of the noble lord at the bar whether upon the speech that he offered at the bar, as it contains objections to the credit and weight of the evidence and complaints of undue practices, whether, upon those complaints, the noble lord at the bar desires the opinion of the lords, whether they will give him further time in order to produce his witnesses?

Lord Lovat—My lords, I was fully determined never to examine any witnesses, when I found I was under such disadvantages, and I humbly beg your lordships' protection and kindness to give me time.

Sixth Day.

Solicitor-General—My lords, the matter now agitated is of the utmost consequence not only to the present, but to all future proceedings of this kind, and I doubt whether it is yet thoroughly understood in its full extent. The witnesses the noble lord now proposes to call are not to his defence or in support of his innocence. If they were, how irregular soever it may be to offer them now, in my own opinion, and, I dare say, the other Managers are of the same, I should be for consenting to their being called. We should never contend, though in strictness we might, that any evidence of this kind came too late to be heard. But the design of calling them, as now opened, is to show that, from some obstruction given to the bringing up his witnesses, his trial ought to be put off to an indefinite time, and that he may have new orders to summon and compel witnesses to come from Scotland. This we oppose, because the application intended to be supported by it cannot now be made. Solicitor-General

The speech made by my lord consisted of two parts—First, a desire to put off his trial indefinitely, and, if your lordships should not think fit to comply with this desire, then he rested his defence upon observations and objections to the force and credibility of that evidence which had been offered to prove his accusation. In this he was very proper, for though a person accused calls no witnesses, yet, if the charge against him is not clearly made out by legal and credible evidence, he ought to be acquitted. Being asked whether he had any witnesses to call, he declared he had none. Had he desired to take your lordships' opinion whether the trial should not stay till he could send to Scotland for witnesses, we should have opposed it. Your lordships calling to the Managers to proceed was a determination that you would not deliberate about staying the trial.

I own freely to your lordships the reason why I did not take particular notice of the noble lord's complaint was because I understood it to be meant as an artifice to palliate his not going into any evidence. And I did not think it necessary, I did not care, to endeavour to wipe off from his apology any varnish of this kind with which he thought fit to colour it. One thing, had I thought of it, I would have taken notice of. He was pleased to say that several witnesses brought up in support of the prosecution were not called by the Managers, because they would have proved the hardships he complains of. I can assure your lordships, and every other gentleman of the Committee will join in what I say, no one witness was left unexamined for that reason. It is true, more persons were brought up to be witnesses than we called, but the reason of not calling them was either because we thought what they had to say not material enough, or else because they were

Solicitor-General

liable to an objection the noble lord had made, which, whether well-founded or ill-founded, we did not care to give your lordships the trouble of disputing.

In consequence of what fell from your lordships, we told the noble lord in the course of the trial that any witness examined by us should attend to be examined by him if he desired it, and would give notice. We should have done the same with regard to any person brought up as a witness, though not examined. As to this whole matter of complaint, the Managers are entire strangers to it. Nothing of that kind has been done with their privity or knowledge. And this brings me to the point whether witnesses shall be now heard at this time to prove any such ground for putting off the trial *sine die.* We oppose it, because, true or false, the trial cannot now be put off, and it would be a most dangerous precedent to go into an *ex parte* examination of such collateral matters. Hearing the evidence supposes your lordships can do something in consequence of it. If you cannot, it would be irregular and improper to go into it. Before your lordships appoint the time of trial you take into consideration the nature of the charge and the place where the facts arise, in order to allow a reasonable time for preparation and bringing witnesses. Your lordships did so in the present case, and, after weighing all circumstances, you appointed the 23rd of February. If, through any accident, the time fixed is too short, your lordships are always open to applications, which must be supported by evidence to show the delay is not affected, that all due diligence has been used, and that the witnesses are material and expected to come within a certain time. Upon the application of the noble lord your lordships deferred this trial to the 5th of March. Upon another application by him you deferred it to the 9th of March, the day named in his petition. If he had any ground sufficient for deferring the trial longer he should have applied to your lordships before it began, but, upon the ground now mentioned, it could not have been deferred, even in that way, because it is plain this matter, whatever there be in it, was within his knowledge at the time of the other applications. Hugh Fraser, his agent, who went down, as his lordship says, to bring up his witnesses, made an affidavit, annexed to a petition presented by his lordship, on the 2nd of March for putting off the trial, and was called in and examined at your lordships' bar. There was likewise an affidavit annexed to his lordship's petition presented on the 3rd of March, and not a syllable of this complaint ever suggested, which shows that they thought no stress could be laid upon it, and that it was not to be supported. In the course of the trial hitherto your lordships have heard nothing of it. On the contrary, you have heard of his witnesses, and what they were to prove.

Sixth Day.

There is no precedent of putting off a trial indefinitely after the evidence for the prosecution is closed. I dare say there never will be such a precedent. At soonest this trial could not come on again before the next session of Parliament. We oppose the attempting to prove a matter upon which your lordships cannot now do anything, but I desire it may be understood that we do not oppose, though it be an improper time, the calling any witnesses upon the merits of his defence, either to disprove the evidence against him or to assert his own innocence. Solicitor-General

Then the Duke of Newcastle moved to adjourn to the Chamber of Parliament, and the Lord High Steward going back to his chair, the House was adjourned accordingly, and then the lords returned in the same order as before.

After some time the lords and others returned into Westminster Hall in the same order as usual, and the peers having taken their places, and the Lord High Steward being seated in his chair, the House was resumed.

Then proclamation was made for silence as usual.

Lord High Steward—Lieutenant of the Tower of London, take the prisoner from the bar, but you are not to take him away to the Tower yet.

Lord Lovat—If your lordships would send me to the Highlands I would not go to the Tower any more.

The prisoner was taken from the bar.[1]

Lord High Steward—Your lordships have heard and considered the evidence in this cause, and everything that has been alleged by the Managers for the House of Commons and by the prisoner. The solemn and established method of your proceedings requires that I should ask your lordships' opinions severally upon the question, whether the noble lord the prisoner is guilty of the high treason whereof he stands impeached or not guilty, and that those opinions should be given in the absence of the prisoner. My lords, this has always been your rule, and after that is done the prisoner is to be brought to the bar

[1] The *Lords Journal* of 18th March, 1747, says that before judgment was pronounced the Archbishop of York, for himself and the rest of the bishops, handed in a Protestation which they desired to be entered. It was as follows:—

"The Lords Spiritual of the House of Peers do desire leave of this House to be absent from the judgment now to be given in the case of Lord Lovat, by protestation, saving to themselves and their successors all such rights in judicature as they have in law, and of right ought to have."

Then His Grace asked leave that they might withdraw, which was agreed to, and they at once departed.

again, and to be acquainted by me with the result of those opinions. Is it your lordships' pleasure to proceed now to give your opinions upon the question of guilty or not guilty?

LORDS—Ay, ay.

Proclamation was then made for silence as before.

Then the Lord High Steward stood up, uncovered, and, beginning with the youngest peer, said, "Henry Arthur, Lord Herbert of Chirbury, what says your lordship? Is Simon, Lord Lovat, guilty of the high treason whereof he stands impeached or not guilty?" Whereupon Henry Arthur, Lord Herbert of Chirbury, standing up in his place, uncovered, and laying his right hand upon his breast, answered—

Lord Herbert—Guilty, upon my honour.

In like manner the several lords aftermentioned, being all that were present, being respectively asked the same question, answered as follows:—

Samuel, Lord Sandys—Guilty, upon my honour.

Richard, Lord Edgecumbe—Guilty, upon my honour.

Stephen, Lord Ilchester and Stavordale—Guilty, upon my honour.

Henry, Lord Montfort—Guilty, upon my honour.

William, Lord Talbot—Guilty, upon my honour.

Robert, Lord Raymond—Guilty, upon my honour.

John, Lord Monson—Guilty, upon my honour.

Matthew, Lord Ducie—Guilty, upon my honour.

Charles, Lord Cadogan—Guilty, upon my honour.

Robert, Lord Romney—Guilty, upon my honour.

Richard, Lord Onslow—Guilty, upon my honour.

Allen, Lord Bathurst—Guilty, upon my honour.

Samuel, Lord Masham—Guilty, upon my honour.

Thomas, Lord Trevor—Guilty, upon my honour.

Francis, Lord Middleton—Guilty, upon my honour.

Bussy, Lord Mansell—Guilty, upon my honour.

George, Lord Hay—Guilty, upon my honour.

James, Lord Somerville—Guilty, upon my honour.

George William, Lord Hervey—Guilty, upon my honour.

Charles, Lord Cornwallis—Guilty, upon my honour.

John, Lord Berkeley of Stratton—Guilty, upon my honour.

John, Lord Ward—Guilty, upon my honour.

William, Lord Byron—Guilty, upon my honour.

Thomas, Lord Leigh—Guilty, upon my honour.

James, Lord Strange—Guilty, upon my honour.

Charles, Lord Maynard—Guilty, upon my honour.

John, Lord St. John of Bletsoe—Guilty, upon my honour.

Francis, Lord North and Guilford—Guilty, upon my honour.

Hugh, Lord Willoughby of Parham—Guilty, upon my honour.

Edward, Lord Wentworth of Nettlested—Guilty, upon my honour.

Verdict of the Lords.

Richard, Lord Willoughby de Broke—Guilty, upon my honour.

Ferdinando Dudley, Lord Dudley—Guilty, upon my honour.

John, Lord Delawar—Guilty, upon my honour.

James, Viscount Leinster—Guilty, upon my honour.

George, Viscount Torrington—Guilty, upon my honour.

Simon, Viscount Harcourt—Guilty, upon my honour.

Hugh, Viscount Falmouth—Guilty, upon my honour.

John, Viscount St. John—Guilty, upon my honour.

Henry, Viscount Lonsdale—Guilty, upon my honour.

William, Viscount Hatton—Guilty, upon my honour.

Charles, Viscount Townshend—Guilty, upon my honour.

Thomas, Viscount Fauconberg—Guilty, upon my honour.

Richard, Viscount Say and Seale—Guilty, upon my honour.

John, Earl of Buckinghamshire—Guilty, upon my honour.

Francis, Earl Brooke—Guilty, upon my honour.

Hugh, Earl Clinton—Guilty, upon my honour.

Thomas, Earl of Leicester—Guilty, upon my honour.

John, Earl of Portsmouth—Guilty, upon my honour.

William, Earl of Bath—Guilty, upon my honour.

Robert, Earl of Orford—Guilty, upon my honour.

Thomas, Earl of Effingham—Guilty, upon my honour.

John, Earl of Ashburnham—Guilty, upon my honour.

Benjamin, Earl Fitzwalter—Guilty, upon my honour.

James, Earl Waldegrave—Guilty, upon my honour.

Robert, Earl Ker—Guilty, upon my honour.

William, Earl Graham—Guilty, upon my honour.

Thomas, Earl of Pomfret—Guilty, upon my honour.

George, Earl of Macclesfield—Guilty, upon my honour.

Philip, Earl of Harborough—Guilty, upon my honour.

Philip, Earl Stanhope—Guilty, upon my honour.

William, Earl Cowper—Guilty, upon my honour.

George, Earl of Halifax—Guilty, upon my honour.

John, Earl of Granville—Guilty, upon my honour.

Charles, Earl of Tankerville—Guilty, upon my honour.

William, Earl of Strafford—Guilty, upon my honour.

Laurence, Earl Ferrers—Guilty, upon my honour.

Edward, Earl of Oxford and Earl Mortimer—Guilty, upon my honour.

Charles, Earl of Portmore—Guilty, upon my honour.

James, Earl of Findlater and Seafield—Guilty, upon my honour.

James, Earl of Moray—Guilty, upon my honour.

George, Earl of Cholmondeley—Guilty, upon my honour.

Francis, Earl of Godolphin—Guilty, upon my honour.

John, Earl Poulett—Guilty, upon my honour.

William, Earl of Jersey—Guilty, upon my honour.

William, Earl of Coventry—Guilty, upon my honour.

William Henry, Earl of Rochfort—Guilty, upon my honour.
George, Earl of Warrington—Guilty, upon my honour.
Robert, Earl of Holderness—Guilty, upon my honour.
Baptist, Earl of Gainsborough—Guilty, upon my honour.
Willoughby, Earl of Abingdon—Guilty, upon my honour.
Augustus, Earl of Berkeley—Guilty, upon my honour.
George Henry, Earl of Lichfield—Guilty, upon my honour.
Anthony Ashley, Earl of Shaftesbury—Guilty, upon my honour.
Richard, Earl of Burlington—Guilty, upon my honour.
Francis, Earl of Doncaster—Guilty, upon my honour.
Henry, Earl of Carlisle—Guilty, upon my honour.
George, Earl of Cardigan—Guilty, upon my honour.
Philip Dormer, Earl of Chesterfield—Guilty, upon my honour.
Daniel, Earl of Winchelsea and Nottingham—Guilty, upon my honour.
Harry, Earl of Stamford—Guilty, upon my honour.
Charles, Earl of Peterborough and Monmouth—Guilty, upon my honour.
John, Earl of Westmorland—Guilty, upon my honour.
Edward, Earl of Warwick and Holland—Guilty, upon my honour.
Henry, Earl of Lincoln—Guilty, upon my honour.
Henry, Earl of Pembroke and Montgomery—Guilty, upon my honour.
Thomas, Marquis of Rockingham—Guilty, upon my honour.
William, Marquis of Lothian—Guilty, upon my honour.
John, Marquis of Tweeddale—Guilty, upon my honour.
Henry, Duke of Chandos—Guilty, upon my honour.
Robert, Duke of Manchester—Guilty, upon my honour.
William, Duke of Portland—Guilty, upon my honour.
Thomas, Duke of Newcastle—Guilty, upon my honour.
Evelin, Duke of Kingston—Guilty, upon my honour.
Peregrine, Duke of Ancaster and Kesteven, Lord Great Chamberlain—Guilty, upon my honour.
Archibald, Duke of Argyll—Guilty, upon my honour.
John, Duke of Montagu—Guilty, upon my honour.
John, Duke of Rutland—Guilty, upon my honour.
Thomas, Duke of Leeds—Guilty, upon my honour.
Charles, Duke of Bolton—Guilty, upon my honour.
Charles, Duke of St. Albans—Guilty, upon my honour.
Charles Noel, Duke of Beaufort—Guilty, upon my honour.
Charles, Duke of Richmond—Guilty, upon my honour.
Charles, Duke of Grafton, Lord Chamberlain of His Majesty's Household—Guilty, upon my honour.
William, Duke of Devonshire, Lord Steward of His Majesty's Household—Guilty, upon my honour.

Lionel Cranfield, Duke of Dorset, Lord President of the Council—Guilty, upon my honour.

Then the Lord High Steward, laying his right hand upon his breast, said—

My lords, I am of opinion that Simon, Lord Lovat, is guilty of the high treason whereof he stands impeached, upon my honour.

Lord High Steward—My lords, there are 117 of your lordships present, and you have unanimously found that Simon, Lord Lovat, is guilty of the high treason whereof he stands impeached. Is it your lordships' pleasure that he should be brought to the bar and acquainted therewith? **Verdict**

Lords—Ay, Ay.

Proclamation was made for silence, and another proclamation for the Lieutenant of the Tower to bring the prisoner to the bar, which was done in the same order as before, and then proclamation was again made for silence as usual.

Lord High Steward—Simon, Lord Lovat, the lords have considered the charge of high treason which has been brought against you by the House of Commons. They have considered the evidence, and all that has been offered to maintain the charge. They have also considered everything that has been alleged in your lordship's defence; and, upon the whole matter, their lordships have unanimously found that you are guilty of the high treason whereof you stand impeached.

Lord President—My lords, I move your lordships to adjourn to the Chamber of Parliament.

Lord High Steward—Is it your lordships' pleasure to adjourn to the Chamber of Parliament?

Lords—Ay, ay.

The House was accordingly adjourned to the Chamber of Parliament, and the lords and others returned in the same order as before.

And the House, being resumed in the Chamber of Parliament, *Ordered* that this House will proceed further, in order to the giving of judgment against Simon, Lord Lovat, to-morrow at eleven of the clock in the forenoon in Westminster Hall, and a message was sent to the House of Commons by the former messengers to acquaint them therewith; *ordered* that the Lieutenant of the Tower of London, or his deputy, do take back Simon, Lord Lovat, and bring him again to the bar of this House in Westminster Hall to-morrow at eleven of the clock in the forenoon.

Seventh Day—Thursday, 19th March [1747].

About eleven of the clock in the forenoon the lords and others came from the Chamber of Parliament in the same order as on the first day into Westminster Hall, where the Commons and their Managers were in the seats prepared for them respectively as before, and the lords took their places in the Court, and the Lord High Steward in his chair.

LORD HIGH STEWARD—The House is resumed. Is it your lordships' pleasure that the judges have leave to be covered?

LORDS—Ay, ay.

Then the Sergeant-at-Arms made proclamation for silence as usual, and afterwards the following proclamation:—

Oyes! Oyes! Oyes! Lieutenant of the Tower of London, bring forth your prisoner, Simon, Lord Lovat, to the bar, pursuant to the order of the House of Lords to you directed.

The Deputy Governor of the Tower brought the prisoner to the bar in the like form as before, and then he knelt down.

LORD HIGH STEWARD—Your lordship may rise.

The Sergeant-at-Arms, by direction of the Lord High Steward, made another proclamation for silence.

LORD HIGH STEWARD—Simon, Lord Lovat, when your lordship was last at this bar I acquainted you that your peers had found you guilty of the high treason whereof you stand impeached, by means whereof you are convicted of that high treason, and I am now to ask your lordship what you have to say why judgment of death should not pass upon you according to law?

Lord Lovat

LORD LOVAT—My lords, I am very sorry I gave your lordships so much trouble in my trial, and I give you a million of thanks for your being so good in your patience and attendance whilst it lasted. I thought myself very much loaded by one Murray, who, your lordships know, was the bitterest evidence there was against me. I have since suffered by another Mr. Murray,[1] who, I must say with pleasure, is an honour to his country, and whose eloquence and learning is much beyond what is to be expressed by an ignorant man like me. I heard him with pleasure, though it was against me. I have the honour to be his relation, though perhaps he neither knows it nor values it. I wish that his being born in the north may not hinder him from the preferment that his merit and learning deserve. Till that gentleman spoke your lordships were inclined to grant

[1] The Solicitor-General, to whom Lovat claimed to be related.

my earnest request and allow me further time to bring up witnesses to prove my innocence, but it seems that has been overruled.

All now that I have to say is a little in vindication of my own character. I was pointed out by the Honourable Managers as a most inveterate enemy of the Royal Family now upon the throne, and the most zealously attached to a family that is not like to come upon the throne. My lords, I humbly beg that your lordships will take notice that my attachment to the family of Hanover is proved without contest after the great services I have done. I was honoured by the King's favour and countenance, that made me so naturally and gratefully attached to his person and family, and, as I was for twelve years in Germany,[1] almost every day in conversation with His Majesty and his family, I thought it necessary to know the history of his family, and I read it very particularly, both the public and private history of it. And I must say that, since your lordships, and this nation in general, thought fit to have a King from Germany, you could not have chosen one from a more illustrious house, so great that several Emperors of Germany have been elected from out of that family, and they always behaved with great distinction, both in the wars and in their own country. I will only give one instance of that, which I had from my dear master, the late King's, own mouth (of glorious memory). I heard him say this to the Emperor's envoy, after the siege of Belgrade, when the envoy told him that there were 40,000 Janissaries killed upon the spot, "Why," says he to the envoy, "I shall be very glad of it, but I know the nature of those animals. If 40,000 of them are killed at night, in the very place of those that are killed 40,000 will rise up the next morning. I have had experience of the war with the Turks. I was with 6000 of my own men at the siege of Buda, and, I believe, they will do me the justice to say that both I and my men behaved as we ought to have done." This shows, my lords, that I always had a true notion of the greatness and illustriousness of the family of Hanover. I gave signal proofs of it in the year 1715, and I beg your lordships will indulge me to repeat a little of what passed at that time, because there are several lords here that were not then born.

My lords, when I came into England in the year 1714, my design was that, with the assistance of my friends, the late Duke of Argyll and the present Duke, I should endeavour to get my remission to go down into my own country, to endeavour to recover my fortune, and to serve the Government faithfully in what I was able. In this situation I was

1 This statement is entirely unsubstantiated, and may be taken as being untrue.

Lord Lovat when my Lord Marischal set up the Pretender's standard at Aberdeen. It did much alarm the Court. I was sent for, and particularly spoken to by the Earl of Sunderland and my Lord Townshend, who were always my friends.

My lords, this present Duke of Argyll was so generous that he would follow his brother to Scotland and expose his life as a Volunteer, and he suffered by it, for at the battle of Sheriffmuir he had a ball went through his side and arm, and had almost lost his life if it had not been by the extraordinary skill and diligence of one Mr. MacGill, a surgeon, who attended him. When he went down, he told me, "Dear Lovat, you must do your best for us now, and I desire you may meet me in Badenoch with all the men you can get together, and I will gather all the men I can in Argyllshire and meet you there." I went down on horseback, and he went down post. Before I came to my own country I found that the rebels were got together in vast numbers, and, as Inverness was the great capital of all those parts, my Lord Marischal resolved to send 2000 men to reinforce the garrison of Inverness, that it might not be surprised. The MacIntoshes and the MacDonalds were gathered together, in order to go to Inverness. When I found it was impossible for the Earl of Islay to come with his men from Argyllshire, I resolved to distinguish myself, even though by a desperate stroke. I had gathered together 200 men at Stratherrick; with these I marched to Inverness, and invested it.[1] Sir John MacKenzie, the then Governor, had 1000 men in the town, so I found there was nothing for it but boldness. I sent a message, which, indeed, looked like a French gasconade, that I would blow him and his garrison, and the castle and the strong steeple, into the air if they did not surrender to me before ten o'clock the next day, though I had not 2 lbs. of powder. At the same time I sent a party of men, in which was a pretty gentleman of skill, one Captain Ross, the laird's brother. Whether Sir John MacKenzie heard this overnight I cannot tell, but he inquired if I was fully resolved to attack the town. He told him positively that I was. Says he, "If Simon be there he is a desperate fellow; I believe I must leave the town to him." And, accordingly, he ran off that night with all his men. This I did, my lords, before any of the loyal clans to this Government were raised.

After this they were pleased to declare me general of the King's forces there. When I got together near 2000 men, of which 1000 were my own, I resolved to attack Lord Seaforth, who was coming with 2500 men to join Sir John MacKenzie at Inverness, or to fight any of the rebels that should meet him. He called them so. He stood his ground

[1] The "Sutherland Book," vol. ii., 53/61, contains an account of the taking of Inverness at this time.

till I came within half a mile of him. I drew up the little army I had in pretty good order, being an officer for many years before. And I can say to your lordships that I believe I am the oldest officer in commission in Great Britain, for fifty years ago I was captain of Grenadiers in King William's army. They were the Sutherland men, Lord Reay's men, and some of the Grants and Munros, but when I came to march up the hill to attack Lord Seaforth, I had none followed me but the Munros. When they found I was come within sight of them they made a precipitate retreat to a bridge that was near them over a river, and afterwards, by Lord President's advice, who was then in the army, Lord Seaforth came and submitted to me as general of King George's forces, promising immediately to lay down his arms, which he did. This submission was brought up and shown to the Ministry. I then went and reduced the Duke of Gordon, who gave me the most ample submission I ever read to the King, and assurances of fidelity to him and to the Government. That submission I likewise showed, and, if they are not consumed in my house that was burnt, they are still extant. My lords, then I pursued the rebels from place to place, and chased them from hill to hill. On this expedition I lost my only brother, who was a very brave young fellow, and I never left off pursuing the rebels till the rebellion was suppressed and extinguished. So that I may fairly say that I assisted to keep the Crown upon the late King's head as much as, if not more than, any one man of my own rank in Britain. Lord Lovat

I had then several invitations to come to Court, and had three letters of thanks from the King's person, by the hands of the great Earl Stanhope, who was Secretary of State then, in which he says that he was so sensible of my extraordinary and signal services, that he would all his life give me such marks of his favour as would oblige all the country to be zealous and faithful to me. Upon this I came to Court, and I was not disappointed. I believe there are lords in this House, I am sure there are a great many yet alive, that know I was a particular favourite of the late King's, I believe more than any one of my own rank in Scotland. I remember my Lord Townshend told me one day, who was my particular friend, that I was certainly a great favourite of the King, and if all the Ministry should join together to hurt me, that it was not in their power to do it, and that he would do me all the service he could, and said the King would not refuse anything he should ask for me; and the King, to my own certain knowledge, reproached the Scotch Ministry that I was not provided for. But that unhappy nation has been always divided amongst themselves, between the family of the Argylls and that of the Montroses, so that they, knowing me to be a relation and partisan of the family of Argyll, never would do anything for

Lord Lovat me. At last the King said he must do it himself, and sent for the Hanoverian Minister and told him that he must immediately fix upon a way to give me a pension. At last it was ordered by the King's particular instruction that I should have a letter or patent for myself for £300 a year, which I enjoyed till now for anything I know. Then all the English Ministers, every one of them, were my friends, and they proposed that I should go into the army. Lord Cadogan, who, in the year 1716, went with an army into Scotland, sent for me, and desired me to bring up 500 men to Badenoch to escort him to Inverness, which I did. They gave out that the Highlanders were to attack him in the woods, but when they heard that I was with him with the best part of my clan, they did not think it proper to attack him. After Lord Cadogan came to Inverness he sent for Sir Robert Munro, who was killed at the battle of Falkirk. He called me into his closet with him and told me, "We are now fully convinced, Lord Lovat, that it was you and a few of the King's friends that were joined to you, that subdued and suppressed the rebellion and extinguished it, and that all that was written in the *Gazette* about Lord Sutherland was all romance. Now, I am so sensible of those services that you have done the Government that, if you will join yourself to the Duke of Marlborough, to the Earl of Sunderland, and to me, that are thought the favourites of the King, we will, in the first place, immediately make you a major-general. You shall have a regiment of foot, or dragoons, and £3000 a year pension during your life." My lords, if I had accepted of that offer, I had now had the best estate in Scotland, and would have been fair for being one of the field-marshals of England, being the oldest officer. But, my lords, the condition was too severe, and I had rather never have any being than be ungrateful.

The late Duke of Argyll, I mean this Duke of Argyll's father, who was one of the greatest men that has been in our country for many ages, he was a father to me, and protected me as his own child. He got me two remissions from King William, and as he was carrying another remission in to be signed by Queen Anne (King William, to my misfortune, having died that year), he found the door shut—that is, he found that three men had turned out all King William's friends, of whom he was one, and the Duke of Queensberry and several others, and that she brought in two families, the Duke of Hamilton and the Marquis of Athol, whom she made a Duke, and to please him, with whom my family unfortunately had a quarrel about an estate—to please him, I say, she put £2000 upon my head, which was £1000 more than ever was usual. So I told the Duke of Argyll that I had nothing for it but to go to Hanover, and there to live and die with fidelity to the Duke of Hanover. He told me that he was well assured that the Duke of Hanover would be glad to receive me, but as he was then declared the Protestant heir, and that succession depended much upon the goodwill of Queen Anne, he must, upon her desire, be obliged to send me back to England, and that he did not know a safe way for me but to go to France, because we were at war with them then; and that was the first thing, my lords, that obliged me to go to France, which was the foundation of my misfortunes.

Now, my lords, after what I have told you, I must humbly submit it to your lordships whether you do not think it is improbable that I should be an enemy to King George and his family—I that received more marks of favour from the late King George than any subject in the north, I that got my estate settled in his time both by the House of Commons and Peers, I that expected never to be out of favour with the Government, being very zealous to promote anything that was for the good of it. My lords, I commanded a Highland company for fifteen years as their colonel, and the country can testify that there was no depredation, theft, or robbery committed there during that time. I took twenty-five Highland robbers in the Highlands in one night, and brought them all prisoners to the Tolbooth of Inverness. I continued to act in the manner that General Wade from time to time ordered me. I own I did not expect that he, who reviewed my company every year, and called it the best company that he ever saw in his life, but I must make the lords laugh upon that occasion: —he told me that Mr. Pulteney, now Earl of Bath, said in the House of Commons that he knew old Lovat very well, that he would never have a company but in his pocket, and now I can tell him that he did not speak truth. General Handaside was present (and his brother, who is a very pretty gentleman) when he declared that he never did see such a fine company in any country that he was ever in. And he appealed to the two Handasides and the other officers that were there whether it was not true, and they all agreed in it. So that, my lords, after this, I very little expected that, without ever blaming me, or imputing any crime to me, my commission should be broke, and not only so, but that I should be ordered to keep 400 men from it in the country, to be put into another company to make up a regiment that General Wade procured for his favourite Colonel Durore. My lords, I was certainly much out of humour to see myself so used, but I never imputed it to the King, nor to his Prime Minister, Sir Robert Walpole, afterwards Earl of Orford. And this is all the grounds of my being out of temper, or that they can lay hold of to say I was against the Government.

So, after what I have told your lordships, and the manner that I have been used, I hope your lordships will not think I was

Lord Lovat capable of any malicious design against the Government. And, indeed, it was a loss to the Government more than to me that my company was broke, because if I had commanded the Highland company, as I did for fifteen years, the country had been peaceable, and there had been no rebellion.

Lord High Steward—My Lord Lovat, I must put your lordship in mind of the question I asked you, whether you have anything to offer in arrest of judgment?

Lord Lovat—Whatever way I may be overruled I will say to my dying hour that I have met with the greatest hardships ever practised in Britain, and I still insist that I shall get the benefit that all subjects have a right to of adducing witnesses that may be for the safety of their lives and interests.

Lord High Steward—Your lordship has heard the opinion of the lords already.

Lord President of the Council—I move your lordships to adjourn to the Chamber of Parliament.

Lord High Steward—Is it your lordships' pleasure to adjourn to the Chamber of Parliament?

Lords—Ay, ay.

Lord High Steward—This House is adjourned to the Chamber of Parliament.

Then the lords and others returned to the Chamber of Parliament in the same order they came down, and the House being there resumed, the proceeding entered in the Journal of the 19th of March, 1715, in relation to the giving of judgment against George, Earl of Wintoun, was read, which being done their lordships were informed that the Commons, with their Speaker and the Mace, were at the door, whereupon they were called in, and Mr. Speaker, at the bar, said—

"My lords, the knights, citizens, and burgesses, in Parliament assembled, did, at this bar, in the name of themselves and of all the Commons of Great Britain, impeach Simon, Lord Lovat, of high treason, and exhibited Articles against him, and have made good the same. I do, therefore, in the name of the knights, citizens, and burgesses, in Parliament assembled, and of all the Commons of Great Britain, demand judgment of your lordships against Simon, Lord Lovat, for the said high treason."

And they being withdrawn, *Ordered* that, when judgment shall be pronounced against the said Lord Lovat, it be the same as was pronounced against the late Earl of Wintoun.

Then the House was again adjourned into Westminster Hall, and the peers and others went down in the same order as before, and the peers being in their places and the Lord High Steward in his chair, and the Commons and their Managers in the seats prepared for them respectively, the House was resumed, and the Sergeant-at-Arms made proclamation for silence as usual.

Lord High Steward—My Lord Lovat, as some time has intervened since I last asked you the question whether you had anything to offer in arrest of judgment, I am now to ask you again whether you have anything to say why judgment of death should not pass upon you according to law. Lord High Steward

Lord Lovat—No; I have said all that I had to say, and beg your lordships' pardon for the rude, long discourse I made to your lordships. I had great need of my cousin Murray's eloquence for half an hour, and then it would have been more agreeable.

Proclamation was made for silence as usual.

Lord High Steward—Simon, Lord Lovat, you have been Impeached by the Commons of Great Britain, in Parliament assembled, of high treason, charged upon you by particular Articles containing different species and various overt acts of that treason.

To these Articles your lordship thought fit to put in an Answer, amounting to a general plea of "not guilty" to the whole, and, after a long and impartial trial, upon the clearest and most convincing evidence, against which you offered no defence by witnesses, your peers have unanimously found you guilty. What remains is the disagreeable, but unavoidable, part of proceeding to that judgment, which is the necessary consequence of such atrocious crimes. Happy had it been for your lordship if, before you engaged in them, you had suffered the terrors of that consequence to have their due weight, when the sacred ties of your allegiance and your oaths were not strong enough to restrain you. In this proceeding the zeal and dutiful affection of the Commons to His Majesty and their country, and the justice of the House of Peers, have shone forth in their full lustre. The Commons found your lordship to be one of the principal conspirators who contrived and carried on the late detestable rebellion to destroy our religion and liberties, and to subvert that legal settlement of the Crown in His Majesty and His Royal Family, under which alone we can live free and happy.

They rightly judged that this, which is the common cause of all the people of Great Britain, ought to be prosecuted by the united voice of the people, that it became them to investigate and lay open in full Parliament the source of those calamities which we have lately suffered, and the deep-laid and long-meditated conspiracy in which your lordship had so considerable and so flagitious a part. They rightly judged that no judicature was equal to such an important proceeding but this High Court, on whose penetration and justice they

Lord High Steward

relied, and before whom in this great assembly public and indubitable satisfaction might be given.

Before your conviction I have spoken to your lordship upon a presumption of your innocence, but now I am bound, by the unanimous decision of my lords your peers, to take the evidence against you to be true, and to address myself to you as a guilty person. Your lordship has, in your Answer, endeavoured to avail yourself of former services to His late Majesty and the Protestant succession, which you have this day enlarged upon at the bar. How unfortunate have you been in referring back to such cancelled merit, since thereby you have furnished an opportunity to the Commons to show for how long a tract of time you have conceived and nursed up this treason in your heart! Whatever your pretences were, so infected was your mind and so forward your zeal in the cause of that Pretender whom you had then abjured, as to engage in that rash and weak attempt from Spain in His late Majesty's reign. Yet, at or very near that time, it appears, by the evidence (out of which every observation I will make shall naturally arise), you were soliciting or accepting favours and trusts from that very Government which you had thus engaged to destroy. What use did you make of those trusts? The instance of Roy Stuart, now an attainted rebel, speaks it too plainly. Whilst you were Sheriff of the shire of Inverness, the largest county in Scotland, and one of the greatest consequence, you suffered that criminal, in the year 1736, to escape out of your public prison, harboured him afterwards in your own house, then charged him with messages and assurances of fidelity to the Pretender, and to procure for you a commission of lieutenant-general and a mock title of honour from that pretended Prince. If anything could surpass this treachery it is the association, which your lordship signed and sealed, together with six other persons, and sent to Rome and Paris, by Drummond of Bochaldie, in the beginning of 1740. The substance of this was to assure the Pretender, whom you always called your "lawful King," of your readiness to appear openly in arms for his service, and to solicit an invasion from France against your native country to support this desperate design.

It should seem by the evidence that the foreign enemies of Britain were less forward in this measure to disturb her than her degenerate unnatural sons. Whether that reluctance proceeded from a distrust of so false a set of men, or from a conviction that the body of this great people was not to be shaken in their loyalty to a King who possesses the throne by the most rightful title, and governs them in justice and mercy, according to their laws and constitution—in either case they were in the right. What dependence could the Court of France have on a few abandoned traitors? What hopes could they entertain that a general infatuation would on the sudden seize and delude a brave, a free, and a happy people to seek their own slavery and ruin? Lord High Steward

From this time till the year 1743 the conspiracy lingered in its progress, though great efforts appear to have been made to render it more extensive and more formidable. Then it happened, as it always has happened, that when France saw such an enterprise, whether successful or not, might be made a convenient engine of her own politics, that Court set about an invasion in earnest. Great preparations were made and ready at Dunkirk, but the Providence of God disappointed them. To be capable to proving transactions of this kind by strict evidence in the forms of law is not common, nor in the nature of the thing ordinarily to be expected. But this the vigilance of the Commons has effectually done, to the conviction of all well-intentioned persons, and to the shame and confusion of those who, though they believed, and perhaps knew it themselves, were industrious to propagate a pernicious incredulity in others. Thus the Commons have traced and brought down the series of the conspiracy to the remarkable era of July, 1745, when the eldest son of the Pretender landed in Moidart, unsupported by any foreign troops, unattended, and almost alone.

The appearing rashness of this attempt gave rise to some apprehensions, some misgivings, in the breasts of your lordship and your fellow-conspirators, proceeding from a concern not for the King or for your country, but for your own private interest and safety. A French invasion had been long solicited. A French force was depended on to secure you against the just vengeance of your native country, and the failure of that damped your hopes and produced your expressions of disappointment. However, such was your zeal that in this rash enterprise your lordship joined, not indeed personally (this you often excused, complaining of your infirmities), but by sending, or rather forcing, out your clan, and committing every other species of the blackest treason which the Articles of Impeachment have charged upon you.

Permit me to stop here a little and lament the condition of part of this United Kingdom, happily united in interests both civil and religious, happily united under the same gracious monarch and the same public policy. And yet the common people in some of the remote northern counties are still kept in such a state of bondage to certain of their fellow-subjects who, contrary to all law and every true principle of government, have erected themselves into petty tyrants over them, as to be liable to be compelled into rebellion against their lawful Sovereign under the peril of fire and sword. Astonishing it is that such a dangerous error in government, such a

Lord High Steward

remnant of barbarism, should have subsisted so long in any quarter of this civilised well-governed island, but, since such is the misfortune, let it be accounted one good fruit of this inquiry that it has appeared in this solemn manner. The knowledge of the disease shows the way to the cure, and it calls aloud for a remedy.

This usurped power was audaciously made use of over your clan. 'Tis true, your lordship's activity in exerting it rose and fell in proportion to the appearances of the good or bad success of the Pretender's cause. But after the advantage gained by the rebels at Prestonpans, which you vainly called "a victory not to be parallelled in history," you thought it time to throw off the mask, and, with less caution, to espouse a party which you then hoped might be espoused with impunity.

I forbear to enumerate the many overt acts of your treason. It would be tedious to this assembly, who have heard them so much better from the witnesses and from the recapitulation of the Managers. It would be grievous to your lordship if your heart is by this time untouched with any remorse for your guilt. But one thing I cannot help observing upon—the excuse you expressly made for this traitorous conduct, even after you were taken prisoner, to which you have this day artfully endeavoured to give a different turn. Being asked how you could act such a part against a Government from which you had received many favours, your lordship's answer was—"It was in revenge to the Ministry for their ill-usage of me in taking away my commission of captain of an independent company of Highlanders," an excuse almost as false as it was profligate—false because some of your treasonable practices were committed whilst you were possessed of that very commission, profligate it was in the highest degree. Is allegiance no duty? Are oaths to His Majesty and his Government no obligation upon the conscience? Is loyalty to our lawful Sovereign and the love of our country to depend on the enjoyment of extraordinary favours and emoluments, which no man has a right to, can in the nature of things be enjoyed but by a few, and are in the pleasure of all Governments to confer or deny? A person actuated by and avowing such principles as these must be lost to all sense of virtue, and of shame, and of every natural, as well as civil, sanction of society.

Sorry, very sorry I am to see this last reflection so strongly verified by the proofs against your lordship. It has appeared that you used your paternal influence over your eldest son, a youth not above the age of nineteen, to compel him to go into the rebellion, and afterwards unnaturally endeavoured to cast the crime and reproach of it upon him. If this be true, 'tis an impiety which makes one tremble. It is the celebrated saying of a wise writer of antiquity, and shows his perfect knowledge of human nature, that "the love of our country includes all other social affections." For we see, when that is gone, even the tenderest of all affections, the parental, may be extinguished with it.

Lord High Steward

I have said these things not with a view to aggravate your lordship's crimes, but, as becomes this place and this occasion, to rouse your mind, which, there is reason to fear, may have been too much hardened, to a just and deep sense of your unhappy and dreadful situation.

Were I to attempt this from topics of religion I should be at a loss whether to apply to you as a Protestant or a Papist. Your open profession, your solemn oaths, and public actions speak on one side; but, if I am to believe the evidence, your private discourse and declarations testify on the other. I will apply no suppositions on this head particularly to your lordship, but from hence I would draw an instructive lesson, which well deserves the serious attention of this whole nation, of what important consequence it is to preserve not only the name and outward form of the Protestant religion amongst us, but the real uniform belief and practice of it. Indifference to all religion prepares men for the external profession of any, and what may not that lead to? Give me leave to affirm before this great assembly that, even abstracted from religious considerations, the Protestant religion ought to be held in the highest reverence as the surest barrier of our civil Constitution. Ecclesiastical usurpation seldom fails to end in civil tyranny. The present happy settlement of the Crown is in truth, and not in name only, the Protestant succession. And the inviolable preservation of that wise and fundamental law made since the Revolution, whereby every Papist, or person marrying a Papist, is absolutely excluded from inheriting to this Crown, will, in future times, be a solid security for our posterity not only against the groundless and presumptuous claim of an abjured Pretender and his descendants, but also to prevent this kingdom from becoming a province to some of the great Popish Powers, who have so long watched for the destruction of our liberties.

But, to return to your lordship, suffer me to exhort you with great earnestness and in great charity to deliberate seriously upon your own case, and to deal impartially with your own conscience. If, according to the evidence given at this bar, you have led a life of craft, dissimulation, and perfidy, consider how that scene has closed, what desolation you have thereby endeavoured to bring upon your country, how fatally it has ended for yourself—consider that the sentence which I am obliged to pronounce may soon send you to a tribunal where no disguise or artifice can avail you.

Sentence.

Sentence

The sentence of the law is, and this High Court doth adjudge, "That you, Simon, Lord Lovat, return to the prison of the Tower, from whence you came, from thence you must be drawn to the place of execution; when you come there you must be hanged by the neck, but not till you are dead, for you must be cut down alive, then your bowels must be taken out and burnt before your face, then your head must be severed from your body, and your body divided into four quarters, and these must be at the King's disposal." And God Almighty be merciful to your soul!

Lord Lovat—My lords, I hope your lordships will not take it amiss that I should let you know, though it be in a very barbarous language, both the affection I had for His late Majesty and the service I did for him and his family. And I must say I have for that the testimony of one of the King's evidence that I declared my affection to his present Majesty. And I have reason so to do, for when he was Regent of these kingdoms, and his father was in Hanover, he was so good as to give me a *noli prosequi* for the great laird of MacIntosh that was at the battle of Preston; and when I complained of the hardships the Duke of Roxburgh put every day upon me, in an audience he was pleased to admit me to, in his closet at Kensington, he was so good as to say that, if he was King, he would defend me against all my enemies, not only the Duke of Roxburgh, but all my other enemies. Now, my lords, when a man has but a very few days in appearance to live, what he says should be relied upon, if there is not immediate evidence to the contrary. I have shown your lordships my esteem for the illustrious House of Hanover. I have shown my attachment for my dear master, the late King, and my respect for His present Majesty, and therefore all that I have further to say is most humbly to implore your lordships' intercession, and to recommend me to His Majesty for mercy.

Lord High Steward—Have you anything further to offer?

Lord Lovat—Nothing, my lords, but that I make the same prayer to the honourable the Members and Managers of the House of Commons, and that I hope, as they have been stout, they will be merciful.

Lord High Steward—Would you offer anything further?

Lord Lovat—Nothing but to thank your lordships for your goodness to me. God bless you all, and I bid you an everlasting farewell. We shall not meet all in the same place again, I am sure of that.

Lord High Steward—Lieutenant of the Tower, take the prisoner from the bar,

Which having been done, proclamation was made for silence as usual.

Then the White Staff being delivered to the Lord High Steward by the Gentleman Usher of the Black Rod, upon his knee, His Grace stood up uncovered, and, holding the staff in both his hands, broke it in two, and declared that there was nothing farther to be done by virtue of the present Commission, and pronounced the same to be dissolved, and then, leaving the chair, came down to the Woolpack, and said, "Is it your lordships' pleasure to adjourn to the Chamber of Parliament?" **Lord High Steward**

LORDS—Ay, ay.

Then the House was adjourned to the Chamber of Parliament, and the lords and others returned in the same order as they had used in coming down, and

The prisoner was carried back to the Tower of London.

Note.—An interesting case of breach of privilege arose out of the trial. Extracts from the debates of the House of Lords and of the trial were printed in the *Gentleman's Magazine* and in the *London Magazine*. The editors, Mr. Cave and Mr. Astley, were arrested and brought to the bar of the House of Lords. They were reprimanded, and expressed their regret for the infringement of Parliamentary privilege as understood at that time. Thereafter they were discharged. The publication of Parliamentary debates is still theoretically a breach of privilege, but the restriction is waived in practice, except where the account is unfair or inaccurate.

APPENDICES

APPENDIX I.

The Last Days of Lord Lovat.

The few weeks between Lord Lovat's condemnation and his execution were spent in the place of his former confinement, the Tower of London, where he met with great kindness from the Governor, General Williamson. The condemned man displayed admirable fortitude to the end. His friends failed in their attempts to induce him to seek a pardon from the King, but he was persuaded to petition His Majesty for the pardon of the Master of Lovat. In doing so he refrained from using any appeal which he thought abject or mean.

Many of his sayings are recorded in an anonymous pamphlet entitled, "A Candid and Impartial Account of the Behaviour of Simon Lord Lovat, April 14, 1747."

The copy warrant for his execution was served on him on 3rd April. On receiving it he exclaimed, "God's will be done!" shook hands with the messenger, and drank his health. Next day he was very cheerful, joked about the guillotine, which was to be substituted for the gallows as the means of execution. He said it would be called "Lord Lovat's Maiden," and that it was a pity his neck was so short. He also averred that he had never shed a drop of human blood with his own hand.

On 5th April (a Sunday) he wrote a long and affectionate letter to his son, and when the major of the Tower came to see him on the following day and asked him how he did—"Do?" he said, "Why, I am about doing very well, for I am preparing myself, sir, for a place where hardly any majors, and very few lieutenant-generals go." When "a certain nobleman" asked him about his religion he said he was a Catholic Jansenist, and when the pair began to discuss the problem of freewill, he quoted the saying of Christ (Matthew xxiii. 37), "O Jerusalem, Jerusalem . . . how often would I have gathered thy children together, even as a hen gathereth her chickens under her wings, and ye *would* not!"

On Tuesday, 7th April, he wrote to his solicitor, William Fraser, asking that his body be placed in a lead coffin and conveyed to Moniack House, near Beauly, prior to burial in the neighbouring family vault at Kirkhill, apologised for the expense this will entail, and hoped that his son will regard the cost as a debt of honour. Next day he was informed that a gentleman had offered to suffer execution as his substitute, and the offer called forth some characteristic comment. He prayed devoutly, talked of his funeral, and discussed the prospects of a future life, expressing the belief that "every straight, honest man bids fair for heaven." Having smoked a pipe, he knocked out the ashes, saying, "The end of all human grandeur is like this whiff of tobacco." His physical vigour is evidenced by his reading without spectacles a book for two hours by candlelight, and saying that, but for his impending death by the guillotine, he would have expected to live for other twenty years.

On 9th April, the day of his execution, he rose at 5 a.m. and read for two hours, arranged about a purse of money as a gift to the executioner, and took leave of his friends with unaltered serenity. The proceedings at the scaffold were rendered memorable by his splendid fearlessness. "Why should there be such a bustle," he asked, "about taking off an old grey head?"

"It's astonishing," wrote Sir Arthur Forbes to Lord President Forbes, "with what resolution and *sang froid* Lovat died to-day." "Lord Lovat, I hear, died well," wrote another of the President's correspondents (Culloden Papers).

The desire of Lord Lovat as to interment at Kirkhill was unfulfilled. The authorities believed that if his body were carried through Scotland, its passage "might spread disaffection and perhaps raise sedition in that country" (*Scots Magazine*, 1747). Transportation by sea would have made public manifestations of opinion impossible, but that method was not adopted. The body was buried in the Tower of London on 17th April, 1747, whence it was removed in 1877 to the crypt of Tower Chapel (St. Peter's).

APPENDIX II.

BIOGRAPHICAL NOTES.

ARGYLL, ARCHIBALD CAMPBELL, first Duke of, a keen supporter of William of Orange, to whom he administered the Coronation oath in 1689; received a grant of his father's forfeited estates immediately thereafter; was the Government's informant of M'Ian's failure to take the oath, and implicated in the subsequent massacre of the MacDonalds at Glencoe; was made a Lord of the Treasury in 1690; created first duke on 23rd June, 1701; died 20th September, 1703.

ARGYLL, ARCHIBALD CAMPBELL, third Duke of, formerly Earl of Islay, born in June, 1682, second son of Archibald, first Duke of Argyll; educated at Eton, Glasgow University, and Utrecht; served as a soldier under Marlborough; appointed Lord High Treasurer of Scotland in 1705; one of the Commissioners for the Union of 1707; created Earl of Islay; made an Extraordinary Lord of Session in Scotland in 1708 and Lord Justice-General of Scotland in 1710; twice wounded at Sheriffmuir; succeeded his brother as Duke of Argyll in 1743; presided at Inveraray in September, 1752, at the trial of James Stewart for the murder of Colin Campbell of Glenure (see volume in "Notable Scottish Trials" series dealing with the case), when Stewart was condemned to death on entirely insufficient evidence; died in London in 1761.

ARGYLL, JOHN CAMPBELL, second Duke of (1678-1743), eldest son of Archibald, first duke; entered the Army in 1694; succeeded to dukedom in 1703; Lord High Commissioner to the Scottish Parliament in 1705; served under Marlborough at Ramillies, at siege of Ostend, at Oudenarde, and Malplaquet; a bitter enemy of Marlborough in after years; said the proposed Union would beggar Scotland and enslave England; Commander-in-Chief in Spain in 1711; and in Scotland during Rebellion of 1715; temporarily in disfavour at Court, 1716-19; defended the city of Edinburgh in debates after Porteous mob; a great soldier and orator; was known as "Red John of the Battles"; died on 4th October, 1743.

Biographical Notes.

ATHOLL, JOHN, first Duke of, born in 1659; as Lord John Murray, was a strong supporter of William of Orange, though his father was inclined to the Stuart side; in 1693 appointed a Commissioner to inquire into the facts of the Massacre of Glencoe, and severely censured the perpetrators of that outrage; in 1694 he was appointed Joint Secretary for Scotland, and in 1696 was created first Earl of Tullibardine; resigned his Government post in 1698, and remained out of politics till the accession of Queen Anne; appointed Lord Privy Seal in 1703; became first Duke of Atholl soon after his father's death on 6th May, 1703; was the object of Lovat's "Queensberry" plot in 1703; quarrelled with the Hanoverians and became temporarily a Jacobite; opposed the Union of 1707; reappointed Lord Privy Seal by the Tory party in 1713; was against the Jacobites in 1715; captured Rob Roy on 4th June, 1717; died 1724.

CAMERON, DR. ARCHIBALD, brother of Lochiel, was born in 1707; studied medicine in Edinburgh and Paris; practised among his clansmen in Inverness-shire; joined them when they rose for Prince Charles in 1745; a staunch friend of the Prince when in hiding; attainted for high treason; escaped to France, and became surgeon to the Albany Regiment; returned to Scotland in 1753 to collect funds, but was arrested at Glenbucket; taken to London, sentenced to death for high treason, and executed. The Government's extreme measures in his case are still remembered by Highlanders with anger.

CAMERON OF LOCHIEL, DONALD, son of John Cameron, who was attainted after the "'15"; disapproved of Prince Charles' landing in 1745, but was taunted by the Prince, and raised his clan; joined the rebels with 800 men; rendered great service all through the campaign; prevented excesses by the troops as far as possible, and ordered two of his men to be shot for theft; was wounded in both ankles at Culloden; was attainted, and lost his estates; lived for four months in hiding, and suffering from wounds; joined the Prince in flight to France at the end of September; commanded a regiment in the French service; died in 1748; was known as "the gentle Lochiel"; on his deathbed he wished he could return to Scotland to "perish with the people I have undone"; a man of noble character, who was honoured by foe as well as friend.

CHISHOLM, THE (Roderick, known as Ruairi 'n Aigh), born in 1697; at the age of eighteen led 200 of his clansmen to Sheriffmuir, although he had previously signed the letter by various chiefs to the Earl of Mar expressing loyalty to King George; married a daughter of Alastair Dubh MacDonell of Glengarry. Most of his lands were forfeited after the Rising of 1715, but some were saved through being under a wadset to Chisholm of Knockfin; wrote to General Wade on 30th August, 1725, promising good behaviour and loyalty to the King; was pardoned on 4th January, 1727; but joined the young Pretender in 1745; lost his youngest son in action, on the Jacobite side, at Culloden, where his two elder sons were fighting on the Hanoverian side; was attainted for high treason, but through the intervention of Lord President Forbes he was let off on payment of a fine; died on 19th August, 1767.

FAWKENER, SIR EVERARD (1684-1758), merchant in London, host of Voltaire during the greater part of his visit to England (1726-9); knighted in 1735; Ambassador to Constantinople, secretary to the Duke of Cumberland in Flanders and during the Highland campaign; visited Lovat at Fort-Augustus; appointed Joint Postmaster-General in 1745; in February, 1747, married Harriet, natural daughter of

Appendix II.

General Charles Churchhill (who was the "young lady" to whom Lovat jocularly alluded at the close of Fawkener's evidence at the trial); died 14th December, 1758.

FORBES OF CULLODEN, DUNCAN, born 10th November, 1685; educated in Grammar School of Inverness; was very wild in his youth; went to Leyden, in 1705, to study law; called to the bar in 1709, and soon appointed Sheriff of Midlothian; his services in suppressing the Rebellion of 1715 were recognised by his appointment as Advocate-Depute; was greatly enraged by the removal of the Jacobite prisoners of 1715 to Carlisle for trial; became M.P. for Ayr Burghs in 1721, for the Inverness Burghs in 1722; was made Lord Advocate for Scotland in 1725; ordered the arrest of the Glasgow magistrates for their neglect in the matter of the Shawfield Riots in 1725; succeeded to Culloden estates in 1735; wrote several theological works; appointed Lord President of the Court of Session in 1737; took a prominent part against the Jacobites in 1745-6, but protested strongly against Cumberland's butcheries; died 10th December, 1747.

FORBES, JOHN, Laird of Culloden, educated in Inverness, where he afterwards led a drunken life. It is recorded that at his mother's funeral he and the party drank so excessively that they left for the graveyard without the body; succeeded to the estates in 1704; member of Parliament for Inverness-shire from 1715 till 1722; many of his letters are preserved in the "Culloden Papers"; died in 1735.

FRASER, MAJOR JAMES, of Castleleathers, was born about 1670. He married a daughter of Sir Robert Dunbar of Grange Hill, near Forres. It is said that he had been sent to the lady by his brother as a suitor by proxy, and that she replied that "he would have done better to have solicited for himself." During his visit to France in search of his chief he received Lovat's promise of the "best davoch of land" on the Lovat estates. In 1716 Lovat said to Mrs. Fraser, "My dear Jannet, I can never part with your husband till once I be settled in my estate, and then, by the living God! you, he, and I shall live together in my country while any of us are alive." There being no signs of the "davoch" after Lovat was established at Castle Downie, the major went to London in 1725 or 1726, and received a promise of his choice of a farm. He chose Tomich, near Beauly, but Lovat secretly wrote to Lady Lovat that "as she wished her own peace, and would be answerable to him, not to let the major in that country." Major Fraser, by favour of Lady Lovat, got entry to the farm of Bruiach, in Kiltarlity, but when Lovat returned he sent men to eject the new tenant. These were driven by the major's womenkind to the gates of Castle Downie, and the tenant completed his revenge by suing Lovat for nine weeks' board incurred by John Fraser of Beaufort, during his last illness in 1716. Bitter enmity continued to separate Lovat and his former "dear cousin" and "bedmate," Castleleathers. In his adversity the major "had no other shift but to go and live within the town of Inverness with his numerous family, children and grand-children, for the benefit of their education. He, having no rent, was necessitate to take a publick house, which was entirely against his graine." After Culloden the major's fortunes revived, for he was appointed by the butcher Cumberland to act as factor on the forfeited Lovat estates. He seemed to have acted faithfully in the interests of the State, for even a clear order from the House of Lords failed to induce him to remit funds to his imprisoned chief. His last days were passed at Inchhaugh, near Auldearn, in the residence of his son, Robert, where he died at the age of ninety years. The "Manuscript" (from which copious extracts appear in this volume) was written in the year 1752, and was first published in 1889, though its existence was known and its information used at earlier dates.

FRASER, SIMON, Master of Lovat, was born in 1726; educated at St. Andrews University; sent by Lord Lovat with part of the clan to join the Prince. The depositions printed in the New Spalding Club's Historical Papers show that he was at Perth at Christmas, 1745, and in Stirling in January, 1746. Mr. Alexander Mackenzie, the Fraser historian, says he was present at Culloden. Mr. Lang states that the Master of Lovat came up too late for the battle. He was attainted by Act of Parliament on 4th June, 1746, surrendered on 2nd August, and imprisoned in Edinburgh till August, 1747; was released about that date, and went to Glasgow, as the Lovat estates had been forfeited; called to the Scottish bar in 1750; one of the Crown counsel at the trial of James Stewart for the murder of Campbell of Glenure in 1752. Soon afterwards he entered the Army, raised a Fraser regiment in 1757, and became lieutenant-colonel; fought at Louisburg under General Wolfe; present at both battles of Quebec, and commanded the left wing at the latter; elected M.P. for Inverness-shire in 1761, but soon saw active service in Portugal and became a major-general; Lovat estates were restored to him in 1774; died a lieutenant-general in 1782; figures in Robert Louis Stevenson's "Catriona," where his character is portrayed in a way that gave just offence to Highlanders.

GORDON OF GLENBUCKET, JOHN, joined Prince Charles after Prestonpans, was present at Clifton, but too ill to take part in the fight. After the meeting of Jacobites of Muirlaggan he escaped to the Continent.

HARDWICKE, PHILIP, first Earl of (1690-1764), Lord Chancellor, was a son of a Dover attorney; called to the bar in 1715; elected M.P. for Lewes in 1719; Solicitor-General in 1720; knighted in same year; Attorney-General in 1724; conducted prosecutions with a moderation that contrasted with the undue zeal of some of his predecessors; made Lord Chief Justice of England and a Baron in 1733; appointed Lord Chancellor, 1737, in Walpole's Ministry; proposed and carried the attainder clauses in the Act of 1744 making correspondence with the Pretender treasonable; presided at trials of Lords Kilmarnock, Balmerino, Cromartie and Derwentwater, and was criticised for his want of magnanimity in that capacity, particularly in the case of Derwentwater; was primarily responsible for the prohibition of kilt-wearing in Scotland after the Rebellion; created Earl of Hardwicke and Viscount Royston in 1754; died 6th March, 1764.

LOUDOUN, JOHN CAMPBELL, fourth Earl of (1705-1782), entered the Army in 1727; succeeded to the earldom in 1731; A.D.C. to the King in 1743; raised a regiment in 1745; fought at Preston; he went north to Cromarty and took up the supreme command of the Hanoverian forces in the north, but did no important service; appointed Governor of Virginia in 1756, and then to the command of a force to operate against the French; again failed to do useful work, and was recalled; was Governor of Edinburgh Castle for some years; died on 27th April, 1782.

MACDONALD OF BARISDALE, Coll, a member of a Glengarry family, born 1698; educated in Rome; about 1735 was appointed Captain of the Watch in the west of Inverness-shire; led the Knoydart men under the Prince in 1745; sent by the Prince in the beginning of the Rebellion to rouse hesitating adherents; made a knight banneret by the Prince after Prestonpans; took no part in the English campaign; rejoined the Prince on his return to Scotland; sent north against Lord Reay, and to raise the Jacobites of Sutherland and Caithness, and did not return in time for Culloden, being then at Dingwall; was considered a man of doubtful loyalty by the chiefs after Culloden; was captured on 10th June, 1746, and taken to Fort-Augustus; was released on condition that he tried to find the Prince; joined the ship that was to convey the Prince to France, and was placed under arrest on a charge of treachery to the Jacobites; was imprisoned in France, liberated in February, 1749; returned to Scotland; was again arrested by the Government, and died in prison, at Edinburgh, on 12th April, 1749, before his trial could proceed. The character of Barisdale is fully analysed by Mr. Lang in his "Companions of Pickle," where the following old epitaph on Barisdale is quoted:—

"If heaven be glad when sinners cease to sin,
If hell be glad when traitors enter in,
If earth be glad when ridded of a knave,
Then all rejoice, MacDonald's in his grave."

MacDonald, Ranald, sixteenth chief of Clanranald, date of birth unknown, was a "quiet and retiring" young man in 1745; became a colonel in the rebel army; brought 250 men to the Prince's standard; was severely wounded at Culloden; remained concealed in his grand-mother's house in Inverness for some days; joined the flying Prince a week later; remained in his own country in secrecy for over a year, and married a Miss Hamilton at Braban Castle, the seat of a political enemy but personal friend; sailed from Cromarty to London and thence to Paris; became A.D.C. to Marshal Saxe; returned to Britain about 1752, and was imprisoned in London; recovered his estates owing to an error in the Act of Attainder, which named him "Donald" instead of "Ranald" (see list of attainted persons, p. 114 *supra*); died in 1777, "a noble, brave, and generous chief."

MacDonell, Æneas (Gaelic, Angus) of Glengarry, second son of John, thirteenth chief, and brother of "Alastair Ruadh." commanded the clan during part of 1745 Rebellion; his men had a great share in the victory of Prestonpans; was sent north thereafter to threaten the clans who would not join the Prince; rejoined the Prince at Stirling in January, 1746; fought at Falkirk, and was killed some days after by the accidental discharge of a musket. The Prince attended his funeral as chief mourner.

Macdonell, Alastair, eleventh chief of Glengarry, was out with Dundee; bore the standard at Killiecrankie; signed a letter to Mar before the Rising of 1715, professing loyalty to King George, but soon after joined the rebels; present at Sheriffmuir with 700 of his clan; made his submission at Inverness; was afterwards made a peer of Parliament by the Pretender; married a sister of Hugh, Lord Lovat; died in 1724. Known in the Highlands as "Alastair Dubh."

MacDonell, Alastair Ruadh, Younger of Glengarry, born about 1725; sent to France in 1738, and held a commission in the French Army; returned to Scotland in 1745, and was sent back to the Pretender with assurance of Highland allegiance; when returning to Scotland was captured at sea, confined in the Tower till July, 1747, so that he was there at the same time as Lovat; is supposed to have stolen the Loch Arkaig treasure in 1749; became a Hanoverian spy on the Pretender, and has been identified by Mr. Andrew Lang with "Pickle the Spy"; became thirteenth chief of the MacDonalds of Glengarry in 1754; died in 1761.

MacDonell, John, twelfth chief of Glengarry, son of Alastair Duhb, did not take personal part in the Rising of 1745; was suspected of Jacobite sympathy; went to Inverness a few days after Culloden to assure Cumberland of his loyalty, but was persuaded to return to his country, which was soon raided by Cumberland's men; was taken prisoner and sent to Edinburgh; released in 1749; died in 1754.

M'Pherson of Cluny, Ewan, was a son-in-law of Lord Lovat, and an officer in the Royal army, but resigned his commission when the rebellion broke out; joined the Pretender at Holyrood, kissed his hands and dined with him; took a prominent part in the fights at Clifton and Falkirk, but did not reach Culloden in time for the battle; had his estates forfeited and castle burned; escaped, and lived for some years in hiding in "Cluny's cage" and other places, not far from his home; escaped to France in 1755, and died in 1756.

Marischal, George Keith, tenth Earl, born about 1693; served under Marlborough; succeeded to earldom in 1712; a strong Jacobite; attended Mar's meeting at Aboyne prior to the Rising of 1715; commanded some cavalry at Sheriffmuir; attainted soon after, and his estates forfeited; quarrelled with Earl of Mar; refused to fly with James; commanded in the farcical invasion of 1719; severely wounded at Glensheil; escaped to Western Isles, and thence to Spain; took offence at some supposed insult, and took no part in Prince Charles' Rebellion; went to Prussia and entered diplomatic service; was appointed Prussian Ambassador at Paris in 1751, and to Spain in 1758; received a pardon from George II. on 29th May, 1759; returned to Scotland, and succeeded to the estates of the fourth Earl of Kintore; died 28th May, 1778.

Middleton, Charles, second Earl of, was born about 1640, accompanied his father in the campaign in Scotland against Cromwell, and then escaped to France; Envoy-Extraordinary to Vienna after the Restoration; succeeded to peerage in 1673; made Secretary of State for England in 1684; remained in England when James VII. fled, and tried to organise a movement for a Restoration, but failed; arrested for high treason in 1692, but released for want of evidence; joined the exiled Court in France in 1693; outlawed by High Court of Justiciary in Scotland in 1694; an enemy of Lord Lovat; responsible in a large degree for the miserable attempt to invade Scotland in 1707; remained loyal to the exiled house till his death in 1719.

Murray, Sir John, Bart., of Broughton (1715-1777), secretary to Prince Charles during the Rising of 1745; second son of Sir David Murray of Stanhope, Peebles; educated at Edinburgh University and at Leyden; visited Rome in 1737; employed in 1741 by the Highland Jacobites to go to Rome to assure the Pretender of their loyalty; had no great belief in the efficiency of the Highland leaders; on hearing of Prince Charles' landing, went from Broughton to join him at Kinlochmoidart, Inverness-shire; is supposed to have been at variance with Lord George Murray and to have contributed to that leader's difficulties with the Prince; took ill on the eve of Culloden and was sent in a litter to Glenmoriston; taken prisoner at Polmood, Peeblesshire, after various wanderings; turned King's evidence against the Jacobites; discharged from prison by the end of 1747; deserted by his own wife on account of his treachery; succeeded his uncle, Sir David Murray of Stanhope as baronet; died 6th December, 1777. He was a client of Sir Walter Scott's father, and occasionally called at his house. There is a well-known story of his being offered a cup of tea by Mrs. Scott, with the result that whenever he left the room Mr. Scott flung out of the window the cup from which he had drunk. "I can admit into my house on a piece of business," said Scott, "persons wholly unworthy to be treated as guests by my wife. Neither lip of me or of mine comes after Murray of Broughton" (Lockhart's *Life of Scott*).

Murray, William, the Hon. (1705-1793), first Earl of Mansfield, fourth son of David, third Viscount Stormont (a Jacobite); born at Scone; claimed by Lovat as a relative; educated at Perth; lifelong rival of William Pitt (Earl of Chatham); called to the bar in 1730, made K.C. and Solicitor-General in 1742; M.P. for Boroughbridge; got freedom of Edinburgh in 1743; a pioneer of Free Trade theories; leader of the House of Commons in 1747. About 1750 he was accused of holding Jacobite opinions; became Attorney-General in 1745; succeeded Sir Dudley Ryder as Lord Chief Justice in 1756, and was created Baron Mansfield; tried the famous Wilkes case in 1768, and several libel cases arising out of the letters of Junius (1770); created Earl of Mansfield in 1776; retired in 1788; died 20th March, 1793, and was buried in Westminster Abbey.

Noel, William (1695-1762), younger son of Sir John Noel, Bart.; called to the bar in 1721; M.P. for Stamford, 1722; K.C. in 1738; appointed by Lord Hardwicke a Justice of the Common Pleas in 1757; Horace Walpole says he was "a pompous man of little solidity"; died 8th December, 1762.

Perth, James Drummond, fourth Earl and first titular Duke of; born in 1648; educated at St. Andrews University; joined Hamilton's party in opposition to Lauderdale; made Justice-General and extraordinary Lord of Session in Scotland in 1682; proved an unfair judge; became a Roman Catholic, and so roused the Edinburgh mob, who attacked his house and caused a riot, for which several men were hanged. When King James VII. was replaced by William and Mary, Perth went to France and joined the Court at St. Germains; was made First Lord of the Bedchamber and a Knight of the Garter, and on James's death he was made first Duke of Perth, in terms of that King's will; died on 11th March, 1716.

Prestonhall, Sir Robert Mackenzie, afterwards Lord; M.P. for Cromarty in 1700, and in 1703 for the burgh of Fortrose; married Margaret, daughter of Archbishop Burnet, and afterwards Margaret Haliburton of Pitcur, widow of Sir George Mackenzie of Rosehaugh.

Ryder, Sir Dudley (Attorney-General), 1691-1756; son of a Nonconformist mercer in West Smithfields; studied at Edinburgh and Leyden; called to the bar in 1725; helped by the influence of Walpole; M.P. for St. Germans, 1733; Solicitor-General in same year; Attorney-General in 1737, and knighted in 1740; took charge in Parliament of the bill of pains and penalties against the city of Edinburgh after Porteous Riots. Horace Walpole described his methods in the Lovat trial as "cold and tedious" (letter to Sir H. Mann, 20th March, 1747); made Lord Chief Justice of the King's Bench in 1754. King signed a patent for making him Baron Ryder of Harrowby, on 24th May, 1756, and was to have kissed hands next day, but he died suddenly during the interval; buried at Grantham; described by Lord Waldegrave as "an honest man and a good lawyer, but not considerable in any other capacity."

SANDYS, SAMUEL, first Baron; a strong opponent of Walpole, for whose removal he moved an address to the King in 1741; became Chancellor of the Exchequer on Walpole's downfall; created a peer on 20th December, 1743; died 1770.

STUART, JOHN ROY, was born in 1700, at Knock, Kincardineshire; served in Scots Greys; became a Jacobite agent, and was thrown into prison at Inverness in 1736; escaped through Lovat's connivance; present in the French army at Fontenoy; joined Prince Charles at Blair Atholl in 1745; present at Prestonpans and Culloden, when he was one of the principal Jacobite leaders; distinguished himself at the fight at Strathbogie; attainted in June, 1746; became a fugitive with a price on his head; escaped to France, where he died in 1752; author of several Gaelic songs.

STRANGE, SIR JOHN (1690-1754), called to the bar in 1718; defended Lord Chancellor Macclesfield at his impeachment; made K.C. in 1736, and Solicitor-General in 1737, in Walpole's Government; M.P. for West Looe, later for Totnes; took part in the debate in Parliament consequent on the Porteous Riots; declined in 1738 the office of Master of the Rolls; made Recorder of London, 1739, and afterwards was made Solicitor-General; knighted, 1740; a member of the Secret Committee for inquiring into his friend Walpole's conduct; gave up his offices and practice in 1742; granted a Patent of Precedence next after the Attorney-General; appointed Master of the Rolls in 1750; died 18th May, 1754.

YONGE, SIR WILLIAM, fourth Baronet (died 1755); M.P. for Honiton in 1714; created K.C.B. in 1725; greatly disliked by George II., who called him "Stinking Yonge," but in 1730 made Commissioner of the Treasury; made Secretary for War in 1735, under Walpole; was impressed during the Lovat trial by the need for allowing counsel to appear and cross-examine for impeached persons, and moved in Parliament accordingly. Reputed "a place-hunting politician."

APPENDIX III.

NOTE AS TO IMPEACHMENTS.

The difficulty of dealing with offenders of high rank and influence was solved by the use of a process of "impeachment." The first recorded instance of its use occurred in 1376, when proceedings were taken against Lord Latimer.

The House of Commons undertakes the prosecution. A member moves that the offender be impeached "in name of the House of Commons and of all the Commons of the United Kingdom." If the motion is carried, the mover is instructed to proceed to the bar of the House of Lords. He there states the nature of the charges, and these are then embodied in Articles of Impeachment and served upon the accused. An arrest follows, and the offender is committed to prison to await his trial.

Appendix III.

The duty of proving the accused person's guilt falls upon the House of Commons, which appoints Managers—usually lawyers of high standing—to conduct the further proceedings. The remaining members of the House go into Committee and attend the trial.

When peers are impeached, a Lord High Steward is specially appointed, but in all other cases the Lord Chancellor presides. In the main the procedure of ordinary criminal trials is followed, but the accusers may add further Articles if necessary. Any crime or offence may be the subject of an impeachment. Witnesses are called and examined on oath. Counsel are not allowed to act for the accused, and, as a result of the hardships imposed on Lord Lovat by his counsel being prohibited from cross-examining, the old rule has been altered, and counsel may now use their usual freedom.

At the conclusion of the hearing the President asks each peer, beginning with the junior baron (according to precedence, not age) for his verdict. The member then rises in his place, replying, "Guilty, upon my honour," or "Not guilty, upon my honour." The President gives his own opinion last. The verdict is then reported to the Commons, and sentence cannot be passed until the Commons demand its pronouncement. It is impossible for the King to pardon an offender so as to prevent his impeachment.

The last British impeachments were those of Warren Hastings, in 1788-95, and Lord Melville, in 1805. The proceedings against Queen Caroline were of a different nature. An ineffectual attempt to use the process of impeachment against Lord Palmerston took place in 1845.

An even more elaborate method of criminal procedure is available in Great Britain—by the use of a Bill of Attainder. Under that process the Commons are judges as well as the Lords.

APPENDIX IV.

Books Dealing with Lord Lovat.

The reader who determines to master Lovatic literature must be prepared to peruse a large number of volumes. It has been suggested to the Editor that a short account of the chief sources of information would prove useful.

The "Memoirs" were written by Lord Lovat in French, and, inferentially, for French consumption. In 1797 an English translation was published, and in 1902 they were edited by Mr. Hugh Keith Fraser, and republished for private circulation by Arthur L. Humphreys. They contain unmistakable evidence of the author's desire to reingratiate himself with the Jacobite Court in France by a highly-coloured account of his doings prior to his temporary conversion to Whiggism. The autobiography ends with the time of the writer's pardon by King George, and it does not seem unfair to suggest that he was careful not to continue his narrative further, so as to avoid emphasising his undoubted services to the House of Hanover in 1715. The pardon itself cut off all chance of the narrative being afterwards used against him in Britain. But for the pardon, the book of the "Memoirs" would certainly have been an official "production" in the treason trial of 1747. It was a convenient opportunity for the crafty autobiographer, and he took advantage of it with his usual astuteness. Though not possessing the distinctive force that pervades his private letters, the "Memoirs" have a value which no student of the period should neglect.

The Inverness Public Library contains a rare volume of papers dealing with Lovat's peerage case. It is more interesting to lawyers than to general readers. It refers to a number of earlier peerage cases, and might prove very valuable to members of the families concerned in them.

The earlier Lives, entitled "The Life of Simon, Lord Lovat" (published by C. Whitefield, London, in 1746), and "The Life and Adventures and Many Great Vicissitudes of Fortune of Simon, Lord Lovat," by "the Reverend Archibald Arbuthnot, minister of Kiltarlity"—a purely fictitious person—(published by R. Walker, London, in 1746), may be ignored. A copy of each book is found in the Reference Department of the Inverness Public Library. Both are anonymous and inaccurate. The former bears evidences of a hasty and uninformed production, doubtless to satisfy the desire of Londoners for information about the noble prisoner who was then in the Tower. The book was translated into French, and published in Amsterdam in 1747. The latter is the produce of some literary rogue. Its contents were first published in tri-weekly parts at a halfpenny each. Its opening and closing pages bear a suspicious resemblance to Whitefield's publication, and the larger middle portion is undiluted fiction of a poor type, introduced, we may assume, to bring in more halfpence. No minister of Kiltarlity could have fathered either the biographical inaccuracies or the fiction without running a danger of ecclesiastical discipline.

Colonel Ferguson, in his introduction to Major Fraser's manuscript, mentions two booklets, "Genuine Memoirs of the Life of Simon, Lord Fraser of Lovat" (London: M. Cooper, 1746), and "Memoirs of the Life of Simon Fraser, Lord Lovat" (Edinburgh, 1747), but the present writer has not been able to get access to either. There is no copy in any of the chief libraries, so far as he can ascertain.

A considerable number of interesting references to Lovat, with accounts of his trial, are contained in the *Scots*, *London*, and *Gentleman's Magazines* for the period covered by his imprisonment and a few months thereafter. Numbers of songs, satires, and pamphlets were current at the time, and several of them have (along with valuable Lovat manuscripts) been preserved in the British Museum. Boswell tells us that in 1747 Dr. Johnson was fond of repeating the following verses by an unidentified author from the *Gentleman's Magazine*:—

On Lord Lovat's Execution.

"Pity'd by gentle minds Kilmarnock died;
The brave, Balmerino, were on thy side;
Radcliffe, unhappy in his crimes of youth,
Steady in what he still mistook for truth,
Beheld his death so decently unmov'd,
The soft lamented, and the brave approv'd.
But Lovat's fate indifferently we view,
True to no king, to no religion true;
No fair forgets the ruin he has done,
No child laments the tyrant of his son;
No Tory pities, thinking what he was,
No Whig compassions, for he left the cause;
The brave regret not, for he was not brave,
The honest mourn not, knowing him a knave."

Appendix IV.

Most important of all, to the examiner of Lovat's life, and the mysteries of human character, are the letters scattered through many volumes, including the "Culloden Papers" (which contain the correspondence with the Lord President and Lord Loudoun), the "Transactions of the Gaelic Society of Inverness," the *Celtic Magazine*, "The Lairds of Grant," the most interesting volume privately printed by Mr. William Burns, solicitor, Inverness (and containing a well-argued "special plea" in Lovat's favour), Alexander Mackenzie's "History of the Frasers," Anderson's "Family of Fraser," Macpherson's "Original Papers," and the appendices to Major Fraser's "Manuscript." An important letter, written to the Master of Lovat from the Tower, on 22nd March, 1747, and now in the possession of Mr. John MacLeod Campbell of Saddell, was published in that excellent magazine, the *Celtic Monthly* (Glasgow), for January, 1911. Lord Lovat was a prolific letter-writer and memorialist. It may safely be assumed that unpublished products of his pen are still numerous, and the hope is now expressed that these will soon be collected, and published with those already known, in a volume which should prove valuable.

Next in importance as direct evidence comes Major James Fraser's "Manuscript," which has been edited by Lieutenant-Colonel Alexander Fergusson (Edinburgh: David Douglas, 1889. Two volumes). Its remarkable interest has been indicated by several quotations in the introduction to this volume. Authors of the major's type are rare. In Scottish literature his "Manuscript" stands alone as a vivid, unpolished, bombastic piece of writing.

Some interesting Lovat stories are recorded in "Historical and Traditional Sketches of Highland Families and of the Highlands," by John MacLean ("the Inverness Centenarian"), first published in 1848, and reprinted by the late Mr. John Noble, Inverness, in 1895. Mr. Noble points out that these sketches were really written by the centenarian's son Finlay, who "was in the habit of adding from other channels matter that the centenarian had not repeated."

The doings of Lord Lovat are recorded, with varied fullness, in almost every volume dealing with Rebellion times. So wide was his influence in the Highlands, for good or ill, that the various historians of the MacDonalds, Mackenzies, Grants, Mackays, Camerons, and other clans have had to record the altered fortunes of the men of those names in consequence of his intrigues.

The "Life" by Dr. Hill Burton (Chapman & Hall, 1847) has only one serious defect, the absence of an index. Mr. W. C. Mackenzie's "Simon, Lord Lovat: His Life and Times" (Chapman & Hall, 1908) contains everything necessary in such a biography, and is written with the vigour and freshness which distinguish its author's other Highland books.

APPENDIX V.

A Perspective View of Westminster Hall, with both Houses of Parliament Assembled on the Tryal of Simon, Lord Lovat.

Also a View of the Peeresses, their Daughters, the Foreign Embassadors, and the rest of ye numerous Company as they were arranged on the Scaffolding erected on that Solemn Occasion.

1. The King's Chair on the Throne
2. Prince of Wales's Seat
3. Duke of Cumberland's Seat

Appendix V.

4. A Chair for the Ld High Steward
5. Ld High Steward removed from his Chair nearer the Bar for conveniency of hearing
6. The two Arch Bishops
7. Bishops on Two Benches
8. The Great Officers of State, Dukes, and Marquises on the front Seat
9. The Barons seated behind the Dukes
10. Earls and Viscounts
11. The remainder of the Barons seated behind the Earls & Viscounts
12. The Master of the Rolls
13. The Head Master in Chancery
14. The Judges Siting on the inside of Woolpacks, and the Masters in Chancery siting on the outside
15. The Serjeant at Mace
16. Lord High Steward's Purse bearer
17. Clerks belonging to ye House of Lords
18. Four Mace Bearers and two Heralds in front, behind them Peers' Sons, all of them standing
19. Four Mace Bearers and Ld. High Steward's Gentlemen, all of them standing.

References to the Scaffolding Round the House of Lords.

A. The Speaker of the House of Commons
B. The Members of the House of Commons on the side seats.
C. Other Members of the House of Commons in front seats
D. The Managers for Ye House of Commons
E. The Soliciters and Clerks belonging to the Managers
F. Lord Lovat at the Bar, with the Lieutenant of the Tower on his Right hand, and the Gentleman jailer, with ye Ax, on his left
G. The Witness giving Evidence
H. The Prisoner's Council
I. Writer taking the Trial
K. The King's Box with a Velvet Chair, and Ladies on 6 Rows of Benches
L. The Prince of Wales's Box. with Ladies Seated on 6 Benches
M. 1 Box with Benches for the Duke of Cumberld., Princesses, and their Attendants, behind this Box was 3 Benches for the use of the Lord High Steward's Family, and 1 Bench for the Lord Chief Justice.
N. The Box where Princs. Amelia sat during ye Trial
O. The Box for Foreign Embassadors
P. Peereses and their Daughters on 4 Benches
Q. Seats for Peers' Tickets, besides these on the Side there were 9 Seats in front for the Peers' Tickets
R. The D. of Ancaster's Gallery at ye South end of ye Hall, containing 17 rows of Seats, holding 860 People. At the North end was another Gallery belonging to the same Duke, filling the whole space behind ye Commons and the Benches for Peers' Tickets
S. Gallery belonging to the Board of Works, and ye Vice Chambern.
T. The Earl of Oxford's Gallery

N.B.—All the Seats were covered, and Scaffolding hung with Red Bays, excepting where the House of Commons Sat, and that was covered with Green Bays. Printed for Thos. Bowles in St. Paul's Churchyard, and John Bowles at ye Black Horse in Cornhill.

INDEX.

Index.